Maya Glyphs: The Verbs

By Linda Schele

Maya Glyphs   The Verbs

University of Texas Press, Austin

To Bob Robertson and Dick Johnson, who were there from the beginning, to Nancy Troike, who made me do it, and to David, who helped me do it.

Copyright © 1982 by the University of Texas Press
All rights reserved
Printed in the United States of America
First edition, 1982

Requests for permission to reproduce material
from this work should be sent to:
   Permissions
   University of Texas Press
   Box 7819
   Austin, Texas 78712

Library of Congress Cataloging in Publication Data
Schele, Linda.
   Maya glyphs, the verbs.
   Bibliography: p.
   1. Mayas—Writing. 2. Maya language—Verb.
I. Title. F1435.P6S27   497'.4   82-7021
ISBN 0-292-75066-8   AACR2

The publication of this book was assisted by a
grant from the Andrew W. Mellon Foundation.

For reasons of economy and speed, this volume has
been printed from camera-ready copy furnished by
the author, who assumes full responsibility for its
contents.

Contents

Acknowledgments

When I was a Visiting Lecturer at the University of Texas at Austin in 1978, I began research on this book with the goal in mind of producing at some time in the far distant future a catalog of Maya glyphic verbs for epigraphers and other Mayanists interested in the writing system. During that semester at UT, Nancy Troike, who participated in and provided logistical support for my classes, encouraged me to enter the Ph.D. program of the Institute of Latin American Studies and to take the Ph.D so necessary in American academia. My initial idea of a verb catalog subsequently became the subject of my dissertation and eventually this book. Nancy was a reader for the dissertation, but more importantly she guided my program and career as a graduate student, enabling me to complete course work and dissertation while teaching full-time at the University of South Alabama. Without her support, encouragement, and friendship, I probably would not have considered taking a Ph.D nor writing a dissertation, and for this reason, I dedicate this book to her.

During my first trip to Mexico in December 1970, I visited Palenque and fell in love with and became obsessed by that beautiful city. At that time, I also met my first real Mayanists--Merle and Bob Robertson. In a kind of magic way, Bob and Merle knew that something profound had happened to me, and from the first moment we met the Robertsons became my dedicated friends. Bob from then until his death in 1981 always offered a haven for me in Palenque with coffee in the morning, rum in the evening, and love and encouragement in between. This book is dedicated to his memory in recognition of the support, love, and great friendship he gave me.

Dick Johnson was a herpetologist from Mobile, Alabama, who as well as being my friend, taught me not to be afraid of snakes and to look at animals carefully, especially reptiles and amphibians, when relating them to Maya iconography and epigraphy. He criticized early papers and tried heroically to teach me to think as a scientist. Dick died in 1982 almost one year after Bob Robertson, and for the profound companionship and for his teaching, this book is dedicated to his memory.

Many other people have made vital contributions to this book. Peter Mathews not only read and corrected the manuscript, but he, Floyd Lounsbury, and David Stuart shared new decipherments and insights with me promptly and freely and gave permission to incorporate them into the commentary in the verb catalog. David Kelley read the manuscript and offered valuable commentary, and he, Floyd Lounsbury, and Peter Mathews have shared ideas, methodology, and information with me completely without reservation since I first met them. Much that I know of glyphs I have learned from them, and this atmosphere of freely shared information has been central to the advances in the study of Maya hieroglyphic writing made in the last decade. When attending the 1978 Workshop on Maya Hieroglyhic Writing at the University of Texas, Kathryn Josserand and Nicholas Hopkins noticed that I could use some help with the jargon and methodology of historical linguistics, and they volunteered their time and home during the following summer to teach me. Any coherent presentations of linguistic data within this book are due to their help; I take responsibility for any errors.

My sincere thanks are given to Ian Graham of the Peabody Museum of Harvard University for permission to publish whole monuments from Yaxchilan and isolated verbs from the *Corpus* project. Without this resource, the study of Maya glyphs would be very much more difficult. I wish also to thank Dr. W.R. Coe of the University Museum of the University of Pennsylvania for permission to publish drawings of several Tikal monuments as well as isolated verbs from all Tikal texts and Claude Baudez, who gave me permission to publish verbs from the monuments of Tonina and Temple 18 at Copan. This project would not have been possible without the cooperation of these people and the drawings and archives they made available in both published and unpublished forms.

I would like to give special thanks to Dorie Reents, Andrea Stone, Christine DeBremaecker, Ruth Krochock, and Constance Cortez, graduate students at the University of Texas, who volunteered their time to check the accuracy of the appendices. It was a boring and difficult job that took many days, but without their help, it would have taken many months.

David, my long suffering husband, deserves perhaps the profoundest thanks of all because he not only suffered through a year and a half of writing and the resulting disruption in our lives, but was also my computer expert and chief programmer. He cheerfully taught me to use the computer and suffered through my often hilarious struggle to understand the contankerous machine that in time miraculously changed into a wonderful tool. David's most heroic sacrifice was to let me take the computer to Austin for nine months in order to finish the book, and those readers who own and love their microcomputers know how great that sacrifice was.

Abbreviations

#	Subnumber on charts in the verb catalog	DH	Death Head monument from Group of the Cross
96G	Tablet of the 96 Glyphs	DN	Distance Number
2ndy	Secondary text	DNIG	Distance Number Introductory Glyph
AD	House AD of the Palace	DO	Dumbarton Oaks Tablet
ADI	Anterior Date Indicator	DPil	Dos Pilas
AEI	Anterior Event Indicator	DRio	Del Rio Throne
AgC	Aguas Calientes	e	East
Agua	Aguateca	Ear	Earplug
Alab	Alabaster vase	Eav	Eave
Alf	Alfarda	ECayo	El Cayo
Alt	Altar	EG	Emblem Glyph
Altun	Altun Ha	EPeru	El Peru
ArP	Arroyo de Piedra	EZotz	El Zotz'
ASac	Altar de Sacrificios	F	Fragment
BCt	Ballcourt	Fig.	Figure
Bon	Bonampak	Frag	Fragment
Bur	Burial	Frt	Front
C	Consonant; House C of the Palace	G	God
		Gp	Group
Cal	Calakmul	H	Head variant
CAlt	Column altar	HS	Hieroglyphic Stairs
Car	Caracol	Imp	Imperfective
Cens	Censor stand	In	Inner
Chin	Chinikiha	Inv	Inverted
Chk	Chinkultic	IS	Initial Series
CItz	Chichen Itza	ISIG	Initial Series Introductory Glyph
Coll	Collection	ISpot	Initial Series pot from Group III
Cop	Copan	Itz	Itzimte
Corn	Cornice	IV	Intransitive verb
CR	Calendar Round	Ixk	Ixkun
Cr	Tablet of the Creation	Ixt	Ixtutz'
CRic	Costa Rica	Jimb	Jimbal
Ctr	Center	Jmb	Jamb
D	House D of the Palace	Jon	Jonuta

L	Lintel	Sach	Sacchana
Lac	Lacanja	Sanc	Sanctuary
LAm	La Amelia	Sarc	Sarcophagus
LC	Long Count	Scb	Scribe
LHig	Los Higos	Scp	Sculpture
LMar	La Mar	se	Southeast
Low	Lower	Seib	Seibal
LP	Leiden Plaque	Slav	Tablet of the Slaves
LPas	La Pasadita	Smj	Simojovel
M	Monument	St	Stela
m	Middle	Stc	Stucco
Mach	Machaquila	Str	Structure
MJos	Motul de San Jose	sw	Southwest
MNAH	*Museo National de Antropología e Historia* in Mexico City	T	Temple; a glyph designation from Thompson's *A Catalog of Maya Hieroglyphics*
MT	Miscellaneous text	Tab	Tablet
n	North	Tam	Tamarindito
Nar	Naranjo	Tbs	Tableritos from the Palace
ne	Northeast	TC	Tablet of the Cross
NimP	Nim Li Punit	TFC	Tablet of the Foliated Cross
NTun	Nah Tunich cave	Thr	Throne
nw	Northwest	TI	Temple of Inscriptions
Oco	Ocosingo	Tik	Tikal
OPT	Oval Palace Tablet	Ton	Tonina
Ora	Orator	Tort	Tortuguero
OVS	Object-verb-subject word order	TS	Tablet of the Sun
p	Provisional	TV	Transitive verb
Pal	Palenque	Uax	Uaxactun
Pan	Panel	Uca	Ucanal
Pass	Passive	Up	Upper
PasTr	Pasadena Tracing	v	Variable vowel
PDI	Posterior Date Indicator	v_1	Vowel echoing stem vowel
PE	Period ending	Var	Variant
PecSk	Peccary Skull	VOS	Verb-object-subject word order
PEI	Posterior Event Indicator	VS	Verb-subject word order
Perf	Perfective	w	West
Pf	Perfect	Xul	Xultun
PN	Piedras Negras	Yax	Yaxchilan
Pom	Pomona	Yxh	Yaxha
Pst	Present		
Pt	Participle		
PTab	Palace Tablet		
PUin	Poco Uinic		
Pul	Pusilha		
Quir	Quirigua		
RAz	Rio Azul		
Res	Resbalon		
Rev	Reviewing stand		
Rm	Room		
s	South		
Sac	Sacul		

Maya Glyphs: The Verbs

Introduction

This work is designed as a study of the verb morphology and syntax of the hieroglyphic writing system used by the Maya during the Classic period (A.D. 293 to A.D. 900). Inscriptions in this writing system are found in the lowlands of the Yucatan peninsula principally in the southern region now occupied by the states of Chiapas, Tabasco, Campeche, and Quintana Roo in Mexico, by the Peten in northern Guatemala, by Belize, and by the western third of Honduras and El Salvador. Most of the extant inscriptions are found in public contexts on upright slabs called stelae; on carved panels of wood or stone mounted as door lintels or engaged into walls; in painted murals; on the outer facades of buildings; and on small portable objects used as a part of costume or ritual regalia. Although the Maya writing system is related to earlier writing systems in southern Mesoamerica (as demonstrated by Michael Coe [1976]), the earliest text which exhibits the full set of features characteristic of the Classic writing system occurs on Stela 29 of Tikal, dated A.D. 293, or 8.12.14.8.15 in the Maya system. Examples of readable signs can now be dated to an earlier time (ca. 50 B.C.) at the site of Cerros (David Friedel, personal communication, 1980), but these examples include only kin and yax signs and are found in iconographic, not inscriptional form. However, their existence indicates that the Classic writing system was in use in the central Maya region by at least A.D. 50.

The study of the Maya hieroglyphic writing system has been underway since the last quarter of the nineteenth century, and its contents are well enough understood to recover a wealth of information about the persons and events of this period in the Mesoamerican past. Particularly important contributions were made by Heinrich Berlin (1958, 1959), who first identified personal name glyphs and emblems associated with local sites, and by Tatiana Proskouriakoff (1960, 1963-1964), who first identified events which occurred in the lives of Classic rulers. Proskouriakoff's "historical hypothesis" posited that the noncalendric residue of undeciphered glyphs in the Classic inscriptions referred, not to astronomical or religious events as had been supposed until 1960, but rather to the activities of the rulers and lords of the Classic period. She identified glyphs referring to birth, inauguration, death, blood-letting, capture, and other kinds of events, as well as name phrases of many of the persons who are recorded as the protagonists of these events. In the two decades since the publication of Proskouriakoff's seminal studies, other scholars have used her methodology and added to the list of known events and rulers of the Classic period.

During the seventies, the number of epigraphers working on the Maya hieroglyphic system increased, and Maya linguists became interested in the writing system as a record of an earlier stage of Mayan languages.

Interaction between these two groups of scholars has suggested that the next important breakthrough in the understanding of the hieroglyphic writing system is likely to result from the application of linguistic methodology to problems in decipherment, and in this context one critical area not yet understood is that of the verb morphology of the writing system. This publication is designed, therefore, as a comparative study of all of the verbal phrases available to me in the resources at my disposal. It is meant to create a collection of data gathered from the viewpoint of the epigrapher and iconographer and presented in a way that can be used by specialists from other disciplines.

The core of this study is a verb catalog listing a large sample of verbal constructions found in the surviving inscriptions. Each example is illustrated in the catalog, and data about syntax, dating, context, and meaning are included in the appropriate listing. The main catalog (Chapter 9) is organized according to the pattern of affixes found on each example; the distribution of these affix patterns is summarized in Appendix 1, and the contents of the catalog are reorganized in Appendix 2 according to the numerical designation of J. Eric S. Thompson's *A Catalog of Maya Hieroglyphics* (1962). Appendix 3 lists each example by site, monument, and glyph block designation, while Appendix 4 list events in chronological order.

References to examples in the verb catalog are listed in the main text as "Chart 21:3," "Chart 37," etc. The first number refers to the chart designation in the catalog, and the second (following the colon) to the individual example on that chart. The traditional orthography used in glyphic studies is employed in all discussions of glyphic texts and individual glyphs. This orthography uses "c" and "k" for the non-glottalized and glottalized "k," while adding " ' " to other consonants to indicate glottalization. This orthography is ossified in the literature, and attempting to change it would result in confusion without a corresponding gain in sense. Linguistic data

not used in direct associations with glyphic readings are written in the following orthography:

b	p	t	tz	ch	k	q		i		u
b'	p'	t'	tz'	ch'	k'	q'	'		ɨ	
		s		x		j	h	e		o
m	n				N				a	
w			y							
	l									
	r									

This book was produced in an unorthodox fashion that I believe is destined in the future to become an important part of scholarly publication. Because of the length of the manuscript and the complex formats used to present catalog and appendices, it was decided in consulation with the editors and designers of the University of Texas Press to produce photo-ready copy using a microcomputer. The computer used was a Heath H89 utilizing at first the PIE word processing program, and later when it became available, converting to the Micropro "Wordstar" program. The most difficult problem in the production of the finished copy arose when the Press designers chose a proportionally spaced type font; our Diablo 630 printer does not have the hardware to support proportionally spaced daisy-wheels. David Schele, my long suffering husband, wrote a program to solve this problem by processing text for proportional spacing before it was sent to the printer; this program is compatible with the embedded commands of the "Wordstar" program. The necessity of using incompatible word processing programs and adapting files to the proportional spacing program proved frustrating and doubled the time needed to produce final copy, but in the process many of the problems inherent in using micro-computers to produce a complicated book were identified and solved.

The use of computers to produce finished copy is not new in publications by university presses, but, in most cases, large university computers have been used, rather than author-owned micro-computers. The extended capabilities provided by these micro-computers offer invaluable new potential to authors in all scholarly fields. Not only does author-produced, photo-ready copy reduce the cost of publication by a large percentage, but the retention of production and editorial controls of the manuscript allows major and minor revisions to be made at no additional cost until the moment when the final copy is printed. This ability to alter text was crucial to the production of the catalog because during and after the time the texts files were being created, new inscriptions at Nah Tunich and Rio Azul as well as other monuments were discovered, and several crucial new interpretations were proposed by Peter Mathews, David Stuart, and Floyd Lounsbury. I was able to include this material in the catalog because of the use of the micro-computer; in any other process, revisions of the catalog would have ceased when the manuscript editing process began.

The use of a micro-computer produces copy not equal in quality to that produced commercially, but I believe that the gain in last minute control over the contents of the text and the possibility of using complex designs and formats that would be prohibitively expensive if produced commercially make the loss of print quality well worth the exchange. If an unusually large number of typos occur in the published text, I take full responsibility; I continued to revise the text after the final Press editing, believing that up-to-date text was more important than perfect copy.

1. A Historical Perspective

The history of the study of Maya hiero-glyphic writing has been summarized criti-cally and in detail by David Kelley (1962a; 1976:3-6), and his commentary need not be recounted here. However, a brief discussion of studies that have focused on or contri-buted to the understanding of the grammar and syntax of the Classic Maya writing sys-tem will be useful. Until 1950, the study of Maya hieroglyphic writing focused on pro-blems in the decipherment of individual glyphs, on arguments about the nature of the system (that is, the question of the pre-sence or absence of phoneticism), and on questions of reading order and calendric and astronomical information. These early stu-dies provided occasional identifications of glyphs as particular events or verbs; for example, Léon De Rosny and Cyrus Thomas identified a glyph for "baptism," and Eduard Seler found glyphs for "capture" and for "drill." However, with few exceptions, the earlier studies did not systematically attempt to identify syntactical and gramma-tical parts of a given text. Paul Schellhas (1904) completed (perhaps unintentionally) the first systematic study of syntax in his comparative study of deity names in the codices. Given the assumption that codical texts record spoken language and, therefore, contain verbs, objects, and subjects, his identifications of deity names are simulta-neously identifications of objects and sub-jects.

Sylvanus G. Morley in his *Introduction to the Study of Maya Hieroglyphic Writing* (1975, originally published in 1915), con-centrated almost exclusively on glyphs recording calendric information, but his work included some very interesting and prophetic speculations. His introductory chapter includes the following passage:

The classification followed herein is based on the general meaning of the glyphs, and therefore has the advantage of being at least self-explanatory. It divides the glyphs into two groups: (1) Astronomical, calendary, and numerical signs, that is glyphs used in counting time; and (2) glyphs accompanying the preceding, which have an explanatory function of some sort, probably describing the nature of the occasions which the first group of glyphs designate. . . . Of the unknown glyphs in both the inscrip-tions and the codices, a part at least have to do with numerical calculations of some kind, a fact which relegates such glyphs to the first group. The author believes that as the reading of the Maya glyphs progresses, more and more characters will be assigned to the first group and fewer and fewer to the second. In the end, however, there will be left what we may perhaps call a "textual residue," that is, those glyphs which ex-plain the nature of the events that are to be associated with the corresponding chrono-logical parts. It is here, if anywhere, that fragments of Maya history will be found recorded, and precisely here is the richest field for future research, since the suc-cessful interpretation of this "textual resi-due" will alone disclose the true meaning of the Maya writings.

(Morley 1975:26)

In his analysis of the text of Quirigua Stela J, Morley (1975:221) applied the me-thod of analysis implicit in his classification system, and as a result he correctly identified for the first time two verbal phrases in a Classic monumental text. We now know these events to be the accession of Two-Legged-Sky of Quirigua and a war event which involved that Quirigua ruler and 18-Rabbit of Copan.

Although identifications of grammatical parts, such as locative prepositions, had occurred during the early period of Maya hieroglyphic studies, the first analysis of a text based on a purely syntactical approach was produced by Benjamin Whorf (1933), although the "readings" he suggested in this study have been universally rejected. Whorf's method was based on a correlation of particular glyphs in a text to elements in the scene which accompanies it. He was able to identify the name of the pictured deity and the glyph which records an object held in the deity's hand, and by elimination, he assumed that the remaining glyph (the initial glyph of each text) was a verb, defined by him as "a word that names the action or status" (Whorf 1933:7). He further demonstrated that the same verbal glyph in other texts appears in the same position and with the same action.

Thompson disagreed with Whorf's proposed readings and his syntactical analysis, as shown in the following statement:

A fundamental misconception has, I think, handicapped nearly all those who have endeavored to decipher glyphs which are above the pictures in the divinatory almanacs of the codices. This misconception, I believe, arises from regarding the glyphs above each picture as serving to explain the pictures. Thus, for example, Whorf (1933) assumed that the glyph of a hand referred to the action of the god depicted below it, and on that assumption based a large part of his argument; Gates (1931:136-139) similarly linked glyphs to pictures. I myself prefer to suppose the opposite, namely, that the pictures are subordinate to the glyphs and supplement them. I believe that whereas one or more of the glyphs, particularly the name glyphs of the gods, are illustrated in the pictures, the actions of the gods do not necessarily correspond to the texts.

(Thompson 1950:263)

Although Thompson was reluctant to allow the consistent association of a pictured action with an accompanying text, he was not reticent in identifying the general syntactical order of codical texts, as shown in the following statement: "The first two glyphs in each text are quite often repeated in all of the compartments of the almanac in question. They may therefore indicate the general subject under discussion, or perhaps be of a still more general nature. I assume one is a verb or verbal noun; the other the object" (Thompson 1950:264).

And in 1959, Thompson advanced the following description of the components of codical texts: "Generally, each compartment holds four glyphs: (1) an action or verbal glyph; (2) the name glyph of the god ruling the days in question, usually the subject; (3) sometimes an object; (4) the last glyph or pair of glyphs recording the augury resulting from the action or influence of the god--abundance, drought, good times, misery, and so forth" (Thompson 1959:357).

Gunter Zimmerman, perhaps the most conservative and methodical of Maya epigraphers, employed major semantic classifications in his 1956 catalog of codical glyphs, but he preferred to apply neutral terms to each category, as follows: (1) nominal glyphs or name glyphs of pictured deities and mythological animals; (2) attributive glyphs, which are distributed in relationship to the glyphs in Category 1; (3) grace-offering glyphs; (4) thematic glyphs; and (5) contact glyphs, which are associated with "certain cosmic fixed points, such as 'cardinal directions, zero date 4 Ahau 8 Cumku, etc.' or are bound to a conspicuous jawless head (main sign 128), both of which belong to the 'offering-grace' group" (Zimmerman n.d.). Of the "thematic" category, Zimmerman gave the following definition: "All those glyphs were designated as 'thematic' glyphs (ThG) which appear mostly in the first or second place of the glyph blocks, showing only slight affix variation. . . . They undoubtedly refer, in some way or other, to the theme treated and also represented in the corresponding passages. For this reason, the neutral label 'thematic' glyph was chosen, so as not to prejudge a particular nuance (as in action perhaps)" (Zimmerman n.d.).

Thompson's and Zimmerman's analyses of codical texts were extended to include Classical monumental inscriptions when Berlin (1959) identified personal name glyphs on the sarcophagus at Palenque. He associated a series of glyphs located adjacent to figures on the sarcophagus sides to similar glyphs in the lid text, and proposed that these glyphs named the persons portrayed. As with the Schellhas discovery of deity names, Berlin's discovery of historical names held syntactical implications. If it is assumed that name phrases in the text of the sarcophagus occur in a readable, linguistic context, they not only record personal names, but also function as the subjects of verbs. And indeed, exactly this syntactical pattern of verb-subject was demonstrated in this text by Floyd Lounsbury (1974) and shown to be the preferred order in Classic texts by Proskouriakoff (1960).

In her seminal work on the inscriptions of Piedras Negras, Proskouriakoff (1960) pointed out repeated patterns in glyph distribution that were associated with particular sculptural motifs. By showing that the particular glyphs found in these patterns were separated by time spans no longer than a human lifetime, she confirmed Morley's earlier speculations about the historical nature of the Classic inscriptions. She identified glyphs recording birth, inauguration, capture, "a rite performed in memory of a dead hero" (Proskouriakoff 1960:470), and blood-letting. In regard to the identification of verbs, she said, "It seems safe to say that glyphs which immediately follow dates and especially those that tend to combine with the 'lunar' postfix make reference to actions, events or ceremonies, and are essentially predicate glyphs. Following them we can expect to find substantives referring to the protagonists of the events, and if the representations are historical, some of these should be appellatives identi-

fying the persons involved" (Proskouriakoff 1960:470).

In the two decades since the publication of Proskouriakoff's study of the inscriptions of Piedras Negras, her "historical hypothesis" has become widely accepted among epigraphers. In his study of the Tablet of the 96 Glyphs at Palenque, Berlin best summarized the impact of the "historical hypothesis" on subsequent approaches to the decipherment of Maya hieroglyphic writing:

Apparently our whole analysis so far has been developed exclusively from the foregoing text. But in reality two basic ideas have crept into the picture from elsewhere: the reflection that the DN's are shorter than a normal human lifetime, and the possibility of actor and action glyphs. The possible actor glyphs we have previously interpreted as the names of Palenque rulers. These ideas were taken from Proskouriakoff (1960) and now applied to this Palenque text. They form part of her "historical hypothesis." We can hope, by just thinking in terms of the structure of history, to understand all those glyphs pertaining to history. If then, as is not unlikely, undeciphered glyphs still remain, their meaning must be looked for in other networks of patterns, such as astronomy or religion. The historical approach will hardly yield interpretational results in the codices, for example. There, the visual structure distinguished between glyphs of action (verbs) and actors, just as the historical approach has done in the inscriptions. As very different verbs are used in the codices from those used in the inscriptions, the nature of the latter could not be identified directly through the former. As we have verbs in the codices and inscriptions, all of them can be subjected to another structural system: grammar.

(Berlin 1968:140)

The use of the "historical hypothesis" has produced in published and not yet published forms detailed analyses of the inscriptions of Yaxchilan, Bonampak, Palenque, Tikal, Quirigua, Naranjo, sites in the Petex Batun region, Tonina, and other sites. Not only have detailed dynastic histories been developed for these and other sites, but the inventory of known events has been extended to include alternative expressions for birth and accession, as well as several glyphs recording death and two forms of a glyph for burial. Events associated with war and sacrifice as well as blood-letting have been identified, and more complicated expressions for period ending rites have been added to those listed in Thompson's *Maya Hieroglyphic Writing: An Introduction* (1950).

This "historical" approach will continue to yield results for many years to come, but it is now evident that the recovery of the original language values of glyphs now understood semantically is not necessarily a by-product of this approach. In recent years, Floyd Lounsbury has pioneered an approach which not only utilizes the historical hypothesis, but also concentrates linguistic methods and information on problems of decipherment. Central to the Lounsbury approach is a paraphrased reconstruction using approximate semantic values in modern languages of the components of a Classic text. As a result of this para-

phrasing technique, Lounsbury (1980:107) has identified couplet structures in verbal phrases and full clauses, as well as patterns of deletion and gapping in which redundant information is eliminated from extended or compound clauses. The new syntactical information resulting from this approach has revealed the need for a working understanding of the verb morphology of the writing system. I suspect that no single person possesses the knowledge necessary to explain fully this verb morphology because not enough information is known about the Mayan languages of the colonial literature and of the Classic inscriptions; however, both areas of study are now receiving growing attention from linguists. Assuming that neither epigraphers nor linguists have the time required to become specialists in each other's fields, this study is designed to provide both sets of scholars with the comparative and distributional data on the Classic inscriptions necessary to bring linguistic information to bear on the problem.

2. Verb Morphology and Syntax of Spoken Mayan

For a number of reasons, some form of early Cholan is accepted by most epigraphers and linguists as the language of the Classic inscriptions. At the time of the conquest, Cholan languages--i.e., Chol, Chontal, Chol-ti, and Chorti--are known to have had a geographical distribution roughly corresponding to that of the Classic Maya inscriptions. Cholan seems to have once been (probably during the Classic period) a prestige language, since Cholan words (such as family names and faunal and floral terms) have been borrowed into adjacent languages, such as Yucatec. And finally, specialized syntactical structures particularly characteristic of Cholan languages have been detected in the Classic inscriptions. In light of the probable identification of Cholan as the language of the inscriptions, it will be useful to review those characteristics of Cholan and other Mayan languages that are likely to be detectable in the writing system. The descriptions of the features are deliberately presented in simplified terms to accommodate those readers who are not familiar with linguistic terminology.

Many Mayan languages are ergative, a term employed to characterize languages in which the subject of an intransitive verb and the object of a transitive verb are expressed by pronouns or nouns in the nominative (or "absolutive") case, while the subject of a transitive verb is expressed by a pronoun or noun in an oblique case, generally called the "ergative" case, which in some langua-

ges--as in Mayan--coincides with the possessive case as employed for the possession of nouns. In other words in most Mayan languages, there are two sets of pronouns which are used in the following contexts (see Bricker 1977 for a more detailed discussion and comparative listing of pronouns from most Maya languages): (1) Set A (the ergative set), which marks the subjects of transitive verbs and the possessors of nouns, and (2) Set B (the absolutive set), which marks the subjects of intransitive verbs and the objects of transitives verbs. These sets of pronouns are listed by Kaufman and Norman (n.d.) in proto-Cholan and proto-Mayan follows:

1. Set A (the ergative set)
   Preconsonantal

	Proto-Cholan	Proto-Mayan
1s	*in-	**nu-
2s	*a-	**aa-
3s	*u-	**u-
1p	*ka-	**qa-
2p	*i-	**ee-
3p	*u-	**ki-

   Prevocalic

	Proto-Cholan	Proto-Mayan
1s	*inw-	**w-
2s	*aw-	**aaw-
3s	*uy-	**r-
1p	*k-	**q-
2p	*iw-	**eer-
3p	*uy-	**k-

2. Set B (the absolutive set)

	Proto-Cholan	Proto-Mayan
1s	*-en	**-in
2s	*-et	**-at
3s	*-∅	**-∅
1p	*-on	**-o'n
2p	*-ox	**-ix (ex)
3p	*-ob'	**-ob'

Some Mayan languages, including the Cholan language Chorti, have a third set of pronouns, which appear to be used only with the incompletive aspect of intransitive verbs (see Appendix 5).

Some dozen or so signs have been identified and accepted by most epigraphers as representing Mayan pronouns. All of these pronoun signs are prefixed and are freely substitutable with each other and with T1, the sign appearing in Landa's "alphabet" as *u*. No postfixed signs have yet been identified as pronouns. Since *u* is the third person pronoun of Set A (the ergative set), and since the equivalent pronoun in Set B (the absolutive set) is -∅, it may be inferred that, to the extent presently understood, the Classic inscriptions are recorded in the third person, and that they conform to the expectations based on the structure of spoken languages, in both transitive and intransitive contexts. Those signs so far identified as third person signs of the ergative set are as follows:

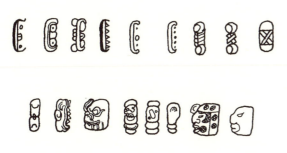

Recently Victoria Bricker (n.d.) has proposed that the Classic writing system reflects not an ergative morphology, but rather that of a split-ergative system, and Barbara MacLeod and Will Norman (personal communication, 1980) have both detected split-ergative morphology in the Cholan languages. To understand split-ergativity, it is necessary to define another characteristic of Mayan languages--tense-aspect. Tense defines an action, event, or state according to whether it is in the future, the present, or the past; in contrast, aspect differentiates an action, event, or state according to whether it is continuing (imperfective or incomplete) or has terminated (perfective or completive), regardless of the tense. Split-ergative languages, such as Cholan and Yucatecan, utilize one or the other of the pronoun sets as subjects of intransitive verbs according to whether the aspect is imperfective or perfective. Bricker (n.d.) defined the expected morphology of an ergative and split-ergative system as follows:

1. Ergative

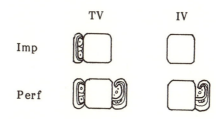

2. Split-ergative

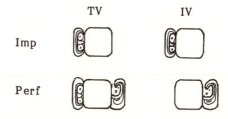

She further posited that T181 -*ah*, one of the most frequently occurring of the inscriptional verbal suffixes, is the marker for the perfective aspect. Although the

distribution of verbal affixing in the inscriptions does not precisely match the
split-ergative pattern, Bricker's proposal
provides the most successful explanation of
the affix patterns in the glyphic system so
far posited, and it explains major anomalies
in which clearly intransitive verbs (i.e.,
the auxiliary verb T757) appear consistently
with a third-person ergative pronoun. The
Classic writing system may well reflect a
split-ergative language.

In Mayan languages, differentiations for
aspect (perfective and imperfective) are
accomplished by the addition of suffixes to
the lexical stem. Several additional differentiations for tense (i.e. present or
past), mode, and further refinements of
aspect are accomplished by particles preposed to the pronouns, or contracted with
them. These tense/aspect particles precede
both the Set A pronouns and the verbal stem
in the following patterns:

1. Transitive

tense- + Set A + stem + perfective + Set B
aspect pronoun   suffix   pronoun

2. Intransitive

tense-   +   stem + perfective + Set B
aspect   suffix   pronoun

Lounsbury (in Mathews n.d.b) has tentatively identified a *tu* (T115) prefix as a
tense-aspect particle + ergative pronoun (*t*
+ *u*) on a burial verb on Stela 8 at Dos
Pilas (see Chart 27). Otto G. Schumann
(1973:23,25) and Viola Warkentin and Ruby
Scott (1980:34) identify *t-* or *ta-* as the
past or completive tense-aspect for Tila
Chol (*tza* in Tumbala Chol), and *t-* is
recorded as the completive aspect for transitives in Colonial Yucatec by Mauricio
Swadesh, Ma. Cristina Alvarez, and Juan R.
Bastarrachea (1970:23), in Itza by Schumann
(1971), in Lacandon by Roberto Bruce (1968:
61), and in Chontal by Smailus (1975:168).
However, the writing system is notable
for the absence of signs which appear in

positions that suggest that they are preposed tense-aspect particles. I was able to
find only six examples which include a *tu*
(T115 or T89) prefix, and with the exception
of pronoun signs (T1 and its equivalents),
only T228, *ah* or *a* (see Chart 130) and T126
(see Charts 62 and 129) are found prefixed
to verbal glyphs. The rarity of tense-aspect
prefixes in the writing system may be explained by the kind of pattern reconstructed
for Colonial Yucatec by Swadesh, Alvarez,
and Bastarrachea (1970:25). For root transitive verbs, they reconstructed the following
pattern:

1. The Present
   Present   Set A + verb stem + -*ik*
   Pres durative *tan* + Set A + verb stem + -*ik*
   Pres habitual *k-* + Set A + verb stem + -*ik*
   Habitual**   *k-* + Set A + verb stem

   ** with implications of the present

2. The Past
   Past   Set A + verb stem + -*ah*
   Past habitual *t-* + Set A + verb stem + -*ah*
   Habitual**   *t-* + Set A + verb stem

   **with implications of the past

Bruce reports a similar pattern from Lacandon in the following statement:

The prefix t- *of the preterite is distinguished from the* t- *of the present by the
simultaneous use of the suffix* -a(h) *of the
preterite instead of the* -ik *of the present.
Examples of its use:*

t-in w-il-ik
"I am seeing it."

t-in w-il-ah
"I saw it."

t-u t'in-ah
"He called it."

Some of the previously mentioned alterna-
tion among the dozen or so preposed glyphic
pronouns may possibly be due to their

reflection of the contraction of preposed tense-aspect particles with the pronoun from Set A.

In addition to transitive and intransitive verbs, a third category--the positional--is important to the study of the writing system. Positionals are special terms used to describe both position and shape in space; for example, there are distinct terms for "lying face down" versus "lying face up." As verbs, these positionals appear with inflectional patterns distinct from those of the intransitive and transitive, and these positional patterns of inflection have been detected in the writing system. T644, the glyph for "to seat" or "to place" (clearly a positional verb) appears with two kinds of verbal suffixes: (1) the suffix -wan (T130.116), the aspectual suffix for the completive reconstructed for proto-Cholan (Kaufman and Norman n.d.); and (2) the suffix -lah (T178.181), possibly a combination of the positional inchoative -l- and the past (perfective?) -ah (see Charts 85 and 112). The presence of either affix pattern on a glyphic verb is probably a good indication that it is a positional verb.

The aspectual suffixes for the three categories of verbs have been reconstructed in proto-Cholan by Kaufman and Norman (n.d.) as follows (incomplete and completive are equivalent to imperfective and perfective):

1. Transitive stems

	Root TV	Derived TV
Incompletive	*CVC-v	*...v-n
Completive	*CVC-v	*...v
Imperative	*CVC-v	*...v-n
Pf pass pt	*CVC-b'il	*...v-n-b'il

     Specification of v:

         -v_1 (Chol, Chorti, Chontal)

         -i, -e (Chontal, Acalan Chontal)

2. Intransitives

Incompletive	*-el
Completive	*-i
Imperative	*-en
Pf pt	*-em
Irrealis	*-ik

3. Positionals

Stative	*-v_ll
Incompletive	*-tɨl
Completive	*-wan-i
Future	*-le-k
Imperative	*-i, -l-en

The contrast between transitive and intransitive inflection patterns is mediated in Mayan languages by several forms. In passive constructions, the patient become the subject of the verb and the verbal inflection utilizes Set B, the absolutive set. In these constructions, the agent may or may not be explicitly expressed, but it is understood though not identified, as in "He was captured." When the agent is expressed, it appears following an agency expression, as in "He was captured *by John*." Yucatec uses the expression *tu men* "by his doing," while several different agency expressions occur in the Cholan languages. *U men(el)* appears in Chorti and Cholti; and *i cha'an* in Chol. In addition *ti k'ɨb'* can occur in Chol when the agent is human.

In the medio-passive (or middle voice), the patient is again the subject of the verb, but in contrast to the passive, the agent is unspecified and general, as in "He got caught." Mayan languages can also reflect the different kinds of circumstances for unspecified agency, as in "He caught because of his nature," "He got caught because of the circumstances," and "He got caught because of an unknown."

Transitive constructions can also be mediated in the antipassive, a term used to describe constructions in which the patient is general or unspecified. These kinds of constructions are in contrast to root transitive verbs in which a patient is understood whether or not it is explicitly named, as in "He ate (it)" versus "He ate." The contrasts in the various degrees of transitivity are important because of evidence from the writing system. *Chuc* "capture" is the one of root transitive verb securely identified in the Classic writing system, and one would expect it to occur most frequently with recognizable transitive inflection, in other words prefixed by *u*. Yet of the forty-five examples recorded in the verb catalog, only two appear with *u* or an equivalent as a prefix. The absence of a preposed ergative pronoun in the remaining forty-three examples suggests that they may be passive constructions in which an explicitly named agent would appear in an agency expression. Fortunately, there are several glyphs that occur between the name phrases of the patient and agent in these contexts: T1.501:102, T1.526:136 *u cab*, and T515: 69var.86, a glyph occurring only on the newly discovered Structure 20 Hieroglyphic Stairs at Yaxchilan. However, eighteen of the "capture" examples are followed by the names of the patient and agent without any intervening glyphs; in three examples, only the patient is named; in fifteen examples, one of the possible agency glyphs appears between the names of the patient and agent; and in the remaining examples, neither the patient or agent is named or the text is too badly damaged to be deciphered. And the distribution of these syntactical patterns is not dependent on any particular suffix pattern.

Statives, another verbal category, are important to the study of the writing system because they have been identified in the Dresden Codex. Statives are equational constructions which reflect a state or condition of the subject. They are formed by the addition of the absolutive pronouns (Set B) to a noun or adjective stem, as in the following Chol examples (the pronouns reconstructed for proto-Cholan are used):

winik-on
"I am a man."

winik-∅
"He is a man."

Notice that in the second example, which is inflected for third person singular, the appearance of the stative in the hieroglyphic system would be that of a noun; only the

syntactical position of *winik* would point to its function as a stative verb.

The statives so far identified in the Dresden Codex are recorded as possessed conditions, as in the following examples (given in proto-Cholan):

u kuch-on Juan
"I am the burden of Juan."

u kuch-∅ Juan
"He is the burden of Juan."

u kuch-∅
"He is his burden."

Notice that the two final examples (both are inflected for the third person singular) display the same surface morphology as would a transitive verb inflected for third person singular in both of the pronoun sets.

Several of the known period ending expression may be possessed statives, as in the following examples from the Temple of Inscriptions at Palenque.

U pat Hun Ahau Katun
It [was] the end of the 1 Ahau Katun

U pat tun.
It [was] the end of the tun.

Possessed statives create problems in decipherment because appearance alone does not distinguish between a possessed stative and a transitive inflected for the third person singular in both the ergative and the absolutive sets of pronouns.

Verb roots in Mayan languages can be derived from any source, i.e., from nouns, adjectives, positionals, onomatopoetic stems, and transitives from intransitives and vice versa, by the addition of derivational suffixes. Those glyphic affixes that occur in distributions similar to derivational affixes in spoken Mayan languages seem to represent phonetic signs without fixed semantic value. In the process of organizing the data for the verb catalog, I noticed that many of the affix signs could appear with nouns as well as verbs or with other grammatical functions. For example, T181 *ah* appears not only as a verbal suffix, but as the male article *ah*; T24 appears as a -*vl* suffix on nouns as well as verbs; and T130 appears as the phonetic complement -*w(a)* in the ahau glyph where it has no semantic value at all. From these and other examples of multiple function, it is clear that in most, if not all, cases verbal affixes represent a phonetic value without being fixed to a particular semantic function. In terms of the writing system, the interesting question about verbal suffixes seems to be not only "What is the passive affix?" but also "What can -*vl* or -*ah* do?"

T181 and others as male article ah (1-3);
T181 as verbal suffix (4)

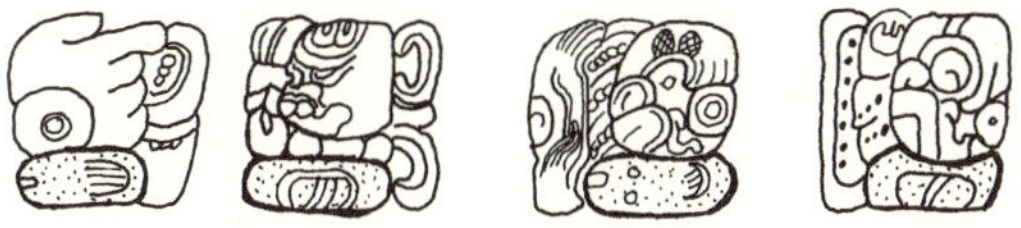

Probable -vl affixes with verbs (1 and 2)
and with nouns (3 and 4)

-wa as a verbal affix (1 and 2)
and as a phonetic complement (3 and 4)

Figure 1. Examples of unrelated semantic
functions for sample affixes.

3. Identification of Verbal Phrases

Whorf's (1933) demonstration of the word order of texts in the codices is still accepted today and was cited by Kelley (1976:188) in his discussion of the Maya writing system. Most working epigraphers are fully aware of the arguments on verb identification, but it is appropriate in the context of this discussion of the glyphic verb to begin with the basic problem of word order and the evidence for the syntactical location of the verb phrase. Since, as noted by Berlin (1968:140), there is direct linkage between the pictorial scenes and glyphic texts in the codices, examples from the Dresden Codex will be used in the discussion. Arguments for widely accepted readings or meanings of glyphs will not be presented; see Thompson (1950) and Kelley (1976) for illustrations and identifications of these glyphs and their readings.

In four scenes on Dresden 30c-31c (Fig. 2), part of a series of nine scenes which illustrate an almanac of 2,340 days, God B is shown seated in a tree. The text accompanying each scene is composed of four glyphs, three of which are identifiable. In all four texts, the glyph in position 2 names the protagonist as God B; position 3 records God B's tree, which in each case is preceded by a color term (red, white, black, and yellow) dependent on the direction glyphs appearing in position 4. The last three glyphs include, therefore, the name of the person shown, the tree in which he is shown, and the color and direction of the tree in the following pattern:

1. God B   red tree in the east
2. God B   white tree   north
3. God B   black tree   west
4. God B in the yellow tree   south

Of the four glyphs in each text, only the initial glyphs (T712) cannot be identified as a part of the scene. This initial glyph must record, therefore, the action in which God B (the only actor pictured in the scenes) is engaged. The precise meaning of the glyph cannot necessarily be deduced from this scene because in the succeeding five scenes in this almanac, the same verb appears with scenes in which God B is shown in an unidentified enclosure, on a sky band, and in three other kinds of trees. And a quick survey of the almanac following that under discussion will show that this same verb accompanies scenes showing God B on stone thrones, in rain, in houses, in a cage, and in various other locations. The event cannot refer specifically to being in a tree, but must express some more general kind of "locational" activity.

The identification of the T712 glyph from Dresden 30c-31c as some sort of "locational" verb is supported by the recurrence of this verb as an initial glyph in texts accompanying thirteen scenes on Dresden 65b-69b. In these thirteen scenes, God B is shown in thirteen locations, but in several cases (Fig. 3), the location appears pictographically following the "locational" verb. In each of the three illustrated examples, the "locational" verb occurs in position 1,

Figure 2. Dresden 30c-31c: verb initial construction.

while the name of the pictured actor (God B) appears in position 3. In the first text, the verb is followed by *ti* (a locative preposition), *yax-te'* "ceiba tree," and God B is shown sitting in a tree. In the second example, God B is shown in a cave-like enclosure marked by *cab* "earth" signs, and the second glyph in the text is *cab*. Note that the upper end of the pictured enclosure is marked with a motif similar to the upper detail of the *zac* "white" glyph that precedes the *cab* glyph in the text above. In the third example, God B sits above two T563 motifs which are clearly the same as the signs in the second glyph of the text above the scene. The word order of all of these texts is: "locational" verb/preposition + the location/actor.

In Whorf's argument and in the discussion of the two sets of examples used here, the verb was identified by a process of elimination and comparison, but there are also examples in the Dresden Codex where the verb

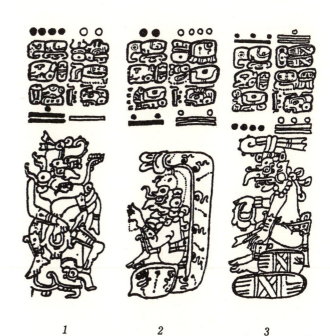

1   2   3

Figure 3. Dresden 67b-68b: verb initial construction.

is graphically a picture of the action shown. On Dresden 68a (Fig. 4), the scene shows God B figures seated back-to-back atop a sky-band. A "lazy-S" floats above the head of each God B, but the right figure is shown seated in rain, while the background behind the left is clear. The text above this scene begins with a glyph composed of two bodies seated back-to-back in a direct reference to the posture of the figures in the scene. The "lazy-S" of the scene occurs as the second glyph, and God B is named in positions 3 and 4, where his name glyph is preceded by a glyph that also appears to refer to the scene. This glyph (position 3) is composed of a seated body attached to a "sky" glyph, and God B is seated on a sky-band. In this text, the glyphs recording the verb and the subject refer pictographically to the scene they explicate.

The initial position of the verbal phrase is characteristic of the texts of the codices, although in some instances directional glyphs may precede the verbal expression (see Dresden 22b). In those examples viola-

ting the verb-initial position, the syntactical construction seems to be that of the stative in which no verb appears. A clear example of this kind of construction is found in the "burden" scenes of the Dresden Codex in which a figure, usually the Young Moon Goddess, is shown carrying another figure or an object in a back bundle (Fig. 5). The texts accompanying these scenes are composed of a glyph naming the object or figure carried (position 1); the "burden" glyph preceded by T1 (*u*) or an equivalent (a third person pronoun of Set A) (position 2); and the name glyph of the person who carries the burden. If this kind of glyphic construction is transitive, then the word order is object-verb-subject (OVS), but it is more likely to be a stative construction composed of the components, "cargo/the burden of/the carrier," paraphrased as "cargo [is] the burden of the carrier."

In Figure 5, the small figures, God B and God A, are the cargo, and their name glyphs appear in position 1 of the text. The glyph in position 2 is *u cuch* "her burden." The

Figure 4. Dresden 68a:
a pictographic verb.

Figure 5. Dresden 16b:
stative constructions.

carrier is named as the Young Moon Goddess in position 3, and Thompson's "augury" (Zimmerman's "attributive") glyph occurs in position 4. These two texts are stative constructions and are paraphrased as follows: "God B [is] the burden of the Young Moon Goddess, 'positive'"; "God A [is] the burden of the Young Moon Goddess, 'negative'."

The Dresden Codex also contains passages that can be identified structurally as verb-object-subject (VOS) in which the components can be clearly associated with element in the pictorial scene. Dresden 67a (Fig. 6) shows two participants, God B and God K. God B is clearly acting upon God K, who sits in a blue and white object held in God B's hand. The text above this scene is composed of six glyphs, the first of which should record the event, and indeed, the first glyph has the T181 "lunar" suffix identified by Proskouriakoff (1960:470) as characteristic of verbal glyphs. The second glyph is the name of God K, who is acted upon in the scene, and the glyphs in positions 3 and 4

name the agent, God B, who is the actor in the scene. The word order in this text is VOS. Whorf's original analysis was based on Dresden 12c (Fig. 7), where the text can be shown to refer to an inanimate object (position 2 in each text) which is held by an animate subject (position 3). The verb occurs in position 1, and the word order is VOS.

The kinds of compound verbs and couplet structures characteristic of the Classic inscriptions are not found in the texts of the codices, but there are examples of the deletion of redundant information and one example of a text with a compound subject. An example from Dresden 67b (Fig. 8) will serve as an illustration of one kind of deletion. The text begins with the "locational" verb previously discussed and a glyph giving the location as a "lake" or "bajo." God B is named in position 2, and the glyphs in positions 4 and 5 are "grace-offerings" associated with agriculture and abundance. The last glyph in the text is a possessed noun, which may record something

Figure 6. Dresden 67a:
verb-object-subject constructions.

Figure 7. Dresden 12c:
verb-object-subject constructions.

like "his gift" or "his offering"; however, the antecedent of the possessive pronoun, which should follow the possessed noun in Mayan grammar, does not appear in the text. It has been deleted from the text, and so must be reconstructed from the information as given, and since God B is the only personage named in the text, he must also be identified as the possessor of this noun.

On Dresden 23b (Fig. 9) a similar kind of deletion occurs, but in a more complex context. The first text of this almanac includes a verb and its subject God N (positions 1 and 2). The object, a fish, is shown being held by the Young Moon Goddess in the single scene below. In the first text, the verb, subject, and object are followed by "her gift" and the name glyph and attributive of the Young Moon Goddess. In the remaining texts of the almanac, the name glyphs and attributives of the Young Moon Goddess are deleted, but they are to be understood from the context. Notice that the word order of this text is apparently VSO because of the complexity of the phrase recording the object.

Compound subjects occur on Dresden 8b-9b in texts which accompany scenes showing two personages engaged in the act of throwing

possessor of noun deleted

Figure 8. Dresden 67b: possessor of noun deleted.

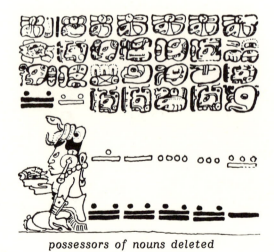

possessors of nouns deleted in the last five texts

Figure 9. Dresden 23b.

Figure 10. Dresden 9b: compound subjects.

dice for an augury. The text on Dresden 9b (Fig. 10) begins with a verbal phrase which Lounsbury (personal communication, 1976) has suggested is *u nuch hax bul* "they join together to cast dice." The verbal phrase is followed by the name glyph and attributive of each of the actors, Itzamna and the Young Maize God. Even if the proposed reading of the verb phrase did not point to the equality of the named persons, the scene shows them acting equally rather than one upon the other; the subject of this text is compound, naming both gods as actors. Notice that the attributives have been eliminated from the name phrase of the second text.

With very few exceptions which are not completely understood, the word order of Classic inscriptions is the same as for the codices. Although the syntax and literary style in the Classic inscriptions can be immensely more complicated than in the later codices, the inscriptions are verb-initial, with the verbal phrase usually found immediately following a date, whether expressed as an Initial Series date with addended data, as a Calendar Round, or as a Distance Number. The simplest clauses are those that utilize the T757 general verb (Fig. 11) to name a person shown in a scene. Such persons can be named without a verbal element in the phrase, but when the T757 general verb appears, there is usually no calendric information in the clause. Simple clauses may be elaborated by the addition of a date, by a complication of the verbal expression, or by elaboration of the name phrase. For

example, in many period ending notations the event may be expressed in two or more verbal phrases before the subject is named. Different events, such as birth and accession, may be linked together, and in many cases redundant information is deleted so that two verbs along with calendric information can be recorded without the appearance of a subject. In almost every instance where a word order seem to violate the VS or VOS order, the exception participates in some such syntactically complex structure.

In contexts where a scene clearly shows one person acting upon another, such as the capture scenes of Yaxchilan Lintel 8 and Bonampak Lintels 1, 2, and 3, the word order is VOS. Proskouriakoff (1960:470; 1963:150-152) first made the correct identification in the Classic inscriptions of the verb for "capture" as well as the name glyphs of the captive and captor. The main text of Yaxchilan Lintel 8 (Fig. 12) is composed of the date, the verb for "capture," the captive Jeweled-Skull, and the captor Bird-Jaguar. The components are clearly verb-patient-agent, although Victoria Bricker (personal communication, 1979) and I have considered the possibility that this is a passive construction with an agency expression between the two names, as in the following paraphrase: "He was captured Jeweled-Skull *by the doing of* Bird-Jaguar."

While there is debate on the syntax of the main text of Lintel 8, as pointed out by Marshall Durbin (n.d.), the syntax of the secondary text is clear. The text opens with

general   name phrase
verb

Figure 11. Yaxchilan Lintel 25, G1-I3:
verb + subject construction.

verb   captive   agency??   captor

Figure 12. Yaxchilan Lintel 8:
"capture" constructions.

the "captor" glyph which is usually considered to be a possessed noun (Fig. 12). In
this text, however, the names of both the
captive and captor follow the "captor" glyph
in word order that is not found with possessed nouns. In Mayan languages, the referent
of the noun precedes it, and the logical
antecedent of a possessive pronoun must
follow the possessed noun. In order for this
text to record "X, the captor of Y," the
name of the captor must precede the possessed noun, but the word order is "captor
glyph/name of captive/name of captor." This
order should not be found with a possessed
noun, but it is characteristic of transitive
constructions, and *u* (T1, the prefix to the
"captor" glyph) is the third person pronoun
of the ergative (the subjects of transitive
verbs as well as the possessors of nouns).
The third person pronoun of the absolutive
set is -∅ in the Yucatecan and Cholan languages, and as expected, the verb above is
shown with only the ergative pronoun. The
syntax of this clause is therefore VOS,
indicating that the transitive word order is
VOS in the Classic writing system as it is
in the inscriptions of the codices.

With the exception of stative constructions in the codices and inscriptions, the
Maya writing system is verb-initial with VS
order in intransitive clauses and VOS in
transitive clauses. Although any word order
can be used in most Mayan languages, the
preferred syntax of Mayan languages is verb-
initial. Thus, the writing system reflects
the structures of the spoken languages.

4. The Directional "Count" Indicators

Most individual clauses and texts of the Classic inscriptions open with some sort of calendric information expressed as a Long Count date, a Calendar Round date, a Distance Number, or a combination of several of these. This calendric information, especially when in the form of an Initial Series date, can be elaborated by noting the position of the day in the Long Count and Calendar Round systems, and by giving its station in the Lords of the Night Series, the Lunar Cycle, and the 819 Day Count. The latter notation usually includes a Distance Number, a Calendar Round date, verb, direction, color, and subject, which as a complete clause can either follow the Initial Series and lunar information or be framed by the tzolkin and haab notations of the Initial Series. Elaborated dates with addended information are usually found at the beginning of Classic texts, but they may also appear within a text (as on Tikal Stela 31 and the Palace Tablet at Palenque) as a means of highlighting an important event.

Many Classic texts include only this kind of Initial Series date (or a less elaborate Calendar Round date) and the verb and subject of a single clause, although either the subject or the verb can occur in very elaborate form. However, in a large number of texts more than one event is recorded, and to prevent ambiguity in time or meaning, these separate events are linked together by means of Distance Numbers (DN), which record the amount of time elapsed between these events. Since the determination of the ear-

lier of two events cannot be made in these contexts without elaborate arithmetical calculations, the Maya used two special glyphs to mark the temporal directions of DNs (Fig. 13). These glyphs, the Anterior Date Indicator (ADI) and Posterior Date Indicator (PDI) were identified by Thompson (1943), who paraphrased them as "count back to" and "count forward to." Thompson's identification of the constants (T741b *xoc*, T513 *mul*, or an inverted vase, and the locative preposition *ti*, T59 or T747b, the head variant) as glyphs for the phrase "count to" appears to be correct, but his paraphrases are less useful because they assume a constant position in the present from which time moves in both directions. Since Classic inscriptions appear to be recorded in the narrative past, and since both the earlier and later of two dates may be marked by these indicator glyphs, they seem to record the two ends of a length of time entirely in the past. Therefore, the paraphrases "count since . . . count until" or "count from . . . count to" have proven much more useful in reconstructing structural paraphrases of Classic texts.

The distinctive feature of the ADI is T126, which appears below or behind the two constants; T679 (or T1), the distinctive feature of the PDI, appears in front of or above the constants. However, these two distinctive signs may function as temporal markers without the presence of the constants by appearing as affixes (prefixed and suffixed in the same pattern) on the main glyph of a verbal expression. The presence of either of these two signs may be considered as diagnostic of the verbal component in an expression which may include modifiers of other grammatical types.

While the PDI or ADI marks a Distance Number as "since" or "until" a certain date, the Anterior and Posterior Event Indicators (AEI and PEI) mark a DN as "since" or "until" a certain event. Any passage with more than one event recorded may contain one or both of either pair of temporal indicators, but usually only one member of a single set is used. If one event or date of a pair is marked as the point from which or to which a

DN is to be counted, the temporal position of the other is abundantly clear from the context. However, in rare texts, all four indicators can appear to mark the dates and events of a text, and in some cases, without intervening date or event, as if the text were saying, "It was so much time count since count until a date." In all of these cases, two dates or events are present in the text, and the DN is to be counted between them.

The recognition of these temporal indicators, especially the AEI and PEI, is particularly important to the study of the syntax of the writing system because they mark

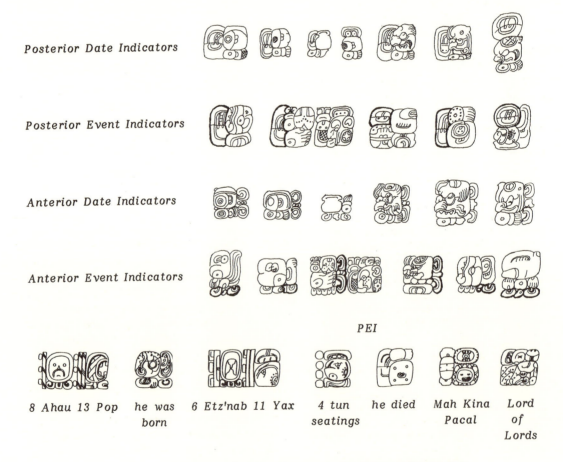

Posterior Date Indicators

Posterior Event Indicators

Anterior Date Indicators

Anterior Event Indicators

PEI

8 Ahau 13 Pop   *he was born*   *6 Etz'nab 11 Yax*   *4 tun seatings*   *he died*   *Mah Kina Pacal*   *Lord of Lords*

Palenque Temple of Inscriptions Sarcophagus 1-9
(lower drawing by Merle Greene Robertson)

Figure 13. Anterior and Posterior Indicators.

clearly the earlier and later of related dates and events. Not only does this feature allow the temporal sequence of events to detected, but the presence of the AEI and PEI on verbal glyphs is also helpful when DNs are associated with two events of which the date or subject of one is deleted. The constants of the ADI and PDI can appear without T125 and T679 as an auxiliary verb which must read *"mul ti (or xoc ti) verbal noun."* In these instances no DN is associated with the verbal phrase.

In terms of the grammatical function of these temporal indicators, Lounsbury (1974:17), in his analysis of the text of the sarcophagus of the Temple of Inscriptions at Palenque, suggested that T679a, the PEI and the variable in the PDI, might be the Chol preposed third person ergative pronoun *i*, based on Thompson's (1962:281) identification of T679 as the allograph of Landa's *i* sign. Regarding the possible function of T679 as an ergative pronoun, Lounsbury made the following comments:

The glyphic u prefix also occurs in Palenque inscriptions as a sign for the third-person pronoun. This does not necessarily militate against recognition of the i sign (if that's what it is) in this function however. There are two possible ways in which these signs could have alternated with each other. One possibility is that the u sign had come to be interpreted as a morpheme sign for the third-person and so could be used for that meaning regardless of the local pronunciation. The other possibility is the 7th-century Chol might have had, as Chorti does today, two sets of preposed pronouns where the other languages have but one. The two third-person preposed pronouns in Chorti are u and a, the choice between them being a function of the grammatical voice of the verb. The second is normal in middle-voice verbs, and "to be born" and "to die" are verbs of that voice. One would have to suppose that the Chol of an earlier period had u and i in these separate functions. The u has precedent in a number of other Mayan languages where it has taken over both functions; the i is the Chol form of today.
(Lounsbury 1974:17)

Lounsbury's earlier assumption that in this Palenque inscription (Fig. 13) T679

could not be functioning as a PEI was based on the absence of an associated DN. However, the "four tun seatings" glyph at 6 must surely be identified as a DN recording the four katun seatings (9.9.0.0.0, 9.10.0.0.0, 9.11.0.0.0, and 9.12.0.0.0) that occurred four katun seatings (9.9.0.0.0, 9.10.0.0.0, 9.11.0.0.0, and 9.12.0.0.0) that occurred between Pacal's birth and his death. DNs recorded in terms of katun endings are also utilized in the opening passages of the Tablet of the Slaves, so that there is evidence that time intervening between events could be recorded in terms of period endings as well as the more expected accumulation of days.

In 1980, Victoria Bricker (n.d.) posited a solution to the problem of the "count" notations that is very similar to Lounsbury's earlier suggestions. She outlined the structural implications of a split-ergative system on the inflection of glyphic verbs in the following pattern:

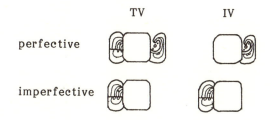

Like Lounsbury, she proposed the existence of two preposed third person pronouns, *u* and *i*, but she linked the appearance of T679 to the imperfective status of transitive and intransitive verbs and to the perfective status of transitive verbs. Utilizing examples from colonial Mayan literature, she proposed that in contexts where two events are linked by DNs, the earlier of the two appears in two appears in perfective form and without preposed pronouns and the later verb appears in imperfective form with T679 as the preposed pronoun, and without T181, the sign she identified as the perfective suffix. She further identified T513, one of the main signs of the PDI, as a verb (*om* "to want"). Her proposal that the main signs of the "count" glyphs are verbs is supported by the occurrence of both T513 and T741b as auxiliary verbs.

Lounsbury's and Bricker's suggestions may eventually lead to a solution to the problem of the "count" glyphs, but neither scheme takes into consideration the AEI and ADI. And both the AEI and PEI can occur with intransitive, transitive, and positional And both the AEI and PEI can occur with intransitive, transitive, and positional verbs without alteration in affixing as well as in addition to normal verbal affixing. The following list is a summary of those verbs in the catalog which occur with the AEI or PEI attached to the main sign. Each affix pattern with which the AEI or PEI occurs is also listed, but the appearance of the ADI and PDI is not noted.

	PEI	AEI
Pattern Ø.Ø	3:6-7	7:11
	5:1	9:2
	5:14	9:13
	8:1	10:18?
	8:3	10:19
	8:5-7	11:6?
	8:9-13	20:2
	10:4	20:5
	13:4	20:14?
	14:4	21:13
	15:6	23:2
	17:6-7	25:2
	18:1	26:5
	19:1	116:1-21??
	21:4	
	21:8?	
	21:10	
	21:26	
	23:3	
	23:5	
	24:1-2	
	24:12?	
	25:1	
	25:3	
	25:12	
	26:4	
Pattern 1.*.Ø	31:2	40:1
	31:4?	
	33:3	
	40:6?	
Pattern 1.*:18	56:4?	
Pattern *.181	67:3	72:7
	69:3-5	
	72:4	

	PEI	AEI
	72:6	
	72:8	
	73:3	
	73:8	
	75:4-5	
	75:7	
	82:7	
	82:21?	
Pattern *:178.181	87:1	84:8
	87:9-10	85:4
		86:2
Pattern *:136.126.181	92:1	92:2
		92:3?
Pattern *:24.181	94:4	
Pattern *:23.181	96:2	96:1
Pattern *:18:181	97:2	
Pattern *:18	101:1-6?	98:2-3
		99:1-4
Pattern *:178:18		100:1-7
Pattern *:136.18		102:1-2
Pattern *:236	105:1	103:1?
	105:4	103:6?
		104:1
		104:3-4
		105:2-3?
		105:5
		105:7?
		106:5?

	PEI	AEI		PEI	AEI
Pattern *:236		108:1	Pattern *:24	119:1 119:3-5	120:4-5
Pattern *:130	110:2 110:5		Pattern *:17	124:3	
Pattern *:130.126	111:3-5		Pattern *:4 or 23	127:2 127:5	
Pattern *:130.116		112:2-4 112:9-15 112:21-23 112:25-29 113:3	Pattern *.116	128:2	
			Pattern 126.T*136	129:5?	
Pattern *:130.18	116:18?	115:1			

See also Charts 86, 87, 90, 101, and 116. In some of these examples, T126 may function as an AEI, rather than as a verbal affix.

5. Syntax of the Writing System

As discussed previously, the word order of the writing system is VOS for transitive constructions and VS for intransitive and positional constructions. The simplest of all texts are those that name persons, who usually are adjacent to the text. These simple phrases include neither calendric information nor a verbal element, and are most frequently found in the context of lintel and pottery scenes. Yaxchilan Lintels 3 and 9 (Fig. 14) are good examples of this kind of text because each of the secondary figures (turned profile to the viewer) is named by verbless phrases positioned next to his legs.

These verbless phrases are relatively rare in monumental texts, and texts designed for naming scene participants often include the verb T1.757 (see Charts 36, 51, 55, 56, 78, 92, 132, and 133). T1.757 is one of the most frequently occurring verbs, but in the context of these name phrases, its meaning must have been general, not specific, because it appears in scenes where the protagonists are engaged in many different activities. It is, therefore, a general verb without explicit reference to the particular actions or state in which pictured figures are shown. The distribution of this general verb is wide, and it may appear in clauses with or without calendric information (see Fig. 15 for examples of both types).

Simple clauses containing no date, but only a subject and a verb (which refers to some specific activity or state) are somewhat rare. The most frequent occurrence of this kind of dateless clause is found on the lintels at Yaxchilan. In some lintel texts, full clauses may accompany more than one figure, but the date is often recorded only in the text of the protagonist (Fig. 16).

In other texts, the date is recorded in a separate frame with its own specification of event or general occasion. Separate verb phrases may then refer to the specific act in which the figures are engaged. Many of the lintels of Yaxchilan follow this pattern of recording the date only once while including a complete clause for each of the pictured personages. On Lintel 41 (Fig. 17), the general occasion is a "shell-star" event that is associated with war activities and Venus stations in other inscriptions; the specific event is the capture of Jeweled-Skull, which interestingly enough is pictured not on Lintel 41 but also on Lintel 8. Lintel 2 (Fig. 18) records the general occasion as the fifth tun anniversary of the accession of Bird-Jaguar, although his name phrase is not directly linked to the anniversary phrase. The two secondary texts record the specific activities of Bird-Jaguar and his son, Shield-Jaguar II, on the occasion of that anniversary.

Any single component of a simple clause (i.e., the date, the verb, or the subject) can appear in greatly elaborated form on Classic monuments. The ways in which dates were elaborated are fully documented in previous studies (see Thompson 1950 and Kelley 1976). Dates may occur as simple Calendar Rounds (CR), as CR with the Lord of

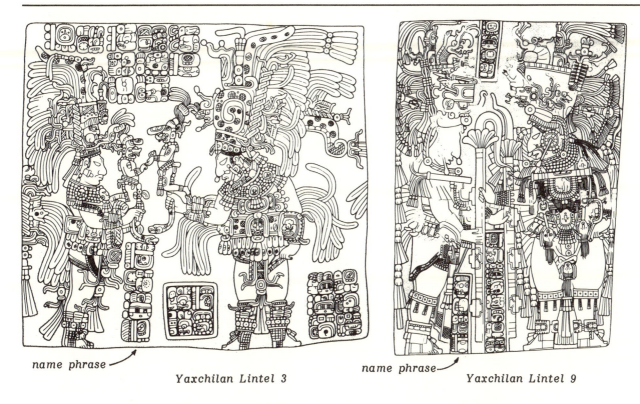

name phrase →   name phrase →

Yaxchilan Lintel 3   *Yaxchilan Lintel 9*

*Figure 14. Name phrases without verbal or calendric components
(drawings courtesy of the Peabody Museum, Harvard
University).*

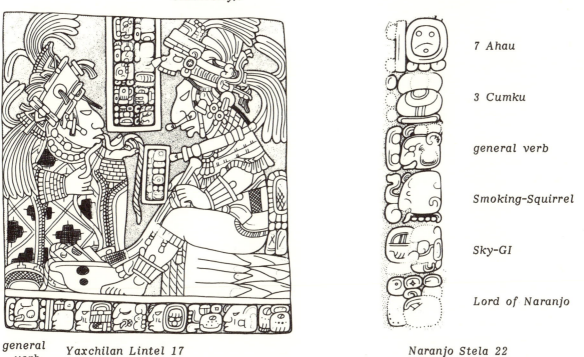

7 Ahau

3 Cumku

general verb

Smoking-Squirrel

Sky-GI

Lord of Naranjo

general
verb   *Yaxchilan Lintel 17*   *Naranjo Stela 22*

*Figure 15. Clauses with the T757 general verb (drawings courtesy of the
Peabody Museum, Harvard University).*

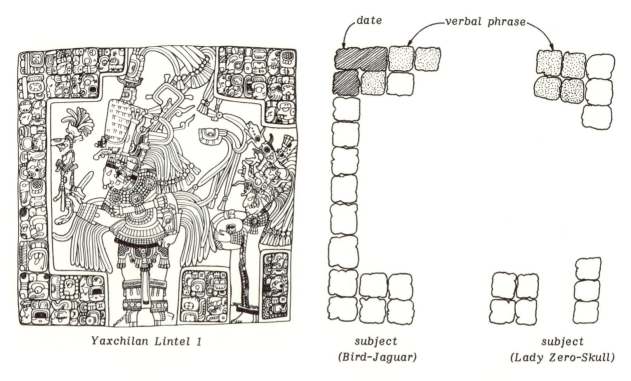

Yaxchilan Lintel 1

subject
(Bird-Jaguar)

subject
(Lady Zero-Skull)

*Figure 16. The date in this text occurs only in the text accompanying Bird-Jaguar
(drawing courtesy of the Peabody Museum, Harvard University).*

date and general
occasion for the
pictured event

was captured
(specific action)

Jeweled-Skull

by (??)

Bird-Jaguar

captor of Ah Cauac

specific action occurring
on the occasion of the
"star-shell" event

*Figure 17. Yaxchilan Lintel 41. The date occurs with the record of the general occasion,
while the specific action is recorded without a date (drawings courtesy of
the Peabody Museum, Harvard University).*

*4 Ahau 3 te Zotz' expired the fifth
tun as ahau of the succession*

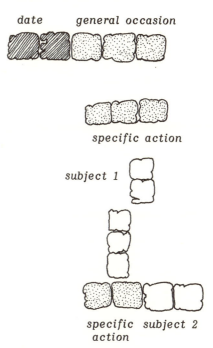

*Figure 18. Yaxchilan Lintel 2. The date occurs with the general occasion and
without a named subject; the specific actions conducted on the
general occasion are recorded with subjects, but without dates
(drawing courtesy of the Peabody Museum, Harvard University).*

the Night, as Long Count (LC) notations, and
as LC notations with any or all of the following information: Lord of the Night, age
of the moon and the station of the lunation
in the lunar half-year, and the station in
the 819 Day Count. Stylistically any of
these forms of calendric notation may be
recorded as geometric signs, as personified
head forms in either anthropomorphic or
zoomorphic versions, or as full-figure
anthropomorphic or zoomorphic personifi-
cations.

Verb phrases are elaborated by a number
of means, including the use of special grammatical forms, such as auxiliary verb + *ti* +
verbal noun constructions (see Chapter 7)
and/or by repeating the event in varied and
contrasted expressions. These couplet and
triplet constructions are especially elaborated at Copan, where a single period ending
may be recorded in five or six variations

before a subject is named. (See Chapter 6
for a discussion of couplet forms.)

Name phrases can also be elaborated in a
variety of ways, and again Copan seems to
have been the champion of the Classic period
in the use of complex name phrases. Personal
names are the "lowest common denominator"
of name phrases; they are the glyphs which
cannot be eliminated from a phrase without
sacrificing the identity of the named person. But a large number of additional glyphs
and phrases can be added to the personal
name glyph to give additional information
about the person, and these added glyphs can
be classified according to their distribution as follows:

1. Titles or other nominal qualities that
   have distribution at all or nearly all
   Classic sites, such as *ahau*, *bacab*,
   batab, and *ahpo*.

2. Titles or qualities that have regional distribution, such as "Sky-God K" at Tikal and "Sky-GI" at Naranjo or *ah nabe* at Palenque and Lacanja.

3. Titles or qualities that have local distribution, but are shared by all or many members of a dynasty sequence, such as the God N title at Piedras Negras.

4. Titles or qualities that are restricted to a particular dynastic name even if reused by successive generations of rulers.

5. Emblem Glyphs, which record a person as a "lord of a local place (or lineage)."

6. Titles or qualities that are restricted to the name of a single person, such as "captor of" notations.

The name phrase of Bird-Jaguar of Yaxchilan Lintel 1 contains examples of these kinds of title/attributive phrases (Fig. 16). Glyphs 1-3 of the name phrase appear in the name phrases of several earlier rulers of Yaxchilan; Glyph 4 is the personal name; Glyph 5 is a personal title not found in other names phrases at Yaxchilan or elsewhere; Glyphs 6-7 and 8-9 are personal "captor of" notations; Glyphs 10-11 and 12-13 are numbered katun titles; Glyphs 14-15 are the double Emblem Glyph of Yaxchilan; and Glyphs 16-17 are "west *batab*," a pan-Maya title phrase. Although many of these titles are used at other sites, the pattern of name phrase elaboration tends to be locally developed, with each site characterized by its special phrases and sequences.

Following suggestions by Christopher Jones (1977:41-42), Mathews, Lounsbury, and I have documented the existence of genealogical statements that are yet another way of elaborating name phrases on Classic monuments (Schele, Mathews, and Lounsbury n.d). These statements are usually associated with events like birth and accession, but at Tikal, they occur with katun endings and other events. The order of these extended name phrases is "Person A, the child of [mother] Lady B, the child of [father] Lord C" or "child--father--mother."

general verb

Lady Ik-Skull

Shield-Jaguar

Figure 19. Yaxchilan Stela 11, rear: name phrases of parents (after Maler).

IS date 9.16.1.0.0 and lunar data on left side of stela

819 Day Count clause and haab   *he was*   *titles*   *Bird-Jaguar*
                                                   inaugurated
                                                   as ahau
                                                   of the
                                                   succession

a. Yaxchilan Stela 11, right side

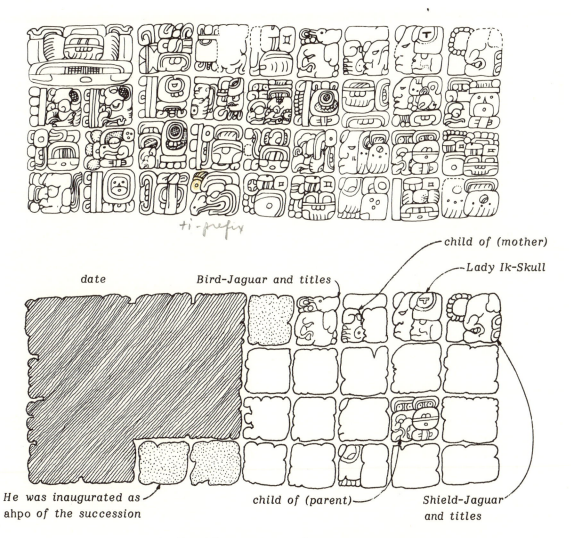

b. Yaxchilan Stela 11, front lower register

Figure 20. Various kinds of clause elaboration.

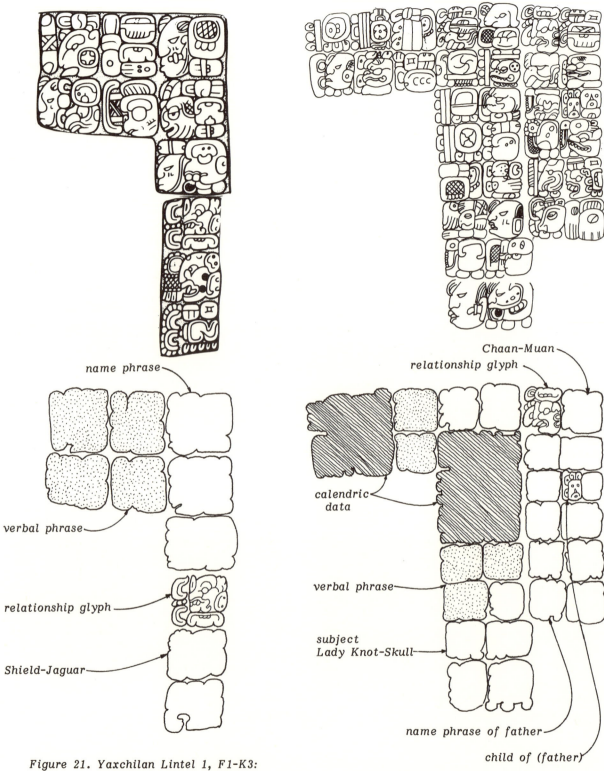

Figure 21. Yaxchilan Lintel 1, F1-K3:
elaborated name phrase
(drawing by Ian Graham).

Figure 22. Bonampak Stela 2.

One of the most interesting examples of the use of the various kinds of elaboration and of redundancy is found on Yaxchilan Stela 11 (Fig. 19), which repeats the genealogy and accession of Bird-Jaguar in a number of varied forms. Portraits of his parents, Lady Ik-Skull and Shield-Jaguar I, appear in the upper registers of both sides of the monument, and their names are included in the extended name phrase of Bird-Jaguar in one of the two accession passages recorded on Stela 11. The first accession record occurs on the sides (Fig. 20a) beginning on the left side with an Initial Series (IS) notation of the date, 9.16.1.0.0, along with the Lord of the Night, lunar data, and an additional phrase not yet understood (the left half of the inscription is not included in the illustration). The right text continues with a DN recording the time elapsed between the 819 Day Count station and the date of the event, and the verb and subject of the 819 Day Count clause. The event is recorded as the T684 "inaugural" verbal phrase, and the subject, Bird-Jaguar, is recorded with a name phrase that includes the Yaxchilan "sky-god" expression, his personal name glyph and a personal title, the Emblem Glyph, and *bacab*.

The text on the front of Stela 11 (Fig. 20b) repeats the same information as the sides, but in variant form. The date is recorded in LC notation as an IS date with the Lord of the Night and lunar data framed by the CR notation. The event is again the T684 "inaugural" phrase, but the name phrase of Bird-Jaguar is very different. It begins with his name glyph, a "captor of" notation, a personal title, and a notation as a "three-katun *batab*." The remaining parts of the name phrase however, record him as a "child of [mother] Lady Ik-Skull, Lady of the God C title, Lady Bacab; [and] child of [parent], 'shell-fist' quality, the "five-katun *ahpo*," Shield-Jaguar, captor of Ah Ahaual, Lord of Yaxchilan, *bacab*." The texts on the sides and front base of Stela 11 record the same information in the same kind of syntactical construction, i.e., a simple date-verb-subject clause, but the two texts are elaborated in different and contrasting ways.

Peter Mathews (1980:61) has identified another convention for the elaboration of subject phrases by the inclusion of genealogical data. The text which accompanies the woman on Yaxchilan Lintel 1 (Fig. 16), includes a verbal expression, the name phrase of the woman (Lady Great-Skull), and a two glyph phrase which includes a "bat" glyph and the name glyph of Shield-Jaguar (Fig. 21). It is reasonable to assume that the "bat" glyph that intervenes between the names of this woman and this man records some relationship between them. The rulers who preceded and followed Bird-Jaguar (the protagonist of Lintel 1) into office both carried the Shield-Jaguar name glyph. Since Bird-Jaguar is named as the child of Shield-Jaguar I, and since Shield-Jaguar II is named as the child of Lady Great-Skull and Bird-Jaguar (Stela 7), it seems unlikely that Lady Great-Skull was a descendant of Shield-Jaguar I. The "bat" glyph is more likely to record the relationship between this woman as a mother and her child, Shield-Jaguar II. The subject of the Lintel 1 verbal phrase is thus identified as "Lady Great-Skull, mother of Shield-Jaguar."

A similar kind of construction is found on Stela 2 at Bonampak (Fig. 22). The first clause of the text (A1-E1) records the "inauguration" of Chaan-Muan, the protagonist of the monument. The second clause records an event, apparently pictured on the monument face, that took place 13.7.9 after the accession event. The verbal phrase (D5-D6) is followed by the name phrase of the woman who is recorded on Stela 1 as the mother of Chaan-Muan. On Stela 2, her name phrase (E6-E8) is followed by the "bat" relationship (F1) and the name phrase of Chaan-Muan (G1-F3), and in turn his name phrase is followed by the T535 "child of [father]" glyph (G3a) and the name phrase of the person who is recorded as his father on Stela 1. The subject of the second clause of Stela 2 is recorded as "Lady Knot-Skull, mother of Chaan-Muan, who was the child of [father] White-Lizard." This Bonampak example is one of the most syntactically complex name phrases known from the Classic inscriptions.

An elaborated simple clause is employed on the Leiden Plaque, the oldest undamaged, dated inscription from the Classic period. The text (Fig. 23) begins with an Initial Series date 8.14.3.1.12 1 Eb G5 (Lord of the Night) seating of Yaxkin. B9 is the "seating" glyph, but in this second occurrence it refers to the "seating" in office of the named and pictured lord. The "seating" verb is followed by the glyph for the office (which is also found on Stela 31, D2). The subject is recorded as a historical person whose name phrase includes the "sky" glyph that occurs in many names phrases of Tikal rulers and an Early Classic version of the Tikal Emblem Glyph also found on Stela 4.

Simple clause constructions are frequent in Classic texts, and they may appear in more or less elaborated form. However, in other cases, texts contain more than one event (and therefore verb and subject) linked together in time by DNs. Such event sequences can contain two or more events within the life of one person, such as the birth and death of a ruler, or different events within the live of different persons. They may also link events in the remote past (historical, legendary, mythological) to events in the historical present. When clause texts relate events in the lives of different persons, all of the components in each clause usually are retained. Such a multiple event series from the west panel of the Temple of Inscriptions at Palenque (Fig.

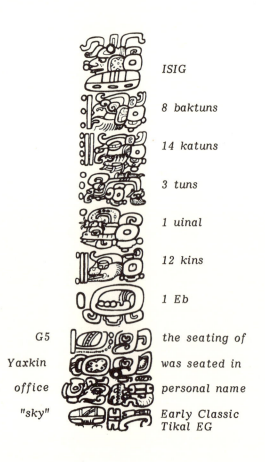

ISIG

8 baktuns

14 katuns

3 tuns

1 uinal

12 kins

1 Eb

G5   the seating of

Yaxkin   was seated in

office   personal name

"sky"   Early Classic
             Tikal EG

Figure 23. The Leiden Plaque: simple clause with elaborated date (drawing by W.R. Coe).

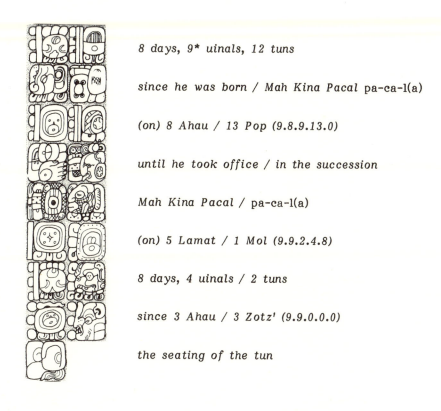

8 days, 9* uinals, 12 tuns

since he was born / Mah Kina Pacal pa-ca-l(a)

(on) 8 Ahau / 13 Pop (9.8.9.13.0)

until he took office / in the succession

Mah Kina Pacal / pa-ca-l(a)

(on) 5 Lamat / 1 Mol (9.9.2.4.8)

8 days, 4 uinals / 2 tuns

since 3 Ahau / 3 Zotz' (9.9.0.0.0)

the seating of the tun

Figure 24. Palenque Temple of Inscriptions, west panel, F1-F9:
clauses linking events with the life of one person.

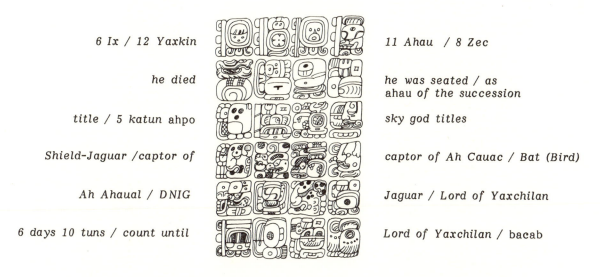

6 Ix / 12 Yaxkin

he died

title / 5 katun ahpo

Shield-Jaguar /captor of

Ah Ahaual / DNIG

6 days 10 tuns / count until

11 Ahau / 8 Zec

he was seated / as
ahau of the succession

sky god titles

captor of Ah Cauac / Bat (Bird)

Jaguar / Lord of Yaxchilan

Lord of Yaxchilan / bacab

Figure 25. Yaxchilan Stela 12, front: clauses linking events within the
lives of two different persons.

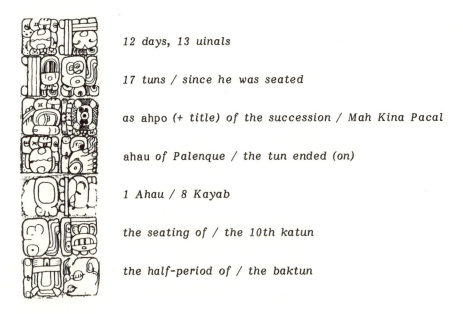

12 days, 13 uinals

17 tuns / since he was seated

as ahpo (+ title) of the succession / Mah Kina Pacal

ahau of Palenque / the tun ended (on)

1 Ahau / 8 Kayab

the seating of / the 10th katun

the half-period of / the baktun

Figure 26. Palenque Temple of Inscriptions, east panel, R9-T4: clauses linking historical events to period endings.

24) links the birth and accession of Pacal to the end of Katun 9. Note that each individual passage retains all of its components--i.e., a CR date, a verb (marked in each case by the Anterior or Posterior Event Indicator), and a subject.

In contrast to the Palenque example, Yaxchilan Stela 12 (Fig. 25) links event within the lives of two different persons, Shield-Jaguar I and Bird-Jaguar, the Great. The first clause records the death of Shield-Jaguar; a DN records the time elapsed between this death and the accession of Bird-Jaguar; and the second clause records the "seating" of Bird-Jaguar. As in the Palenque example above, all of the components (i.e., date, verb, and subject) are retained in each of the two clauses, and

the DN simply leads from one date and event to the others.

However, in the more extensive and complicated texts of Palenque, one or more of the redundant components can be deleted. The first two and one-third panels of the Temple of Inscriptions record a series of katun histories between 9.4.0.0.0 and 9.13.0.0.0. Each of these histories opens with a passage linking the last accession within a katun to the appropriate katun ending (with the lahuntun and oxlahuntun used if more than one accession occurred within a particular katun). These passages are very similar in form and include information organized in the following formula: "It was so much time since he was seated as lord, name, until the tun ended, date of the tun." The CR dates of the accession are deleted, possibly because these dates are not the featured information; the focus is on the sequence of katun endings in which the lords of Palenque were "seated." One of the most typical of these katun histories is that of Pacal (Fig. 26). In this clause as in the others, the CR date of the "seating" is deleted, and the "seating" verb is marked by the AEI. The katun ending not only is named with its CR date, but also is specified as the "seating of the tenth katun, the half-period of the baktun." Compare the pattern of this clause to that of the clause from the west panel (Fig. 24) which all of the components are retained.

The deletion of a date within a clause sequence is usually easy to detect, and the deleted information readily reconstructable. However, other clause components can also be deleted, especially when a sequence records different verbs that have the same subject. This deletion of subjects and the resulting gapping of clauses have caused many problems in decipherment because it was assumed until recently that DNs occur between progressively spaced dates that are all recorded in a text or are easily recovered if deleted. (Thompson called this deletion of dates "suppression.") However, this assumption cannot be made about the Tablet of the Cross, which records the dynastic sequence of Palenque from the mythological past into the historical past of the protagonist of the monument, Chan-Bahlum. Like the text of the Temple of Inscriptions, this text from the interior of the Temple of the Cross relates information in a repeated formula that is slightly varied with each usage. Here the components of the full formula are as follows: DN, verb, subject, date, until verb, subject, date; or, "It was so much time since he was born, subject, on a date until he acceded, subject, on a date." In each usage of this pattern, the sequence of components is slightly varied, and redundant or nonessential components are deleted in a varied pattern. Summary paraphrases with deletions marked as **** are displayed in

Figure 27. (Problems with calendric data are not treated in the paraphrases, and complex phrases for accession are paraphrased simply as "he acceded.")

The DNs in this text from the Tablet of the Cross do not link together a series of successive dates, but rather they record the elapsed time between two internally related events, in each case the birth and accession of a ruler. Because only one of the two involved dates need be recorded (the other is implied by the DN), either date could be deleted without loss of information. Syntactical and poetical variation was achieved by changing the patterns of inclusion (both dates could be recorded) or deletion (either date could be eliminated, thus focusing on the other). And since it is obvious from the text that the person born was also the person who acceded, only one subject needed to be named. Again, variation was achieved by alteration of the patterns of inclusion and deletion. Additional variation was generated by the deliberate repetition of information; for example, the birth event is recorded twice in Passages 3 and 5, but only once in the other passages. The extent of variation based on the utilization of redundancy and deletion within the text of the Tablet of the Cross suggests that the scribe was consciously manipulating literary conventions and deliberately avoiding repetition of a single syntactical pattern. Most of the possible patterns of deletion and redundancy appear in the text.

Deletion is rare at Yaxchilan, where simple clauses are more common; it is much in evidence at Palenque, where the texts are longer and more complicated; and it is found in the later texts at Tikal, where accession events are linked to katun endings. Stela 16 is a good example of the use at Tikal of a simple clause to record a katun ending. The text begins with the CR date of the katun ending and a verbal couplet that records the period ending as "the completion of the fourteenth katun" and "the end of the tun." The remaining glyphs in the text record the

Passage 1 (E5-F8)

 ****

(it was) 2.1.7.11.2   she was born   until she acceded   Zac-Kuk   (on) 9 Ik 0 Pop

**** deleted: subject and date of birth

Passage 2 (E10-Q3)

   ****

(it was) 3.6.10.12.2   count since   9 Ik   until he was born   U-Kix-Chan

**** deleted: verb and subject for 9 Ik date

 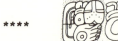 ****

(it was) 1.6.7.13   he was born   U-Kix-Chan   until he acceded   U-Kix-Chan   (on) 11 Caban 0 Pop   EG

**** deleted: date of birth

Passage 3 (P4-Q9)

(on) 5 Cimi 14 Kayab   he was born   Kuk   (it was) 1.2.5.14   since he born

****  ****

until he acceded   (on) 1 Kan 2 Kayab   title or EG

**** deleted: subject of birth and accession verbs; date of birth

Passage 4 (P10-S2)

(on) 11 Lamat 6 Xul   he was born   "X"   (it was) 13.3.9   since he was born   "X"

 ****

(until) 2 Caban 10 Xul   (it was) 6.3   (since) he acceded   "X"

Figure 27. Patterns of deletion on the Tablet of the Cross at Palenque.

count until   8 Ahau 13 Ceh   PE   9 baktuns   PE

**** *deleted: verb and subject of 2 Caban 10 Xul*

Passage 5 (R3–S7)

   **** ****

(it was) 1.8.1.18   he was born   Manik   until he acceded   (on) 3 Etz'nab 11 Xul

**** *deleted: date of birth; subject of accession verb*

Passage 6 (R8–R13)

   ****

(it was) 1.16.7.17   he was born   (on) 5 Ahau 3 Zec   Chaacal   until he acceded   (on) 5 Caban 0 Zotz'

**** *deleted: subject of accession verb*

Passage 7 (S13–S17)

   ****  ****

(It was) 1.19.6.11   he was born   Kan-Xul   until he acceded   (on) 5 Kan 12 Kayab

**** *deleted: date of birth; subject of accession verb*

Passage 8 (T1–U6)

 ****

(it was) 2.2.4.17   he was born   until he acceded   Chaacal II   (on) 1 Imix 4 Zip

**** *deleted: date and subject of birth verb*

Passage 9 (U11–U17)

    ****

(it was) 2.8.4.7   he was born   Chan-Bahlum I   (on) 11 Chicchan 13 Ch'en   until he acceded

**** *deleted: date and subject of accession verb*

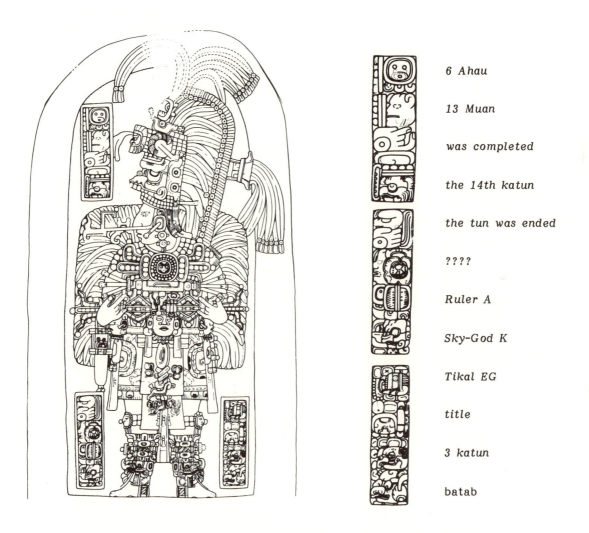

6 Ahau

13 Muan

was completed

the 14th katun

the tun was ended

????

Ruler A

Sky-God K

Tikal EG

title

3 katun

batab

Figure 28. Tikal Stela 16: simple clause recording a period ending event
(drawing by W.R. Coe).

name phrase of the protagonist and subject of the verb, Ruler A (Fig. 28).

Tikal Stela 22 (Fig. 29) records the same class of information as Stela 16, but the structure of the text is much more complicated. The text again opens with the period ending CR date (13 Ahau 18 Cumku) and the appropriate verbal expression, "the seventeenth katun, the tun was ended." The remaining glyphs before the next set of calendric data record the name phrase of Ruler C, including a notation of his genealogy as the "child of Ruler B." The second part of the text begins with a DN of two tun and thirty-six days that links the katun ending above to the accession of Ruler C. This passage is paraphrased as follows: "[It was] sixteen and twenty days, two tuns 11 Kan 12 Kayab since he was seated as *batab* of the succession until he scattered." Both verbs are marked by the appropriate indicators: the AEI suffixed to the "seating" verb, and the PEI infixed into the "scattering" verb. The appearance of the temporal indicators and the DN clearly shows that the "scattering" event occurred on the katun ending, and the portrait of Ruler C shows him engaged in exactly this activity.

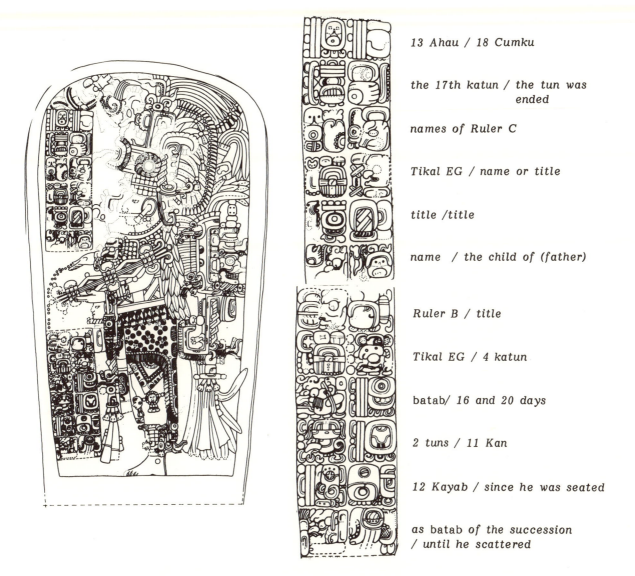

13 Ahau / 18 Cumku

the 17th katun / the tun was
                        ended

names of Ruler C

Tikal EG / name or title

title /title

name / the child of (father)

Ruler B / title

Tikal EG / 4 katun

batab/ 16 and 20 days

2 tuns / 11 Kan

12 Kayab / since he was seated

as batab of the succession
/ until he scattered

Figure 29. Tikal Stela 22: clauses linking period ending rites to accession.
(drawing by W.R. Coe).

The subjects of both the final events in the Stela 22 text have been deleted, but their identity is clear from the context. Ruler C is named as the subject of the first period ending verb, and since the "scattering" event occurred on the same day and on the occasion of the katun ending, it can be assumed that Ruler C is also the actor in the "scattering" event. Finally, since no other person is named as a subject of any of the three verbs (the name phrase of Ruler B occurs as part of the extended name phrase of Ruler C), Ruler C is clearly the subject of the "seating" verb as well as of the period ending event and the "scattering."

Deletion of the subject of a verb is also found in texts that repeat a previously recorded event as the base of a DN. One of the clearest examples of this deletion pattern is found on the Tablet of the Foliated Cross at Palenque (Fig. 30). The first part of the passage records the birth and acces-

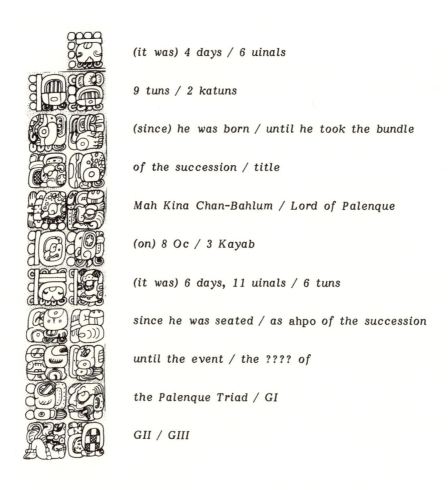

(it was) 4 days / 6 uinals

9 tuns / 2 katuns

(since) he was born / until he took the bundle

of the succession / title

Mah Kina Chan-Bahlum / Lord of Palenque

(on) 8 Oc / 3 Kayab

(it was) 6 days, 11 uinals / 6 tuns

since he was seated / as ahpo of the succession

until the event / the ???? of

the Palenque Triad / GI

GII / GIII

*Figure 30. Palenque Tablet of the Foliated Cross, M17-O10:
verbs repeated as the base of Distance Numbers.*

sion of Chan-Bahlum II as follows: "[It was] 2.9.6.4 since he was born until he acceded, Chan-Bahlum, Lord of Palenque, [on] 8 Oc 3 Kayab." The next phrase of the text connects the accession event to an event that occurred six tuns later, but the accession event is repeated in the alternative form of the T644 "seating" expression with the subject deleted as redundant information. This passage not only illustrates deletion of redundant information; it also provides evidence that the T713/757 "accession" expression does not record the taking of an office distinctly different from that recorded by the T644 "seating" phrase, but rather that these two verbal phrases are alternative expressions describing the same ritual occasion.

As can be seen from the examples under discussion, deletion can occur in many different patterns in the Classic inscriptions, but it is most frequently found in contexts where two or more verbs have the same subject; where an event is repeated as the base of a DN; where a verb occurs in a redundant passage; and where an event, such as a period ending, is recorded repeatedly in alternative forms. In all of these contexts, the identity of the subject is clear from the context; where it would not otherwise be clear, the subject of the verb has been explicitly recorded.

6. Redundancy, Couplets, and Style

The redundancy of Classic inscriptions is documented at many sites, including Copan, Palenque, Naranjo, Piedras Negras, and Yaxchilan. For example, on Stela 11 at Yaxchilan the accession of Bird-Jaguar is recorded on the sides and front lower register (Fig. 20), and his genealogy is proclaimed not only by the portraits of his parents in the upper registers of both sides of the monument, but by the explicit record of it contained in his name phrase in the text of the front lower register. Bird-Jaguar's accession is linked to his birth in the texts of Lintels 29, 30, and 31, and it is associated with the death of his father, Shield-Jaguar I, on Stela 12. The accession and its fifth tun anniversary are again recorded on Lintels 1 and 3 of Structure 33.

The redundancy of the Classic Maya inscriptions is especially notable at Palenque, perhaps because its longer texts allowed for greater complication in syntax and stylistic convention. Longer texts in general seem to be much more redundant at all Maya sites; and at sites like Yaxchilan, where texts tend to be short, redundancy is built into the inscriptions by repeating events in several formats on one monument or on several monuments. In the texts of the Group of the Cross at Palenque, redundancy is a major feature of the inscriptional composition. The accession of Chan-Bahlum II is recorded five times; his heir-designation, nine times; and the eighth tropical year anniversary of his accession, seven times. The record of his designation as heir as recorded in the final columns of the Tablet of the Sun is a most interesting example of redundancy because this passage illustrates the manner in which variation and deletion were used to retain interest in highly repetitive texts.

The first section of this passage associates the heir-designation of the ancestral ruler Kan-Xul I to that of Chan-Bahlum II and to the conclusion of this rite five days later (Schele n.d.a). This section may be paraphrased as follows (Fig. 31): "[It was] 7.6.12.3 [since] 12 Ahau 8 Ceh since he took office as heir of the succession, Kan-Xul I; count since the 'heir-designation' count until 9 Akbal 6 Xul, he took office; five days later he became the sun, Mah Kina Chan-Bahlum, *balan-ahau* of the Palenque succession, related to GI." Notice that the earlier event is recorded twice, and in its second occurrence it lacks a subject and is framed by the Anterior and Posterior Date Indicators. In the verbal phrases recording the later event, only the "mirror-in-hand" verb is recorded for the 9 Akbal 6 Xul event, and both the glyphs recording the "office" and the name of the subject are deleted. This verb is gapped to the next event, which occurred five days later, but which can be identified as part of the same ceremonial sequence by a comparison of all of the expressions recording this heir-designation event. Note also that the verbal glyph (*oc te'*) of the event five days later is a

Section 1

(it was) 3 days, 12 uinals

6 tuns / 7 katuns

(since) 12 Ahau / 8 Ceh

since he took office / as heir of the succession

Kan-Xul I / count since

the "heir-designation" / count until

(on) 9 Akbal / 6 Xul

he took office / on the 5th day later

he became / the sun oc te' kin-kin

Mah Kina Chan-Bahlum / balan-ahau of the Palenque succession

relationship or agency / GI

Section 2

(it was) 17* days, 2 uinals / 6 tuns

(since on) 2 Cimi / 19 Zotz'

he was born / until he was heired

Section 3

(it was) 12 days, 8 uinals / 1 tun, 13 Ahau

18 Kankin / 10 tuns

(since) he was "designated" /as heir of the succession

Figure 31. Palenque Tablet of the Sun, O16-Q16: redundant record of heir-designation.

variant of the noun appearing as the office in the first occurrence of Kan-Xul's heir-designation event.

In the second section of this passage, the heir-designation is again recorded, but now linked by DN to Chan-Bahlum's birth, as follows: "[It was] 6.2.18* [since on] 2 Cimi 19 Zotz' he was born until he was 'heired.'" In this section, the subjects of both verbs are deleted, but it is clear from the context and from a comparison of other expressions used in this text that the second event is the heir-designation of the previous section, and that the subject of both the birth and heir-designation is to be understood as Chan-Bahlum. This assumption is supported by the arithmetic, although there is an error of one day in the DN; 2 Cimi 19 Zotz' is recorded as the birth date of Chan-Bahlum on the Tablet of the Foliated Cross, and the DN required between 2 Cimi 19 Zotz' and 9 Akbal 6 Xul, the date of the heir-designation, is 6.2.17. Note that the main sign of the heir-designation event in this section is identical to the noun in the Kan-Xul section above (both are variants of the *oc* glyph), but that it appears with the verbal affix T181 -*ah*.

The third section of this passage again records the heir-designation event, but now linked by DN to the period ending 9.10.10.0.0 as follows (Fig. 31): "[It was] 1.8.12 [until] 13 Ahau 18 Kankin, the lahuntun [since] he 'was designated' heir of the succession." In this, the fourth consecutive record of Chan-Bahlum's heir-designation, the subject of the verb, although deleted, is clearly identifiable because of the context and the repetition in the text. This same event is recorded twice more in the secondary text of this tablet, twice on the Tablet of the Foliated Cross, and once on the Tablet of the Cross. Note that in the final section of the text under discussion, the DN does not lead from the 9 Akbal 6 Xul event to the lahuntun, but rather from the event recorded

* The DN (6.2.18) is recorded incorrectly but can be reconstructed arithmetically as 6.2.17.

five days after the heir-designation, suggesting that the heir-designation was a rite of five days' duration, rather than two events occurring five days apart.

The redundancy of the Classic inscriptions resembles a stylistic form noted by Munro Edmonson as a major characteristic of the Quiche *Popol Vuh* and of Quiche discourse:

It is my conviction that the Popol Vuh is primarily work of literature, and that it cannot be properly read apart from the literary form in which it is expressed. That this form is general to Middle America (and even beyond) and that it is common to Quiche discourse, ancient and modern, does not diminish its importance. The Popol Vuh is in poetry, and cannot be accurately understood in prose. It is entirely composed in parallelistic (i.e., semantic) couplets.
(Edmonson 1971:xi)

Lounsbury (1980) has discovered the presence of semantic couplets as a major feature of the texts of the Group of the Cross at Palenque, and once the presence of couplet structures is recognized, they can be detected as a major feature of many Classic texts. Several of the texts already discussed are structured in the form of semantic couplets: the text of Tikal Stela 22 (Fig. 29) is organized in the form of a couplet, and the last passage of the Tablet of the Sun (Fig. 31) is in the form of a triplet.

Lounsbury (1980:107) first detected couplet structures in the left half of the Tablet of the Cross, where their presence had long caused difficulties in the interpretation of calendric data. In this series of passages, couplet structures are relatively easy to detect, and I will use them as illustrative examples here. The first section of these repetitive passages opens with a DN that leads from the birth of an unnamed person to 4 Ahau 8 Cumku, here expressed as the "completion of thirteen baktuns" (Fig. 32). The second passage opens with another DN counted from 4 Ahau 8 Cumku, but the era event is expressed with a different phrase, thereby forming a parallel couplet with the

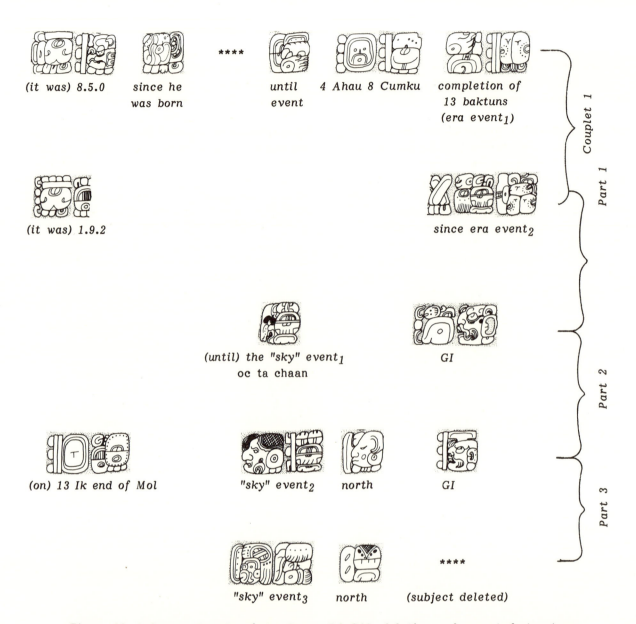

Figure 32. Palenque Temple of the Cross, D2-C13: deletion and repeated structures.

previous era expression. Note that the first era expression is the event to which a DN is to be counted, and the second is the event from which another DN is to be counted.

The second era expression above is also a part of another couplet; it is the event from which the DN 1.9.2 is counted until an event expression composed of the verb *oc*, the locative preposition *ta* (T103), and *chaan* "sky." The subject of this event, GI of the Palenque Triad, must also be identified as the deleted subject of the birth event in the first clause. The calendric data in the first part of this second repetitive section is recorded as the time elapsed since the 4 Ahau 8 Cumku event until the *oc ta chaan* event. The actor is recorded as GI the First (written as GI' in the illustrations), who was the father of the Palenque Triad (Lounsbury 1980).

Section 2 of the passage begins with the CR date 13 Ik end of Mol, reached by adding the DN from the previous passage (1.9.2) to 4 Ahau 8 Cumku. In other words, the dates of the two section are identical, but one is written as the time elapsed since the beginning of this era and the other as the correct CR date. The verbal phrase of Section 2 includes a "sky" glyph, but it occurs within a different verbal construction and is qualified as "north" in order to contrast to the *oc ta chaan* phrase in the first section of the triplet. The subjects of both sections are recorded as GI the First.

The third section of the triplet repeats the same event, but in yet another form that includes a "sky-elbow" with God C and a "house" glyph. An alternative form of "north" completes this section, and since this is the second repetition of the event, the subject (GI the First) is deleted. This triplet includes two versions of the date and three of the verb, but all refer to exactly the same information--an action involving the sky and enacted by GI the First one and one-half years after the beginning of the current era.

The text of the Tablet of the Cross continues with yet another couplet structure organized like the triplet above. The first part of this couplet (Fig. 33) begins with a DN counted since the "sky" event (in yet another form) of GI the First until the

birth of another personage, whom Lounsbury (1980:114) had identified as GI of the Palenque Triad. (Lounsbury [1980:114] has shown that the GI recorded in the earlier passages is the father of the Palenque Triad, and distinct from this supernatural bearing the same name.) The second half of the couplet begins with the CR date 9 Ik 15 Ceh, which is 1.18.3.12.0 (the recorded DN) after 13 Ik end of Mol, the date of the earlier "sky" event. The subject is recorded with the same titular glyph that occurs in the first half of the couplet, but here the personage is identified as the "child of" the ancestral goddess whose birth is recorded in the first clause of this inscription. The verb is an alternative expression for birth based on a metaphor still extant in Chol--"to experience the world" (Lounsbury 1980:112-114). This second couplet, like the first, records the first part as "It was so much time since event 1 + subject until event 2 + subject"; and the second part records the CR date of the second event as "On this date was event 2 + subject."

Other texts at Palenque utilize different forms of couplet, triplet, and quadripartite redundancies. On the Palace Tablet, Chan-Bahlum's accession is recorded in a couplet in which all calendric data is deleted from the second part (Fig. 34). The accession of Kan-Xul on this same tablet is recorded in four successive passages of which only the

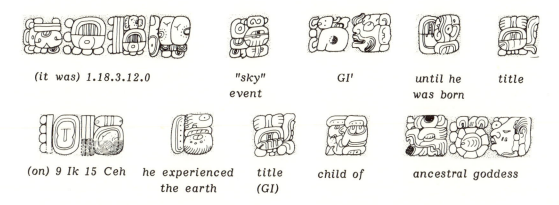

| *(it was) 1.18.3.12.0* | *"sky"* *event* | *GI'* | *until he* *was born* | *title* |

| *(on) 9 Ik 15 Ceh* | *he experienced* *the earth* | *title* *(GI)* | *child of* | *ancestral goddess* |

Figure 33. Palenque Tablet of the Cross, D13-F4: couplet recording the birth of GI of the Palenque Triad.

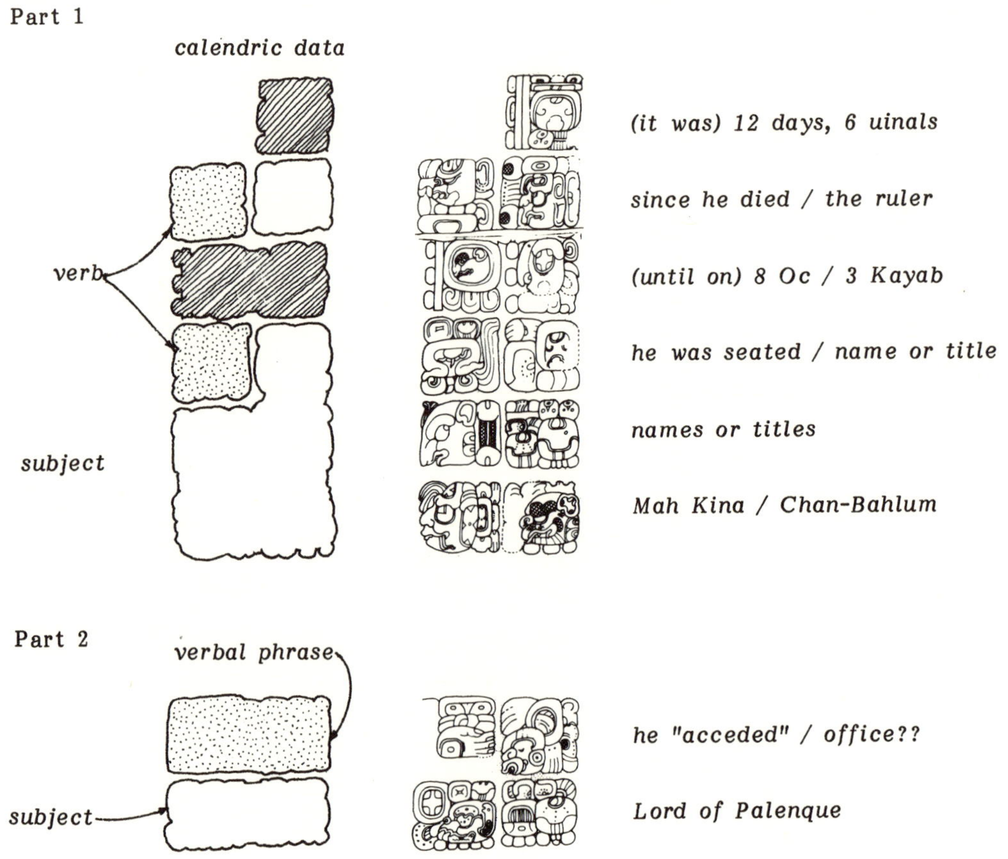

Part 1

calendric data

verb

subject

(it was) 12 days, 6 uinals

since he died / the ruler

(until on) 8 Oc / 3 Kayab

he was seated / name or title

names or titles

Mah Kina / Chan-Bahlum

Part 2

verbal phrase

subject

he "acceded" / office??

Lord of Palenque

Figure 34. Palenque Palace Tablet, J14-L11: couplet recording the accession of Chan-Bahlum.

first contains calendric data, and of which the last is linked to the accession of Pacal, the father of both Chan-Bahlum and Kan-Xul (Fig. 35). On this tablet, Chan-Bahlum's death is recorded as the amount of time elapsed since his accession and in temporal relationship to 9.13.10.0.0, the nearest period ending (Fig. 36).

Tikal Stelae 19, 21, and 22 (Fig. 29) record period ending events in couplet form in which the second part of the couplet relates the katun ending "scattering" event to the accession or first katun anniversary of the accession of the current ruler. The analysis of the difficult text of Lintels 3 from Temples I and IV at Tikal is also aided by the assumption that each text contains

redundant structures. Lintel 3 of Temple I begins with a phrase establishing the LC position of all dates in the text by tying them to 9.13.3.0.0. The second clause records an event which appears to be related to war. Great-Jaguar-Paw of "Site Q" (an undiscovered site earlier thought to be Calakmul) is named either as the subject of this event or, more likely, as its object, in which case the deleted subject would be Ruler A of Tikal. The The third clause (Fig. 37) includes a verbal couplet of which the second half can be identified as a "blood-letting" expression. Ruler A is named as the subject of this verbal couplet, and his name phrase includes notation of his genealogy. The date of this event has been recognized

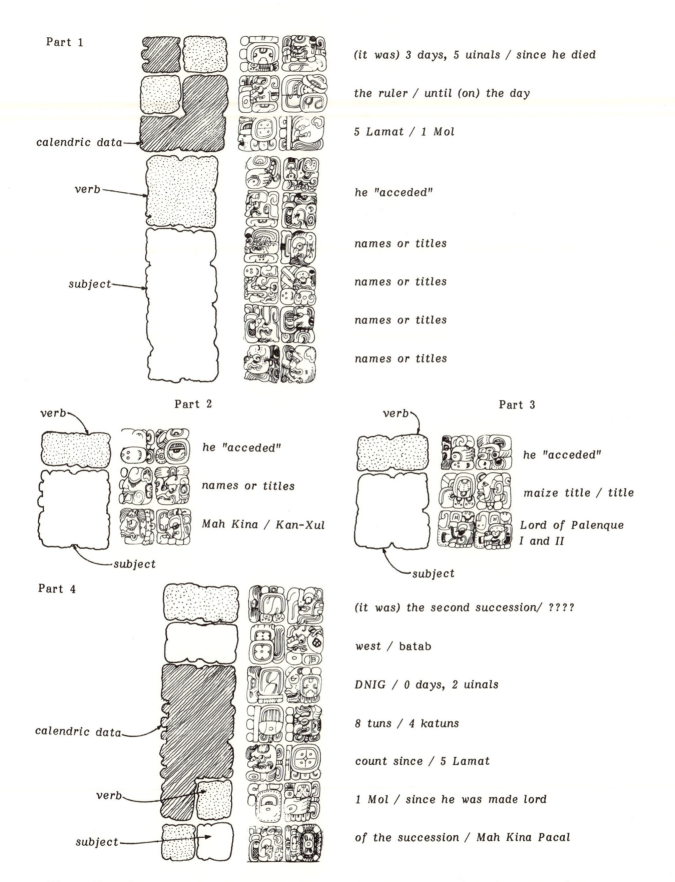

Part 1

calendric data ———

(it was) 3 days, 5 uinals / since he died

the ruler / until (on) the day

5 Lamat / 1 Mol

verb ———

he "acceded"

subject ———

names or titles

names or titles

names or titles

names or titles

Part 2

verb

he "acceded"

names or titles

Mah Kina / Kan-Xul

subject ———

Part 3

verb

he "acceded"

maize title / title

Lord of Palenque I and II

subject ———

Part 4

calendric data ———

verb ———

subject ———

(it was) the second succession/ ????

west / batab

DNIG / 0 days, 2 uinals

8 tuns / 4 katuns

count since / 5 Lamat

1 Mol / since he was made lord

of the succession / Mah Kina Pacal

Figure 35. Palenque Palace Tablet, M13-R1: quadripartite record of the accession of Kan-Xul.

Part 1

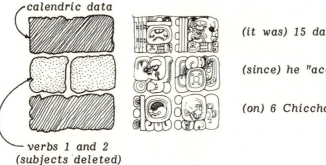

calendric data

*verbs 1 and 2
(subjects deleted)*

(it was) 15 days, 6 uinals / 18 tuns

(since) he "acceded" / until he died

(on) 6 Chicchan 3 Pop

Part 2

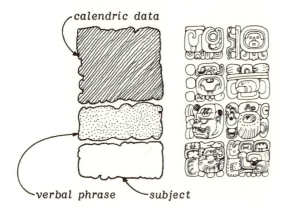

calendric data

verbal phrase   *subject*

(it was) 5 and 20 days / since 7 Ahau

3 Cumku / the half-period

(until) he died

Mah Kina Chan-Bahlum / Lord of Palenque

Figure 36. Palenque Palace Tablet, M6-N12: couplet recording the death of Chan-Bahlum.

as a thirteen-katun anniversary of the last surviving date on the Early Classic monument, Stela 31, so that the blood-letting ritual recorded here may be involved in rites of ancestral recall. The remaining glyphs in this text form the second part of the couplet by relating the anniversary event to the accession of Ruler A as follows: "[It was] 13.10.2 [since] 5 Cib 14 Zotz' since he was seated as lord of the succession, Ruler A, Sky-God K, Lord of Tikal, until he took part in the anniversary event (subject deleted)."

The precise meaning or reading of this anniversary expression is not known, but a variant of it appears on the last half of Lintel 3 of Temple 4. The first half of this text records a "star-shell" event and an-

other event one day later. The second half of the text records the three-tun anniversary of the latter event. The anniversary record is divided into five semantically parallel parts (Fig. 38) of which the second and fourth list GVI (of the Palenque god lists [see the introduction to Chapter 9]) as the subject. The event phrase in Part 2 also occurs on the center upper stair of Structure 44 at Yaxchilan, where Shield-Jaguar is the subject. In the Tikal text, Parts 3 and 5 record Ruler B as the subject of the events, and the verbal component of Part 3 is the same as the anniversary verb from Temple I (Fig. 37). Furthermore, the verb in Part 5 is found at Palenque in association with anniversary dates (see Chart 87:3-11). Ruler B's genealogy is included in this

Part 1

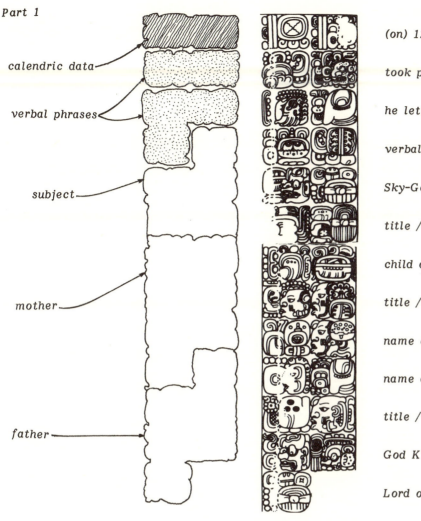

calendric data — (on) 12 Etz'nab / 11 Zac

took place the anniversary event

verbal phrases — he let blood

verbal phrase / Ruler A

subject — Sky-God K / Lord of Tikal

title / name or title

child of (woman) / name or title

title / name or title

mother — name or title / Lady Jaguar-Throne

name or title / child of (parent)

title / name or title

father — God K title / Shield-Skull

Lord of Tikal

Part 2

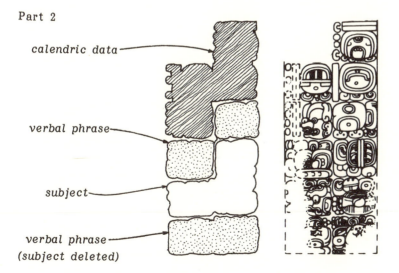

calendric data — (it was) 2 days, 10 uinals

13 tuns / 5 Cib

verbal phrase — 14 Zotz' / since he was seated

as lord of the succession / Ruler A

subject — Sky-God K / Lord of Tikal

verbal phrase — until the anniversary event
(subject deleted)

Figure 37. Tikal Temple 1, Lintel 3, C1-F12: couplet recording
an anniversary (drawing by W.R. Coe).

Part 1

3 tuns (until) 13 Akbal 1 Chen

Part 4

Part 2

Part 5

Part 3

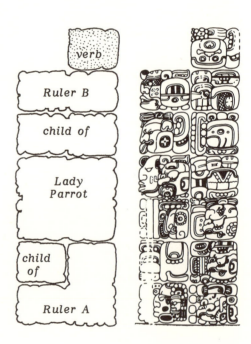

Figure 38. Tikal Temple 4, Lintel 3, F1-H9: five-part record of an anniversary
(drawing by W.R. Coe).

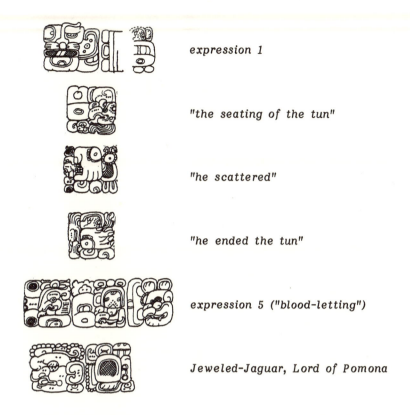

	expression 1
	"the seating of the tun"
	"he scattered"
	"he ended the tun"
	expression 5 ("blood-letting")
	Jeweled-Jaguar, Lord of Pomona

Figure 39. Pomona Wall Panel: six-part record of a period ending.

final occurrence in the text of his name phrase. Notice that this passage exhibits an internal structure of the following pattern:

A   B   C

B   C

Since very few of the individual glyphs in this long, complicated passage are understood, it is difficult to determine whether the five parts of the text represent different ways of recording a single act and subject, or different actions by different persons on the occasion of the anniversary. However, the repetition of the same subject in Parts 2 and 4 and in Parts 3 and 5 suggests that some of the five parts record the same action in alternative form and the same actor.

Couplet structures are particularly associated with period ending notations. In these contexts, the subject of each individual verb phrase is often deleted (as occurred in the text of Tikal Temple I, Lintel 3 [Fig. 37]) resulting in sequences of as few as two and as many as six semantically parallel phrases. A good example of sequenced verbal expressions is found on a wall panel from Pomona on which five distinct verbal phrases follow the initial date and precede the name phrase of the protagonist of the text (Fig. 39).

Copan is particularly notable for the complication of its period ending texts, resulting from the use of many semantically parallel passages. The texts of two Copan stelae will serve as examples. Stela 6 (Fig. 40) celebrates the period ending 9.12.10.0.0 in a succession of passages beginning with the "scattering" expression, here marked as the half-period 8 Ahau (the numerical coefficient of the day should be 9 as is record-

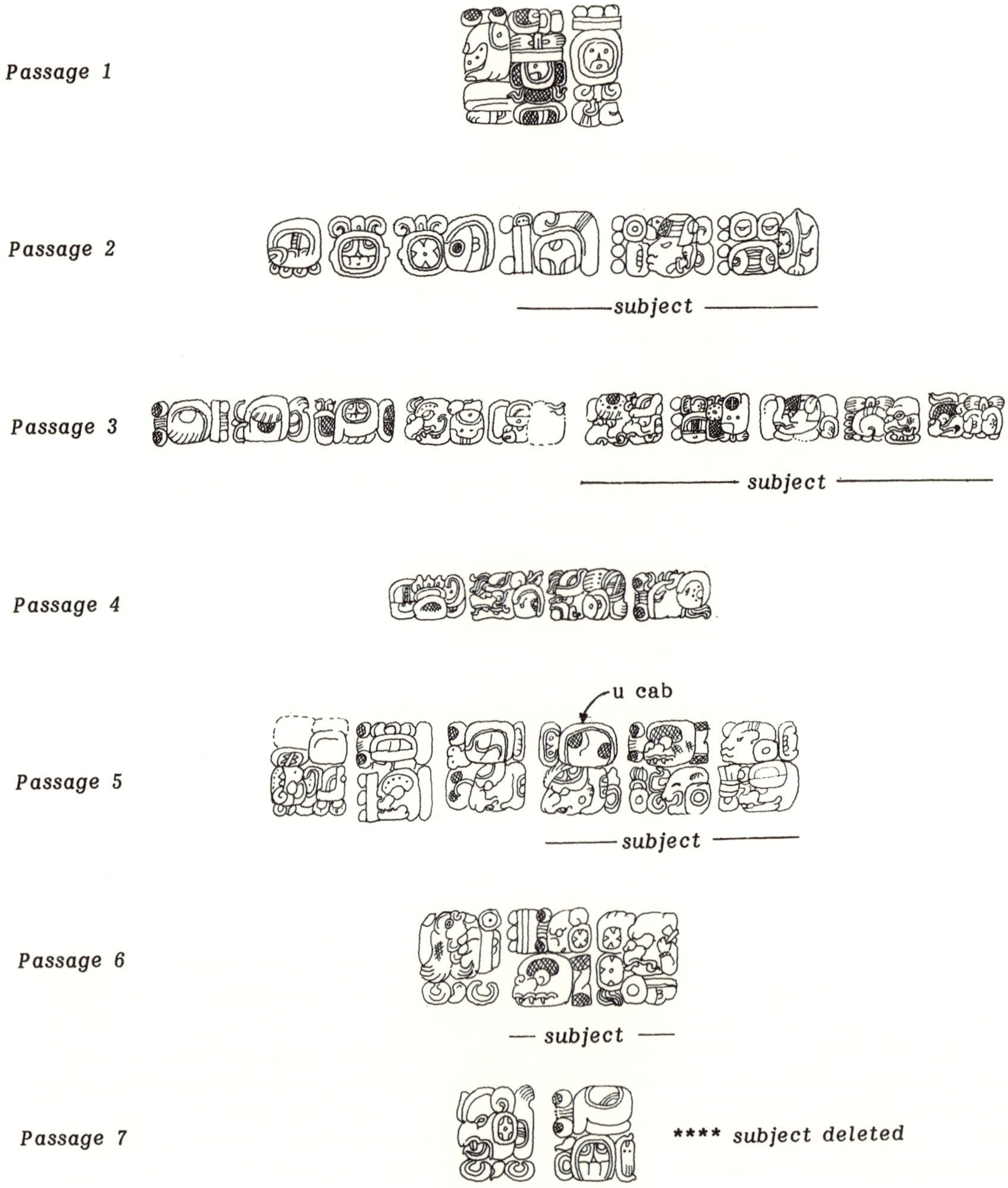

Passage 1

Passage 2

——— subject ———

Passage 3

——— subject ———

Passage 4

u cab

Passage 5

——— subject ———

Passage 6

— subject —

Passage 7   **** subject deleted

Figure 40. Copan Stela 6: seven-part record of a period ending.

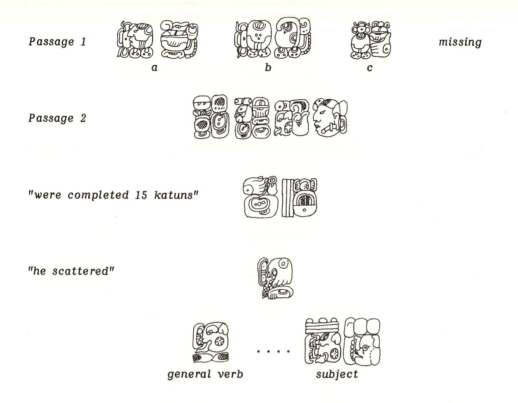

Figure 41. Copan Stela B: eight-part record of a period ending.

ed in the IS date). The "scattering" expression is followed by an "akbal-kin" phrase associated with period endings not only at Copan, but also at Naranjo and other sites. The subject of this second passage seems to be recorded with a "4-Ahau/IV-Rodent-Bone-Kankin" title series. The third passage records both a T712 "blood-letting" event and a period ending in which the main sign is an eye with vision lines emerging from the side of the block. This latter verb is prominent in period ending expressions at Pomona (see the listing under T819 in Appendix 2). The subject of this event is recorded with an "Imix (water-lily)-God K" compound and a series of titles. The fourth passage features the T601 period ending verb that is found at many sites, but no recognizable subject expression can be identified in the text. Passage 5 is the most difficult because the first half of the expression is

destroyed. The subject, who appears to be the contemporary ruler of Copan, is named following an u cab glyph. The final two passages of the text are arranged in a couplet structure and record a a blood-letting event of which 18-Rabbit is the subject. The verb in the in the first half of the couplet is "fish-in-hand," and in the second half it is the T712-"akbal" expression associated with blood-letting. It should be be noted that the text of Stela J records the "seating" of 18-Rabbit one katun after the date of Stela 6, so he was not involved in these period ending rites as a ruler of Copan.

The number of different clauses that are associated with the one date on Stela 6 is not unusual for the inscriptions of Copan. One may choose between two assumptions about the meaning implied in this text: (1) that only the first clause is associated with the recorded date and that the remaining clauses refer to a series of events occurring after that date, but without the specification of a particular temporal framework; or (2) that all of the clauses refer to the same date. In the case of the former assumption, it must be supposed that Copanecs alone of Classic Maya peoples were not concerned with a fixed temporal framework for historical events, and this is a very unlikely possibility. If the latter assumption is accepted, then the multiplicity of clauses is viewed as a property of literary convention, and the study of Copan inscriptions is much simplified.

The text of Copan Stela B supports the analysis of Stela 6 as a series of semantically parallel passages referring to a single period ending because many more of its verbal phrases are recognizable as PE expressions. The first section of the text (Fig. 41) opens with an Initial Series date followed by three or four parallel phrases. The constant in these phrases is composed of the zero sign prefixed to the kan "maize" glyph. This constant is followed in the first instance by a "sky" glyph; in the second, by an "earth" glyph; and in the third, by a "1-sky-in-hand" glyph. The fourth part is now destroyed.

The second section features the T601 period ending glyph followed by "were com-pleted fifteen katuns" and the "scattering" verb. The subject of all these period ending verbs is recorded in the remaining glyphs of the text as 18-Rabbit, but his name phrase is preceded by the T757 general verb which has been previously discussed as a verb introducing name phrases without reference to specific acts or states. Here and in other Late Classic Copan texts, the T757 verb appears to function as a means of highlighting the name phrase of the subject after a long, complicated series of verbal phrases that occur with deleted subjects.

The kinds of redundant structures discussed in this chapter now appear to represent a major stylistic feature of the inscriptions from the Classic period. The recognition of the presence of couplets and more complicated patterns of semantically parallel structures not only has given insights into many of the more obscure texts of the Classic period but also has provided means of identifying semantically equivalent verbal expressions. The virtuosity of the Maya scribe in the substitution of phonetic, semantic, and graphic metaphors and puns is most easily detectable within the context of this kind of parallel and redundant structures, and the presence of such semantically parallel substitution patterns often provides important clues for decipherments.

7. General Verbs and Auxiliary Verb Constructions

Both Thompson (1962:354) and Proskouriakoff (1968) have commented upon the frequent occurrence of the T1.757 glyph immediately after a date or at the beginning of a text without a date. Proskouriakoff, in her study of this glyph, suggested the following interpretation of its function:

The precise meaning of the opening glyph (T1.757 or T1.788) is unknown, but because it is used in a wide range of contexts, almost always occurs at the beginning of a passage, and often appears in direct association with individual figures, it must stand for some widely applicable expression, such as for example: "Here is portrayed (or recorded) . . .," "In commemoration of . . .," or some such phrase directing attention to the subject of the accompanying picture.
(Proskouriakoff 1968:247)

In her analysis of the T1.757 verb, Proskouriakoff pointed out the multitude of different contexts in which it can appear. The variety of actions associated with it indicates that it cannot refer specifically to any one of these various actions, but rather must serve some general function appropriate to many different actions and states. As a general verb, T1.757 can appear with the following functions:

1. It may function as a verb in clauses identifying persons shown in a scene. In this context the verb does not refer directly to the specific action shown pictorially.

2. On Naranjo Stela 22 (Fig. 15) and on Tikal Stela 5, T1.757 occurs as the verb in clauses associated with a PE date, but again it cannot refer directly to a specific action conducted in celebration of the period ending.

3. At Copan and Yaxchilan, T1.757 may precede a name phrase after a sequence of verbal phrases that have deleted subjects. The presence of this verb between such verbal sequences and name phrases seems to function as a method of highlighting the name of the person who is the subject of all the recorded events (Fig. 41).

4. In parentage statements, T1.757 is frequently found preceding the T1.I:606:23 "child of mother" glyph, which is grammatically a possessed noun paraphrased as "the child of . . ." The subject of the verb in this context is the noun "child," not the female name phrase naming the possessor of the noun (or, in other words, the mother). The function of T1.757 in this context seems to be similar to that in third category--to highlight the name phrase of the mother within a lengthy and complex passage (see Chart 133).

5. T1.757 may also appear in the T712 "child of parent" expression, but the grammatical function in this context is not the same as that of the the general verb. This expression can be shown to be identical in form to the verbal expression of

"blood-letting" in either verb + complement or auxiliary verb + *ti* + verbal noun constructions (see Chart 132).

See Charts 36, 51, 55, 56, 78, 92, 98, 101, and 133 for the cataloged examples of T1.757 as a general verb.

In the texts on the bones from Tikal Burial 116, T1.501:102 seems to occur in contexts parallel to those of T1.757, and the same glyph can substitute for T1.757 in verb + complement and auxiliary verb + *ti* + verbal noun constructions. Finally, there are several cases where T513 *muluc* and its upright version T580 appear to function in contexts parallel to those of T1.757 (see T513 in Appendix 2 for a listing of examples).

T1.757 also occurs frequently in other kinds of verbal expressions in which additional glyphs are added in order to specify the exact nature of the verb. These additional kinds of structures are of two types: verb + complement and auxiliary verb + *ti* + verbal noun. The latter construction especially has been associated with similar verbal morphology in modern Chol and other

languages (Josserand, Schele, and Hopkins n.d.). Although the full epigraphic and linguistic evidence for these identifications will be published in the *Fourth Palenque Round Table*, it is appropriate to discuss the major points of evidence within the context of this study.

In verb + complement constructions, the complement may or may not carry verbal affixation in addition to that appearing on the T757 verb. The two clearest examples of this kind of verb construction are found on Tikal Stela 4, dated 8.17.2.16.17, and La Mar Stela 1, dated 9.17.18.6.19 (Fig. 42). Both texts record the accession of a ruler with a well known "accession" expression (the T684 "inauguration" phrase at Tikal and the T713/757 "accession" at La Mar), but in both cases these "accession" verbs function as the complements of the T1.757 verb. And in both, the verbal components of the "accession" phrases carry the T181 verbal affix in addition to the inflectional affix (third person pronoun of Set A) on the T757 verb. All other examples of the T1.757 + complement construction now known in the Classic inscriptions appear either without affixing

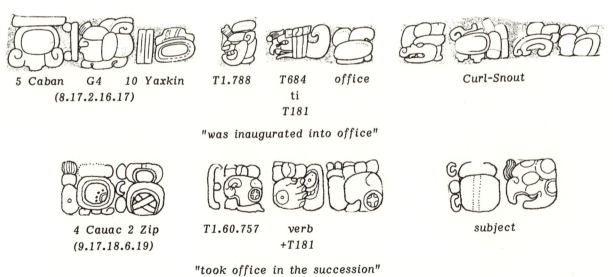

5 Caban   G4   10 Yaxkin   T1.788   T684   office   Curl-Snout
      (8.17.2.16.17)   ti
                                                              T181

"was inaugurated into office"

4 Cauac 2 Zip   T1.60.757   verb   subject
(9.17.18.6.19)   +T181

"took office in the succession"

Figure 42. Tikal Stela 4 and La Mar Stela 1: general verb + inflected verb constructions (Tikal drawing by W.R. Coe).

of any kind on the complementary glyphs or with T1 (or an equivalent) prefixed to them. In the latter context, some of the complementary glyphs may well be nouns, rather than verbs.

The second kind of verbal construction includes T1.757 as an auxiliary verb, the particle *ti* or a functional equivalent (such as T103 *ta*), and a glyph that specifies the action in the form of a verbal noun. Two comparative examples will serve to illustrate the contrast between a normally affixed verb and an auxiliary verb construction utilizing the same main sign in different grammatical form. The T684 "inaugural" expression can appear without verbal suffixing; with T181 in its full form (T180) infixed into the bundle sign; with some other infix and T181 as a suffix; and with various other affix patterns (see T684 in Appendix 2 for a full list of these affix patterns). In contrast to this kind of affixed construction, T684 appears on Naranjo Stela 20 following T1.757 + *ti* (Fig. 43) without any apparent change in meaning.

The fact that T684 retains T180 as an infix in the main sign causes some problems because a verbal noun should not be marked with this verbal affix. However, the bundle grapheme is very ancient and may have become conventionalized with T180 as a part of it, or T180 may have been retained as a device to fill the glyph block, since the bundle strap alone is an awkwardly shaped grapheme. The problem of the retention of T180 in the Naranjo example does not occur in the auxiliary verb construction of another "accession" expression, T168.518 (Fig. 44). On the west panel of the Temple of Inscriptions at Palenque, this glyph, which appears with the positional affix pattern *-wan*, records the accession on 5 Lamat 1 Mol of the ruler Pacal and the accession of a mythological personage some half million years earlier. The same "accession" expression appears on the Early Classic Lintel 12 (dated 9.4.0.0.0) from Piedras Negras, where it occurs as the verbal noun in an auxiliary verb construction. This verbal phrase occurs without a date in the secondary text above the main figure. However, in the main text of this lintel, the same T518 verb (with normal verbal affixing) and name phrase are associated with the date 9.4.0.0.0 13 Ahau 18

Yaxchilan Stela 11
no affixing

Bonampak Stela 2
T181 as suffix

Yaxchilan Lintel 30
T180 as infix

auxiliary verb 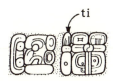 verbal noun

Naranjo Stela 20
auxiliary verb + ti + T684

Figure 43. T684 in various verbal constructions.

Yax. This auxiliary verb construction from the secondary text is the oldest example of the *ti* construction so far known.

After I showed these kinds of verb + complement and verb + *ti* + verbal noun constructions in the inscriptions to Nicholas Hopkins and Kathryn Josserand, who were working on Chol grammar at the time, we discovered that these kinds of constructions are prominent in Chol and are used in contrast to transitive, intransitive, and stative constructions. Aulie and Aulie described these auxiliary constructions as follows:

The nominative verb is invariable (i.e., it does not form reflexive, passive, participial, or other constructions), since it acts as a nominal subordinated to the intransitive verb woli "to be" (estar) in the present progressive tense, and as the complement of the transitive verb cha'len "to do" (hacer) in the other tenses. After woli, the nominal verb has preposed to it the prepositional element ti, but ti is not used after cha'len. Examples:

woli ti alas
"he is playing"

tsi' cha'le alas
"he played"

The nominalized verbs express verbal concepts of intransitive action, which in Spanish (and other languages) are expressed by means of intransitive verbs.

(Aulie and Aulie 1978:189,
translation by Hopkins and
Josserand)

In their treatment of these kinds of verbal constructions in Chol, Josserand and Hopkins distinguish between the following kinds of constructions:

1.   chonkol pɨk'ob
"they are planting"

An auxiliary verb (chonkol) precedes an inflected main verb, which has transitive (-ob third person plural) inflection.

2.   mik kahel hk'ux
"I'm going to eat"

Kahel is inflected with a transitive pronoun (-k first person), but the second construction is ambiguous. Hk'ux could be interpreted as a possessed noun complement of kahel ("I begin my eating") or as a second

Palenque Temple of Inscriptions

west panel, H12-G1

west panel, H2-H3

verb with
inflectional
affixes

subject

Piedras Negras Lintel 12

auxiliary verb   ti verbal
noun

subject

Figure 44. Auxiliary verb construction with T168:518.

transitive verb ("I begin I eat" or "I begin
to eat"). *(This latter interpretation may be
related to the T1.757 + complement constructions found in the inscriptions.)*

3.　　　tza mahliy-on ti t'an
　　　　"I went to speak"
　　m i k-mahlel ti paxial
　　　"I'm going to go for a walk"

*In the first example, mahl, the auxiliary
verb, is inflected for the intransitive (-on
first person), and the semantically important
element, the action referred to, appears as
a noun following the locative particle ti.
The second example is similar to the first,
except that the auxiliary verb is inflected
for the transitive. (These constructions are
the equivalent of the ti constructions in
the Classic inscriptions.)*
　　(Josserand, Schele, and Hopkins n.d.)

Josserand and Hopkins (personal communication, 1979) report that in their 1978
field work with Salto de Agua Chol, they had
difficulty eliciting normal intransitive
expressions for several tense-aspects. *Woli
ti* "to be doing something" and *sami ti* "to
be going to do something" are the normal
intransitive expression for those tense-
aspects. They suggest that the difference in
transitive and intransitive inflection on
the auxiliary verb appears to reflect a
slight difference in meaning. The transitive
forms seem to imply that the action has
already been done several times, and the
intransitive forms that the action is completed for the first time. This suggested
contrast does not seem to exist in the Classic writing system; however, the differen-
tiation in inflection may well reflect a
split-ergative system both in modern Chol
and in the inscriptions.

There are many auxiliary verbs used in
Chol, and this kind of construction is now
known to exist in other Mayan languages as
well. Prominent auxiliary verbs documented
in Chol are as follows:

woli　　"to be doing something"
sami　　"to be going to do something"
chonkol　"to be doing something"
yikel　　"to be doing something"

kahel　"to begin to do something"
mahlel　"to go to do something"
ochel　"to enter upon doing something"
la　　"let's do something"
uhti　"to finish or to just have done
　　　　something"

A number of auxiliary verbs have been
identified in the writing system, including
T1.757, T516:103, T3.580, and T1.501:102,
and, in some cases, the main signs of the
Anterior and Posterior Date Indicators
(T513:59 *mul ti* and T741b:59 *xoc ti*) can
function in parallel contexts. For verb +
complement constructions, see Charts 3:8,
17?, 35, 37, 52, 57, 107:10, and 132:2,4,5,
14; for auxiliary verb + *ti* + verbal noun
constructions, see Charts 3:2,5,8, 5:12,
9:5, 18, 21:8, 35:3,5-6, 38, 48, 53, 55:5-7,
121:9, and 132:15-17. Although most of the
constructions, see Charts 3:2,5,8, 5:12,
9:5, 18, 21:8, 35:3,5-6, 38, 48, 53, 55:5-7,
121:9, and 132:15-17. Although most of the
examples of these kinds of verbal constructions are included in the verb catalog, it
is appropriate here to discuss those examples that are involved in new identifications of events or that are confirmations of
previously suggested readings.

Proskouriakoff (1973:168) suggested that
the "God K-in-hand" event might record the
receiving of the God K scepter by a ruler.
Her suggestion is confirmed by a series of
texts at Yaxchilan and Palenque that accompany scenes of rulers holding God K either
as a manikin or as a scepter. Yaxchilan
Lintel 1 pictures an event occurring on the
day of Bird-Jaguar's accession. In the scene
(Fig. 45a), Bird-Jaguar stands holding the
God K scepter and a woman holds a bundle.
The event phrase in the Bird-Jaguar text is
a couplet, both parts of which are auxiliary
verb constructions (Fig. 46). The semantically critical component of the first phrase
is "ahau-in-hand"; the second phrase utilizes T516:103 as the auxiliary verb, but
the verbal noun is not yet understood.
Lintel 3 of the same structure at Yaxchilan
(Fig. 45b) again shows Bird-Jaguar holding a

a. Yaxchilan Lintel 1

b. Yaxchilan Lintel 3

c. Palenque Tablet from Temple 14

Figure 45. The God K scepter event at Yaxchilan and Palenque (Yaxchilan
drawings courtesy of the Peabody
Museum, Harvard University).

God K scepter, but on the occasion of the
hotun of Katun 16, four tuns after his
accession. Again, the verbal phrase (Fig.
46) is a couplet with the semantically critical element of the first phrase recorded
as "ahau-in-hand." But while the acts shown
on Lintels 1 and 3 are the same, the occasions for them are different, and that difference seems to be reflected in the second
halves of the couplets, which are different.
On Lintel 3, T516:103 is the auxiliary verb,
but the glyphs following the *ti* sign are not
the same as those on Lintel 1. This pattern
is found throughout the inscriptions of
Yaxchilan; displaying the God K scepter was
a rite that could occur on many different
occasions which are often recorded in the
second half of the verbal couplet.

The identification of "ahau-in-hand" as a
reference to the holding of the God K scepter and as a semantic equivalent of "God K-
in-hand" can be supported by the text of
Tablet 14 at Palenque. The scene on this
tablet shows a woman in the act of rising
from a seated position as she hands a God K
manikin toward Chan-Bahlum, who is seen
dancing. Because of the probable Long Count

position of the historical date (3 haabs and 1 tzolkin after Chan-Bahlum's death), the scene (Fig. 45c) can be identified as posthumous (Schele n.d.c). The text associates the historical event with its first occurrence far in the mythological past, and as a result both the ancient and the historical events are recorded four times in forms of interest to the Yaxchilan texts. In three of these occurrences (Fig. 46), the main sign is "ahau-in-hand" (or the variant of ahau that occurs as the day sign on Piedras Negras Lintel 12), and in two of these three examples, the forehead mirror diagnostic of God K is suffixed to the "ahau-in-hand" as a semantic determinative specifying the God K manikin. In the fourth example (marked with

yax as the "first God K-in-hand"), the mirror replaces the ahau sign in the T670 hand. Thus, the "ahau-in-hand" and "God K-in-hand" are alternative versions of the same action, "the display or holding" of the God K scepter, and this ritual display could occur on many different occasions. The T670 hand appears to be a graph showing a human hand poised in the instant before it grasps a vertically oriented object. The hand represents the action; the ahau and the "God K mirror" graphemes appear to represent the object grasped.

Through similar comparative analysis of other Yaxchilan texts, it can be shown that a conflation of the cauac sign and a bat head (Fig. 47) refers to the holding or dis-

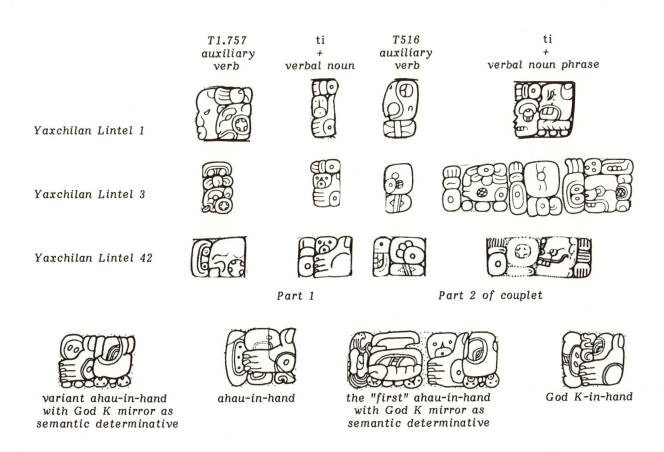

event glyphs from Tablet 14 at Palenque

Figure 46. Ahau-in-hand in auxiliary verb expressions (Yaxchilan drawings courtesy of the Peabody Museum, Harvard University).

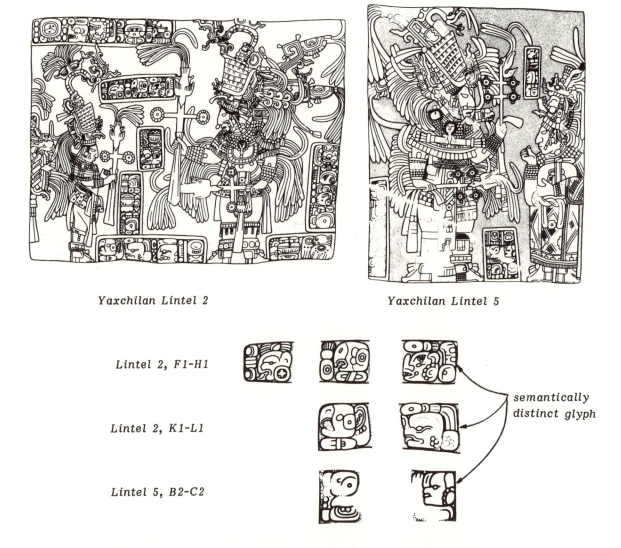

Yaxchilan Lintel 2   *Yaxchilan Lintel 5*

Lintel 2, F1-H1

Lintel 2, K1-L1

Lintel 5, B2-C2

semantically distinct glyph

Figure 47. Verbal phrases associated with the "bird-scepter" event (drawings courtesy of the Peabody Museum, Harvard University).

play of the bird scepter or to a rite involving this scepter in some manner. Stela 11 and Lintels 33, 9, and 54 record a verbal noun phrase referring to the ritual use or possession of a cloth staff (Fig. 48). Components of this verbal noun phrase occur as the office taken at accession (recorded with the T684 "inauguration" verb) on El Cayo Lintel 1, and the ruler is shown holding the same staff. The glyph phrase associated with this staff is also used to specify the office assumed at accession (recorded with the T644 "seating" glyph) on Lintel 1 of Lacanja, and elsewhere it occurs as a title in name phrases, presumably as a reference to the possession of the staff. And finally, the basket-God K staff on Yaxchilan Lintels 6 and 43 is recorded by a "zip" glyph (Fig. 49).

One of the most interesting auxiliary verb constructions so far identified is one associated with period ending rites and blood-letting (Fig. 50). On the Pomona wall panel (Fig. 39) and Panel X, this expression

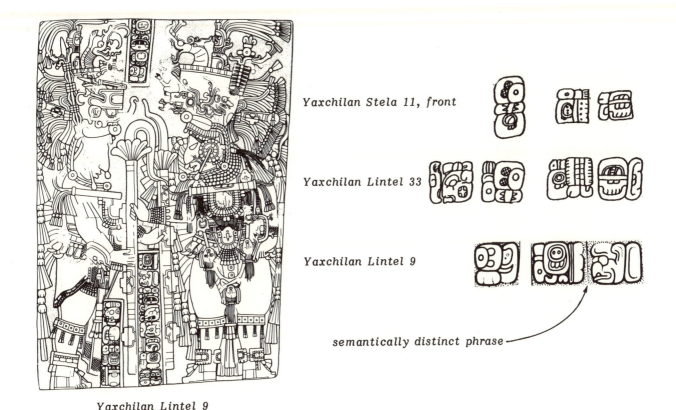

Yaxchilan Stela 11, front

Yaxchilan Lintel 33

Yaxchilan Lintel 9

semantically distinct phrase —

Yaxchilan Lintel 9

Figure 48. Verbal phrases associated with the "cloth-staff" event (drawings courtesy of the Peabody Museum, Harvard University).

occurs with the period endings 9.17.0.0.0. and 9.18.0.0.0, respectively; while on Quirigua Stela J it occurs with the date 9.16.5.0.0. In the two Pomona examples, the phrase consists of the T1.757 auxiliary verb, "yax-mul-ta" (T16.580:102), "hun uinic" (TI032), and "na-chan" (T4.25:764). The last three glyphs of the Pomona examples occur in the Quirigua text, but the auxiliary verb is replaced by a T501 glyph unique to that text. On Step VII of Yaxchilan Structure 33, a verbal phrase identical to the Pomona examples occurs following a "ball playing" verb (Chart 13:6) and a "scattering" event (Chart 3:12); however, the date of these events is not a period ending, but rather 9.15.13.6.9. The scene shown is one of a ballgame, but the text indicates that the historical events are reenactments or in some way associated with events far in the mythological past. The key to the meaning of these phrases is found on Yaxchilan Lintels 13 and 14, both of which display scenes of blood-letting. On both these lintels, the text associated with the female actors utilize forms of a known blood-letting verb-- "fish-in-hand." However, the texts associated with the male actors, also shown engaged in blood-letting activities, use the newly discovered phrase under discussion. On Lintel 13, the verb is composed of the T757 auxiliary verb and the "hun-uinic" glyph, while on Lintel 13 the verbal phrase contains the T757 auxiliary verb, the "yax-mul" glyph, and T712, the blood-letting lancet that occurs as the verbal noun in the *ti*

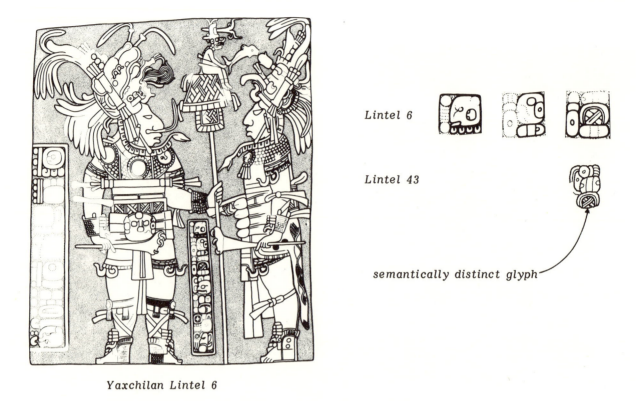

Yaxchilan Lintel 6

Lintel 6

Lintel 43

semantically distinct glyph

Figure 49. Verbal phrases associated with the "basket-staff" event
(drawings courtesy of the Peabody Museum, Harvard University).

construction for blood-letting on Yaxchilan Lintel 24. The association of this "yax-mul/hun-uinic/na-chan" expression with the blood-letting scenes on Lintels 13 and 14 is a clear indication that the expression is a reference to a blood-letting rite, an identification strongly supported by the presence of the T712 lancet in the Lintel 14 text (see Charts 21:14, 38:13, and 52:6-9).

The use of the general verb + complement and auxiliary verb + *ti* + verbal noun constructions added enormous versatility to the manner in which events could be recorded in the Classic inscriptions. This versatility and deliberate variation of verbal phrases has caused problems to epigraphers because until the recognition of these structures it could not be assumed that such variations were semantic equivalents. The verbal phrases associated with the blood-letting rite and its attendant "vision" scenes are perhaps the best examples of the kind of variation that could be used to record a single event (see Fig. 51). Since one of the phrases used to record blood-letting also functioned as a metaphor for "child of parent," examples from that context, as well as from verbal contexts, have been used to illustrate the available patterns of variation. The skill and virtuosity of the Maya scribe can most easily be detected in the patterns of variation used in the manipulation of grammatical and syntactical forms of these kinds.

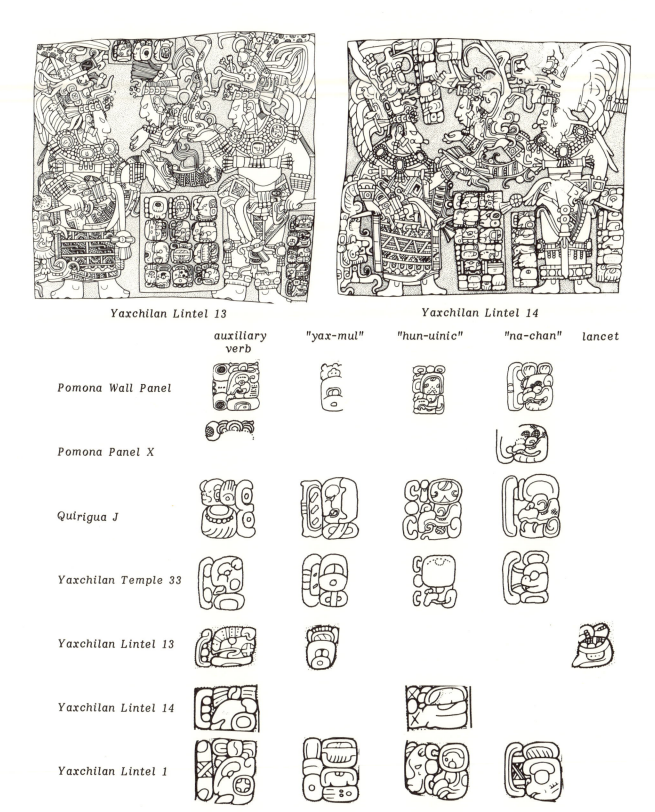

Yaxchilan Lintel 13   Yaxchilan Lintel 14

Figure 50. Verbal phrases associated with the "na-chan" blood-letting events
(Pomona and Yaxchilan drawings courtesy of the Peabody Museum,
Harvard University).

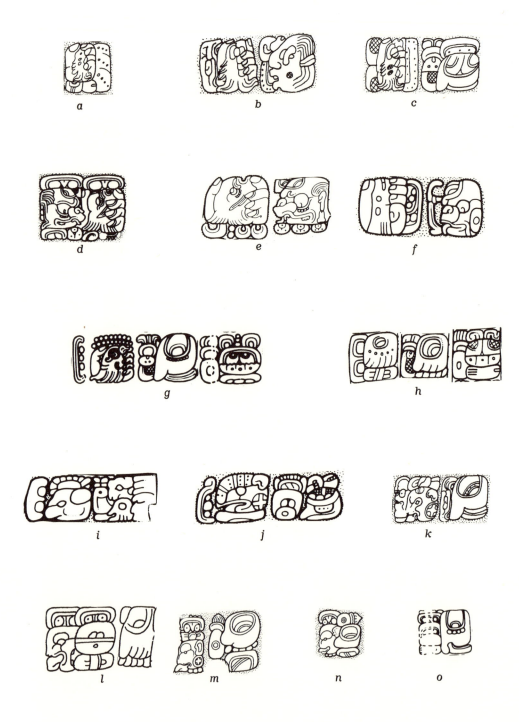

Figure 51. Various verbal expressions associated with "blood-letting."

(a) *Palenque Tablet of the Sun, O13.*

(b) *Palenque Temple of the Foliated Cross, C9-D9. The "water-group" suffix appears in the form of an anthropomorphic head variant.*

(c) *Palenque Temple of the Foliated Cross, M10-L12. Two intermediate glyphs are not included in the illustration. The T712 lancet appears following T89, the locative tu. The construction is verb + complements + tu + verbal noun.*

(d) *Yaxchilan Lintel 25, B1. Additional glyphs in the event phrase are not included. Verb + complement.*

(e) *Yaxchilan Lintel 25, M1-L2. This is a redundant statement of the previous verb, but neither of its components is inflected with T1 u.*

(f) *Yaxchilan Lintel 14, D2-E2. The suffix T181 is in contrast to the affix patterns of the first five examples.*

(g) *Tikal Temple 1, Lintel 3, C3-C4. The main verb is "fish-in-hand," but here it is followed by tu + T712 and ti + akbal. The construction is verb + tu + verbal noun + ti + verbal (?) noun.*

(h) *Yaxchilan Stela 18, A9-A11. This expression is exactly parallel to that above,*

except that the "fish-in-hand" verb is replaced by the auxiliary verb T1.501: 102. Auxiliary verb + tu + verbal noun + ti + verbal (?) noun.*

(i) *Yaxchilan Lintel 13, C1-D1. "Fish-in-hand" is now the verbal noun in an auxiliary verb + tu + verbal noun construction.*

(j) *Yaxchilan Lintel 14, G1-G2. General verb + complements.*

(k) *Palenque Tablet of the Sun, C11-D11. General verb + complement. This is a metaphor for "child of parent."*

(l) *Yaxchilan Stela 11, front lower register. Auxiliary verbs + ta + verbal noun. The auxiliary verb is reduplicated as T1.757 and T1.580. This is a metaphor for "child of parent."*

(m) *Yaxchilan Lintel 24, C1-D1. Auxiliary verb + ti + verbal noun.*

(n) *Yaxchilan Lintel 24, G1. Auxiliary verb + ti + verbal noun. The woman pictured on this lintel is named as the subject of this verb, and the action shown is tongue mutilation.*

(o) *Tikal Temple 1 Lintel 3, F4. Auxiliary verb (T3.580) + ti + verbal noun. This is a metaphor for "child of parent."*

8. Some Unusual Examples of Syntax

In the inscriptions, there are two examples in which an unrelated verbal phrase and its subject are embedded within another verbal phrase or sequence of verbal phrases with completely different subjects. The first example occurs on Yaxchilan Lintel 17 (Fig. 52), which does not display a date, although the scene is clearly one of blood-letting. The main text within the pictorial space opens with a four-glyph auxiliary verb + *ti* + verbal noun phrase, but unfortunately the semantically critical glyphs are eroded. However, none of these eroded glyphs is likely to have recorded a subject because both the second and third glyphs in the text are preceded by *ti*, and the fourth is preceded by a pronominal (Set A third person) sign.

The text continues with a "birth" verb and the personal name glyph of Bird-Jaguar's son, Shield-Jaguar II. This two-glyph phrase apparently records the occasion (the birth of a son) on which the blood-letting rite was conducted. This suggestion is supported by the text on another blood-letting monument--Lintel 13, which explicitly records the birth of Shield-Jaguar II as one of the primary events celebrated (Fig. 53). The Lintel 17 text (Fig. 52) continues with another verbal phrase that has as its main verbal glyph a T501 compound. The second glyph of this phrase seems to be a "yax-mul" compound identical to the second glyph in the "fish-in-hand" verbal expression on Lintel 15 (another blood-letting/vision monument), and apparently related to the "yax mul/hun-uinic/na chan" expression for blood-letting discussed in the previous chapter. The remaining part of the Lintel 17 text names the subject as Bird-Jaguar. The structure of this text seems to be composed of the following sequence of components: auxiliary verb + *ti* + verbal noun + *ti* + verbal noun--"he was born, Shield-Jaguar II"--*ti* verb + complement, subject. The occasion for the pictured blood-letting rite--the birth of Shield-Jaguar II--is embedded in the verbal sequence recording the specific rites conducted in celebration of the occasion.

A similar kind of structure is found on the door jamb panels from Temple 18 at Palenque (Fig. 54). The last long clause of this text opens with a DN that leads from a birth to an accession, but the subjects of both are deleted. The text continues with another DN that associated the historical accession with the accession of the ancestral goddess whose birth and accession are recorded in the first half of the Tablet of the Cross (Lounsbury 1976, 1980). The short clause recording her accession utilizes the same verb as that recording the historical accession, and her name phrase is included in the clause. The text continues with another series of glyphs which Lounsbury (personal communication, 1978) believes contains a "death" reference. Mathews (personal communication, 1978) and I are not yet convinced of the presence of another verbal phrase, but the identification of a fourth verbal phrase is not critical to this analy-

first verbal phrase

embedded clause: "he was born Shield-Jaguar II"

second verbal phrase

Bird-Jaguar (subject)

Figure 52. *Yaxchilan Lintel 17. An embedded clause (drawings courtesy of the Peabody Museum, Harvard University).*

he was born

Shield-Jaguar II

Figure 53. *Yaxchilan Lintel 13: Shield-Jaguar II's birth record (drawings courtesy of the Peabody Museum, Harvard University).*

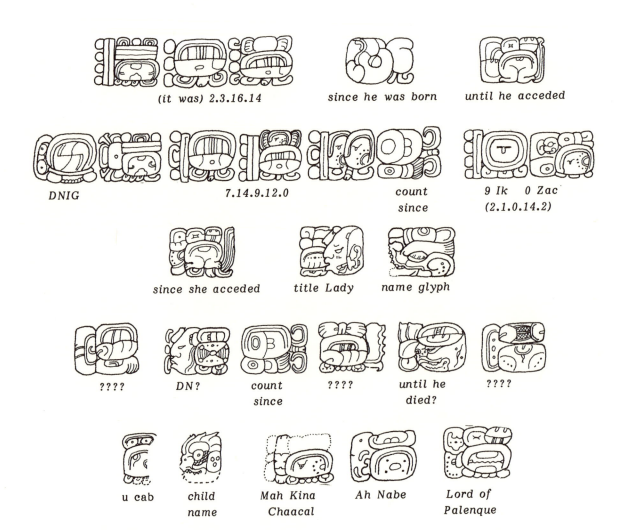

(it was) 2.3.16.14   since he was born   until he acceded

DNIG   7.14.9.12.0   count since   9 Ik   0 Zac (2.1.0.14.2)

since she acceded   title Lady   name glyph

????   DN?   count since   ????   until he died?   ????

u cab   child name   Mah Kina Chaacal   Ah Nabe   Lord of Palenque

Figure 54. Palenque Temple 18 Jambs, D5-C18: an embedded clause.

sis because in either case, Chaacal (named in the final phrase of the text) is also the deleted subject of the birth and accession that began this passage. The structure seems to be as follows:

DN since he was born (deleted subject) until he acceded (deleted subject)

DN since she was seated, the ancestral goddess (deleted: "until he acceded, subject")

Possible verbal phrase *u cab*, child name, Mah Kina Ah Nabe Chaacal, Lord of Palenque.

Two unusual features are evident in this passage. An event with a different subject is inserted between two verbs and the record of the missing subject of those verbs. And the event to which the second DN is to be counted is not recorded; the only way in which the accession event of the ancestral goddess can be related to the historical accession of Chaacal is to work out the calendric arithmetic.

The name phrase of Chaacal is preceded in this text by the glyph *u cab*, which Kelley (1962b:324) discussed as a possible appellative indicator. Kelley called attention to the Yucatec uses of *cab* as "town," "place," and "world." In our own studies of the inscriptions of Palenque, Lounsbury, Mathews, and I had entertained a meaning of "second" for *u cab* because its distribution seemed to be in contrast to *ah nabe*, which can be interpreted as "first." However, it is clear now that Kelley's suggestion is more likely to be correct; for example, in the passage from the Temple 18 jambs discussed above, both *u cab* and *ah nabe* appear in Chaacal's name phrase (Fig. 54).

Because of Kelley's speculations and our awareness of the importance of *u cab* as a signal of name phrases at Palenque, the occurrences of *u cab* are recorded in the verb catalog. This assembly of information has shown that *u cab* can appear in the two following contexts: (1) verbal phrase, *u cab*, name phrase; and (2) verbal phrase, name phrase, *u cab*, name phrase. In the latter context, the second name phrase is almost always identifiable as the contemporary ruler of the appropriate site, a fact that is suggestive of an agentive construction. However, *u cab* is associated with too many different verbal affix patterns and with too many different syntactical and semantic contexts to construct a convincing argument for this identification of its function. It seems more likely that Kelley's reference to the meaning of *u cab* as "his town," "his earth," "his world," or "his nation" points in the right direction. At present, I believe *u cab* can be tentatively paraphrased as "during the tenure of . . .," "under the auspices of . . .," or some sort of equivalent phrase. A listing of the catalog numbers of the examples of *u cab* is as follows:

11:4	21:3	75:8	99:7

11:5	21:15	75:10	111:6
12:1	39:5	79:6	114:3
12:9	54:1	80:3	121:4
12:10	58:1	82:1	122:4
13:5	69:8	89:10	124:1
14:2	74:17	95:17	128:4
14:4	75:3	98:17	128:5

T1.501:102 is another glyph that occurs in many of the same contexts as u cab; most particularly it appears between the patient and agent in "capture" records (see Chart 34). However, this T501 glyph is also related to the T757 general and auxiliary verb because it occurs in auxiliary verb expressions (see Chart 35:5), and on the Tikal bones it introduces name phrases in contexts which resemble the introduction of name phrases by the T.757 general verb (Chart 36).

The occurrence of T1.501.102 between the patient (the one acted upon) and the agent (the actor) in "capture" records suggests that this glyph is some sort of agency expression (Fig. 55a-b). The components of this glyph are as follows: T1, a third person pronoun of the ergative set (Set A); T501, phonetic *ma* or *ba*; and T102, phonetic *-al*. Together, the individual signs are read as *u mal* or *u bal*. In nine of the forty-nine examples of "capture" events listed in the verb catalog, *u mal* occurs between the patient and agent, and in one (Fig. 55c), it occurs following the verb and preceding the patient and agent. The occurrence of T1.501:102 in these contexts may point to its function as an expression of agency, but one related example on the Dos Pilas Hieroglyphic Stairs (Fig. 55d) suggests that it is a second verb inflected for the transitive or the intransitive imperfective. In the Dos Pilas example, the name of the patient follows the "capture" verb, and an alternative form of the T501 agency expression follows the agent and precedes the patient. This alternative form is T501:178.181, read as *ma:la.ah* or *ba:la.ah*. Since the context of the Dos Pilas example is exactly

	verb	*patient*	*mal*	*agent*
a. Yaxchilan Lintel 43				
b. Yaxchilan Lintel 46				
c. Yaxchilan Structure 44 center lower step				
d. Dos Pilas Hieroglyphic Stairs, east				

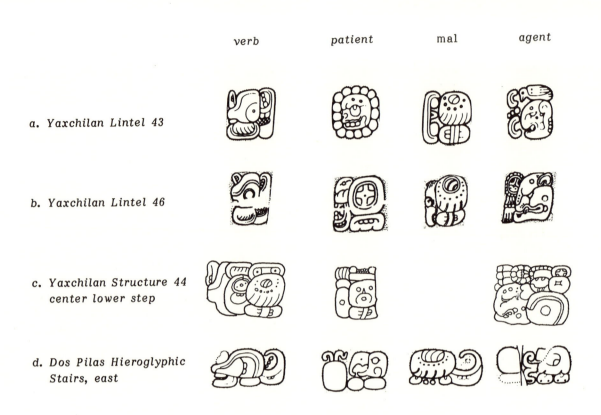

Figure 55. Capture constructions with possible agency expressions.

parallel to the T1.501:102 examples, the different affix patterns can be interpreted as different inflection patterns on the same verbal stems.

In many Mayan languages, agency expressions are composed of some form of the verb "to do," "to make." Various agency expressions documented for Mayan languages and a comparative list of the verbs for "to do" and "to make" are as follows:

Agency expressions:

Yucatec	*u men, tu men*
Chontal	*u men(el), u k'al*
Chorti	*u men(el)*
Cholti	*u men(el)*
Chol	*i men (?)*
	cha'an
	ti k'ɨb' (with human agency)
Tzeltal	*xkah*
Tzotzil	*xkoh*
Jacaltec	*u*
Mam	*u'n*
Quiche	*umal*
Sacapultec	*amal*
Sipacapa	*amal*
Cakchiquel	*umal*
Pocoman	*u'uum*
Pokonchi	*u'uum*
Kekchi	*xk'aba', xmak*
Huastec	*abal, k'al*

"To do, to make, to work"

Yucatec	*men*	"to do, to make, to work"	Jacaltec	*munil*	"to work for another person for pay"
Mopan	*men*	"to do, to make, to work"			
Lacandon	*men*	"to do"	Kanjobal	*munil*	"to work"
Cholti	*k'ale*	"to do"	Teco	*munil*	"responsibility"
Chol	*mel*	"to do"	Aguacatec	*ban*	"to do, make"
	cha'le	"to do"	Mam	*ban-*	(in *bancham* "to do")
Tzeltal	*mel-*	(in *meltza'an* "to fix, mend")	Uspantec	*ban*	"to do, make"
			Quiche	*ban*	"to do, make"
Tzotzil	*mel-*	(in *meltzan* "to make, to build, to prepare")	Cakchiquel	*ban*	"to do, make"
			Kekchi	*uxman*	"to do"
Tojolobal	*uman*	"to do"		*ban*	"for"
Chuj	*munil*	"work"	Huastec	*umal*	"to do"

9. The Verb Catalog

The goal in structuring this verb catalog is to provide a tool that can be used in different kinds of studies of the Classic Maya inscriptions. Proskouriakoff and Berlin in terms of the "historical hypothesis" and Knorozov in terms of his "phonetic hypothesis" provided the basic methods and approaches that have yielded our present understanding of Classic dynastic history and the phonetic values of a limited number of signs. Most advances in the last two decades of study have resulted from a application of these two approaches, but prospects of further gains in the understanding of the inscriptions seems limited if our method remains only the extension of the presently available methods of analysis to sites that have not been thoroughly studied. New kinds of information and approaches are being developed that focus on the application of linguistic methods of analysis to the inscriptions, with one of the most obvious areas being a study of the verb morphology of the writing system. Such a study can add to the inventory of deciphered events and, therefore, to our reconstruction of the history of the Classic period. Moreover, a reconstructed grammar and syntax of the writing system of the Classic period will be enormously important to historical linguists, ethnohistorians, and other specialists who work directly with the Mayan languages. A written record does exist of the language(s) spoken between A.D. 293 and A.D. 900.

Personal experience has led me to suspect that no single individual is likely to command all the specialized information about the writing system and historical linguistics required to produce a complete analysis of the verb morphology of the inscriptions. This catalog is designed, therefore, to provide a compendium of information about phrases occupying the syntactical position of the verb in the Classic inscriptions. This body of information is presented from an epigrapher's and iconographer's point of view for the use of other people with the same specialties, as well as for the use of linguists, ethnohistorians, and other scholars who may wish to pursue studies of the inscriptions from their own point of view.

In 1978, I began to establish a file of verbal phrases including calendric and syntactic information on and an illustration of every verbal phrase available to me in my archives. This information was mounted on Key-sort cards with any single card limited to examples in which the main signs and affix patterns of the glyphs were identical. Each example was accompanied by the following information: location, monument and glyph block designations, date of the event, object if any, subject, and date of dedication, which I determined to be the nearest hotun ending after the latest date on the monument or in the architectural setting. The cards were punched for this information and for the affix patterns, as well as for the meaning, if known, of the verb.

Based on the experience gained in making the card file, I organized the final catalog according to the affix patterns of the writing system, rather than according to T-numbers or the meaning of particular verbs, in order to concentrate on the verbal grammar. The resulting catalog is organized in the following arrangement: (1) all phrases occurring with no affixing of any kind; (2) all phrases occurring with the prefix T1 or an equivalent; (3) all phrases occurring without prefixes and with the suffix T181; and (4) all phrases occurring with any other affix pattern.

The charts in the catalog are numbered consecutively with examples subnumbered. In a designation such as "107:11," the first number refers to the chart and the second to the individual example on that chart. At the top of each chart appear its number, the affix charted, the affix cluster in which and main sign with which that sign appears, and, when appropriate, general commentary on the class of verbs contained on the chart. The examples are then listed, with the following information for each example: its location, the date of the event, the "patient" and "agent", and the date of dedication of the monument. The terms "patient" and "agent" are used, rather than object and subject, in order to cope with the problem of passive constructions in which the "patient" (the one acted upon) becomes the subject of the verb. However, both sets of terms are used in the commentary on individual examples, with "object" and "subject" used in the grammatical sense and "patient" and "agent" used in the semantic sense. The terms "patient" and "agent" head the appropriate columns on each chart in order to more accurately reflect those recorded as acting versus those acted upon. The lack of an entry in either the agent or patient column signals that nothing is explicitly recorded in the original texts; however, when I could detect patterns of deletion, they are noted in the appropriate columns.

After experimenting with various formats, it was decided to include an illustration of each example in order to avoid relying on T-numbers. That system is opaque to the uninitiated, and it simply cannot cope with subtle variation in graphic configuration or with glyphs not originally recorded by Thompson.

Commentary on many examples, often including explanations of particular decisions, follows the basic data. These notes also include any commentary or speculation about meaning, and call to attention syntactical patterns of interest and associations with other events. This commentary is intended to record my present thinking about certain patterns of meaning, and not to represent final, irrevocable conclusions; nor is it intended as a summary of all past and present commentary in the literature on the Maya inscriptions. The catalog should be used with this in mind.

Where possible each chart records only one verbal main sign, but in many cases, only one or two examples of a particular verb are known in the Classic inscriptions. In order to conserve space, these verbs of restricted occurrence are grouped together on large charts of miscellaneous organization. The location of these verbs can be quickly identified by the use of the appendices which list the contents of the catalog in the following patterns: (1) Appendix 1, according to the affix patterns; (2) Appendix 2, according to the T-numbers of the main signs of the verbs; (3) Appendix 3, according to site and monument designations; and (4) Appendix 4, according to a chronological summary of the dates of each event. Each major section of the catalog begins with period ending expressions (the largest category of verbs) listed in the following order: T218 "completion of"; T713 "end of the tun"; "scattering"; T601 expressions; and, any miscellaneous period ending phrases. Known dynastic events, such as birth, accession, death, capture, etc., follow the period ending expressions. Because continuous texts were necessarily fragmented in order to list verbs with different affix patterns under the proper affix category, the commentary are heavily cross-referenced, directing the reader to other parts of a verbal sequence, as well as to other occurrences in different texts of similar verbal constructions.

In many texts, the boundaries of a verbal phrase are difficult to identify because when five or six glyphs appear in an undeciphered phrase, some of the components may record an object or be part of a name phrase. In these cases, I have included all glyphs that follow a Distance Number or date and precede the first recognizable glyph in a name phrase. Some of these glyphs are very probably not verbal, but it seemed to me that it would be better to have all potentially relevant glyphs in ambiguous phrases present and subject to elimination, than to have users of the catalog assume that all such glyphs were present when some had been eliminated.

I have included in the catalog verbal phrases from monuments now located in private and public collections because these texts contain important information for the study of verb morphology. The largest single group of monuments comes from the site tentatively identified as "Calakmul" by Marcus (1973). However, although this Emblem Glyph does occur on monuments from Calakmul, it also occurs at Dos Pilas, Resbalon, Tikal, and elsewhere, so that a secure identification of the Emblem Glyph as Calakmul is not possible at present. Peter Mathews (n.d.a) has identified twenty-five monuments from this unknown site, which he designates as "Site Q," the term used in this catalog.

Monuments from "Site Q" designated according to Mathews' summary and other looted monuments are recorded in the catalog as "Coll 1," "Coll 2," etc. These collection designations refer to the following monuments:

Coll 1 Panel 2 from Site Q, a panel with incised glyphs listed as No. 6 in Mayer 1980.

Coll 2 A wall panel located in the Kimbell Art Museum in Fort Worth. See Mayer 1980, No. 14.

Coll 3 A stela, possibly located in Zurich.

Coll 4 Panel 5 from Site Q. The scene shows a male and female in "scattering" rites. Photograph provided by Irmgard Groth.

Coll 5 A panel probably from Yaxchilan showing a female seated in a moon sign Dutting 1979, 187, Fig. 6.

Coll 6 The Randall stela. See Mayer 1980, No 43.

Coll 7 A stela possibly from the Bonampak region. See Mayer 1978, No. 1.

Coll 8 A round pedestal stone throne in the Chicago Art Institute. See Mayer 1980, No. 7.

Coll 9 Glyphic Panel 8 from Site Q. See M.D. Coe 1973, Fig. 6 and Mayer 1980, No. 48.

Coll 10 A small incised bone said to be from the Palenque region.

Coll 11 Panel 4 from Site Q. See Mayer 1980, No. 2.

Coll 12 An Early Classic glyphic panel in the William Rockhill Nelson Gallery in Kansas City, Missouri. See Mayer 1980, No. 17.

Coll 13 A panel from the Yaxchilan region now located at the Cleveland Museum of Art. See Mayer 1980, No. 8.

Coll 14 Panel 1 from Site Q. See M. D. Coe 1973, No.3 and Mayer 1980, No. 45.

Coll 15 Glyphic Panel 6 from Site Q. It records the birth of Great-Jaguar-Paw of Site Q. See Mayer 1978, No. 17.

Coll 16 A stela with a standing female figure. Located in the Dallas Museum of Fine Arts. See Mayer 1980, No. 10.

Coll 17 Stela 2 from Site Q. Located in the Cleveland Art Museum. See J. Miller 1974 and Mayer 1980, No. 9.

Coll 18 Fragment of a wall panel from the north facade of the Palace at Palenque. Located in Art Museum of the University of Indiana. See Mayer 1980, No. 10.

Coll 19 Stela 4 of Site Q. Located in the Tamayo Collection in Oaxaca.

Coll 20 Glyphic Panel 4 of Site Q. See Mayer 1978, No. 48.

Coll 21 Glyphic Panel 7 from Site Q. See Mayer 1978, No. 18.

Coll 22 Glyphic Panel 9 from Site Q. Located in the Barbachano Collection.

Coll 23 Ballplayer Panel 3 from Site Q. Present location unknown.

Coll 24 Dumbarton Oaks Stela. See Mayer 1978, No. 44.

Coll 25 Stela in Musees Royaux d'Art et d'Histoire, Brussels. See Mayer 1978, No. 2.

Coll 26 An alabaster bowl on exhibition at the University of Virginia Museum, 1982.

Several other looted monuments can be attributed to Bonampak because of the presence of recognized named phrases and the Bonampak Emblem Glyph in these texts. These panels were assigned letter designations as follows:

Bonampak A An Early Classic wall panel dated at 9.3.10.0.0. The panel is composed of six columns of glyphs without an accompanying scene. See Mayer 1980, No. 6).

Bonampak B An Early Classic wall panel with two seated figures flanking a central text dated at 9.4.8.14.9. The same persons named on Bonampak A also occur in this text. See Mayer 1980, No. 44.

Bonampak C A stela showing a standing male figure marked with blood-letting

iconography. See Joralemon 1974, Fig. 18 and Mayer 1980, No. 65.

Bonampak D A column with a glyphic text. See Liman and Durbin 1975 and Mayer 1980, No. 56.

Abbreviations of site names and technical terms used throughout the catalog and appendices are listed at the beginning of this book. In several texts from Palenque, Tikal, and elsewhere, various supernaturals are identified as the agents of verbal phrases. The designations used in the catalog are drawn either from Schellhas (1904) or from Berlin's (1963) identification of the Palenque Triad. In addition, there is an extended list of deity names associated with the Palenque Triad in the Tablet of the Foliated Cross and the Palace Tablet at Palenque. I have assigned roman numerals to these name glyphs, using the three gods of the Triad as the initial three numerals. The designations and illustrations of these seven deities are as follows:

GI　　　GII　　　GIII　　　GIV

GV　　　GVI　　　GVII

CHART 1   Affix Ø   in Cluster Ø.*.Ø   with Main Sign T218

This glyph is a period ending expression usually given the interpretation "completion of."

#	LOCATION	DATE (EVENT)	PATIENT	AGENT	DEDICATION	
1.	Tik 31 H15	9. 0. 0. 0. 0	9 cycles	Stormy-Sky	9. 0.10. 0. 0	

This verbal phrase is preceded by T617:126 and followed by TIX.528.528 "9 cycles," but here the period sign usually taken to represent baktuns must record the katun period.

#	LOCATION	DATE (EVENT)	PATIENT	AGENT	DEDICATION	
2.	Nar Alt1 K6-K7	10. 0. 0. 0. 0	10 cycles	none	9. 8. 0. 0. 0	

This verb is followed by

#	LOCATION	DATE (EVENT)	PATIENT	AGENT	DEDICATION	
3.	Pal Slav G5a	9.14.18. 9.17	3 katuns	deleted (Chac-Zutz')	9.15. 0. 0. 0	

This verbal phrase records the 3rd katun anniversary of the birth of Chac-Zutz', and although his name is deleted from this clause, it is clear from the context that he was understood to be the agent.

#	LOCATION	DATE (EVENT)	PATIENT	AGENT	DEDICATION	
4.	Tort 6 P2	13. 0. 0. 0. 0 1 Ahau 3 Kankin	13th baktun	missing	9.12. 0. 0. 0	
5.	PN Alt1 K2	13. 0. 0. 0. 0 4 Ahau 8 Cumku	13 baktuns	missing	9.13. 0. 0. 0	

CHART 2   Affix Ø   in Cluster Ø.*.Ø   with Main Sign T528:713

This glyph is a period ending expression with an approximate meaning of "it ended, the tun" or "the end of the tun." Note that T116, the phonetic complement -n(i), can be attached to the tun glyph (T528) or to the entire block.

#	LOCATION	DATE (EVENT)	PATIENT	AGENT	DEDICATION	
1.	Cop PecSk	8.17. 0. 0. 0	tun	Capped-Ahau	8.17. 0. 0. 0	

Chart 2   81

2.	Bon A C8	9. 3. 0. 0. 0	tun	none	9. 3.10. 0. 0	
3.	Bon A E3-F3	9. 3.10. 0. 0	tun	none	9. 3.10. 0. 0	
4.	Nar 23 G19	9.14. 0. 0. 0	tun	Smoking-Squirrel	9.14. 0. 0. 0	

This verb follows a "completion of the 14th katun" expression.

5.	Nar 29 H12-I13	9.13. 3. 0. 0	tun	Lady 6-Sky of Tikal	9.14. 3. 0. 0	
6.	Nar 29 H17	9.14. 3. 0. 0	tun	Lady 6-Sky of Tikal	9.14. 3. 0. 0	
7.	Cop N B18b	????	tun	missing	9.16.10. 0. 0	

The date of this period ending is 14.18.3.0.0.0 before 4 Ahau 8 Cumku and 14.17.19.10.0.0 before 9.16.10.0.0, the dedication date of Stela N. The two and one-half glyph blocks following this passage are badly eroded, and therefore it is not possible to ascertain if the remaining glyphs referred to the period ending or to a supernatural agent.

8.	Tik TI D14	9. 4. 0. 0. 0	tun	eroded	9.16.15. 0. 0	
9.	Tik 22 B2	9.17. 0. 0. 0	tun	Ruler C	9.17. 0. 0. 0	
10.	Tik 20 A4	9.16. 0. 0. 0	tun	Ruler B	9.16. 0. 0. 0	
11.	Nar 1 F6-E7	9.13.10. 0. 0	tun	eroded	9.13.10. 0. 0	

| 12. | Nar 22
G20-H20 | 9.13.10. 0. 0 | tun | none | 9.13.10. 0. 0 |  |

This phrase closes the inscription, and the agent, if any, is not recorded.

13.	Nar 24 E15-D16	9.13.10. 0. 0	tun	Lady 6-Sky of Tikal	9.13.10. 0. 0	
14.	Nar 21 E10	9.13.15. 0. 0	tun	Smoking- Squirrel	9.13.15. 0. 0	
15.	Nar 13 A3-A4	9.17.10. 0. 0	tun	Ruler IIIb	9.17.10. 0. 0	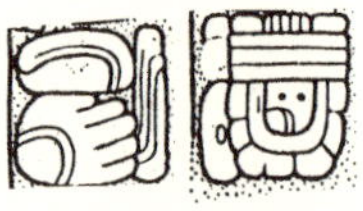
16.	Nar 13 E10	9.17.10. 0. 0	tun	Ruler IIIb	9.17.10. 0. 0	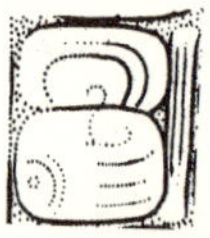
17.	DPil 8 H5	9.14. 0. 0. 0	tun	Shield-God K	9.15. 0. 0. 0	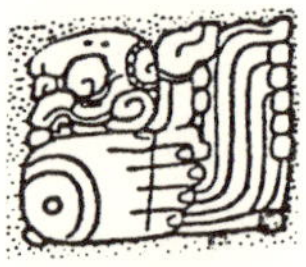
18.	Tik 12 B4	9. 4.13. 0. 0	tun	*u cab* Curl-Head	9. 4.13. 0. 0	
19.	Tik 16 B1	9.14. 0. 0.0	tun	Ruler A	9.14. 0. 0. 0	

CHART 3   Affix Ø   in Cluster Ø.*.Ø   with Miscellaneous Main Signs

The majority of verbal phrases on this chart are associated with period ending dates or occur as the final passage of a text and seem to function as some kind of dedicatory expression. Several "scattering" expressions not associated with period endings or final passages are included because they appear to record the same rite as these period ending expressions.

#	LOCATION	DATE (EVENT)	PATIENT	AGENT	DEDICATION	
1.	Car 1 E1-F1	9. 8. 0. 0. 0		Ruler 3	9. 8. 0. 0. 0	

Chart 3   83

2.   Pal T18   none   none   9.14.15. 0. 0
     Jamb D17

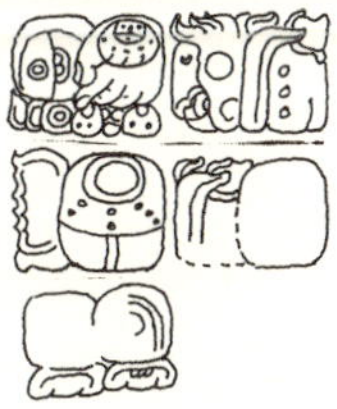

This expression occurs as the final passage of the Temple 18 jambs and
appears to be a dedicatory expression for the inscription. It includes a
couplet contrasting "water," represented by the waterlily glyph, and
"sky," and it seems to be a neutral event, which is cosmological in
nature, requiring a supernatural subject or none at all. This same couplet expression is found with other dedicatory expressions at Palenque
and is especially prevalent with anniversary events (see 87:3,5–11). The
first part of the verb includes the *mul ti* constants of the ADI and PDI,
but the variable (either T679 or T126) is missing. Here *mul ti* must
function, not as part of the "count" glyph, but rather as an auxiliary
verb + *ti* construction with "scattering" as the verbal noun. *Xoc ti*
occurs in similar construction in #5. The "scattering" verb is accompanied by two phonetic complements: T502 *ma* infixed into the main sign
and T178 *la* suffixed to it. Combined, these signs support the *mal* reading
suggested by Kelley (1976:51–52). See #12 and #13 for occurrences of
alternative "spellings" of *mal*.

3.   Tik T4   9.15.10. 0. 0   none   9.16. 0. 0. 0
     L3   A2

4.   Mach 4   9.19.10. 0. 0   none   9.19.10. 0. 0
     A2a

5.   Pal TIw   9.12. 0. 0. 0   supernatural?   9.12.15. 0. 0
     A11–B12

The *xoc ti* in this expression appears to function as an auxiliary verb +
ti as does the *mul ti* in #2; however, it should be noted that this phrase
is parallel to two others (see 31:1–2) in which a third person pronominal
sign from the ergative set occurs instead of the *xoc* glyph. *Xoc* may
function, therefore, as a substitute for this pronoun, rather than as an
auxiliary verb. This event phrase is followed by two glyphs that do not
occur elsewhere as personal names in the inscriptions of Palenque. These
glyphs may refer to the period ending event or they may record an unknown
personage or supernatural as the agent.

6.   Pal TIw   9.12. 0. 0. 0   supernatural?   9.12.15. 0. 0
     A10–B10

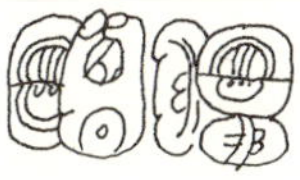

This phrase follows a "tun seating" expression. As in examples #5 and #7,
the glyphs following this expression are not known dynastic names.

7. Pal TIw   9.13. 0. 0. 0   supernatural? 9.12.15. 0. 0
    D2

This expression is parallel to #6, but it records an event that would
have occurred in the future at the time of the composition of this
inscription.

8. Pal PTab   none   none   9.14.10. 0. 0
    R18-R19

This expression, like #2 from the Temple 18 jambs, closes the inscription
and appears to function as a dedicatory phrase. *Mul* again appears to function as an auxiliary verb, but the damaged state of these glyph makes it
impossible to determined if *ti* was also present.

9. Coll 18   9.13.10. 0. 0?   none   9.14.10. 0. 0
    Pal Frag
    pA6-pB6

This is the final passage on a panel fragment which stylistically should
come from the north facade of the Palace. The verbal phrase is associated
with the day 7 Ahau, which corresponds to 9.13.10.0.0, a date 25 days
before the death of Chan-Bahlum. It could refer to this period ending date
or, like #2 and #8, it may be the final dedicatory phrase of the inscription. Note that T580 (upright muluc) occurs as a phonetic complement to the
"scattering" hand.

10. Pal Thr1   9.11. 0. 0. 0   quarter-   Pacal II   9.11. 0. 0. 0
    G1   katun PE

11. Pal TIw   9.11. 0. 0. 0   tun   none   9.12.15. 0. 0
    K9a

12. Yax Str33   9.15.13. 6. 9   deleted   9.16. 6. 0. 0
    Step 7 R2   (Bird-Jaguar)

This phrase is the second in a series of three events; it is preceded by
a glyph that Peter Mathews (personal communication, 1980) has tentatively
identified as a verb for the ballgame (13:6), and this text accompanies a
ballgame scene. It is followed by an expression associated with blood-
letting (see 52:9). All of these event phrases are associated by DN with
a series of mythological events that took place in the far distant past.
Note that this "scattering" verb is followed by phonetic complements--
T501 *ba* or *ma* and T178 *la* forming *mal* as do the complements in #2.

Chart 3   85

13. Pal T18   missing   missing   9.14.15. 0. 0
    Stc 472

This stucco glyph was not found in situ, so it cannot be associated with
a date or agent. It is important as a confirmation of the reading of the
"scattering" hand as *mal*. Here the phonetic complement is composed of
T74, Landa's *ma*, in lieu of T502 in #2 and T501 in #12. The lower glyph
is the head variant of T178 *la*, an "inverted ahau."

14. Bon 2   9.17.18.15.18   Lady Cauac-   9.18. 0. 0. 0
    D6   Skull

This phrase is the third part of a verbal series that records an event
clearly shown in the accompanying scene to be blood-letting. This direct
association of the "scattering" glyph with an act of blood-letting and the
consistent occurrence of blood-letting iconography, such as the personified
blood-letter (Joralemon 1974), with "scattering" scenes are evidence that
"scattering" was an act of blood-letting. The sign below the "scattering"
hand is T103, a locative preposition, but the second of these two glyphs
is not understood.

15. Yax Str33   no date   ??-Chaan   9.16. 6. 0. 0
    Step 7 T1

This verb occurs in the secondary text next to the ballplayer in the scene.
It appears to function as a general verb much like T1.757 in introducing a
name phrase.

16. Yax L26   no date   Shield-Jaguar   9.14.15. 0. 0
    T1b-U2

This expression is the second part of a verbal couplet of which the first
half is a *ti* construction with T684 as the verbal noun (see 48:6). The
scene shows Shield-Jaguar dressing is battle gear with a woman in attend-
ance. This lintel is part of a blood-letting sequence, and the woman is
shown with blood around her mouth.

17. NTun   no date   Chaan-   9.16.10. 0. 0
    GpIVj   Ah Cauac
    A1

18. Yax Str44   9.12. 9. 8. 1   deleted   9.15. 0. 0. 0
    Ctr up   (Shield
    D10-C11   Jaguar I)

This phrase is the first part of a verbal couplet recording the accession
Shield-Jaguar. Either his name phrase was deleted and was to be understood as the agent from the context, in which he is the only person
named as an agent, or his name was recorded on the unphotographed riser
of this step (Mathews, personal communication, 1980).

19. Cop 23   9.10.18.12. 8   missing   9.11. 0. 0. 0
     E5-F5

20. Hauberg   3 Kan 12 Zotz' or   Bone-Deer   Late Pre-Classic
     A7-A8   3 Kan 12 Xul

The CR date on this monument occurs in an unothodox form, suggesting that
at this early time the Maya had not yet decided upon a format for pre-
senting the CR (Mathews, personal communication, 1982). The text begins
with an ISIG followed by the haab position, designated as 12 with an
animal head. The month is either Zotz' or Xul, but without examination of
the original monument, identification of the particular animal head is
not possible. The haab is followed by two glyphs, the first of which has
the shape of the kin-helmet of the Quadripartite Monster (although the
center is entirely obscured by erosion) and an eroded set of signs within
a day sign cartouche. These two glyphs are followed by what appears to be
Glyph C of the lunar series; however, it has a coefficient of seventeen,
a number impossible in the Lunar Series of the Classic Period. A6 records
the tzolkin position 3 Kan, with a head variant marked as Kan by maize
signs along the top of the head. The possible LC positions of 3 Kan 12
Zotz' and 3 Kan 12 Xul are as follows:

7.16.18. 4. 4	3 Kan 12 Zotz'	September 20, 21 B.C.
7.19.10.17. 4		A.D. 32, October 8
8. 2. 3.17. 4		A.D. 84, September 24
8. 4.16. 7. 4		A.D. 136, September 13
8. 7. 9. 2. 4		A.D. 188, August 31
8.10. 1.15. 4		A.D. 240, September 19
8.12.14.10. 4		A.D. 292, September 5
7.14.17.14. 4	3 Kan 12 Xul	December 9, 61 B.C.
7.17.10. 9. 4		November 26, 9 B.C.
8. 0. 3. 4. 4		A.D. 44, November 14
8. 2.15.17. 4		A.D. 96, November 1
8. 5. 8.12. 4		A.D. 148, October 19
8. 8. 1. 7. 4		A.D. 200, October 8
8.10.14. 2. 4		A.D. 252, September 15
8.13. 6.15. 4		A.D. 304, September 13

The verb is composed of two glyphs: (1) a version T712 blood-letting that
also occurs on Tikal Stela 10 (76:7) and Caracol Stela 3 (128:5) and (2)
an early version of God C. This God C has the mirror infixes characteris-

Chart 3   87

tic of the God C variant frequently shown on loin cloths; however, since
it is preceded by the locative + preposition *tu* (T89) and is in association with a blood-letting verb, I suspect it is an early version of the
God C "water-group" head (T41), now known to represent blood. The verbal
phrase is followed by four glyphs recording the name of the subject. The
first of these glyphs, a long bone adjoined to a long-eared skull, I
assume is the personal name of the subject. It is followed by an open-
mouthed monster; a vulture, marked as the locative *ta* by the presence of
a "torch" (*tah*) in his forehead lock; and a glyph that may be an Emblem
Glyph. The main sign of this possible EG is T563, superfixed by T168 *ahpo*
in the reversed order characteristic of Late Classic inscriptions. The
"blood" glyph usually found preceding EGs may be recorded as the set of
beads enclosing the other signs; blood is shown in this manner around the
lips of the woman on Yaxchilan Lintels 24 and 26 and in Yaxchilan "scattering" scenes. This text accompanys a scene showing a ruler holding a
serpent whose tail is marked as flint by etz'nab signs; this serpent
appears to be the proto-type of the blood-letting serpents shown on Yaxchilan Lintels 13 and 14, Tikal Temple 4, Lintel 3, and Copan Stela D.

21. SDiego   ???? 18 Yax   Turtle-Shell   Late Pre-Classic
     Clift
     A4-B4

Like #20, the CR date of this inscription does not occur in orthodox
order. Mathews (personal communcication, 1982) has suggested that since
no tzolkin date occurs in the surviving inscription and one eroded glyph
block is located above the ISIG, the order was tzolkin, ISIG, haab (18
Yax), and Glyphs G and F. Although this order does not match that of the
Hauberg stela, it is similar enough in its unorthodoxy to suggest that
both inscriptions were recorded during a time of experimentation with
format. It is interesting to note that the use of a ISIG with a CR and
Lord of the Night notation, and without an LC date, also occurs on Tikal
Stela 4, which may deliberately echo this very early tradition. The verb
appears to consist of the T757 auxiliary verb (here without inflection)
and the T712 blood-letting sign. See #20, 21:21, 35:2,4-6, 37:25. 38:28,
39:3,7, 55:5-6, 40:3, 76:7, 98:5,9, 101:2, and 132 for related verbs.

CHART 4   Affix Ø   in Cluster Ø.*.Ø   with Main Sign T644

This period ending expression is generally accepted as the "seating (or placing) of the tun."
However, in the context of period ending expressions, it occurs fourteen times with "zero"
affixing and six times with the possessive pronoun *u* prefixed to it. The lack of occurrence with
other affix patterns suggests that this is a compound noun expression, such as "tun seating."

#	LOCATION	DATE (EVENT)	PATIENT	AGENT	DEDICATION	
1.	Chin Thr1 K	9. 7. 0. 0. 0	tun	none	9.10. 0. 0. 0	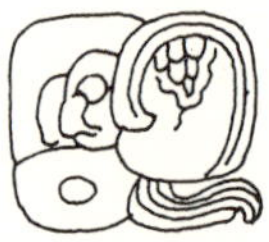
2.	Pal TFC Jamb B11	9.13. 0. 0. 0	tun	none	9.13. 0. 0. 0	
3.	Pal DH F2	9.13. 0. 0. 0	tun	none	9.13. 0. 0. 0	
4.	Pal DO A3	9.11. 0. 0. 0	tun	none	9.14.15. 0. 0	

This "seating" phrase is an earlier event from which a DN is counted to
a later and featured event.

#	LOCATION	DATE (EVENT)	PATIENT	AGENT	DEDICATION	
5.	Pal Slav J3a	9.15. 0. 0. 0	tun	none	9.15. 0. 0. 0	
6.	Pom Stela Frag	9.13. 0. 0. 0	tun	none	9.18. 0. 0. 0?	
7.	Pom PanX pB3	9.18. 0. 0. 0	tun	none	9.18. 0. 0. 0	

This event phrase is preceded by an "inverted bat" event and an "18 katuns"
glyph. The two glyphs following it are eroded, but the surviving text
suggests that it was followed by a third event expression which included
the T1.60:757 verb. See 52:8 and 64:3.

#	LOCATION	DATE (EVENT)	PATIENT	AGENT	DEDICATION	
8.	Pom PanY pC1	9. 8. 0. 0. 0	tun	none	9.18. 0. 0. 0	

Chart 4 89

This glyph is followed by  and by the name "Mah Kina 5-Jaguar."
The subject of the second event may also function as the agent of
this "seating" event.

9. Pom PanY   9. 9. 0. 0. 0   tun   none   9.18. 0. 0. 0
    pB1

This verb is following by the same glyphs as #8, but the agent of this
event is recorded as "GI-Jaguar."

10. Pom Wall   9.17. 0. 0. 0   tun   none   9.17. 0. 0. 0
    Pan pG1

This glyph is part of a series of verbs and is followed by the "scattering" and "end of the tun" (T204.528:116:713:130) events. The sign
usually found infixed into T644 has been placed below the main sign,
rather than inside it. See 41:4, 43:7, 52:7, and 66:9.

11. Pal TIw   9.12. 0. 0. 0   tun   none   9.12.15. 0. 0
    B9

12. Pal TIw   9.13. 0. 0. 0   tun   none   9.12.15. 0. 0
    C2

13. Pal T18   missing   tun   missing   9.14.15. 0. 0
    Stc 411

14. Pal Thr1   9.11. 0. 0. 0   tun   none   9.11. 0. 0. 0
    N1b

15. Pal TC   9.12. 0. 0. 0   tun   none   9.12.10. 0. 0
    Cens1 H2

16. Pal TIe   9. 8.13. 0. 0.   tun   Ahc-Kan   9.12.15. 0. 0
    N3

17. Pal TIe   9.10. 0. 0. 0   tun   none   9.12.15. 0. 0
    S2-S3

| 18. | Pal TIw E9 | 9. 9. 0. 0. 0 | tun | none | 9.12.15. 0. 0 | |

| CHART 5 | | Affix Ø | | in Cluster Ø.*.Ø | | with Miscellaneous Main Signs |

#	LOCATION	DATE (EVENT)	PATIENT	AGENT	DEDICATION	
1.	Cop Str11 Rev S1	9.17. 0. 0. 0		New-Sky-at-Horizon	9.17. 0. 0. 0	
2.	Cop AltD' E-D	9.17. 0. 0. 0		New-Sky-at-Horizon	9.17. 0. 0. 0	
3.	Itz 12 C1-D1	10. 2. 0. 0. 0	tun	local ruler	10. 2. 0. 0. 0	
4.	Quir Fw B15a	9.15.10. 0. 0	tun	none	9.17. 0. 0. 0	
5.	Yax L31 K5	9.17. 0. 0. 0	tun?	none	9.17. 0. 0. 0	
6.	Tort Box C2-D2	9.12. 6.17.18		Ahpo-Balam	9.12.10. 0. 0	

This verbal phrase follows a CR, a DN of two days, and the PE 9.12.7.0.0.
If the verbal refers to the PE, then there is no date associated with the
initial CR. Since the PE is most probably used to lock the CRs of this
text into the LC, it seems likely that the verb refers to the initial CR.

| 7. | Pal Cr I1 | eroded | | none | 9.16. 0. 0. 0? | |

See 14:4.

| 8. | Cop AltD' E1 | 9.17. 0. 0. 0 | | deleted (New-Sky-at Horizon) | 9.17. 0. 0. 0 | |

Chart 5   91

This verb is the second part of a verbal triplet of which #2 is the first part and a T1.757:126:82 general verb is the third part. The subject for all three phrases is named as New-Sky-at-Horizon.

9.   Pal Thr1   9.11. 0. 0. 0   deleted   9.11. 0. 0. 0
     D1   (Square-Nosed-
                                           Beastie)

The verbal phrases under #9 and #10 occur in the text of the subterranean throne of the Palace. These two phrases form a couplet which follows an initial phrase in which the verbal component is too eroded to be read. Note that the first halves of these phrases are identical, but that #9 includes a *ta* locative and a "sky" glyph while #10 includes a *ta* locative and the phonetic glyph *ca-b(a)*, *cab*-"earth". The subject of both phrases is a square-nosed zoomorphic head which appears as the subject of a possible astronomical event of the east panel of the Temple of Inscriptions (N10).

10.   Pal Thr1   9.11. 0. 0. 0   Square-Nosed- 9.11. 0. 0. 0
      E1   Beastie

11.   Pal Thr1   9.11. 0. 0. 0   12 Ahau   none   9.11. 0. 0. 0
      L1   8 Ceh

12.   Pal T14   9 Ik 10 Mol   *u cab* Moon   9.13.15. 0. 0
      A2-B2   Goddess

This verbal phrase is one of several (see 3:2, 3:5, and 3:8) which incorporate components of the Anterior and Posterior Date Indicators as auxiliary verbs. In all of these examples, the distinctive signs of the ADI (T126) and the PDI (T679) are not included when these two glyphs (T513:59, *mul ti*, and T741b, *xoc ti*) function as auxiliary verbs. The verbal phrase is followed by *u cab*, with the *cab* sign occurring in head variant form. The agent is expressed by three glyphs, the first of which is the T1000a female head with T181 attached to its rear. The syntactical location of this female head is that of a noun, not a verb, so that T181 cannot function here as a verbal suffix. Rather it seems to be a semantic determinative for the female head, which without additional information would be taken to mark the general class of female names and not the moon goddess specifically. Here T181 is literally the moon, marking the female head as that of its prototype--the moon goddess. Her name is followed by two aged male heads, each with a numerical prefix, but since their name glyphs are unique to this inscription, they have not been so far identified. To identify one of the agents of this event as the moon goddess is in keeping with its very ancient date.

| 13. | Pal T18 Stc 464 | missing | 8 katuns | none | 9.14.15. 0. 0 |  |

| 14. | Pal TC K10 | 9.10.10. 0. 0 | | none | 9.13. 0. 0. 0 |  |

CHART 6   Affix ∅   in Cluster ∅.*.∅   with Miscellaneous Main Signs

These glyphs represent rare period ending and anniversary expressions.

#	LOCATION	DATE (EVENT)	PATIENT	AGENT	DEDICATION	
1.	Cal 43 B8-A9	9. 4. 0. 0. 0		none	9. 4. 0. 0. 0	

This verbal phrase is the first half of a verbal couplet. See 82:19 for the second half of the couplet.

| 2. | Tik MT 38a-b | none | | deleted | 9.15. 0. 0. 0 | 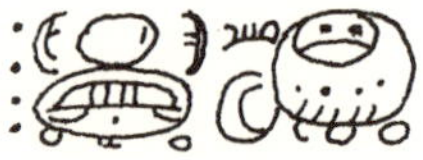 |

This anniversary phrase closes the text in both examples, and since Ruler A is recorded as the subject of the immediately preceding event, he is understood to be the agent of this closing event also.

CHART 7   Affix ∅   in Cluster ∅.*∅   with Main Sign T684

Proskouriakoff (1960) identified this expression as one recording "inauguration" of a ruler.

#	LOCATION	DATE (EVENT)	PATIENT	AGENT	DEDICATION	
1.	Cop 9 F3	9. 6.10. 0. 0?		Waterlily-Jaguar	9. 6.10. 0. 0?	

T684 is preceded by a "water-group" prefix (T35), and the head of the sun god appears in the succeeding block. Another zoomorphic head of the sun god (T1017a) appears with a cartouche as the infix of T684. These head glyphs may refer to the office to which this ruler acceded.

Chart 7   93

| 2. | PN 25 A15 | 9. 8.10. 6.16 | | Ruler 1 | 9. 8.15. 0. 0  |

| 3. | PN 25 I12 | 9. 8.10. 6.16 | | Ruler 1 | 9. 8.15. 0. 0  |

This event is the same as that recorded as #2, but in this case, it is linked by DN to a period ending event.

| 4. | PN L2 K'1-L'1 | no date | | Ah Cauac | 9.11.15. 0. 0  |

This verbal expression occurs in the secondary text framing the smaller figure behind the protagonist of the scene. In the context of the historical environment associated with this lintel, the event cannot be the accession to the office of ruler, but rather it must represent a ritual involving some other office, perhaps that of heir-designate.

| 5. | PN 36 B8 | 9.10. 6. 5. 9 | | Ruler 2 | 9.11.15. 0. 0  |

| 6. | Yax 11 Sides C'11 | 9.16. 1. 0. 0 | | Bird-Jaguar | 9.16. 5. 0. 0  |

| 7. | Cop Str11 nStep K2 | 9.16.12. 5.17 | | New-Sky-at-Horizon | 9.17. 0. 0. 0  |

| 8. | Cop Stone Table | 9.16.12. 5.17 | | New-Sky-at-Horizon | 9.16.15. 0. 0  |

| 9. | Cop Str11 nDoor e D2 | 9.16.12. 5.17 | | New-Sky-at-Horizon | 9.17. 0. 0. 0  |

| 10. | PN L3 A'1-Z2 | 9.16. 6. 9.16 | Bat-Jaguar | *u cab* God N title | 9.16.10. 0. 0  |

The name immediately following this verb is Bat-Jaguar, but in turn his name is followed by *u cab* and the God N title that appears prominently in the name phrases of Rulers 2 and 4. Since the God N title appears in more than one ruler's name at Piedras Negras, it cannot be used in this clause

to identify a particular ruler. But in addition to the problem of subject
identity, the syntactic structure of this secondary text is not entirely
clear. It begins with a verbal phrase (21:26) of which the same Bat-
Jaguar is named as subject. That initial verb is followed by the CR 2
Cauac 2 Muan (9.16.6.10.19); another verb (21:27); a DN of twenty-three
days; this clause; a second CR (9.16.6.9.16 2 Cib [19] Mac); and a final
clause (21:28). The first CR is the later of the two, so I am tentatively
assuming that this inaugural verb records the event from which the DN is
to be counted. If this analysis is correct, the verb following the 2 Cib
19 Mac date can be identified structurally as the second part of a
couplet construction.

11. Seib 7   9.17. 0. 0. 0   Ah Tah   9.18.10. 0. 0
    B2

T126, the AEI, is postfixed to T684, and the affix above the AEI may be a
verbal suffix.

12. Nar 32   9.19. 4. 1. 1   18-Rabbit 9.19.10. 0. 0
    R3

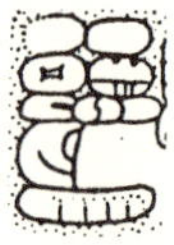

13. PN 25   9. 8.18. 6.16   Ruler 1   9. 8.15. 0. 0
    I8a

CHART 8   Affix Ø   in Cluster Ø.*.Ø   with Main Signs T60:713/89.60:757

This "accession" compound is an expression composed of a verb (T713), identified
as such because all verbal affixing and "temporal" indicators are always attached to it, and a
prepositional phrase introduced by T89 *tu*, a contraction of the locative *ti* and pronoun *u*. It is
my belief that this prepositional phrase records a metaphor for the concept of "succession," and
that the office taken is recorded by the glyphs above the T713 hand. Many of these glyphs appear
as titles in name phrases and can occur as the designation of office with other accession glyphs.

#	LOCATION	DATE (EVENT)	PATIENT	AGENT	DEDICATION	
1.	Pal TIw E4-F5	9. 9. 2. 4. 8		Pacal II	9.12.15. 0. 0	

The sign above the T713 hand is the knot from the T684 bundle, and the
verb may refer to the possessing or taking of the bundle by the incumbent
ruler. The PEI is prefixed to the verb, reflecting the fact that it is a
later date to which a DN is counted.

Chart 8   95

2. Pal TIw   9.12.11.12.10   Chan-   9.12.15. 0. 0
    S9-T9   Bahlum II

The glyphs above the T713 hand are the glyphic version of the Jester God, which appears as the term for office of ruler on the east panel of this temple (see 112:9-10, 12), and as a semantic determinative for Ahau (see Palace Tablet, D11, and Tablet of the 96 Glyphs, J1).

3. Pal TFC   9.12.11.12.10   Chan-   9.13. 0. 0. 0
    O2-P3   Bahlum II

This event is marked with the PEI because it is linked by DN to Chan-Bahlum's birth.

4. Pal TFC   9.12.11.12.10   Chan-   9.13. 0. 0. 0
    F7-E4   Bahlum II

The glyphs above the T713 appear in titles in the Chaacal name at Palenque and throughout the inscriptions of Tikal.

5. Pal TC   2. 1. 0.14. 2   ancestral   9.13. 0. 0. 0
    F7-E8   goddess

PEI; the accession is linked by a DN to birth.

6. Pal TC   5. 8. 17.15.17   U-Kix-Chan   9.13. 0. 0. 0
    P1-Q1

PEI; the accession is linked by a DN to birth.

7. Pal TC   error   Kuk I   9.13. 0. 0. 0
    Q7-P8

PEI; the accession is linked by DN to birth; however, the DN does not work with the recorded CRs, and no explanation for the error has been discovered.

8. Pal TC   8.19.19.11.17   Ruler 2   9.13. 0. 0. 0
    Q15-P16

9.   Pal TC   9. 2.12. 6.18   Manik   9.13. 0. 0. 0
     R6-S6

'PEI; this accession is linked by DN to birth.

10. Pal TC   9. 3. 6. 7.17   Chaacal I   9.13. 0. 0. 0
     S11-R12

PEI; this accession is linked by DN to birth.

11. Pal TC   9. 4.14.10. 4   Kan-Xul I   9.13. 0. 0. 0
     R16-S16

PEI; this accession is linked by DN to birth.

12. Pal TC   9. 6.11. 5. 1   Chaacal II   9.13. 0. 0. 0
     T3-U3

PEI; this accession is linked by DN to birth.

13. Pal TC   9. 6.18. 5.12   Chan-Bahlum I 9.13. 0. 0. 0
     T17-U17

PEI; this accession is linked by DN to birth.

14. Pal TS   9.12.11.12.10   Chan-   9.13. 0. 0. 0
     L2-M2   Bahlum II

15. Pal TC   9.12.11.12.10   deleted   9.13. 0. 0. 0
     O4   (Chan-Bahlum)

This verb occurs as a redundant expression from which a DN is counted to
a later and featured event. Because it repeats information recorded fully
in the immediately preceding clause, the prepositional phrase usually
found following the verb as well as its agent are deleted as redundant
information.

16. Pal Slav   9.14.11.12.14   Chac-Zutz'   9.15. 0. 0. 0
     C2

Notice that the smoking mirror characteristic of God K is infixed into
the bundle knot.

Chart 9 97

| 17. | Pal T18
Ste 449 | missing | missing | 9.14.15. 0. 0 | 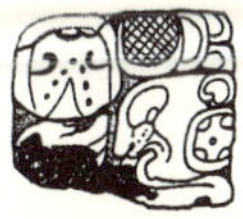 |

| 18. | Chin 1
A2 | 7 Cib 13 Pop | Ah Cauac | Late Classic | 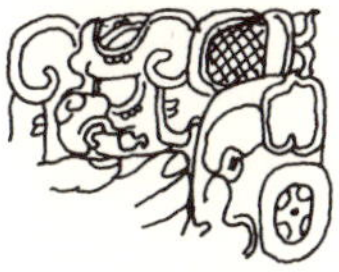 |

CHART 9   Affix ∅   in Cluster ∅.*.∅   with Miscellaneous Main Signs

All these expressions are associated with the taking of an office.

#	LOCATION	DATE (EVENT)	PATIENT	AGENT	DEDICATION	
1.	Tik 31 E10-F10	8.17. 2.16.17		Curl-Snout	9. 0.10. 0. 0	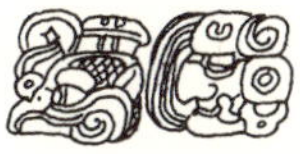

This verb is associated with a date which occurs on Stela 4 with the accession of Curl-Snout (see 37:4).

| 2. | Coll 1
E4 | 9. 8.12.12. 9 | | deleted
(Ah Naab-Chan) | 9. 9. 0. 0. 0 | 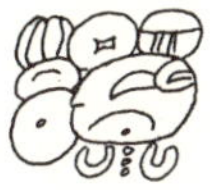 |

AEI; a DN is counted from this event to a subsequent one in a structure that can be paraphrased as follows: "it was so much time since the seating as lord until. . ." Since the agent of this event is named in the immediately preceding clause, his name is deleted from this repetitive phrase. The protagonist (Ah Naab-Chan) is clearly understood from the context to be the agent of this verb also.

| 3. | Cop AltQ
B4-A5 | 9.15. 6.17. 0 | | New-Sky-at-
Horizon | 9.17. 5. 0. 0 | 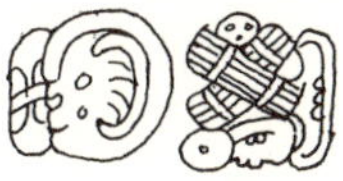 |

This event occurred three days after a "God K-in-hand" event and seems to record some sort of ritual for the taking of office, but both events precede the event in which New-Sky-at-Horizon became ruler of Copan.

| 4. | Nar 24
D2-E2 | 9.13. 7. 3. 8 | | deleted | 9.13.10. 0. 0 | 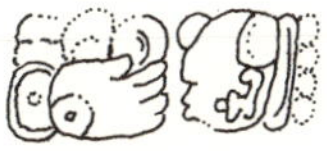 |

This event expression is the first part of a verbal triplet restating the event recorded on the front of Stela 24 in the form of T1.757 + *ti* + the

T1001 female title. The agent is deleted within the sequence of verbal phrases, but it is recorded as Lady 6-Sky of Tikal after the conclusion of the final phrase. See #5, 38:5, and 52:1.

5.   Nar 24   9.13. 7. 3. 8   deleted   9.13.10. 0. 0
     D3

This phrase is the second part of the verbal sequence described above. It is composed of an auxiliary verb in the form of T580, the locative *ti*, and a verbal noun, the meaning of which is not known. For other examples of this T580 auxiliary verb, see 132:9,15,16,17.

6.   Bon Scp1   9.12.11.6. 9   Ah Hun-   9.13. 0. 0. 0
     B1   Chu-??

7.   Yax L49   no date   m ssing   9. 8. 0. 0. 0
     B3

The T700var verbs listed in ##7-12 are preceded by ordinal constructions that are numerically ordered from 5th through 10th. Although the numbers preceding #7 and #8 are now missing, they can be reconstructed from the context. Since the main sign of these ordinal glyphs is known to appear in DNs at Palenque (TC, O8; TFC, L10; and TS, N13 and Q7), and since the main sign is a variant of the T573 hel glyph, these ordinals appear to mark the T700var "accession" events according to their numerical order in the history of the succession of the dynasty of Yaxchilan.

8.   Yax L49   no date   Ta-??-Skull   9. 8. 0. 0. 0
     B7

This verb is preceded by "6th succession."

9.   Yax L49   no date   Moon-Skull II 9. 8. 0. 0. 0
     D4

This verb is preceded by "7th succession."

10. Yax L37   no date   Bird-Jaguar I 9. 8. 0. 0. 0
     B1

This verb is preceded by "8th succession."

Chart 10 99

11. Yax L37   no date   Knot-Eye-   9. 8. 0. 0. 0
    B7   Jaguar

This verb is preceded by "9th succession."

12. Yax L35   no date   Ta-??-   9. 8. 0. 0. 0
    B2   Skull II

This verb is preceded by "10th succession."

13. Quir O   9.14.13. 4.17   Two-Legged-   9.18.10. 0. 0
    Y2-Z2   Sky

AEI.

14. Hauberg   ????   eroded   Late Pre-Classic
    B13

This verb follows a possible DN of 2.12; however, the main sign of this
DN is not a uinal sign, but rather a disk carved in the same manner as
the disks (jade?) worn by the protagonist. The main sign of this verb
seems to be T518 with a variant of T168 above. I suspect this is the same
verb used to record the accessions of Pacal and a supernatural at Palenque (113:1-2) and heir-designation of Smoking-Squirrel at Naranjo (130:
2). Most of the glyphs immediately following the verb are very badly
damaged, and, as a result, it is not possible to determine whether the
subject of this verb is the same as that of the first clause (see 3:20).

CHART 10   Affix Ø   in Cluster Ø.*.Ø   with Main Sign T510

Kelley (1977) first suggested that these "star" events are associated with astronomical intervals.
Closs (1979) associated a limited number of them with the maximum eastern and western elongation
of Venus, and more recently, Lounsbury (n.d.) has found others associated with other phases of
Venus, especially with Venus as Evening Star. It should be noted that these events occur
frequently in association with the "Tlaloc" blood-letting complex of iconography, and that
most, if not all, "star" events were occasions for raiding and war.

#	LOCATION	DATE (EVENT)	PATIENT	AGENT	DEDICATION	
1.	Car 3 F3	9. 9.18.16. 3	????	eroded	9.10. 0. 0. 0	

Lounsbury (n.d.) has associated this date with the observation of the
first appearance of Venus as Evening Star.

2. Nar HS   9.9.18.16. 3   ????   Ruler 4   9.10.10. 0. 0
    N1b   of Caracol

3. Nar HS   9.10. 3. 2.12   18-Rabbit   Ruler 4   9.10.10. 0. 0
    B1   of Caracol

4. Tort 6   9.10.11. 9. 6   ????   deleted   9.12. 0. 0. 0
    A10-A11

This example seems to be composed of a triplet structure in which two of
the sections are marked by the PEI T679. The first section includes the
"flint-shield" glyph which is also associated with a "star" event at Dos
Pilas. The main head in the first part is an *oc* while in the second, it
is the front head of the celestial monster. This monster's head is preceded by the T565 locative preposition and an an "inverted sky" glyph
marked as a verb by T181. The last part includes "star-over-earth" and a
glyph not yet understood, but probably part of the verbal phrase, rather
than a patient or agent. These events are linked by DN to the accession
(T644 "seating") of Ahpo-Balam.

5. Tort EarB   9.10.17. 2.14   ????   deleted   9.12. 0. 0. 0
    C-D

This "star-over-earth" event is followed by a bundle glyph that appears
to function as a part of the verbal phrase. A very similar bundle (with
an "inverted sky" glyph enclosed) follows this same glyph on the sarcophagus (see #7); furthermore, the dates of these two events are the same.
If the second glyph is part of the verbal phrase, then there is no agent
named in this clause, or the agent is deleted and the clause gapped to
the following one, which contains a second "star-over-earth" event (see
#6). Ahpo-Balam is named as the agent of this second event.

6. Tort EarB   9.10.19. 8. 4   Ahpo-Balam   9.12. 0. 0. 0
    I

7. Tort Sarc   9.10.17. 2.14   *u cab* Ahpo-Balam   9.12.10. 0. 0
    43

This "star-over-earth" event is followed by a series of glyphs which
includes a variant of the "capture" glyph. The name Ahpo-Balam is found
at the end of this passage following an *u cab* glyph. See 74:2.

8. DPil HSe   9.11.17.18.19   see note   9.12.12. 0. 0
    A4

Chart 10   101

This "star-shell" event is followed by a series of glyphs, none of which
can be identified as local personages. The additional glyphs either
qualify the event or name unknown agents, perhaps supernaturals. The T575
"shell" sign appears in other contexts which suggest its function as a
verbal suffix, and it may therefore be a verbal suffix in ##8-9, 12, 14,
16-17, 19-23, and 24.

9. DPil HSw   9.12. 5. 9.14   Twist-Skull   9.12.12. 0. 0
    A3-A4a

10. Ton M122   ????   none   9.14.15. 0. 0
    A3

This "star" event is not followed by any glyph, but the name glyph of
Kan-Xul and the Emblem Glyph of Palenque appear on the thigh of a bound
captive immediately adjacent to this text. It is interesting to note that
Kan-Xul's death is not recorded in the surviving texts of Palenque, and
that the accession of the next ruler, Xoc, is recorded in the final
passage on the Palace Tablet in a manner suggesting that it was not part
of the original composition of the tablet. It seems that on the occasion
of this event the people of Tonina took captive the aging ruler of
Palenque. The haab station in the CR is either Yax, Ceh, or Chen, but the
distinctive characteristics of the superfix were never carved.

11. Tik   9.11.19. 4. 3   Paddlers   9.15. 0. 0. 0
    MT 38a-c

The "star-over-earth" event appears with canoe scenes on two of the bones
from Burial 116 at Tikal. In each text, the "star" event is followed by
glyphs which have been identified by David Stuart (personal communication, 1980) as the names of the paddlers of the canoe. The agents of the
event seem to be both paddlers, and this subject of this clause is,
therefore, compound.

12. Agua 2   9.15. 4. 6. 4   none   9.15. 5. 0. 0
    A2

Lounsbury (n.d) has identified the occasion for this event and #13 as
the first appearance of Venus as Evening Star. The Emblem Glyph main sign
(with locative prefix) infixed into the center of the glyph is that of
Seibal, and Jaguar-Paw-Jaguar, a Seibal lord recorded in the text of the
Hieroglyphic Stairs at Seibal, is recorded as the patient of one of the
subsequent events. See 54:1-2 and 95:11-12.

13. DPil 16   9.15. 4. 6. 4   none   9.15. 5. 0. 0
     C1

This text records the same series of events as the inscription on Aguateca Stela 2. See #12, 54:1-2, and 95:11-12.

14. Tik T4   9.15.12. 2. 2   none   9.16. 0. 0. 0
     L3; D4

See #15.

15. Tik T4   9.15.12.11.13   none   9.16. 0. 0. 0
     L2; B8

Both this event and that of #14 are followed by a series of glyphs
including T1044, an anthropomorphic head which appears in a list of
supernaturals on the Tablet of the Foliated Cross and the Palace Tablet
at Palenque (see the introduction to the verb catalog). The signs flanking this glyph are in an unusual configuration that allows their identification as water because the rectangular motifs appear in the Tikal
canoe scenes and at Palenque as the distinguishing marks for water.

16. Yax L41   9.16. 4. 1. 1   none?   9.16. 5. 0. 0
     A2-B2

The second glyph in this phrase may name the agent or location of the
event or provide additional information about the event. If this second
glyph does not name the agent, the event is recorded without one.

17. Ton M91   missing   Kin-Te'-Mo'   Late Classic
     pA-pB

This event appears on a fragmentary stela base on which no calendric
information survives. The second glyph of the phrase seems to be the
"flint-shield" glyph that occurs with "star" events (see ##4 and 5), but
the flint sign appears in head variant form.

18. ASac Pan4   9.14. 2. 0.14?   destroyed   Late Classic
     pC6-pD6

This text is in very poor condition with only the CR date and this verb
in readable condition.

Chart 11 103

19.	DPil HSw A2-B1a	9.12. 0. 8. 3		none	9.12.12. 0. 0 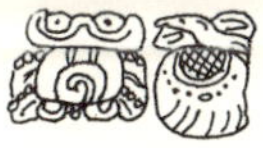

AEI.

20.	Yax L10 A4a	9.18.17.12. 6		none?	9.19. 0. 0. 0 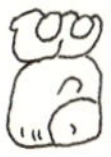

This "star" event from Lintel 10 is part of a sequence of verbal phrases
including an "ahau-in-hand" event (see 129:6-7) and a "capture" event
(see 74:27).

21.	DPil 25 K1-L1	9.13. 4.17.14		*u cab* Shield-God K	9.14. 0. 0. 0 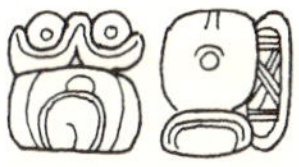
22.	PN 35 B12a	9.11. 9. 8.12		eroded	9.11.10. 0. 0 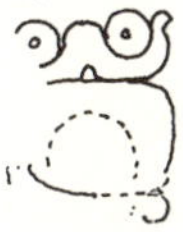
23.	PN 37 C7	9.11.16. 11. 6		*u cab* Ruler 2	9.12. 0. 0. 0 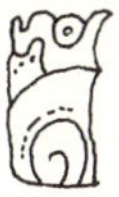
24.	PN 12 D1a	_____ 10 Zotz'		eroded	9.18. 5. 0. 0 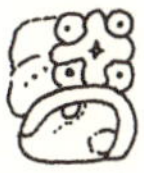
25.	DPil 1 G3a	9.13.13. 7. 2		Shield-God K	9.13.15. 0. 0 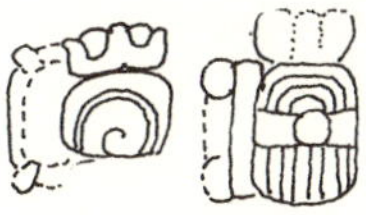

CHART 11	Affix 𝜙	in Cluster 𝜙.*.𝜙	with Miscellaneous Main Signs

These verbal phrases seem to be related to the complex of events which includes the "star" and
"flint-shield" events.

#	LOCATION	DATE (EVENT)	PATIENT	AGENT	DEDICATION
1.	Nar 22 E16	9.13. 1. 9. 5		none	9.13.10. 0. 0 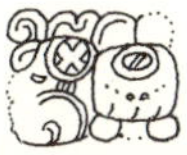
2.	Nar 22 F18-E19	9.13. 1.13.14		none	9.13.10. 0. 0 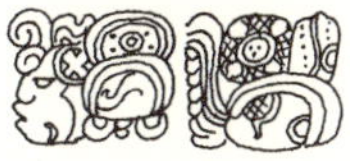

3.   Nar 22   9.13. 5. 4.13   none   9.13.10. 0. 0
      G12-H12

The events listed under ##1-3 are related and occur successively in the
text of Stela 22. This event series seems to have been initiated by the
assumption of a T518 title by Smoking-Squirrel at the age of five. The
event listed as #1 occurred shortly thereafter at age 5.13.18; #2 at age
6.0.7; and #3 at age 9.9.6. No name glyphs follow these verbal phrases,
but it may be assumed that they are associated with Smoking-Squirrel's
assumption of office.

4.   Nar 22   9.13. 6.10. 4   Kan-   *u cab* Smoking-   9.13.10. 0. 0
      H14   Flint   Squirrel

This version of the event is followed by Kan Flint (T281:23.168:86:529),
the name appearing in the phrase immediately in front of the sacrificial
victim on the front of the stela. This victim's name is followed by *u cab*
and the name phrase of Smoking-Squirrel. If *u cab* is taken as "under the
auspices of. . ." or some equivalent phrase, then Kan-Flint would be the
subject of the verb. I suspect that Kan-Flint is the patient and Smoking-
Squirrel the agent. Mathews (personal communication, 1980) has noticed
that the Kan-Flint glyph also occurs as the Ucanal EG and suggested that
such a reference may be intended here.

5.   Nar 23   9.13.18. 4.18   ????   *u cab* Smoking-   9.14.10. 0. 0
      E9-E10   Squirrel

The boundary of this verbal phrase is not clear from the context, but
T712 (blood-letting lancet) is the likely candidate for the terminal
glyph of the phrase. These three glyphs are followed by an eroded block
and what might be the Emblem Glyph of Yaxha. The T518 title glyph then
occurs, but it is not clear whether it functions as a second verb or as a
nominal glyph. This clause concludes with the T126.522:23 "wife" glyph,
the name "Lady of Tikal," and the name phrase of Smoking-Squirrel. The
presence of *u cab* before Smoking-Squirrel's name may indicate that the
"Lady of Tikal" is the subject of the verb, and that the rite was enacted
under his authority.

6.   Tik   ????   ????   9.15. 0. 0. 0
      MT 29

Since no other glyph follows this verbal phrase, the second head (the
head variant of ik and the number 3) may function as a part of the verb
or as the subject. This event is preceded and followed by death events
occurring on different dates.

Chart 12   105

7. DPil HSw   9.12. 5.10. 1   Flint-Sky-   9.12.12. 0. 0
    A5   God K

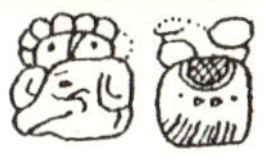

This event occurred seven days after a "star-shell" event. See 10:9.

CHART 12   Affix ∅   in Cluster ∅.*.∅   with Main Sign T266.21:575

In all of these examples, T575 appears in a postfixed position which may identify it as a
verbal affix. In other contexts, such as the T218 "completion" glyph, the optional appearance
of T575 almost certainly identifies it as a verbal suffix. However, since it appears not to be
optional in this compound, I am tentatively identifying T575 as a part of the main sign and not
as a verbal affix.

#	LOCATION	DATE (EVENT)	PATIENT	AGENT	DEDICATION

1. Car 3   9. 9.13. 4. 4   He of   *u cab* Ruler 4   9.10. 5. 0. 0
    D17   Naranjo?

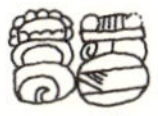

The second glyph in the clause includes the male article *ah* T12, suggesting that it records the name of a person. Since the main sign of this
second glyph is the Emblem Glyph of Naranjo, and since one of the "star"
events involving Naranjo and Caracol occurs within five years of this
date, I am tentatively identifying the second glyph, "he of Naranjo," as
the patient of the verb.

2. DPil HSw   9.12. 6.16.17   ????   ????   9.12.12. 0. 0
    D2-C3

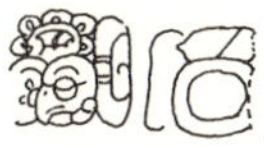

None of the glyphs following this verbal expression are recognizable names
from the Dos Pilas dynastic list. However, the contemporary ruler of Dos
Pilas, Flint-Sky-God K, is the protagonist of this text, and he is the
agent of a now eroded verbal phrase following this event.

3. Pal TS   9.10. 8. 9. 3   deleted   9.13. 0. 0. 0
    P16-Q16   (Chan-Bahlum)

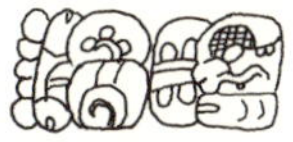

The event phrases of both #3 and #4 consist of a verb + prepositional
phrase (recording the office of heir-designate). This example closes the
main text of the Tablet of the Sun and appears without an agent. However,
this phrase is at the end of a long passage recording the same event four
times; in the preceding three records, Chan-Bahlum is clearly recorded as
the subject, and he is to be understood as the subject of this verb.

4.   Pal TS   9.10. 8. 9. 3   Chan-   9.13. 0. 0. 0
      I1-J1   Bahlum II

5.   Tik T1   9.13. 3. 7.18   Jaguar-Paw   deleted   9.15. 0. 0. 0
      L3; A4-B4   of Site Q   (Ruler A?)

This event occurred 40 days before the rite celebrating the 13-katun
anniversary of the last date on Stela 31. The event is followed by the
name phrase of Great-Jaguar-Paw of Site Q. This same person was identified by J. H. Miller (1974:155) as the protagonist of Stela 2 of Site Q,
now located in the Cleveland Art Museum. Jaguar-Paw may well be named as
the subject of this verb, but his name is followed by a glyph containing
the main sign (a bone) of the Palenque Emblem Glyph. Certainly this
"bone" glyph does not identify Jaguar-Paw as a person from Palenque, but
the word for "bone" (*bac*) also is a term for "captive." Furthermore, a
stucco relief on Structure 5D-57 shows the disposition of a captive 13
days after this event. Since this captive event occurs in such close
temporal proximity to the Lintel 3 event, and since the name phrase of
Jaguar-Paw contains a glyph which may name him as "captive," I am tentatively assuming that he is the patient, rather than the agent, of this
verb. If this proposed syntactical structure is correct, Ruler A would
also be the deleted subject of this first event. It should be noted that
the texts of Jaguar-Paw record his birth as 9.10.16.16.19 3 Cauac 2 Ceh
(Site Q Glyphic Panel 6 and Calakmul Stela 9); his accession at age 36 as
9.12.13.17.7 6 Manik 5 Zip (Cleveland Stela and Dos Pilas Stela 13), and
the Tikal event at age 46 on 9.13.3.4.18 11 Etz'nab 11 Chen. See 95:13.

6.   Nar 22   9.13. 1. 4.19   Chikin-Cab   deleted   9.13.10. 0. 0
      F14

The glyph Chikin-Cab (T671[544]:82.526) follows this verbal glyph, but it
apparently does not record the agent of the event. This same name glyph
appears on the thigh of the sacrificial victim on the base of Stela 24, a
monument dedicated to Lady 6-Sky of Tikal, the probable mother of Smoking-
Squirrel. The identification of Chikin-Cab as a sacrificial victim suggests that he was the recipient rather than the perpetrator of the act.

7.   Nar 22   9.13. 2.16. 0   ????   Smoking-   9.13.10. 0. 0
      H1-G2   Squirrel

This version of the event seems to include the main sign of the Tikal
Emblem Glyph, but the sign which precedes the Tikal bundle is now destroyed and it is not possible to ascertain whether or not it was a
locative preposition. The illustrated phrase is followed by the "capture"
glyph ([87]515a:25?.25?.181) without the captor named and a birth glyph

Chart 13   107

(T741:missing.181). The name phrase of Smoking-Squirrel is then recorded, presumably as the agent of all three events. This event occurred to him at age 6.11.3.

| 8. | Tik
MT 39a-b | 9.13. 3.13.15 | Bone-Imix | Split-Earth
of Site Q | 9.15. 0. 0. 0 | |

This glyph occurs as the verb on MT 39a and 39b, which both show a standing bound captive. In both texts, the verb is followed by a three-glyph phrase presumably naming the captive; by *u cab*, possibly specifying the authority under which the event occurred; and by a final name glyph (Split-Earth), presumably the agent of the event. This same "Split-Earth" glyph appears in the secondary texts in the following sequence: (1) *ox-kal-te'* (TIII.683:87); (2) *ahpo-ix-il(?)* (T168:524:24); (3) *u-??* (T1.747var); (4) "Split-Earth" (T249:526.nn); and (5) the Site Q Emblem Glyph. The first two glyphs should name the captive, although only *ix* and a jaguar head (both referring to jaguars) are common elements in the name phrases of the main and secondary texts. Glyph 3 is a possessed noun in which the noun refers to the first two glyphs and the possessive pronoun refers to the last two. The secondary texts many be paraphrased as follows: "Ox-Kal-Te', Ahpo-Ixil, the something (captive?) of 'Split-Earth,' Lord of Site Q." It is interesting to note that a lord of Site Q appears in this text as well as that of Temple 1 Lintel 3 (see #5).

9.	Bon L4 A2-A4	9. 8. 9.15.11	Ah ??- Imix	*u cab* Chaan-Muan	9. 9. 0. 0. 0	
10.	Car 3 C19-C20	9. 9.14. 3. 5		*u cab* Ruler 4	9.10. 5. 0. 0	
11.	Pus D D13	9. 8. 1.12. 8		local ruler	9.10.15. 0. 0	

CHART 13   Affix Ø   in Cluster Ø.*.Ø   with Main Sign T331 or T32.843

The most likely graphic identification for this main sign is a footprint on the profile of a pyramidal facade. The meaning of this event is not known, but it is an important part of the Primary Standard Sequence (M.D. Coe 1973) in inscriptions on ceramics.

#	LOCATION	DATE (EVENT)	PATIENT	AGENT	DEDICATION	
1.	Tik 31 E6-E7	missing		Curl-Snout	9. 0.10. 0. 0	

The glyphs immediately before this passage are destroyed so that the date of the event cannot be established.

2. Car 16   ????   supernaturals 9. 5. 0. 0. 0
    D9

The name phrase following this verb includes the "sky god" (Tmissing.74?: 561:23/1013c), a skull, and the head of the sun god (T1010).

3. ASac 5   9.10.11.12.17?   a female   9.11. 0. 0. 0
    C3-C4

4. Cop AltZ   9.17. 0. 0. 0   New-Sky-at-   9.17. 0. 0. 0
    B3   Horizon

This particular version of the T843 verb may not be equivalent to the first two examples. The superfix is the same, but the main sign is more like T515. Furthermore, the event on Altar Z is clearly a period ending, and this same version of the T843 verb (with the addition of T74 *ma* as a superfix) is associated with a period ending on Copan Altar GII.

5. Cop AltQ   9.17. 5. 0. 0   *u cab* New-Sky-at- 9.17. 5. 0. 0
    F1-E2   Horizon

6. Yax Str33   9.15.13. 6. 9   deleted   9.16. 6. 0. 0
    Step 7
    Q2

Mathews (personal communication, 1980) suggests this glyph may graphically represent a ball striking the profile of a ballcourt, and this verb is the principal one in a text accompanying a ballgame scene.

7. PN Thr1   9.17. 9. 5.11   deleted   9.17.15. 0. 0
    B'1b-C'1   (Ruler 7)

This may not be a verb, but if it is, the deleted agent would be Ruler 7.

8. NimP 2   12 Ahau?   missing   9.15.10. 0. 0
    K1-L1

9. PN L7   ???? 8 Kayab   missing   9. 9.10. 0. 0?
    Y17-X18

Chart 14   109

CHART 14   Affix Ø   in Cluster Ø.*.Ø   with Main Sign T333

The main sign of this glyph is an "axe." Some examples found at Quirigua, Aguateca, and Dos Pilas are associated with war and conquest events and with "star" events.

#	LOCATION	DATE (EVENT)	PATIENT	AGENT	DEDICATION	
1.	Pal HS F1	9.11. 1.16. 3	Crossed-Bands-Sky of Site Q	????	9.11.10. 0. 0	

The identification of the agent of this verb is difficult because it is followed by a series of glyphs including "Crossed-Bands-Sky, Lord of Site Q" and the names of all three members of the Palenque Triad. In addition, the T518 title glyph precedes the "Crossed-Bands-Sky" name. I suspect that the Site Q lord may be the patient and the Triad gods, the agent.

#	LOCATION	DATE (EVENT)	PATIENT	AGENT	DEDICATION	
2.	Quir Fe C17b-C18	end of 13 cabaltuns	????	u cab eroded	9.17. 0. 0. 0.	

This event occurs in a series of dates counted with very large DNs. The name of the agent is eroded, but it was preceded by u cab.

#	LOCATION	DATE (EVENT)	PATIENT	AGENT	DEDICATION	
3.	LMar 3 A6	9.18. 1. 8.18	????	eroded	9.18. 5. 0. 0	

#	LOCATION	DATE (EVENT)	PATIENT	AGENT	DEDICATION
4.	Pal Cr J1-I2	no date	????	u cab Chac-Rodent-Bone	9.16. 0. 0. 0?

The left half of the Tablet of the Creation is so badly eroded that the text leading to this "axe" verb is undecipherable. The verbal phrase is preceded by a PEI and an "imix" compound which may be a period ending glyph. It is followed by two pairs of glyphs which may record the patients of the verbs. The agent is recorded following an u cab glyph as Chac-Rodent-Bone (T109.758:110[203]); the Palenque EG with ahau as the main sign; and two versions of GI of the Palenque Triad. The Chac-Rodent-Bone name does not appear elsewhere in the Palenque dynasty lists, but "rodent-bone" is a prominent title in Palenque name phrases. It should be noted that an alternative interpretation of the syntax of this clause would be that the glyphs I have identified as patient may record the agents, and that this event took place "under the auspices of" Chac-Rodent-Bone.

CHART 15   Affix Ø   in Cluster Ø.*.Ø   with Main Sign T714

The T714 "fish-in-hand" glyph can be associated with blood-letting rites.

#	LOCATION	DATE (EVENT)	PATIENT	AGENT	DEDICATION	
1.	Cop AltX A2-B2	9. 5.19.12.18 or 9. 8.12. 7.18		eroded	9. 5.15. 0. 0 or 9. 9. 0. 0. 0	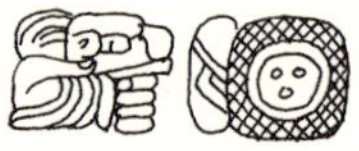
2.	Quir L A2-A3	9.13.13.16.11		Smoking- Turtle	9.14.15. 0. 0	
3.	Tik MT 32	9.12.14. 3.11		Ahpo-Kin	9.15. 0. 0. 0	
4.	Tik MT 33	9.13. 2. 4.11		18-Rabbit Lord of Tikal	9.15. 0. 0. 0	

The agent of this verb and that listed under #5 is 18-Rabbit (TXVIII. 1:757), presumably the same person who is named on Lintel 2 of Temple 1.

#	LOCATION	DATE (EVENT)	PATIENT	AGENT	DEDICATION	
5.	Tik MT 36	9.13. 2. 4.11		18-Rabbit Lord of Tikal	9.15. 0. 0. 0	
6.	Yax L15 F2-G3	9.16.17. 2. 4		none	9.16.18. 0. 0	

This phrase is the second part of a verbal couplet, the first section of which is "fish-in-hand" (T714.181); *yax mul* (T16.513H); *na chan* (T4.764); *u balan ahau* (T.539:126); and God K (T1030b:142). No subject is named in the main text, but the name Lady Ahpo-Ik appears in the secondary text next to the figure, who is involved in a serpent vision scene associated with blood-letting. See 76:2.

Chart 16 111

CHART 16   Affix ∅   in Cluster ∅.*.∅   with Main Sign T207var

All of these verbal phrases appear to be related to a set of rites which at Palenque are involved with ancestral anniversary celebration, and at Yaxchilan with ancestral anniversaries and blood-letting rites.

#	LOCATION	DATE (EVENT)	PATIENT	AGENT	DEDICATION	
1.	Pal DH A2-B2	9.12.19.14.12		GVI or Chan-Bahlum	9.13. 0. 0. 0	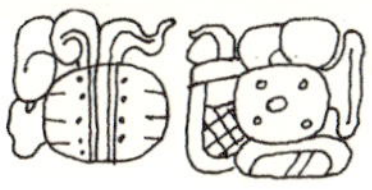

This event occurred on the occasion of the eighth tropical year anniversary of the accession of Chan-Bahlum. The same date is recorded on the alfardas and jambs of the TC and TFC, but in those texts, the main verb is T22:60:515.4, which suggests that the "fire" event is in some way equivalent to this more common expression. The agent of this verb is either GVI of the Palenque god list or Chan-Bahlum; both names follow the verb.

#	LOCATION	DATE (EVENT)	PATIENT	AGENT	DEDICATION	
2.	Yax L31 J4	9.16.13. 0. 0.		Itzam	9.17. 0. 0. 0	

The main sign in the name glyph following this verb has been identified by Mathews (personal communication, 1980) as the front head of the Celestial Monster, usually thought to be Itzamna. I have used the provisional name Itzam for the name glyph, although I suspect Bird-Jaguar is the intended agent of this event. This verb is the first part of a couplet in which the event expression of the second part includes a "house" glyph. This "fire" event may be related to the class of events included on this chart, or it may refer to the dedication of the building housing Lintels 29, 30, and 31. See 126:3.

#	LOCATION	DATE (EVENT)	PATIENT	AGENT	DEDICATION	
3.	Yax L26 H2-J2	9.14.14.13.17		Lady Xoc	9.15. 0. 0. 0	

The subject of this event is almost totally eroded, but the head variant of the "na-baat-cab" (T1000a."axe":526:23), which is also present in regular form in the name phrase of Lady Xoc on Lintel 24, appears in the eroded area. This substitution of the anthropomorphic head for the "axe-over-earth" title can be confirmed in the name phrases of Kan-Xul on the Palace Tablet at Palenque (Schele 1976:Fig. 21).

4. Yax L23   9.14.14.13.17   Lady Xoc   9.15. 0. 0. 0
    M5a-M6b

This event from Lintel 23 is parallel to that on Lintel 26, but here the
date is clearly 9.14.14.13.17.

5. Yax L56   9.15. 6.13. 1   Lady Rodent-   9.15.10. 0. 0
    H1-J2   Bone

Lady Xoc is the subject of this event as well as those of Lintels 26 and
28. In this text and that of Lintel 26, her name phrase concludes with a
passage that appears to record a relationship between her and Shield-
Jaguar.

6. Yax L28   9.16. 4. 6.17   Lady Xoc   9.16. 5. 0. 0
    W1-X1

This verbal phrase concludes a series of events, including the deaths of
Lady Pacal and Shield-Jaguar. The text begins on Lintel 28, continues to
Lintel 59.

7. Tik TI   9.16.14.17.17   missing   9.16.15. 0. 0
    I'3-J'3

8. Coll 6   10. 1.14. 5.12   Bat   10. 1.15. 0. 0
    D3-D4

9. Ton F92   ???? 13 Kayab   missing   Late Classic
    pC2-pD2

10. Yax Str44   9.11.18.15. 1   Shield-Jaguar   9.15. 0. 0. 0
    Ctr low
    B1-A2a

This verbal phrase is the first part of a verbal couplet; see 52:3 for
the second half.

11. Bon T1   9.18. 1. 2. 0   Chaan-Muan?   9.18. 5. 0. 0
    Rm1
    P2d-Q2c

This final event in the main text of Room 1 occurred 236 days after the
IS date (one which the child in the upper register was designated heir

Chart 17   113

[M. Miller 1981]) on the day that Venus first appeared as Evening Star
(Lounsbury n.d.). The text which names the agent is badly damaged, but
enough detail can be seen to identify a "sky" glyph, one of the principal
glyphs of Chaan-Muan's name. Mary Miller (1981:88) has proposed that this
verb corresponds to the processional scene in the lower register. Two
badly eroded glyphs were once between the two illustrated glyphs, but I
cannot see them well enough in any of my sources to produce a drawing.

CHART 17   Affix Ø   in Cluster Ø.*.Ø   with Main Sign T1014a

Since the shell glyph is one of the distinctive features of God N, I have categorized these
examples as "zero" affixing, but it is possible that some of the shell signs are verbal suffixes.
In these phrases, the God N glyph seems to function as an auxiliary verb.

#	LOCATION	DATE (EVENT)	PATIENT	AGENT	DEDICATION
1.	Pal TC C10-D11	13. 0. 1. 9. 2		GI the First	9.13. 0. 0. 0

These two sets of glyphs represent parts of a triplet recording some
activity conducted by GI the First, the god identified by Lounsbury
(1980:114) as the father of the Palenque Triad, 1.9.2 after 4 Ahau 8
Cumku. The "6-Sky" glyph appears in other texts as a title in GI's name,
and the event may involve the assumption of that title. See 20:1 and
32:13.

#	LOCATION	DATE (EVENT)	PATIENT	AGENT	DEDICATION
2.	Pal TFC M6-L8	9.12.18. 5.17		Chan- Bahlum II	9.13. 0. 0. 0

This event is the second in a series of three events spanning a period of
four days which are conducted by Chan-Bahlum in commemoration of the
seventy-fifth tropical year anniversary of the death of his father, Pacal.
The fourth glyph is a special version of the "house" glyph used on the
tablets of the Group of the Cross. The third glyph, *mah kina*, has been
identified by Mathews (n.d.d) as a substitute for "west," the glyph that
appears in the same position in #3.

#	LOCATION	DATE (EVENT)	PATIENT	AGENT	DEDICATION
3.	Pal TS O8-N10	9.12.18. 5.17		Chan- Bahlum II	9.13. 0. 0. 0

This event is the parallel version from the Tablet of the Sun to the
anniversary event above. The only variation between the two passages is
the substitution of the "west" glyph for *mah kina*.

4.   Yax L25   9.14.11.15. 1   Lady Xoc   9.15. 0. 0. 0
     O2-Q1

The event is linked by a DN of 2.2.7.0 to the accession of Shield-Jaguar, recorded glyphically and pictorially on the bottom of this lintel as a blood-letting rite. Lady Xoc is named as the person pictured in the scene and as the agent of this "God N" event.

5.   Yax L24   9.13.17.15.12   Turtle-GI?   9.15. 0. 0. 0
     H1-H2

This phrase occurs as an unframed secondary text on the bottom of Lintel 24. The agent seems to be recorded as a variant of GI of the Palenque Triad. The suffix to this God N, as well as the one in #4, may function as a verbal suffix, but it should also be noted that the shell in #3 is a diagnostic feature of God N. The "bat" glyph (T61.756c) also occurs as an independent verb (see Chart 22).

6.   Yax L26   9.14.18. 6.12   GI?   9.15. 0. 0. 0
     D1-F1

This event follow a CR and appears in an unframed text on the bottom of Lintel 26. The agent seems to be a version of GI of the Palenque Triad.

7.   Pal TIw   9. 9.13. 0. 7   Lady Ahpo-   9.12.15. 0. 0
     R4-Q5   Hel

In the clause that follows this one, a DN is counted from the "seating" of Lady Ahpo-Hel to her death. Since the calendric arithmetic of this and the following clause makes it clear that the "seating" event and this God N event occurred on the same day, the God N expression must represent some alternative expression for "seating" or for an "accession" ritual of some sort.

8.   DO Alab   9.15.13.12. 1   Ah God C-   9.15.15. 0. 0
     4-7   Shell-Imix

The meaning of this event phrase is unknown, but it appears in the rim text on an alabaster vase which shows a scene related to the traditional accession scenes at Palenque. A male figure sits in the center, holding a square-nosed, jeweled serpent, and facing a male figure holding the 7-Ek-Kan god. A female sits on the other side holding the "9 god" that is paired with 7-Ek-Kan in many contexts. The name glyphs surrounding the principal figure in the scene are also recorded as the agent of this verb.

Chart 18 115

9. RAm Alt1   9.10.10. 2.16   Rodent-Bone-   9.11. 0. 0. 0?
    M2-P2   Turtle

This verbal phrase may be preceded by the T757 auxiliary verb.

CHART 18   Affix ∅   in Cluster ∅.*.∅   with Main Sign T516:103

These examples are auxiliary verb + *ti* + verbal noun constructions.

#	LOCATION	DATE (EVENT)	PATIENT	AGENT	DEDICATION	
1.	Coll 1 F4-E5	9. 8.18.12.12		deleted	9. 9. 0. 0. 0	

PEI; this phrase records the event to which a DN is counted from an
earlier event. This verb is on Site Q Panel 2.

2.	DPil 25 F1	9.14. 0. 0. 0		Shield-God K	9.14. 0. 0. 0	

This verbal phrase follows T218 "completion" (of 14 katuns) and T528.116:
713 "end of the tun" expressions. Since no new date occurs between these
period ending expressions and the auxiliary verb construction, it must
record some period ending rite.

3.	Yax L42 C2-C3	9.16. 1. 2. 0		Bird-Jaguar	9.16. 5. 0. 0	

This verbal expression is the second part of a couplet which includes as
its first part an auxiliary verb (T1.757) + *ti* + "ahau-in-hand" (T533:
670) expression. The first part of the couplet refers to the act shown in
the scene; i.e., the holding of the God K scepter by Bird-Jaguar (see
38:8). Since the display of God K can occur on many different occasions,
the second part of the verbal couplet may record the specific ritualistic
context in which God K is displayed. This same event is recorded on
Lintel 7. T228 *ah*, which appears as a prefix to T516:103, occurs option-
ally with this auxiliary verb, but it is not known whether it functions
as a preposed pronoun or as a phonetic complement. See Chart 130 for
other examples of T228 prefixed to verbs.

4.	Yax L3 C2a-D2	9.16. 5. 0. 0		Bird-Jaguar	9.16. 6. 0. 0	

This verbal expression, like that of example #3, follows an auxiliary verb + *ti* + "ahau-in-hand" compound. Bird-Jaguar is again shown holding the God K scepter, although on a different date and ritualistic occasion. See 38:10.

5. Yax L1   9.16. 1. 0. 0   Bird-Jaguar   9.16. 6. 0. 0
    C1b-D1

This expression follows the same "ahau-in-hand" auxiliary verb expression as #3 and #4, but the occasion as recorded elsewhere in the inscriptions of Yaxchilan is the accession as ruler of Bird-Jaguar. See 38:9.

6. Cop E   ????   missing   9. 9. 5. 0. 0
    Alt

CHART 19   Affix ∅   in Cluster ∅.*.∅   with Main Sign T21:23.585

This event has been identified by Lounsbury (1974) as "death."

#	LOCATION	DATE (EVENT)	PATIENT	AGENT	DEDICATION	
1.	Pal TI Sarc 7 PEI	9.12.11.5.18		Pacal II	9.12.15. 0. 0	
2.	Pal TI Sarc 17a	9. 4.10. 4.17		Chaacal I	9.12.15. 0. 0	
3.	Pal TI Sarc 19a	9. 6.11. 0.16		Kan-Xul I	9.12.15. 0. 0	
4.	Pal TI Sarc 21a	9. 6.16.10. 7		Chaacal II	9.12.15. 0. 0	
5.	Pal TI Sarc 26a	9. 7. 9. 5. 5		Chan-Bahlum I	9.12.15. 0. 0	
6.	Pal TI Sarc 29a	9. 8.11. 6.12		Lady Kanal-Ikal	9.12.15. 0. 0	

Chart 20   117

#	LOCATION	DATE (EVENT)	PATIENT	AGENT	DEDICATION	
7.	Pal TI Sarc 33	9. 8.19. 4. 6		Ac-Kan	9.12.15. 0. 0	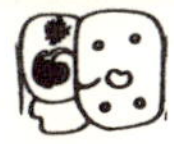
8.	Pal TI Sarc 39	9.8.18.14.11		Pacal I	9.12.15. 0. 0	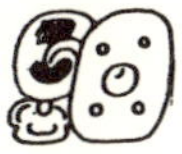
9.	Pal TI Sarc 47a	9.10. 7.13. 5		Lady Zac-Kuk	9.12.15. 0. 0	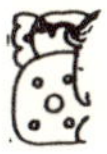
10.	Pal TI Sarc 50a	9.10.10. 1. 6		Kan-Bahlum-Mo'	9.12.15. 0. 0	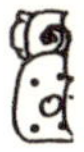
11.	Pal TIw S6a	9.12.11. 5.18		Pacal II	9.12.15. 0. 0	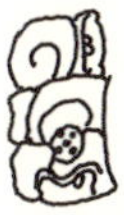

CHART 20	Affix Ø	in Cluster Ø.*.Ø		with Miscellaneous Main Signs	
#	LOCATION	DATE (EVENT)	PATIENT	AGENT	DEDICATION	
1.	Pal TC D7	13. 0. 1. 9. 2		GI the First	9.13. 0. 0. 0	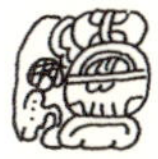

This phrase is composed of verb and prepositional phrase. The verb is *oc*, the term for "to enter" or "to begin." The prepositional phrase includes the locative *ta* (T103) and *chaan* "sky" (T561), suggesting this event took place in the sky or heavens. The agent is GI the First, the parent of the Triad. This verbal phrase represents the first section of a triplet construction in which this "sky" event is recorded in three different forms (see 17:1 and 32:13).

| 2. | Tik Alt5 3-4 AEI | 9.12.19.12.19 | | Lady Cauac | 9.14. 0. 0. 0 | 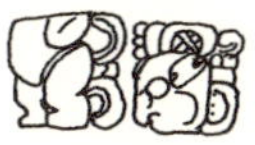 |
| 3. | Pal T18 Stc 443 | missing | | missing | 9.14.15. 0. 0 | 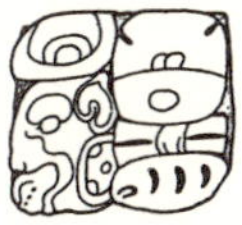 |

4.   Tik T4   9.15.12.11.12   Ruler B   9.16. 0. 0. 0
      L3; B4

5.   Xul 3   10. 0. 3. 3. 8   deleted   10. 1.10. 0. 0
      A4a

This "birth" glyph is part of a passage linking it to the period ending
10.1.10.0.0. It appears in the same glyph block as the "end of the tun"
glyph (T1:528:713.116), and since it records already-known information,
the subject is deleted.

6.   Mach 7   10. 0. 0.14.15   deleted   10. 0. 5. 0. 0
      E5b

7.   PN L12   9. 4. 3.10. 1   eroded   9. 4. 5. 0. 0
      N1

See 127:4-6.

8.   Pal T14   9 Ik 10 Mol   deleted   9.13.15. 0. 0
      D4

This event occurs immediately after a DN leading from this mythological
event to a historical one. The earlier 9 Ik 10 Mol event is recorded in
detail in the first half of the inscription as an event celebrated
perhaps by the moon goddess many hundreds of thousands of years in the
past. This occurrence of the verb is designed to insure that the initial
event of the sequence is understood as the base of the DN, and therefore
the agent of the event is not included in the restatement of the event.
The glyph preceding the "ahau-in-hand" glyph reinforces the reference of
the verb; it is composed of a possessive pronoun (T204), *na* (T4), *ta* or
ti (T565), and *la* (T178), combining to form *u na:ta:l(a)*. From another
occurrence of this glyph on the east panel of the TI (30:4) functions to
mark the katun seating on 9.9.0.0.0 as the "first" katun ending of Pacal's reign. The possessive pronoun is present to mark the construction
as an ordinal, and the T565:178 *-tal* suffix occurs with other ordinal
constructions utilizing numbers. The stem for "first" is then the *na*
sign, and *nahil* is "first" in modern Chol and other adjacent languages.
The "ahau-in-hand" glyph clearly refers to the monument scene which
records the presentation of God K. The God K mirror in the second half of
the verbal glyph functions as a semantic determinative to insure that
the identification of the scepter as God K is understood. The earlier
mythological event occurred 5.18.11.7.8.13.18 before its reenactment in
historical times. See #2, 23:7, 45:11, 87:10, and 121:4.

Chart 21   119

| 9. | Sac 1
B10a | 9.16. 8.16. 1 | | Shell-Hand | 9.16.10. 0. 0 | 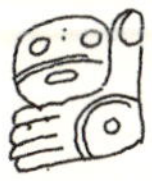 |

| 10. | Pal T18
Stc 425 | missing | | missing | 9.14.15. 0. 0 | 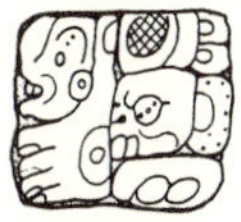 |

| 11. | Sac 1
A8 | 9.16.10. 0. 0 | | Lady 5-Sky?? | 9.16.10. 0. 0 | 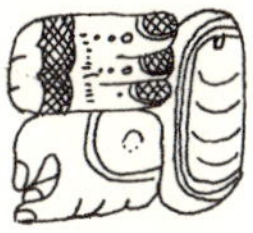 |

| 12. | Pal PTab
E7 | 9.10.18.17.19 | | Kan-Xul II | 9.14.10. 0. 0 | 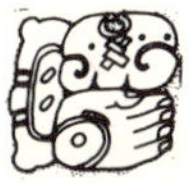 |

This verb is the first part of a verbal couplet recording an event that occurred to Kan-Xul II at age 7.0.19. The meaning is not known, but the sign held in the hand later occurs as a title in the name phrase of Kan-Xul II (Palace Tablet, P4). See 92:6 for the second part of the couplet.

| 13. | Bon A
F5 | 9. 3. 0. 0. 0 | | none or
deleted | 9. 3.10. 0. 0 | 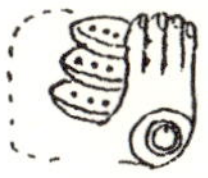 |

| 14. | Cop J
20a | 9. 0. 0. 0. 0 | | Yax-Mo' I? | 9.13.10. 0. 0 | 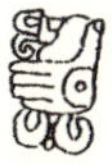 |

| 15. | PN 12
B21 | 9.18. 4.16. 7 | | Ruler 7? | 9.18. 5. 0. 0 | 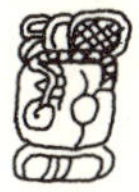 |

This phrase records the forty-sixth tun anniversary of Ruler 7's birth.

CHART 21	Affix ∅		in Cluster ∅.*.∅		with Miscellaneous Main Signs
#	LOCATION	DATE (EVENT)	PATIENT	AGENT	DEDICATION
1.	Tik 31 D2	missing		*u cab* GIII	9. 0.10. 0. 0 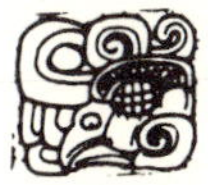

This verb occurs following a rare "count" glyph in which a skeletal variant of chuen is the main sign. The immediately preceding phrase is located in a partially destroyed area so that the temporal context of the event is unclear. The subject appears to be GIII of the Palenque Triad, whose name follows an *u cab* glyph at the end of the clause. It should be

noted that this vulture sign is identical to that following the seating
event on the Leiden Plaque (see 97:1), and that it may, therefore, refer
to some sort of office.

2.   Car 16   9. 4. 0. 0. 0   GIII   9. 5. 0. 0. 0
      A12-B12

3.   Nar Alt   9. 7.10.11. 3   *u cab* Ruler I   9. 8. 0. 0. 0
      H1-H2

4.   Tort 6   9.11.16. 8.18   deleted   9.12. 0. 0. 0
      E6-F6   (Ahpo-Balam)

PEI. The subject of this verb is deleted, but structurally it is clearly
to be understood as Ahpo-Balam, the protagonist of the monument. This
phrase follows a DN of 1.5.5.8 and "since he was seated, Ahpo-Balam
until . . ." T181 is suffixed to the second glyph in this verbal phrase,
suggesting that it consists of a two-word phrase which is suffixed as a
whole. Because of this alternative interpretation, this example is listed
both under "zero" affixing and under -T181 (see 82:21).

5.   Pal TS   9.10. 8. 9. 3   Chan-   9.13. 0. 0. 0
      P8-Q8   Bahlum II

This *oc-te* event occurs five days after the heir-designation of Chan-
Bahlum; however, structural comparison of the texts recording this heir-
designation suggests that it consisted of a rite of five days' duration,
rather than two separate rites five days apart. The second glyph *kin-kin*
appears to record the office (Schele n.d.a).

6.   Pal TS   9. 3. 1.15. 0   deleted   9.13. 0. 0. 0
      P4   (Kan-Xul I)

This glyph, like the expression under #5, must record an alternative
expression for heir-designation. It stands between an ADI (counted from
an heir-designation event) and a PDI, marking the CR date of a later
heir-designation, in the following context: Event 1 + Subject 1 count
since *Event 1* count until Date 2 + Event 2.

7.   Pal TS   9.12.19.14.12   GIII   9.13. 0. 0. 0
      Alf   G1

A structural comparison of the texts from all the alfardas from the three
temples of the Group of the Cross suggests that this verb must be equivalent in some way to the verb T221.60:515.4. The subject of the verb is
named as T74.184.217var.nn:526, but structurally the name following the

Chart 21 **121**

lent in some way to the verb T221.60:515.4. The subject of the verb is
named as T74.184.217var.nn:526, but structurally the name following the
5 Eb 5 Kayab event on the TS alfardas should be GIII or a title for him.

8. Pal TFC   9.12.18. 5.16   GI   9.13. 0. 0. 0
    M14-L14

PDI. This passage is parallel to a passage from the TS in which
T79:[178] 180 is recorded as the verb. I suspect tha the same event is
recorded in this phrase, but with a noun phrase in which the verb has
been deleted. See Chart 87 for examples of the T79 verb.

9. Pal T14   9 Ik 10 Mol   deleted   9.13.15. 0. 0
    A10

This event glyph occurs in a passage delineating the temporal directions
for the counting of a very long DN. Structurally, it occupies the position in which the earlier event (occurring on 9 Ik 10 Mol) is expected,
and must be equivalent in some way to the "ahau-in hand" event. The 9 Ik
10 Mol date of this text occurred 5.17.15.13.14.16.18 before 4 Ahau 8
Cumku.

10. Pal T18   missing   missing   9.14.15. 0. 0
    Stc 483

PEI. Mathews (personal communication, 1980) has called to my attention
that this glyph occurs on bundles both at Yaxchilan and in scenes on
pottery.

11. Tik   9.14.15. 6.16   ????   9.15. 0. 0. 0
    MT 30

The boundary of this unknown verbal phrase is not clear from the context,
and the name glyph of the agent cannot be identified at this time.

12. Tik   no date   GI   9.15. 0. 0. 0
    MT 51a-b

This verb is the graphic representation of a canoe, reflecting the canoes
in the scenes it accompanies. The syntax of both texts is not yet clear.
Each begins with the "canoe" verb followed by the name of GI, who appears
as the actor in each scene. However, in both cases, GI is followed by *u
mal* (T1.501:102) and the name phrase of Ruler A (see 34:3). In the
capture texts Yaxchilan, this *u mal* glyph appears in a structurally
similar context; i.e., between the names of the captive and the captor

(or patient and agent), where one expects an expression of agency. Since the texts on MT 51a and b are structurally identical, the *u mal* glyph may record "agency" or represent a second verb inflected with *u* and recorded with a different agent. See 32:5 and 99:6 for other "canoe" verb.

13. Pal PTab   9.10.10.11. 2   God K   9.14.10. 0. 0
    C2

AEI; this is an 819 Day Count verb.

14. Bon Scp1   9.13. 0. 0. 0   ????   9.13. 0. 0. 0
    C2b-D2a

See 82:32-33 for additional examples of this verb.

15. PN Thr1   9.17.10. 6. 1   *u cab* Ruler 7   9.17.15. 0. 0
    D'1

This event phrase is the first unit of a very complicated sequence occurring on the legs of this throne. The repetitious pattern of phrases seems to be as follows: "On this day was Event 1 of Ruler 7 (Z1-Z'1); it was 1.0.10 until Event 2 of Ruler 7 (A'2-E'1); count since Event 1 [subject deleted] (E'1-G'2) to the day of Event 2 [subject deleted] (F'3-F'6); it was 3.3 until Event 3 (accession) of Ruler 7; it was 4.8.16 until 9.17.15. 0. 0, a period ending." The characterization of each event phrase has been simplified, but the comparison below will show the existence of common elements in each example of the two events:

Event 1, form 1   

Event 1, form 2   

Event 2, form 1

Event 2, form 2

See 82:32-33 for other events in this series.

16. PN Thr1   9.17. 9. 5.11   deleted   9.17.15. 0. 0   
    E'3-F'1   (Ruler 7)

Chart 21   123

17.   Pal TC   9.10. 8. 9. 3   Chan-   9.13. 0. 0. 0
      I1-K1   Bahlum II
                                                       (by title)

This event from the secondary texts of the TC records the heir-designation event of Chan-Bahlum II, perhaps as a direct reference to the front of the Temple of Inscriptions, where the piers show the presentation of Chan-Bahlum as God K. It should be noted also that a child appears prominently in the Bonampak murals in what may be heir-designation rites in which he is presented from the front of a pyramid. This event occurs in many different forms in the inscriptions of the Group of the Cross; for other examples, see #5, #6, #18, 12:3-4, 38:4, 82:7, and 113:3-4.

18.   Pal TS   9.10. 8. 9. 3   Chan-   9.13. 0. 0. 0
      E2-F2   Bahlum II
                                                       (by title)

This event phrase from the Tablet of the Sun is parallel to #17, but the office is now recorded with the *oc-te* glyph that functions as the main verb in #5.

19.   Cop HS   missing   missing   9.17.10. 0. 0

20.   Quir J   9.16. 5. 0. 0   Two-Legged-   9.16. 5. 0. 0
      C4-C5   Sky

This blood-letting expression also occurs with period endings on the monuments of Pomona and at Yaxchilan. See 38:13-14, 52:6-9, and 76:2.

21.   Pus D   9.10.15. 0. 0   local ruler   9.10.15. 0. 0
      H10-H12

22.   Tort 6   9.10.11. 9. 6   none   9.12. 0. 0. 0
      A10

This is the first part of a verbal triplet that includes "inverted-sky" (75:7) and "star-over-earth" (10:4) events. T761 *chi/ti* hand may function as a phonetic complement specifying the Cholan pronunciation *och* versus the Yucatecan *oc*.

23.   Tort 6   9.11.16. 8.18   eroded   9.12. 0. 0. 0
      F11

24.	Tort 6 J2	8 ???? 8 Mac		Flint-Quetzal	9.12. 0. 0. 0
25.	PN Thr1 A'1b	9.17. 9. 5.11		none	9.17.15. 0. 0
26.	PN L3 X1-X3	no date	*u cab* Bat-Jaguar		9.16.10. 0. 0

The second and fourth glyphs have T228 *ah* as prefixes, which may identify them as nouns. See 7:14 for a discussion of the structure of this secondary text.

27.	PN L3 X7-Y7	9.16. 6.10.19		deleted (Bat-Jaguar?)	9.16.10. 0. 0
28.	PN L3 A'5-Z6	9.16. 6. 9.16		missing	9.16.10. 0. 0
29.	Coll 26 D2	9.16.16. 2. 5	Ti-Kab-Cauac		9.17. 0. 0. 0

This verb occurs on an alabaster vase with a two column text on either side and is linked by DN of 5.5.8.2 to a "wing-shell" death event occurring on the earlier date (25:19). The verb consists of a canoe glyph, marked as wood by the presence of the *te* sign and shown atop a series of stacked rectangles now known to signal the surface of water. The most extraordinary feature of the glyph, however, is the presence inside the canoe of an aged human head wearing a jaguar helmet. This Aged Jaguar God is the same as the jaguar paddler in the canoe scenes from Burial 116 at Tikal. Since the canoe verb on the alabaster vase occurs in the first half of a parallel couplet in which the second verb is a known "death" verb (see 24:11 and 12), it confirms the Tikal scenes as metaphorical references to death. See #12 and 32:5.

Chart 22 125

CHART 22   Affix Ø   in Cluster Ø.*.Ø   with Main Sign T61.756c

None of these examples is associated with a date or followed by a name phrase with a recognizable dynastic name, although there does seem to be a pattern in these phrases. Since there are no dates associated with any example and since I cannot identify particular glyphs as patient and agent, I will list these examples under a different format containing #, location, date of monument dedication, and full illustration of each clause. All examples are located in secondary texts.

#	LOCATION	DEDICATION	
1.	PN L4 Frame Pan a	9.11.10. 0. 0	
2.	PN 6 Front a	9.12.15. 0. 0	
3.	PN 6 Front b	9.12.15. 0. 0	
4.	PN 6 Front c	9.12.15. 0. 0	
5.	PN 6 Front d	9.12.15. 0. 0	
6.	PN 11 left	9.15. 0. 0. 0	

This clause appears to name the standing figure.

7.	PN 13 Front a	9.17. 0. 0. 0	
8.	PN 13 Front b	9.17 0. 0. 0	
9.	PN 15 Front c	9.17.15. 0. 0	

10.	PN 15 Back a	9.17.15. 0. 0
11.	PN Thr1 Pan a	9.17.15. 0. 0
12.	PN Thr1 Pan b	9.17.15. 0. 0
13.	PN 12 Pan a	9.18. 5. 0. 0

This clause is located in front of the left standing figure.

| 14. | PN 12
Pan b | 9.18. 5. 0. 0 |

This clause is located below the main figure.

| 15. | PN 12
Pan c | 9.18. 5. 0. 0 |

This clause is located at the leg of the main figure.

| 16. | PN 12
Pan h | 9.18. 5. 0. 0 |

This clause is located at the knee of the right standing figure.

| 17. | PN 12
Pan j | 9.18. 5. 0. 0 |

This clause is located above the ankle of the left standing figure.

| 18. | PN 12
Pan k | 9.18. 5. 0. 0 |

This clause is located below #17.

Chart 22 127

19. PN 14
     Pan a

     9.18.10. 0. 0

This clause is located adjacent to the incense bag.

20. PN 14
     Pan b

     9.18.10. 0. 0

This clause is located on the cloth behind the female.

21. PN 14
     Pan c

     9.18.10. 0. 0

22. PN 14
     Pan d

     9.18.10. 0. 0

23. PN 14
     Pan e

     9.18.10. 0. 0

24. PN 14
     Pan f

     9.18.10. 0. 0

25. Yax L45
     D1

     9.15. 0. 0. 0

This clause is located behind Shield-Jaguar.

26. Yax L46
     H1

     9.15. 0. 0. 0

This clause is located in front of the head of Shield-Jaguar.

27. Bon Scp2
     A1-A2

     Late Classic

28. Bon L4
     F1

     9. 9. 0. 0. 0

29. Bon 1
     P1

     9.17.10. 0. 0

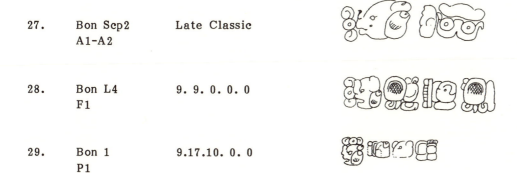

30.   Bon 1   9.17.10. 0. 0
           Q1

31.   Pal DH   9.13. 0. 0. 0
           A1

32.   Pal 96G   9.17.15. 0. 0
           L4

This phrase follows "completion of the 1st katun as ahau"; it may be part of a name phrase.

33.   Nar 14   9.18. 0. 0. 0
           G1

This clause is located on the lower frame of the main text.

34.   Nar 12   9.18.10. 0. 0
           H1

This clause is located on the frame below the main text.

35.   ArP 1   Middle Classic
           C1-C2

36.   Agua 7   9.18. 0. 0. 0
           G1-H1

37.   Agua 7   9.18. 0. 0. 0
           I1-I4

38.   LAm 2   Late Classic
           C1

39.   LAm 2   Late Classic
           D1

Chart 22   129

40.   LMar 1   9.18. 0. 0. 0
      E1

This clause is located on the right outer frame.

41.   Cal 51   Late Classic
      G1

42.   Cal 51   Late Classic
      G3

43.   Coll 19   Late Classic
      Site Q 4
      I1

44.   Coll 2   9.17.15. 0. 0
      FtWorth Pan
      K1

The clause is located adjacent to the kneeling attendant.

45.   Coll 6   10. 1.15. 0. 0
      K1

46.   ECayo L3   9.15. 5. 0. 0
      K1

47.   Coll 17   9.13. 0. 0. 0
      Site Q 2
      a1

48.   Coll 17   9.13. 0. 0. 0
      b1

49.   Coll 17   9.13. 0. 0. 0
      d1

50.   Coll 17   9.13. 0. 0. 0
      i1

51.   Coll 17   9.13. 0. 0. 0
      j1

52.	Coll 17 k1	9.13. 0. 0. 0	
53.	Coll 17 L1	9.13. 0. 0. 0	
54.	PN 12 Pan 1	9.18. 5. 0. 0	
55.	PN 12 Pan m	9.18. 5. 0. 0	
56.	Yax L24 H1-H4	9.15. 0. 0. 0	

See 17:5.

| 57. | Yax L25 O2-Q1 | 9.15. 0. 0. 0 | |

See 17:4. Lady Xoc is named as the subject of this event.

| 58. | Yax L26 O3-R1 | 9.15. 0. 0. 0 | |

See 17:6.

| 59. | DO Alab 4-7 | 9.15.13.12. 1 | |

See 17:8.

| CHART 23 | Affix Ø | in Cluster Ø.*.Ø | with Miscellaneous Main Signs |

#	LOCATION	DATE (EVENT)	PATIENT	AGENT	DEDICATION
1.	Bon A C2-D3	9. 3. 3.16. 4		Kan-Batz'	9. 3.10. 0. 0

Chart 23   131

This verbal phrase accompanies the Initial Series date on this monument. The first glyph seems to be a local variation of the "chuen" count glyph found on Stela 31 of Tikal and Monument 6 of Tortuguero. The final glyph is preceded by a locative preposition (T51) and a glyph which could represent a house. The central two glyphs compose the verbal phrase, the meaning of which is not known.

2.   Tort EarA   9.11.17. 3.10   Ahpo-Balam   9.12. 0. 0. 0
     EarA F-H

AEI. This event took place on the occasion of the twenty-sixth tun anniversary of the accession of Ahpo-Balam, who is recorded as the agent of the verbal phrase. An AEI is attached to the initial "house" glyph, suggesting that it is the verb while the two additional glyphs are complements of some kind. The two additional glyphs are particularly interesting in relationship to ##3-6 because they contain elements prominent in these latter expressions (an "inverted sky" glyph and T568 *lu*), which are also associated with anniversary rites.

3.   Pal TC   9.12.18. 5.16   GI   9.13. 0. 0. 0
     O5-O6

PEI. I have included an illustration of the entire clause under this number because of the difficulty of identifying the agent. The verbal glyph is followed by a possessed noun with the possessor recorded as the introductory glyph of the Palenque Triad. This glyph may refer to all three gods or only to the patron of this temple, GI. This possessed noun can be analyzed as either the agent or the patient of the verb, as follows: " he acted the X of GI" or "he acted upon his X, GI." At present Iprefer the second interpretation because of the text of the Dumbarton Oaks Tablet, which records an event of the same kind. That text begins with a couplet in which GI is the agent of the first part and Kan-Xul I, of the second. It seems best to interpret this couplet as a structure giving two sets of information: (1) that on the occasion GI acted, and (2) that Kan-Xul also acted, perhaps while impersonating GI (Schele n.d.c). The record of this TC event appears in a very similar structure on the TFC (#5), where it occurs in a couplet with the Palenque Triad and additional gods following the first verb and with Chan-Bahlum the agent of the second verb (see 82:6). This couplet structure suggests that the Triad gods are the agents of this anniversary event. Lounsbury (personal communication, 1981) has found evidence that this event occurred in association with a prominent Jupiter hierophony, and it was also part of the celebration of the seventy-fifth tropical year anniversary of Pacal's accession.

4.   Pal TFC   9.12.18. 5.16   GII and GIII   9.13. 0. 0. 0
     L2-M3

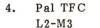

The possessed noun is the same as #3, but the agents of the verb are now named as GIII (recorded with his portrait head) and GII.

5.   Pal TFC   9.12.18. 5.16   Palenque   9.13. 0. 0. 0
     N8-O8   Triad
                                                     (by title)

PEI. The deities named as the agents of this event include the Palenque Triad and four additional supernaturals (see the introduction to this catalog). The verb occurs as the first part of a couplet (see the note to #3).

6.   Pal TS   9.12.18. 5.16   GIII   9.13. 0. 0. 0
     N5-O5

The possessed noun of the previous phrases (T1.671.23:59:116) is replaced here by *u balan ahau* (T204.539[585]:24?). Barbara McLeod (personal communication, 1980) has suggested that the infix T585, known to have a phonetic value of *be* or *bi*, may with T24 form the participial suffix for Chol *-bil*. The noun would then be read *u balbil ahau* "his hidden lord," perhaps as a reference to the dead Pacal, whose accession anniversary is associated with this event series. This suggestion is supported by the texts of Yaxchilan Stela 12, which records the death of Shield-Jaguar. On the reverse side (see 55:7), an additional event (without additional date) is recorded as auxiliary verb + *ti balan-ahau*. The absence of an additional date suggests that this *balan-ahau* event in some way refers to Shield-Jaguar's posthumous state.

7.   Pal T14   9.13.13.15. 0   Chan-Bahlum? 9.13.15. 0. 0
     C6-D6

This posthumous event occurred 3 haabs and 260 days after the recorded death date of Chan-Bahlum, the male figure shown dancing in the scene (Schele n.d.c). This event is tied by an enormous DN to events in the mythological past. Structurally, the ancient mythological event can be identified as an "ahau-in hand" verb, and, in the earlier text marking the base events of this DN, the earlier event is called the "first (T203.4:565:178) ahau-in-hand" and "yax God K-in-hand" (*yax* is the term for "first" in Yucatec). Note that the initial sign of this glyph also appears in the T585 death glyph (see Chart 19) and a series of "fire" events (see Chart 16). The appearance of T11 (an equivalent of T1, the third person singular ergative pronoun) over the "impinged bone" glyph may mark the latter part of this expression as possessed nouns. Finally, a number of name glyphs follow the verbal expression. These include among other GI and GIII of the Palenque Triad, but since the name phrase of Chan-Bahlum ends the text without the appearance of another verbal phrase, I am tentatively identifying him as the agent. See 20:8.

Chart 23   133

8.	Pal 96G B5-B6	9.11. 2. 1.11	Pacal II	9.17.15. 0. 0	

This is the event to which subsequent accession expressions on this tablet are related, and although the meaning is not understood, it is interesting to note that the second glyph appears as a title in each of the name phrases (Kan-Xul II, Chaacal III, and Kuk II) following this clause. The initial glyph is badly damaged, but enough survives to tentatively identify the prefix as a variant of T207. The remaining part the glyph is a head variant of unusual configuration, but I suspect that the superfix was T122 and that it is the head variant of the "fire" glyph. If this idenitfication is correct, the verb is equivalent to those on Chart 16.

9.	Pal C Eav A1-D2	no date	????	9.11.10. 0. 0	

This long passage is found at the beginning of the text on the underside of the eaves of House C. It is probable that the passage includes more than one verbal phrase, with the second phrase beginning perhaps with the fourth glyph, but all are included because I cannot securely establish the boundary of the verbal phrase(s). This passage is followed by four pairs of glyphs (which include a deity name and TI.23:565:314) arranged in the following pattern: (1) Bolon-Yocte and constant; (2) decapitated body and constant; (3) God K and constant; (4) "water-group/God C" and constant. The last God C glyph is identical to the fifth glyph in the drawing above. I suspect these four pairs of glyphs may constitute a compound subject. See 5:9-10 for a comparison to the sixth through eighth glyphs above.

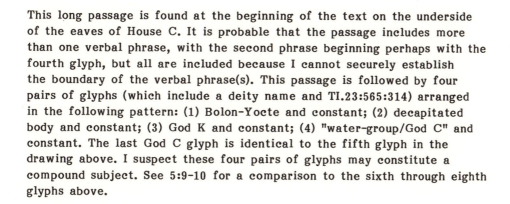

10.	Coll 21 B3	9. 8.17.15.15 + 1 or 2 CRs?	Smoking- Jaguar	9.12. 0. 0. 0	

This verb is from Site Q Glyphic Panel 7.

11.	PN 23 I8-J8	????	deleted or missing	9.14.15. 0. 0	

CHART 24   Affix Ø   in Cluster Ø.*.Ø   with Miscellaneous Main Signs

All of these examples appear to record death events.

#	LOCATION	DATE (EVENT)	PATIENT	AGENT	DEDICATION	
1.	Pal PTab M11-N11	9.13.10. 1. 5		Chan-Bahlum	9.14.10. 0. 0	
2.	Pal T14 Stc 500	missing		missing	9.14.15. 0. 0	
3.	Tik MT28a A3	9.14. 9. 0.12		Personage 1	9.15. 0. 0. 0	
4.	Tik MT28a A16	9.14.10. 3. 3		Personage 2	9.15. 0. 0. 0	
5.	Tik MT28a A24	9.14.10.13.12		Personage 3	9.15. 0. 0. 0	
6.	Tik MT28b A3	9.14.15. 1.19		Shield-God K of Dos Pilas	9.15. 0. 0. 0	

Although the two name glyphs of the subject of this death verb are badly
eroded, there is good evidence that this clause records the death of
Shield-God K, a contemporary ruler of Dos Pilas. Not only does the EG of
Tikal as local emblem of Dos Pilas, but the same date is recorded on
Stela 8 of Dos Pilas as the death of Shield-God K, and on Stela 8,
"death" is written with the more common "wing-shell/ahau-ik" expression
(see 25:4).

#	LOCATION	DATE (EVENT)	PATIENT	AGENT	DEDICATION	
7.	Tik MT28b A8	9.14.15. 4. 3		18-Rabbit	9.15. 0. 0. 0	
8.	Tik MT28b A25	9.14.15. 6.13		Lady Lahuntun	9.15. 0. 0. 0	
9.	Tik MT30a A3	4 Ben ????		eroded	9.15. 0. 0. 0	

Chart 25   135

The CR in this clause contains the tzolkin day 4 Ben, but the haab
position is not readable. The glyph found in this position is identical,
however, to a month sign representing Uayeb on Caracol Stela 14. Unfortunately, no recognizable number precedes the month sign in the Tikal text,
so that the CR cannot be determined with the present information.

10.	Tik MT30a A10	9.15. 1.12.13	Ik	9.15. 0. 0. 0+	
11.	ECayo L3 J1a	9.15. 1. 6. 3	Turtle-Shell	9.16. 5. 0. 0	
12.	Cop AltF' B2b	9.17. 4. 1.11	deleted	9.17. 5. 0. 0	
	PEI.				
13.	Coll 26 D5	9.16.16. 2. 5	Ti-Kab-Cauac	9.17. 0. 0. 0	

This verb occurs in the second half of a clause couplet in which a canoe
with the Aged Jaguar God is verb of the first part. See 21:30.

CHART 25   Affix Ø   in Cluster Ø.*.Ø   with Main Sign T77:575

Proskouriakoff (1963:162-163) identified this phrase as an expression for "death." It has two
elements: the "wing-shell" glyph to which all verbal and temporal affixes are adjoined; and the
"zac-ahau-ik," which is usually preceded by T1, marking it as a possessed noun. T575 appears to be
a necessary element in the verbal glyph of this expression, but since it behaves like a verbal
suffix in other contexts, the possibility that it functions as a verbal suffix in the expression
cannot be eliminated.

#	LOCATION	DATE OF EVENT	PATIENT	AGENT	DEDICATION	
1.	Pal TIw Q9-R10	9.12. 0. 6.18		Lady Ahpo-Hel	9.12.15. 0. 0	
	PEI.					
2.	Pal PTab J10-I11	9.12.11. 5.18		Pacal II	9.14.10. 0. 0	

3. Pal T18   missing   missing   9.14.15. 0. 0
   Stc pC2-pD2

   PEI

4. DPil 8   9.14.15. 1.19   Shield-God K   9.15. 0. 0. 0
   I10

5. Yax 12   9.15.10.17.14   Shield-Jaguar   9.16. 5. 0. 0
   A2-B2

6. Yax L27   9.13.13.12. 5   Lady Pacal   9.16. 5. 0. 0
   A2-B2

7. Yax L27   9.15.10.17.14   Shield-Jaguar   9.16. 5. 0. 0
   F2

8. Yax L28   9.15.19.14. 3   Lady Ik-   9.16. 5. 0. 0
   S1b-T1   Skull-Sky

The name phrase of this woman is badly eroded, but it includes a sequence
of the T1001 female head, a skull, a sky sign, and the head variant of
the "water-group" affix specified for a female. This same sequence occurs
in the name of the female on Lintels 32 and 53 and in the name phrase of
Bird-Jaguar's mother as recorded on Stelae 11 and 12.

9. Yax L59   9.15.17.15.14   Lady Xoc   9.16. 5. 0. 0
   L1-M1

10. PN L3   9.16. 6.11.17   Ruler 4   9.16.10. 0. 0
    U2-V2

11. Ton MNAH none   deleted   Late Classic
    Disk

This phrase occurs after the date 9 Ahau, an eroded verb, and a name
phrase, but no calendric glyphs are located between the first clause and
this "death" phrase. In turn, this phrase is followed by the day 13 Akbal
and an additional series of name glyphs. If the 13 Akbal glyph is accepted as a name rather than as a date, the subject of the "death" event is
recorded as "13 Akbal, Ah Zac, Ah Mol (and so on)."

Chart 25 137

12. Cop HS   missing   missing   9.17.10. 0. 0

     PEI.

13. Ton F33   missing   Lady Ahpo-?? Late Classic
     pB-pC

This phrase occurs on a monument on which no calendric information survives. It is followed by a female name in which the center element is
eroded. The first sign of the verbal phrase does not look like a wing,
and the second, a turtle head, is not expected in the "wing-shell/ahau-
ik" expression. This example, therefore, may not record death.

14. Pal C   9. 9. 6.10.19   Pacal II   9.11.10. 0. 0
     Eav I1

This event occurs after the death date of Pacal I, so that the subject
must be the later Pacal. The "wing-shell" element of the death phrase
does not appear in this example; instead, the "ahau-ik" compound, which
appears as a possessed noun in the "death" expression, functions here as
the main verb. It is interesting to note that the date of this event is
7.14.8 (2,808 days or 2 x 3 x 4 x 9 x 13 days) after the death of Pacal
I; this event could be the commemoration of that death.

15. ASac 4   9.10. 3.17. 0   eroded   9.10.10. 0. 0
     B6-A7

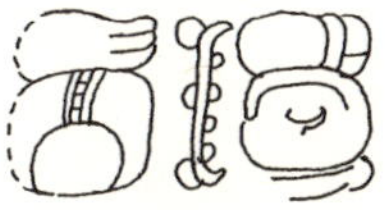

16. Ton M69   9.17. 4.12. 5   Chaan   9.17.10. 0. 0
     D1

17. Pal TC   7 ???? 8 Xul   Batz'-Ah Kin   9.12.10. 0. 0
     Cens1
     H7-G8

18. PN 7   9.12.14.10.14   Ruler 2   9.14.10. 0. 0
     C3

19. Coll 26   9.11.10.12.13   Sky-Uinal   9.17. 0. 0. 0
    A4-B4

This death is linked by a DN of 5.5.8.2 to a later event recorded in a
couplet structure in which a canoe verb (21:30) is the verb of the first
part and a T736 "death" glyph (24:13) is the verb of the second part.

CHART 26	Affix Ø	in Cluster Ø.*.Ø	with Miscellaneous Main Signs

#	LOCATION	DATE (EVENT)	PATIENT	AGENT	DEDICATION	
1.	Nar Alt1 F1	9. 6.11. 0.17		Ruler I	9. 8. 0. 0. 0	

The T79 sign appears at Palenque in phrases associated with anniversary
events, and this Naranjo example occurs 2.2.6.3.3 or 834 tropical years +
11 days after an earlier event.

| 2. | Nar Alt1
F11-G12 | 9. 6.11. 0.17 | | deleted
(Ruler I) | 9. 8. 0. 0. 0 | |

This phrase is a restatement of the event in #1, from which a new DN is
counted to a later and featured event. The subject is deleted because it
is redundant information.

| 3. | Coll 7
pD3-pE4 | 9. 8. 0. 0. 0 | | Kankin? | 9. 8. 0. 0. 0 |  |

This passage follows a DN of 1.1.13.13, and it is immediately followed by
a parentage statement, the presence of which leads me to suspect that one
or more of the last three glyphs in this passage records the name of the
subject.

| 4. | Tort 6
D11-D12 | 9.10.15. 1.11 | | none | 9.12. 0. 0. 0 | |

| 5. | Tort 6
C17-D17 | 8.15.16. 0. 5 | | none | 9.12. 0. 0. 0 | |

Chart 26   139

AEI. The event phrases listed as #4 and #5 are identical in form, but #4 is a historical event occurring 3.16.1 after the accession of Ahpo-Balam, and this one occurred during Cycle 8. Presumably, the later event is a reenactment, recurrence, or remembrance of the earlier one; the time between the two events, 14.19.1.6, is 10 days short of 294 haabs.

6.	Pal T18 Stc 510	missing		missing	9.14.15. 0. 0
7.	Yax L16 A2a	9.16. 0.13.17	Ah-??-Kab	Bird-Jaguar	9.16.18. 0. 0
8.	Cop HS	missing		missing	9.17.10. 0. 0
9.	Nar 32 M2-N2	9.19. 4. 1. 0		18-Rabbit	9.19.10. 0. 0
10.	Nar 32 U2-W2	9.19. 9.15. 0		18-Rabbit	9.19.10. 0. 0
11.	Nar 32 A'2-Y3	9.19. 4.15. 1		none	9.19.10. 0. 0

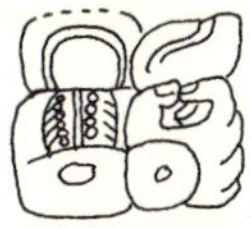

This phrase is the second half of a couplet; see 62:20.

12.	Nar 32 Z4-A'4	9.19. 5. 9.12		none	9.19.10. 0. 0

This phrase is the first part of a couplet; see 62:21.

13.	Pul D D11-D12	9. 8. 0. 0. 0		u cab local ruler	9.10.15. 0. 0

This period ending phrase is part of a set of expressions using the generalized "tree" sign (T767) and the T528 tun glyph (see 67:1, 68:3, 69:3, 84:6, and 131:2-3). The first glyph can be identified as "fire" by a comparison to #14, a parallel passage in which the head variant of "fire" occurs. Note that T669, phonetic *ka*, functions as a phonetic complement for *kak* "fire," and that the usual semantic determinative (T122) for "fire" is missing.

14.	Pul D F12-E13	9. 8. 0. 0. 0	*u cab* local ruler	9.10.15. 0. 0
15.	Cop T18 Wall Pan pB1-pC1	missing	missing	9.18.10. 0. 0
16.	NTun Gpĭa B2	9.15.13.11.10	Muan	9.16.10. 0. 0
17.	NTun GpIVb A3	9.15. 2. 1. 5	local person	9.16.10. 0. 0
18.	NTun GpIVi A3-A5	9.15.16. 9. 3	local person	9.16.10. 0. 0

See 82:29,31, 98:12, and 116:20-21.

19.	NTun GpIVl A1	no date	13-????	9.16.10. 0. 0
20.	NTun GpIVm A3	9.15.12. 9.15	Ek-??-Cab	9.16.10. 0. 0
21.	NTun GpVIa A2-B2	12 Ix? 4 Zac	local person	9.16.10. 0. 0
22.	NTun GpVIa E1	4 Cib 7 Zac	local person	9.16.10. 0. 0
23.	NTun GpVIb A3	9.16.11.12. 4	Chaan- Ah Cauac	9.16.10. 0. 0

Chart 27 141

| 24. | NimP 2 H3 | 9.14.15. 4.14 | | *u cab* 6-Gourd/ Black-Bat | 9.15.10. 0. 0 |  |

| 25. | Yax Str20 HS 169 | 9.18. 9.10.10 | Ahpo-Pah | Shield-Jaguar II | 9.18.10. 0. 0 |  |

CHART 27   Affix *tu*   in Cluster *tu.*.various   with Miscellaneous Main Signs

Thompson (1950:57) identified T89 as *tu* (a contraction of *ti* and *u*), and Lounsbury (personal communication 1976) has identified T115 as *tu* or some close approximation because of its frequent presence with the *otoch* "house" glyph in contexts where a locative and pronoun are predicted. In the contexts of these verbal expressions, *tu* may well record a contraction of the preposed tense-aspect particle *t* or *ta* with the pronoun *u*.

#	LOCATION	DATE (EVENT)	PATIENT	AGENT	DEDICATION	
1.	Pal C Eav A1	no date		????	9.11.10. 0. 0	

See 23:9.

| 2. | Pal TC Sanc w B1 | 9.12.11.12.10 | | deleted (Chan-Bahlum) | 9.13. 0. 0. 0 |  |

This verb is located on the outer, west sanctuary panel of the TC, but there is good evidence that this same event was also recorded on the now damaged outer panels of the TFC. The TC text begins with a DN ("the tenth day [changeover] after") and an identical DN appears as the first glyph on the south panel of the TFC, although no verbal glyphs survive. However, on the TFC north panel fragments of a turtle glyph, identical to the second glyph in the TC phrase, precedes the name of Chan-Bahlum, who is also recorded as the subject of the TC event. Although no CR is recorded on any of these panels, the occasion can be assumed to have been the accession of Chan-Bahlum (9.12.11.12.10) because (1) the absence of a specified date suggests that the event was readily known to any viewer; (2) these outer panels were designed to record the assumption by Chan-Bahlum of the position and regalia of ruler; and (3) accession is the event featured pictorially in both temples, and since any event unmarked calendrically must be dated from the context of known information, surely an undated event must refer to the action featured in the epigraphic and

pictorial systems, i.e., "accession." This event phrase is likely, therefore, to be an alternative expression for "accession". See 21:5 for
another event in which T765 *oc* is the main sign, and see 111:5 for the
event which occurred ten days after this "accession."

TC DN   TFC DN   TFC "turtle"

3. DPil 8   9.14.15. 2. 3   Shield-God K   deleted   9.15. 0. 0. 0
   H14

This event has been identified by Mathews (n.d.b) as an expression for
"to bury." See 73:4 for more extensive commentary and for other examples.

4. Yax L10   9.18.17.12. 6   Zero-Skull   9.19. 0. 0. 0
   C1-D1ᴄ

This expression concludes a long series of event expressions (including a
"star" event and a "capture") by restating the phrase which began the
series (see 129:6). The intervening events are then framed by the initial
occurrence of this event phrase and this restatement.

5. Pal PTab   9.14. 8.16.18   Xoc   9.14.10. 0. 0
   R15

This "house" event occurs following a DN of "three and twenty" days
counted since the accession of Xoc. I suspect it may refer to the dedication of the north building of the Palace in which this tablet was
mounted. A similar kind of "house" expression also occurs on Yaxchilan
Lintel 31 (see 126:3) in a clause which may also record the dedication of
a structure.

6. Ton M69   9.17. 5. 7. 5   Chaan   9.17.10. 0. 0
   N1

This event occurred 260 days after the death of the person named as
subject.

Chart 28 143

CHART 28   Affix T1   in Cluster 1.*.∅   with Main Sign T528.116:713

This glyph is a period ending term, such as "it ended, the tun" or "the end of the tun." T1 refers to all signs which can stand for the third person pronoun of Set A.

#	LOCATION	DATE (EVENT)	PATIENT	AGENT	DEDICATION	
1.	Tik 27 D2	9. 3. 0. 0. 0	tun	Jaguar-Paw-Skull I	9. 3. 0. 0. 0	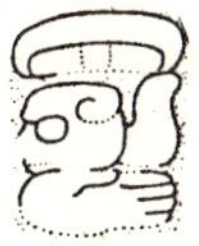
2.	Nar Alt1 H5	9. 6. 0. 0. 0	tun	none	9. 8. 0. 0. 0	
3.	Nar Alt1 H7	9. 7. 0. 0. 0	tun	none	9. 8. 0. 0. 0	
4.	Nar Alt1 H9	9. 8. 0. 0. 0	tun	none	9. 8. 0. 0. 0	
5.	Nar 38 A6	9. 6. 0. 0. 0	tun	none	9. 8. 0. 0. 0	
6.	Nar 38 A8	9. 7. 0. 0. 0	tun	none	9. 8. 0. 0. 0	
7.	Nar 38 B2	9. 8. 0. 0. 0	tun	none	9. 8. 0. 0. 0	
8.	Car 6 D6	9. 6. 0. 0. 0	tun	Ruler 2	9. 8.10. 0. 0	
9.	Car 6 D8	9. 7. 0. 0. 0	tun	Ruler 2	9. 8.10. 0. 0	
10.	Tort 1 A2b	9.10.13. 0. 0	tun	Ahpo-Balam	9.11. 0. 0. 0	

This verb is preceded by [glyph] and followed by [glyph] .

11.	Pal TIe G8	9. 6.13. 0. 0	tun	none	9.12.15. 0. 0	
12.	Pal TIe L5	9. 8. 0. 0. 0	tun	none	9.12.15. 0. 0	
13.	Pal TIe M1	9. 8.13. 0. 0	tun	none	9.12.15. 0. 0	
14.	Pal TIe O2	9. 9. 0. 0. 0	tun	none	9.12.15. 0. 0	
15.	Pal TIe R12	9.10. 0. 0. 0	tun	none	9.12.15. 0. 0	
16.	Nar 14 A3	9.18. 0. 0. 0	tun	Ruler IIIb	9.18. 0. 0. 0	
17.	Nar 10 A8	9.19. 0. 0. 0	tun	Ruler IIIb	9. 19. 0. 0. 0	
18.	Mach 7 D1-D2	10. 0. 0.13. 0	tun	One-Fish-in-Hand	10. 0. 5. 0. 0	
19.	Xul 3 A4b	10. 1.10. 0. 0	tun	none	10. 1.10. 0. 0	

This period ending glyph following a DN of 1.6.14.12 leading from an an earlier birth to this lahuntun.

| 20. | Uca 4 A2 | 10. 1. 0. 0. 0 | tun | none | 10. 1. 0. 0. 0 | |
| 21. | Ixk 1 E7 | 9.18. 0. 0. 0 | tun | Rabbit-God K | 9.18. 0. 0. 0 | |

There is an error in the Initial Series, but the date must be 9.18.0.0.0.

Chart 29   145

22.	MJos 2 C5	9.14. 0. 0. 0	tun	none	9.14. 0. 0. 0	

This phrase is followed by the CR and the "completion of the 14th katun."

23.	PN 39 D2	9.12. 5. 0. 0	tun	Ruler 2	9.12.10. 0. 0	
24.	PN 6 A18	9.12.15. 0. 0	yax-tun	Ruler 3	9.12.15. 0. 0	
25.	PN 12 B12	9.18. 5. 0. 0	tun	Ruler 7	9.18. 5. 0. 0	

CHART 29   Affix T1   in Cluster 1.*.∅   with Main Sign "Scattering"

These events record a period ending rite involving the dropping of some substance into a brazier or other kind of container. Scenes showing this rite often display blood-letting regalia, and since the substance dropped in "scattering" scenes at Yaxchilan can be identified as blood by comparing it to the motif around mouths in tongue laceration scenes, "scattering" can be identified as a "blood-letting" rite. The glyph can appear with or without the suffixes T95 and T758var, the functions of which are not known. They can appear with many additional affix patterns. When with "scattering," I have tentatively classified them as part of the "scattering" expression, rather than as verbal affixes.

#	LOCATION	DATE (EVENT)	PATIENT	AGENT	DEDICATION	
1.	Car 6 E18-F18	9. 8.10. 0. 0		Batz'-Ek (by title)	9. 8.10. 0. 0	
2.	Agua 2 G13	9.15. 5. 0. 0		Spangle-Head	9.15. 5. 0. 0	
3.	Sac 1 A5	9.16.10. 0. 0		Ahau-Kin	9.16.10. 0. 0	
4.	Yax 1 B3	9.16.10. 0. 0		Bird-Jaguar	9.16.10. 0. 0	

| 5. | Bon 1 G3 | 9.17.10. 0. 0 | | Chaan-Muan | 9.17.10. 0. 0 | |

This "scattering" glyph is preceded by a "half-period" glyph and by the "end of the tun" glyph (T204.528.116:713:130).

6.	Nar 19 A2-B2	9.17.10. 0. 0		Ruler IIIb	9.17.10. 0. 0	
7.	Bon 3 A3-B3	9.17.15. 0. 0		Chaan-Muan	9.17.15. 0. 0	
8.	Ixlu 2 A3	9.18. 3. 0. 0		eroded	9.18. 3. 0. 0	
9.	Quir A B16	9.17. 5. 0. 0		Two-Legged-Sky	9.17. 5. 0. 0	
10.	NimP 1 C3	9.15.10. 0. 0		Lahun-Chaan	9.15.10. 0. 0	
11.	PN 40 A17	9.15.15. 0. 0		Ruler 4	9.15.15. 0. 0	

| CHART 30 | Affix T1 | | in Cluster 1.*.∅ | | with Main Sign T644.528.116 |

#	LOCATION	DATE (EVENT)	PATIENT	AGENT	DEDICATION
1.	Pal Sarc 6	none	tun	Pacal II	9.12.15. 0. 0

This glyph is probably not verbal. It follows 8 Ahau 13 Pop and "birth," and 6 Etz'nab 11 Yax and "death"; and it precedes the name phrase of the subject of both the "birth" and "death" verbs, Pacal II. This glyph functions as a DN, specifying the four "katun seatings" that occurred between these two events.

| 2. | Pal Sarc 24a | 9. 7. 0. 0. 0 | tun | Chan-Bahlum I | 9.12.15. 0. 0 |

Chart 30   147

This glyph and that listed under #3 record the two period ending dates used to lock all the CRs in the sarcophagus text into proper position in the LC. Each example is followed by the name of the ruler who was in office at that particular katun ending. Note that these dates represent the one-third points of the nine katun endings (Katun 4 through Katun 13) recorded in the katun histories of the upper panels.

3.   Pal Sarc   9.10. 0. 0. 0   tun   Lady Zac-Kuk 9.12.15. 0. 0
     45a

4.   Pal TIe   9.10. 0. 0. 0   tun   Pacal II   9.12.15. 0. 0
     S9-S10

This glyph records a katun ending, but as it relates to the reign of Pacal II, not as it relates to the LC. It is preceded by an ordinal construction for "first" (T232.4:565:178), marking it as the first katun ending in the reign of Pacal. See 20:8.

5.   Pal TIm   9.11. 0. 0. 0   tun   Pacal II   9.12.15. 0. 0

This glyph records the second katun ending of the reign of Pacal II. It is preceded by T205, which has the phonetic value *ca* and may represent, therefore, the number 2. However, T205 also can function as a third person pronoun of Set A and, therefore, as the pronoun in the ordinal construction. It is possible that T205 is fulfilling both these functions in this glyph. The main part of the construction includes T168 *ahpo*, marking the katun as one of a "reign."

6.   Pal TIm   9.12. 0. 0. 0   tun   Pacal II   9.12.15. 0. 0
     F9-F10

This glyph records the third katun ending of Pacal's reign, and it is preceded by the ordinal "third." "Reign" is recorded by the prepositional phrase *tu ahpo le* (T89.168:188).

CHART 31   Affix T1   in Cluster 1.*.∅   with Miscellaneous Main Signs

All of these examples are expressions associated with period ending dates.

#	LOCATION	DATE (EVENT)	PATIENT	AGENT	DEDICATION	
1.	Pal TIw C3	9.13. 0. 0. 0		????	9.12.15. 0. 0	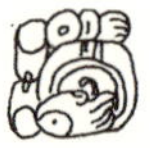

This period ending expression and that listed as #2 record the ends of
periods which are later than the dedication date of this inscription and,
therefore, these events may be classified as ones of the future. Both
event expressions are followed by a series of nouns naming the agents,
perhaps as a supernatural.

2.	Pal TIw C8-D8	10. 0. 0. 0. 0		????	9.12.15. 0. 0	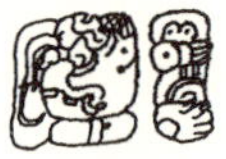

3.	Pal TIe R2	9. 9. 0. 0. 0	3 Ahau Katun	none	9.12.15. 0. 0	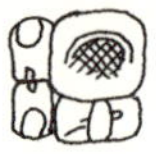

This verb is an event in a period ending formula used to record the katun
histories of Pacal's reign. The verb is composed of *pa* (T586) and either
ti (T59) or *ta* (T103) to form *pat* "the end of something." *Pat* is inflected with a third person singular pronoun of Set A. *U pat* is followed by "3
Ahau Katun," the name designation of the katun which ended and presumably
the object of the verb. This construction is either transitive or stative, but in either case, no agent is named.

4.	Pal TIe O7	9. 9. 0. 0. 0		none	9.12.15. 0. 0	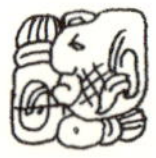

This *pat* event occurs in a context different from those of #3 and #5. It
heads the section of the katun history which records the particular
nondynastic event characteristic of the final day of the katun. The
function of the prefixed sign--a conflation of *ti* and T679 *i*--is not yet
understood.

5.	Pal TIe T7	9.10. 0. 0. 0	1 Ahau Katun	none	9.12.15. 0. 0	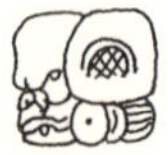

This example is parallel to #3 and is followed by "1 Ahau Katun, the
first seating of the tun," referring to its ordinal position in Pacal's
reign. See ##2-3 and 30:4.

Chart 31   149

6. Pal TIm   9.11. 0. 0. 0   12 Ahau   none   9.12.15. 0. 0
    D1   Katun

This glyph is very badly eroded, but since it occurs in a passage parallel to #3 and #5, and since it is followed by "12 Ahau Katun," it is
almost certainly an *u pat* glyph.

7. Pal TIm   9.12. 0. 0. 0   ????   GI by title   9.12.15. 0. 0
    I8

The phonetic value of this verb appears to be *u tup* (T204 *u* or an
equivalent; T89 *tu*; and T586 *pa*), but a meaning for it has not been
demonstrated. This event occurs within a section of the text documenting
the relationship of the members of the Palenque Triad to the end of Katun
12. The verb is followed by a glyph featuring the forehead symbol of the
Quadripartite Monster, the motif at the base of the cross on the TC and
TI sarcophagus. This "quadripartite" symbol may be an alternative name
for GI, but I suspect that it is the object of the verb; that the subject
is deleted; and that this clause is gapped to the succeeding one in
which GI is named as the subject. See Chart 70.

8. Pal TIm   9.12. 0. 0. 0   ????   GII by title   9.12.15. 0. 0
    K7

This *tup* glyph is followed by a variant of the xoc glyph especially
associated with GII, who is the subject of the succeeding clause. This
passage is parallel to those in #7 and #9.

9. Pal TIm   9.12. 0. 0. 0   ????   GIII by title   9.12.15. 0. 0
    M3

This *tup* glyph is followed by the T1030o glyph especially associated with
GIII, who is the subject of the succeeding clause. T1030o is the glyphic
version of the Jester God. This passage is parallel to those in #7 and
#8.

10. Cop AltZ   9.17. 0. 0. 0   none   9.17. 0. 0. 0
    A2

The glyphs in ##10-14 occur immediately before period ending CRs in contexts which suggest that this glyph is parallel to the "quarter-katun"
glyph, T1.44:563:142.

#	LOCATION	DATE (EVENT)	PATIENT	AGENT	DEDICATION	
11.	Cop Str11 Rev Q1a	9.17. 0. 0. 0		none	9.17. 0. 0. 0	
12.	Cop Str11 Rev E'3	9.17. 0. 0. 0		none	9.17. 0. 0. 0	
13.	Cop AltS G1a	10. 0. 0. 0. 0		none	9.15. 0. 0. 0	
14.	Cop T21 In Door Q1a	9.17. 0. 0. 0		none	9.17. 0. 0. 0	
15.	NimP 2 D4-E1	9.15. 7. 0. 0		local ruler	9.15.10. 0. 0	
16.	PN Alt1 L2	13. 0. 0. 0. 0 4 Ahau 8 Cumku		paddlers	9.13. 0. 0. 0	

CHART 32	Affix T1		in Cluster 1.*.∅		with Miscellaneous Main Signs	
#	LOCATION	DATE (EVENT)	PATIENT	AGENT	DEDICATION	
1.	Pal TC E2	1.18. 5. 3. 2		GI by title	9.13. 0. 0. 0	

The glyphs in ##1-4 are metaphorical expressions for "birth" (Lounsbury 1980:113), consisting of a third person pronoun (T204, T11, or T1), a hand (T217), and either the phonetic, T25:501 *ca-b(a)*, or logographic, T526 *cab*, glyph for "earth." This metaphor still survives in modern Chol in several forms, all of which are various ways of expressing "to experience the world for the first time." The subject of #1 is written with a title glyph (T74:565:178.117) that can occur in the name phrases of all three gods of the Palenque Triad. The identification of GI as the proper Triad member in this passage can be confirmed by the text from the alfarda of the TC (#2), where GI is named with the expected head glyph (T1011). GII is the subject of #3, and although the personal name of the subject of the alfarda text from the TS is missing, it was clearly GIII. In the main text, GIII is named as the subject of a "birth" glyph that took place on the same date, and in that record, "birth" is recorded with the standard "birth frog" (T741).

Chart 32   151

2. Pal TC   1.18. 5. 3. 2   GI   9.13. 0. 0. 0
    Alf A2

3. Pal TFC   1.18. 5. 4. 0   GII   9.13. 0. 0. 0
    Alf A2

4. Pal TS   1.18. 5. 3. 6   GIII   9.13. 0. 0. 0
    Alf A2

5. Tik   no date   Ruler A   9.15. 0. 0. 0
    MT 38a-b

    See 21:11.

6. Pal Slav   no date   Chan-   9.15. 0. 0. 0
    B2   Bahlum II

The date of this event is not recorded by LC or CR, but rather by an
unusual phrase recording the three katun endings between the accession of
Pacal II on 5 Lamat 1 Mol and this event, the "seating" of Chan-Bahlum.
The element prefixed to the "seating" glyph is the locative preposition
ti, which here contains T180 *ah* as an infix, functioning perhaps as a
phonetic complement specifying the locative *ta*. The presence of the tun
glyph (T528.166) seem incorrect, unless the reference of *tun* is intended
to be to a "stone" bench throne. The tun glyph is similarly infixed into
the period ending "seating" glyph in the preceding block.

7. Pal Slav   no date   Kan-Xul II 9.15. 0. 0. 0
    C9a

One katun ending is recorded as having occurred between this "seating"
and the previous one of Chan-Bahlum. The subject is clearly named as Kan-
Xul II, but there is only one seating glyph, not two, as in the previous
clause (#6). This one glyph should refer, therefore, both to the "seating" of the tun and to the "seating" of Kan-Xul.

8. Pal 96G   9.13.10. 6. 8   deleted   9.17.15. 0. 0
    D5   (Kan-Xul II)

This "seating" expression occurs as the second half of a couplet recording the accession of Kan-Xul II. The "seating" glyph is shown resting on
a throne pillow covered with a jaguar pelt. It is followed by a possible
title glyph (T58.nn:528.4), which also appears in parallel passage recording the accessions of Chaacal III and Kuk. It is possible that this

title names the agent (Kan-Xul) by title, or it may qualify the "seating" event in some way. If the latter is the correct interpretation, the subject of this second clause of the couplet is deleted.

9.   Pal 96G   9.16.13. 0. 7   deleted   9.17.15. 0. 0
      G4

This example records the same "seating" expression as #8. The same title follows in the next block, but this expression restates the accession of Kuk. The prefixed head is another version of the third person pronoun of Set A.

10.   Yax L46   no date   Knot-Eye-   9.15. 0. 0. 0
      F8   Jaguar

On both Lintels 46 and 45, this glyph appears following the clause recording a capture by the contemporary ruler, Shield-Jaguar. The purpose of this event phrase and the clause in which it is found seems to be to relate this Shield-Jaguar "capture" to earlier ones, which are recorded not only on these two lintels, but on the steps below them. The glyphs following this verb on Lintel 45 are now missing, but on Lintel 46, it is followed by Knot-Eye-Jaguar (who is named as the agent of a "capture" in the text of the step below this lintel); by a "capture" glyph; and by the name glyph appearing as the patient of the "capture" event in the text of the step. The syntactical order of this clause appear to be VSVO or VSVO [subject deleted].

11.   Yax L45   no date   missing   9.15. 0. 0. 0
      C6

12.   Pal TIw   no date   deleted   9.12.15. 0. 0
      S12a   (Pacal II)

This is the last event recorded on the panels of the Temple of Inscriptions. It is followed by *u cim-il* "his death" and the name phrase of Pacal II.

13.   Pal TC   13. 0. 1. 9. 2   deleted   9.13. 0. 0. 0
      C12-C13   (GI the First)

The event phrase is the third part of a verbal triplet recording a mythological event 1.9.2 after 4 Ahau 8 Cumku. The deity who has been identified by Lounsbury (1980:114) as the father of the Palenque Triad (GI the First) is recorded as the agent of this event in its first two

Chart 32   153

occurrences and he is implied here. See 17:1 and 20:1 for the first two
verbs in this series.

| 14. | Yax L8 B1 | no date | Ahpo-Muluc | Kan-Tah | 9.16. 5. 0. 0 |

In a presentation given at the Taller Maya IV in 1979, Marshall Durbin
identified this clause as a transitive construction. Since the captive's
name is incised on his leg, the glyph naming him can be identified in the
adjacent text as immediately following the verb. If this expression
records a noun phrase, such as "the captive of . . ." or the "captor of
. . .," the referent of the possessed noun should precede the noun and
the antecedent of the pronoun should follow it. However, the name phrase
of both the captive and the captor follow this glyph in a sequence which
must be identified as VOS. Durbin further proposed that other "captor"
statements found within the name phrases of Classic rulers are embedded
transitive constructions. I am not full convinced of his identification
of embedded transitive constructions in name phrases, but his argument on
the syntactical order of this Lintel 8 text seems to be correct.

| 15. | Yax 5 B2 | 9.18. 6. 5.11 | | Shield- Jaguar II | 9.18.10. 0. 0 |

This glyph immediately follows a *chucah* "capture" verb and precedes two
glyphs that are very difficult to see in published photographs. The
location of this glyph is unusual and can be explained in two ways. If
this "captor" glyph is a verb, the verbal components of this text occur
in the form of a couplet contrasting two forms of "capture." If the glyph
is identified as a possessed noun, the text would be paraphrased as
"Shield-Jaguar II captured the captor of someone."

| 16. | Pal OPT A1 | no date | Pacal II | Lady Zac-Kuk | 9.11. 0. 0. 0 |

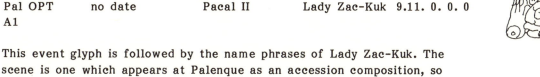

This event glyph is followed by the name phrases of Lady Zac-Kuk. The
scene is one which appears at Palenque as an accession composition, so
there is little doubt about the general meaning of the verb, but the
identification of the patient and agent is of the text is more difficult.
In this regard, it is helpful to know that at Palenque the Oval Palace
Tablet portrays the only accession in which all of the recorded participants were alive at the time of the event; in all others, the parents of
the incumbent ruler, who give objects of office as a testimony of his
legitimate position, are shown posthumously. And this is the only accession text at Palenque that names both a patient and an agent. Syntactically, the order--verb/Lady Zac-Kuk/Pacal--would identify Lady Zac-Kuk as
the patient and Pacal as the agent, but the texts of the Temple of
Inscriptions identify Lady Zac-Kuk as the mother of Pacal. She also

acceded to office shortly before his accession, and she lived through the
first twenty-five years of his reign. In addition, the scene clearly
shows her in the act of giving the drum-major headdress to Pacal, who
sits passively to receive it. Therefore, according to both the historical
background and the action as recorded pictorially, Lady Zac-Kuk acts upon
(crowns) her son; she must be the agent and he, the patient. The usual
syntactical order (VSO) may have resulted from the demand of this kind of
accession composition in which the principal secondary figure must be
positioned on the right side (or compositional left) of the main figure.
With this arrangement, the normal VOS word order would have placed Pacal's name next to Lady Zac-Kuk and and hers next to Pacal. I suggest
that the usual VSO order was used in order to insure that each name
phrase remained adjacent to its appropriate figure.

| 17. | Yax Str20
HS 126 | 9.18. 8.10.12 | | Shield-
Jaguar II | 9.18.10. 0. 0 | |

This glyph looks very much like a DNIG, but here it stands between the
CR date and Shield-Jaguar's name glyph.

| 18. | Cop Str11
Rev W1-X1 | 9.17. 0. 7. 0 | | New-Sky-at
Horizon | 9.17. 0. 0. 0 |  |

| CHART 33 | Affix T1 | in Cluster 1.*.∅ | | with Main Sign T713 or T670 |

#	LOCATION	DATE (EVENT)	PATIENT	AGENT	DEDICATION	
1.	Pal TIm F4-E5	9.11. 0. 0. 0	????	Pal Triad	9.12.15. 0. 0	

This expression seems to record some activity of the gods of the Palenque
Triad that occurred in association with the end of Katun 11, the second
katun ending of the reign of Pacal II. The signs (T741.23) appearing in the T713 hand can be
shown by a comparison of this example to #2 to be a substitute for T1030o, a title which can
stand for ahau. The second glyph of the phrase is very rare and as a result not understood.
It may record an object or it may be a component of the verbal phrase. See 129:2 for the
third example of this event phrase.

| 2. | Pal TIw
B3-A4 | 9.12. 0. 0. 0 | ???? | Pal Triad | 9.12.15. 0. 0 | |

This expression is parallel to #1, but records activity of the Triad in
association with the end of Katun 12, the third katun of Pacal's reign.
Neither #1 nor #2 contains a CR date within the clause, but both are part

Chart 33 155

of the katun histories of their appropriate katuns.

3. Pal TC   13. 0. 0. 0. 0   ????   deleted   9.13. 0. 0. 0
    C3   (GI the First)

This glyph records an event that occurred on 4 Ahau 8 Cumku. It is linked
by DN to a clause recording a birth, the subject (GI the First) of which
has been deleted. Lounsbury (1980) assumed that this event is related to
similar ones recorded on the Palace Tablet (92:6) and the jambs from
Temple 18 (59:8). In his interpretation, the subject of this verb, like
the birth, been deleted, and both clauses are gapped to the succeeding
one in which GI the First is subject. However, it is also possible that
this glyph refers to some era event, in which case there is no agent.

4. Pal T18   missing   missing   9.14.15. 0. 0
    Stc 435

This stucco glyph appears to combine two different expressions for accession found at Palenque. A very similar expression is found on the Palace
Tablet (O10-P10), but in that example the two components occupy different
glyph blocks and the "elbow" contains the T1016 God C head. In the Temple
18 example, the two components (T522:712:24 and T205.187) are conflated.
T24 does function as a verbal suffix in other contexts, but since it is
adjoined only to T713 and not to the entire glyph block, I am classifying
the entire block as one with no suffixing.

5. PN 3   9.13.19.13. 1   Lady Ahau-   9.14. 0. 0. 0
    E3   Katun

6. Quir Ew   9.14.13. 4.17   Two-Legged-   9.17. 0. 0. 0
    A8   Sky

This "God K-in-hand" event occurred on the date recorded as Two-Legged-
Sky's accession in other Quirigua texts.

7. Cop AltQ   9.17. 5. 3. 4   deleted   9.17. 5. 0. 0
    F6   (New-Sky-
                                               at-Horizon)

This phrase closes the text and has no recorded agent. However, New-Sky-
at-Horizon is the protagonist of this monument and the subject of all
preceding events; he is to be understood as the subject of this verb as
well. Compare the second glyph to #1 and #2.

8. Seib 9   10. 1. 0. 0. 0   Ah Bolon-Tun 10. 1. 0. 0. 0
    C2

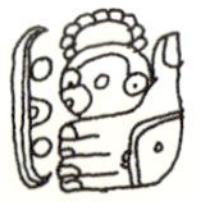

This event follows a period ending phrase without the intervention of an
additional CR date. The protagonist is shown holding a double-headed bar
in the form of the Celestial Monster.

9. CItz   none   missing   Late Classic
    Jade

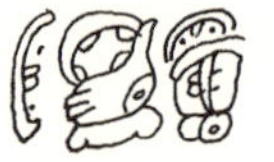

See Proskouriakoff 1974:118 and Fig. b.

10. Bon 2   9.17.18.15.18   Lady Cauac-   9.18. 0. 0. 0
    E6   Skull

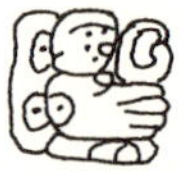

This is the second part of a verbal expression recording a blood-letting
event. See 3:14 and 76:3.

CHART 34   Affix T1   in Cluster 1.*.∅   with Main Sign T501:102

This verb appears to be substitutable with T757 in contexts where both can be identified as
general verbs without reference to a specific action. Many of these examples appear to function as
general verbs, while others occur in contexts which favor a function as expressions of "agency."

#	LOCATION	DATE (EVENT)	PATIENT	AGENT	DEDICATION

1. Coll 3   ?? Ahau 3 Xul   eroded   Late Classic
    pA4

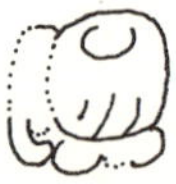

The coefficient for the Ahau is 11, 13, or 18, none of which is found
with 3 Xul on a seventh tun ending during the Late Classic period. The
"seventh tun" notation must then refer to some sort of anniversary celebration or to an ancient date, such as 8.10.7.0.0 13 Ahau 3 Xul.

2. Yax Str44   9.12. 8.14. 1   Ah Ahaual   Shield-Jaguar 9.15. 0. 0. 0
    Ctr Up
    A3-B3a

This phrase is one of the most unusual examples of a capture expression
known in the Classic inscriptions. Most capture expressions are recorded
in the following syntactical patterns: (1) capture-captive; (2) capture-
captive-captor; or (3) capture-captive-agency-captor. Examples of the
proposed agency expressions are ##12-17; in all of those examples,
T1.501:102 stands between the name phrase of the captive and the captor

Chart 34   157

where one expects an agency expression in association with a passive construction. In this passage, however, the T1.501:102 glyph immediately follows the "capture" verb, and the name of the captive (Ah Ahaual) is recorded with a locative preposition (*ti*) as prefix.

3.   Tik   no date   Ruler A   9.15. 0. 0. 0
     MT51a-b

The function of T1.501:102 in these texts on MT 51a and b seems to parallel that in ##12-17. Each text begins with a "canoe" verb (21:12) and its subject, GI of the Palenque Triad. T1.501:102 follows the name of GI and precedes the name phrase of Ruler A. This verb may be an expression of agency or a second verb delineating the activity of Ruler A.

4.   Tik   no date   Ruler A   9.15. 0. 0. 0
     MT43-44

5.   Tik   no date   Personage 1   9.15. 0. 0. 0
     MT42a-b
     A2-A4

The texts from MT 42a and b (##5-8) are composed of a list of names, each of which is introduced by T1.501:102. This use of T501:102 seems parallel to those inscriptions in which names are preceded by T1.757 without reference to specific actions. See Chart 36.

6.   Tik   no date   Personage 2   9.15. 0. 0. 0
     MT42a-b
     A5-A7

7.   Tik   no date   Personage 3   9.15. 0. 0. 0
     MT42a-b
     A8-A10

8.   Tik   no date   Lord of   9.15. 0. 0. 0
     MT42a-b   Palenque (?)
     A11-A12

9.   Tik   no date   Lord of   9.15. 0. 0. 0
     MT40   Tikal
     A12-A15

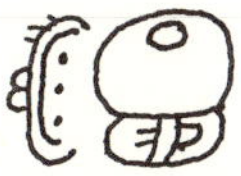

10. Tik   no date   Lord of   9.15. 0. 0. 0
     MT 181   Tikal

11. Tik   no date   Ah Chac   9.15. 0. 0. 0
     MT 180

The texts of MT180 were found in Burial 196 along with a cylindrical vase
displaying the same name glyph as the subject of this text. He may well
be the occupant of the tomb.

12. Yax 15   9.12. 8.14. 1   Ah Ahaual   Shield-Jaguar 9.15. 0. 0. 0
     A3

The remaining six examples on this chart appear to function as agency
expressions in "capture" contexts. A summary of the syntactical order is
as follows:

St 15	was captured	Ah Ahaual	T1.501:102	Shield-Jaguar I
St 19	was captured	Ah Ahaual	T1.501:102	Shield-Jaguar I
L 45	was captured	Ah Ahaual	T1.501:102	Shield-Jaguar I
L 46	was captured	Ah Kan	T204:501:102	Shield-Jaguar I
L 41	was captured	Jeweled-Skull	T1.501:102	Bird-Jaguar III
L 8	was captured	Jeweled-Skull	T1.501:102	Bird-Jaguar III

The name phrase of the captive on Lintel 45 is missing, but since the
date of his capture corresponds to that on Stela 15, the captive can be
securely identified as Ah Ahaual. In addition his name phrase is found
elsewhere on Lintel 45.

13. Yax 19   9.12. 8.14. 0   Ah Ahaual   Shield-Jaguar 9.15. 0. 0. 0?
     A8   or Death

14. Yax L45   9.12. 8.14.1   [Ah Ahaual] Shield-Jaguar 9.15. 0. 0. 0?
     A2b

15. Yax L46   9.14. 1.17.14   Ah Kan   Shield-Jaguar 9.15. 0. 0. 0?
     F5

16. Yax L41   9.16. 4. 1. 1   Jeweled-   Bird-Jaguar   9.16. 5. 0. 0
     C3   Skull

17. Yax L8   9.16. 4. 1. 1   Jeweled-   Bird-Jaguar   9.16. 5. 0. 0
     E1   Skull

Chart 35   159

CHART 35   Affix T1   in Cluster 1.*.Ø   with Main Sign T501:102 or T757

These examples utilize either T501:102 or T1.757 as auxiliary verbs in related expression concerning period endings and/or blood-letting.

#	LOCATION	DATE (EVENT)	PATIENT	AGENT	DEDICATION	
1.	Cop 2 D1-D2a	9.10.15. 0. 0		Bat-Uinal	9.12. 0. 0. 0	

This expression is possibly the second half of a couplet construction recording a period ending.

2.	Cop I C5	no date		Copan EG	9.12. 5. 0. 0	

This expression is not associated with a CR date, but, like #1, it may be the second half of a period ending couplet, or it may record a blood-letting rite as do #4 and #5.

3.	Nar 30 A4-A5	9.14. 3. 0. 0		Smoking-Squirrel	9.14. 3. 0. 0	

4.	Pal Ora A1-B1	no date		Chaacal III	9.15. 0. 0. 0	

This phrase is the verbal component in a passage marked as information spoken by the figure on the Orator. It is parallel to #5 and to a similar passage on Lintel 3 of Temple 1 at Tikal (see 39:7). All three of these expressions record some sort of blood-letting rite. The initial glyph is the T501 auxiliary verb, but here as in some other examples it occurs without T102 *al* (see 38:23-24, 28 and 132:8). In this example, it is followed by the head variant of T580 (or T513), another auxiliary verb. See the second glyph in 76:3 for another example of the T580 head variant.

5.	Yax 18 A9-A11	9.14.15.17.11		Shield-Jaguar by title	9.15. 0. 0. 0	

This phrase occurs following a "capture" verb and the name of the captive, Ah Chuen. T712, the second component, can be identified as a blood-letting lancet, and this event is surely blood-letting, possibly executed upon the captive. This particular construction appears to be an auxiliary verb construction in which T712 and akbal are verbal nouns; both glyphs is preceded by a locative sign—T89 *tu* and T59 *ti*, respectively. Shield-

Jaguar is named as the agent of this blood-letting event, and if the agent is deleted from the initial "capture" clause, he is named as the subject of that event as well. His personal name does not appear in the name phrase, but several of the titles are found in his name phrase in other texts. See 74:7.

6. Tik CAlt1   9.15.17. 0. 4   7-Gourd   9.16. 0. 0. 0
    A1-A2

This verbal phrase is parallel to the blood-letting expression under #5, but it does not include the akbal element. The scene shows a bound sacrificial victim.

7. Nar 13   9.17.10. 0. 0   Ruler IIIa   9.17.10. 0. 0
    A5-A7

This expression is parallel to the period ending phrase of #1, #3?, and #8. The kin and akbal elements appear as visual motifs within the scene on Naranjo Stela 19. David Stuart (personal communication, 1981) has accumulated evidence that the kin and akbal signs when they appear in these special cartouches, and especially with a *na* sign attached to kin and a *ti* sign to akbal, refer to the Old Jaguar God and the Old Stingray God who appear as paddlers in the canoe scenes of Tikal Burial 116. If his analysis is correct, then the T757 verbs would function in these instances as general verbs, rather than as auxiliaries, and the kin and akbal glyphs would refer to the agents of the verb. See 129:8,11 for parallel examples utilizing a different verbal glyph.

8. Nar 19   9.17.10. 0. 0   none   9.17.10. 0. 0
    A8-A10

The latter two glyphs appear as part of the scene.

CHART 36   Affix T1   in Cluster 1.*.Ø   with Main Sign T757 or T788

In all these examples, T757 or its Early Classic equivalent T788 functions as a general verb introducing name phrases in many different contexts. This verb cannot refer to the specific activity in an accompanying scene. These listed examples are only those found on Classic monuments, but it should be noted that during the Early and Late Classic periods, this glyph was used prominently as a general verb and introductory glyph to name phrases in text on ceramic vessels.

#	LOCATION	DATE (EVENT)	PATIENT	AGENT	DEDICATION	
1.	Uax Mural	no date		see note	Early Classic	

Chart 36 161

All of the examples of T1.60:788 as a nominal introducing glyph in the Uaxactun murals are included under this one entry because drawings available to me are not accurate enough to risk identifying personal name glyphs. See Thompson (1962:375) for a full listing of each individual occurrence. Each of the texts in which this general verb is found stands next to one of the individual figures as a naming phrase. T1.60:788 also functions as the verb in the longer featured text, but these examples are listed as 37:1-3.

2.	Car 14 G1	no date	eroded	9. 6. 0. 0. 0	

This example occurs in a text accompanying a small seated figure isolated from the main composition. Two glyphs follow the general verb, but the personal name (the second glyph is the text) is too badly damaged to be read.

3.	Tik 7 B2	9. 3. 0. 0. 0	Jaguar-Paw-Skull I	9. 3. 0. 0. 0	
4.	Bon B E1	no date	Kan-Chuen	9. 4.10. 0. 0	

The examples under #4 and #5 begin the secondary texts located in front of each seated figure. The names following each example appear in the main text as the subjects of an event which occurred on 9.4.8.14.9.

5.	Bon B F1	no date	Fish-Fin of Bonampak	9. 4.10. 0. 0	
6.	Cop P E5	no date	Serpent-God C	9. 9.10. 0. 0	

The glyph immediately following this example is completely destroyed. Since no personal name is recognizable in the series of titles following the eroded block, it may have recorded the personal name of the agent. However, it is also possible that a verbal complement occurred in this position.

7.	Bon C B1	no date	Bolon-Yocte-Chul	9.13.15. 0. 0 

This example occurs in a secondary text located adjacent to the head of the protagonist and isolated from the main text. The Chul name (T116.515

[568]) occurs throughout the main text, but the Bolon-Yocte glyph (TIX.765:87.35) only appears in this text. It is possible, therefore, that Bolon-Yocte is not a title as I am classifying it, but rather a part of the verbal phrase.

8.   Tik 5   9.15.13. 0. 0   Ruler B   9.15.15. 0. 0
     D5

This Tikal example follows a period ending date which has no other period ending notation; T1.60:757 must function as the verbal expression for that date.

9.   Tik Alt8   no date   7-Gourd   9.16. 0. 0. 0
     A1

This example appears above a bound sacrificial victim whose name includes many of the elements found in the name of the victim on Column Altar 1 (see 35:6). The last glyph in the name includes a numerical coefficient 7 in both texts. Although the first glyph of the name phrase is almost entirely destroyed on Column Altar 1, the prefix in both texts seems to be the same. Details in the remaining glyphs are similar enough to risk identifying them as the same. I am tentatively calling this captive 7-Gourd because of the similarity of the last glyph on Column Altar 1 to a gourd (or jaguar-caller) glyph in the text of the Hieroglyphic Stairs at Dos Pilas (see 82:23).

Column Altar 1   Altar 8   Dos Pilas HS

10. PN L12   no date   Personage 1   9. 4. 5. 0. 0
     Q1

The verb in this clause and those in #11 and #12 introduce the name phrases of three kneeling figures in the left half of the scene. The subject of #12 is Knot-Eye-Jaguar of Yaxchilan, suggesting that all three persons were foreign visitors.

11. PN L12   no date   Personage 2   9. 4. 5. 0. 0
     S1

12. PN L12   no date   Knot-Eye-   9. 4. 5. 0. 0
     U1   Jaguar of
                                                      Yaxchilan

Chart 37   163

13. LMar 2   no date   Chuen-Ah Kan 9.18. 0. 0. 0
     A1

14. Car F56   missing   missing   ????
     pB1

This glyph is from a small fragment with only two partial glyphs on it. It follows a tun sign (T528.116), suggesting that it is the first glyph following a period ending notation, but this speculation must remain very tentative. The animal head has features of T757, including a lolling tongue and short ear, but the ear is clearly marked with the "etz'nab" lines characteristic of T759. The suffix appears to be T25 *ca*. This verb may be the auxiliary verb under discussion, or it may be related to the one other occurrence in the Classic inscriptions of T759 as a verb (see 83:1).

15. DPil 17   9.12.10. 0. 0   none   9.12.10. 0. 0
     A1

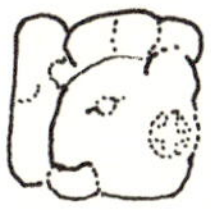

This verb is followed by the day sign and the verb *malah* (T510H:178.181). See 77:3.

16. Nar 19   9.17. 5. 8.12   Ruler IIIb   9.17.10. 0. 0
     C4

Since this general verb is not followed by a phrase specifying the particular event, and since the date is different than the initial one (a PE), it is not possible to determine which of these two dates corresponds to the scene shown.

CHART 37   Affix T1   in Cluster 1.*.∅   with Main Sign T757 or T788

In all these examples, T757 functions as an auxiliary verb with the meaning of the particular event specified by one or more complements. The complements may occur with or without inflectional affixes, and no *ti* sign occurs between the auxiliary verb and its complements

#	LOCATION	DATE (EVENT)	PATIENT	AGENT	DEDICATION	
1.	Uax mural A1-A4	no date	????	Mah Kina Rodent	Early Classic	

This verbal phrase occurs in the main text of the Uaxactun mural, but because of the poor reproductions of this mural, glyph identifications posited here must be considered tentative. The glyph immediately follow-

ing T1.788 seems to be the aged human head found on Tikal Stela 31 (#6).
The glyph at B2 appears to have *ti* as a prefix, suggesting that it is
part of the verb. The glyphs from A3–A8 seem to name the agent with the
Early Classic version of the *mah kina* title (T1010b.365.74) occurring at
A8, followed by three glyphs. A9 is the T788 head with an object in its
mouth. The same glyph occurs in the second clause in the location where a
subject is expected.

2.   Uax mural   no date   Rodent   Early Classic
       C1–C2

The last verbal phrase in the main text occurs at C1–C2 followed by the
same turtle head as that recording the agent of the initial clause.

3.   Cop AltX   9. 8.12. 7.18   deleted   9. 8.15. 0. 0
       H1–G2

4.   Tik 4   8.17. 2.16.17   Curl-Snout   8.17. 5. 0. 0
       C4–B5

This phrase records the accession of Curl-Snout with the T684 "inaugural"
expression functioning as the complement of the T788 auxiliary verb. The
ti locative (T747b) infixed into the bundle glyph (T684) should refer to
the glyph of office following the bundle, rather than to the auxiliary
verb preceding it. T684 carries the verbal suffix T181, which does not
generally occur with complements in auxiliary verb + complement constructions. See #20 for a parallel example using an alternative expression for
accession.

5.   Tik 31   no date   Curl-Snout   9. 0.10. 0. 0
       I1–J1

The verbal complement found at J1 is the head of an aged god, a glyph
prominent in auxiliary verb + complement constructions in Early Classic
texts, especially those found in texts on pottery. The aged head is
followed by a katun glyph and the T168:518 title. The *po* section of the
ahpo title seems to be conflated with the *ti* sign, suggesting that these
two glyphs may have read as "a katun of the T518 title." If this identification of the conflation is correct, the "katun of title" expression
may function as part of the verbal phrase or as the object.

6.   Tik 31   no date   Curl-Snout   9. 0.10. 0. 0
       M1–N1

Curl-Snout's name phrase immediately follows the T1.788 + "aged head"

Chart 37   165

construction on this side of Stela 31. The meaning of the "aged head" is not known.

7.   Tik 13   no date   Kan-Chitam   9. 2. 0. 0. 0?
     B1-B2

8.   Tik 9   9. 2.19.12.19?   Kan-Chitam   9. 3. 0. 0. 0?
     B1-B2

The date of Tikal Stela 9 is problematic. The period ending notation which begins the text appears to have the numerical coefficient 2 in front of the katun glyph and the tzolkin date 4 Ahau, correct for 9.2.0.0.0. However, this period ending notation is followed by a DN of 5.5 which is marked as a "count" from a date (with a coefficient of 1) earlier than the katun ending. Arithmetically, the subtraction of 5.5 from 9.2.0.0.0 yields the CR date 3 Men 13 Muan, but the date in the text is 1 Men. However, if 5.5 is subtracted from 9.3.0.0.0, the resulting CR is 1 Men 13 Yax, a date that matches the text. If the katun intended on Stela 9 is 9.3.0.0.0, the two central dots of the Ahau coefficient must be considered to be an eroded filler, and the coefficient of the katun glyph must be identified as an error. I have listed the 9.3.0.0.0 date in this chart, but I do not eliminate the possibility that 9.2.0.0.0 is the correct PE.

9.   Tik 15   9. 3. 0. 0. 0   Jaguar-Paw-   9. 3. 0. 0. 0
     B2-B5   Skull I

The Tikal EG and Jaguar-Paw-Skull I immediately follow the two complements included in the verbal phrase, but either or both of these glyphs may be part of the name phrase of the agent, rather than part of the verb. If so, this example of T1.788 is comparable to the general verb of Tikal Stela 5 (see 36:8).

10.   Tik 8   9. 3. 2. 0. 0   Bird-Claw   9. 3. 2. 0. 0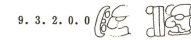
     A1-A2

This verbal phrase is followed by the Jaguar God of the Underworld (GIII) and two other glyphs which seem to record titles. Since GIII appears consistently as a part of Early Classic Tikal name phrases, I am assuming that these titles refer to the human protagonist of the stela named at B3-B8. An alternative interpretation would identify GIII as the supernatural agent of the verb.

11.   Xul 19   no date   local ruler   Early Classic
     A1-B1

No date survives on this Early Classic monument from Xultun. The T1.757 +
complement phrase is found in a secondary text (which never included a
date) on the front of the monument near the head of the protagonist. The
name of the subject is destroyed, but the scene show a standing ruler
holding an anthropomorphic jaguar (GIII) manikin.

12.   Xul 9   no date   Rabbit   9.??.10.??.??
      E1-E2

Not much of the Initial Series date of this stela survives, but the style
is Late Classic. The fish head (T205) preceding T60:757 is equivalent to
T1. This secondary text occurs (without a date) in front of the headdress
of the ruler, who is holding a GIII scepter. This ruler is named as the
subject of the verbal phrase by a T1.757 or T1.758 glyph.

13.   Tik   9.12.18. 9.16   Shield-Yax-   9.15. 0. 0. 0
      MT35   Animal-Head

The date of this text is recorded as 4 Cib 14 Ceh, and its LC position
may be one CR later than listed. The animal head does not have an *u*
prefix or the kan-cross characteristic of the T757 verb, but I am tentatively assuming that this verbal phrase is in the same category as other
auxiliary + complement constructions. The complement is recorded with the
verbal suffix T4 postposed to the main sign.

14.   Tik   9.12.14. 3. 11   Chan   9.15. 0. 0. 0
      MT31

This verbal phrase is badly damaged, but enough detail remains to suggest
that it was the same as #13. The LC position of the date (9 Cimi 9 Zac)
may be one CR later.

15.   Tik   9.12.17. 3. 7   Chan   9.15. 0. 0. 0
      MT34

Like #14, this verbal phrase is badly eroded, but it appears to be the
same as that on MT 35 (#13). The date may be one CR later, and the
subject of this verb and #14 are the same person.

16.   Xul 15   no date   eroded   9.14. 0. 0. 0
      C1-D1

17.   Xul 16   no date   eroded   Late Classic
      A1-B1

Chart 37 167

18. DPil 17   9.12.10. 0. 0   Flint-Sky-   9.12.10. 0. 0
    C1-D1   God K

The date of the verbal phrase is recorded only as 9 Ahau.

19. ASac 12   no date   Parrot-Ahau   9. 4.10. 0. 0
    A1-A2

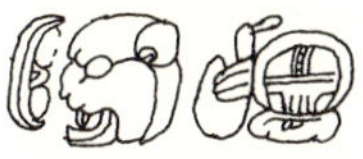

20. LMar 3   9.17.18. 6.19   local ruler   9.18. 5. 0. 0
    A2-A3

This accession expression is equivalent in structure to that on Tikal
Stela 4 (see #4), except that whereas the T684 "inaugural" expression is
used on Stela 4, this La Mar example utilizes the T713/757 "accession"
phrase as the complement. In both examples, the verbal affix T181 is
postfixed to the verbal component of the "accession" expression.

21. Coll 27   9.16.15.18. 9   Ek-Chaan   Bird-   9.17. 0. 0. 0
    C1-D1   Jaguar III

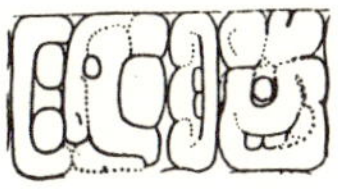

The patient of this verb also is recorded on the rear of Yaxchilan Stela
10. The complement is a verb associated with the sacrifice of captives
and with blood-letting rites conducted by rulers and members of their
families (see Chart 95).

22. NimP 15   9.14.10. 0. 0   18-Rabbit   9.14.10. 0. 0
    G1-H1

23. Nar 19   none or eroded   Lady Scroll   9.17.10. 0. 0
    I1-J1

This verbal phrase is on the rear of Stela 19 and presumably refers to
the blood-letting ceremony shown on that side. The upper part of the
scene includes a now-eroded date and clause, but the event should have
occurred close to the featured date on the front, 9.17.10. 0. 0. The
name glyphs following the verb appear to be the T1000a female head and
the T578 scroll.

24. RAm Alt1   9.10.10. 2.16   Rodent-Bone- 9.11. 0. 0. 0?
    M2-P2   Turtle

25. LHig   9.17.10. 0. 0   missing   9.17.10. 0. 0
    D8-D9

This phrase records the T712 blood-letting expression either as a verb or or in a parentage statement.

26. Cop AltY   9. 7. 1. 2. 6   local ruler   9. 7. 5. 0. 0
     E2-F2

CHART 38   Affix T1   in Cluster 1.*.∅   with Main Sign T501 or T757

All of these examples are auxiliary verb + *ti* (or an equivalent) + verbal noun constructions.

#	LOCATION	DATE (EVENT)	PATIENT	AGENT	DEDICATION
1.	PN L12 V1-V2	no date		eroded	9. 4. 5. 0. 0 

This verb occurs in a secondary text immediately behind the head of the protagonist in the right side of the scene. The verbal noun is the T168:518 title that appears prominently in Classic royal name phrases and as a verb for accession on the west panel of the Temple of Inscriptions at Palenque (see 113:1-2). "Accession" cannot be assumed in this case, however, since the same verb appears as some nonaccession event that occurred to Smoking-Squirrel of Naranjo at age 5 (see 128:3). T168:518 must represent some title which could be assumed at different times in the lives of rulers and which was not directly linked to the taking of the throne as ruler. It should be noted that the composition and iconographic program of Lintel 12 are linked to those of Lintels 2 and 4 at Piedras Negras.

2. Coll 4   9.11.10. 0. 0   Zac-Balam   9.11.10. 0. 0
    A3

The verbal noun in this phrase is the "scattering" expression associated with period ending rites. This phrase occurs on Site Q Panel 5.

3. Xul 5   no date   Rabbit   9.12. 0. 0. 0
    E1-E2

This verbal phrase is located on the front of Stela 5, the scene of which show a standing ruler holding manikin scepters of GI and GIII of the Palenque Triad.

4. Pal TFC   no date   Chan-Bahlum   9.13. 0. 0. 0
    G1-G2   (by title)

Chart 38   169

Although no date occurs with this verbal expression, it can be associated with the heir-designation event (on 9.10.8.9.3 9 Akbal 6 Xul) recorded on all the main tablets of the Group of the Cross. The locative (T565) + verbal noun following the auxiliary verb is equivalent to the prepositional phrase that records the office of heir-designate at Q3 and Q16 on the TS. Chan-Bahlum is recorded as the agent by a series of titles that also occur in his name phrase in the secondary text of the TS (I1-K3). See 12:3; 21:5-6,17-18; 88:11; and 113:3.

5.	Nar 24 A3-A5	9.13. 7. 3. 8	Lady 6-Sky of Tikal	9.13.10. 0. 0	

The two glyphs following the auxiliary verb do not occur as independent verbs in other contexts; rather they appear with wide distribution as titles in female name phrases. For this reason, it is highly possible that this title is a part of a preposition + noun phrase, rather than the auxiliary verb + *ti* + verbal noun constructions treated under this category. In either case, the most likely interpretation of the verbal expression is that Lady 6-Sky took the T1001 title on this occasion.

6.	PN 1 G10-G11	9.13.14.13. 1	Lady Ahpo-Katun	9.13.15. 0. 0	

This event occurred on the occasion of Ruler 3's one-katun anniversary of accession.

7.	Nar 2 A1-A2	no date	Smoking-Squirrel	9.14. 2. 0. 0	

8.	Yax L42 C1-B2	9.16. 1. 2. 0	Bird-Jaguar	9.16. 5. 0. 0	

This expression is the first half of a verbal couplet which accompanies a scene showing Bird-Jaguar holding a God K scepter. See 18:3 for the second half of the couplet.

9.	Yax L1 B2-C1a	9.16. 1. 0. 0	Bird-Jaguar	9.16. 6. 0. 0	

This expression also accompanies a scene of Bird-Jaguar holding a God K scepter, but the occasion is his accession, rather than the rite forty days later recorded on Lintel 42 (#8). The second half of this verbal couplet is listed as 18:5, and since it is different from the equivalent half of the couplet on Lintel 42, it may well record the specific ritual environment in which the scepter was displayed.

10. Yax L3   9.16. 5. 0. 0   Bird-Jaguar   9.16. 6. 0. 0
     D1b-C1a

This text accompanies the display of the God K scepter, but on the occasion of a hotun ending. The second half of the couplet, which is different from the equivalent passages on Lintels 42 and 1, is listed as 18:4.

11. Yax L2   9.16. 6. 0. 0   Shield-   9.16. 6. 0. 0
     F1-H1   Jaguar II

This verbal phrase accompanies a scene in which Shield-Jaguar II holds a bird scepter. The verbal expression accompanying Bird-Jaguar on this lintel (see 79:11) contains only the T516 auxiliary verb and the "cauac-bat" verbal noun. Since T516:103 appears in many contexts as an auxiliary verb (see Charts 18 and 79), it is possible to identify the "cauac-bat" glyph as that element specifically referring to the bird scepter. T1.60: 757 is the auxiliary verb to which have been added a second auxiliary verb in the form of a verbal noun and the verbal noun specifying the particular event. This same kind of construction can be seen on Lintel 33 (see #15).

12. Yax L13   no date   Lady Zero-   9.16. 5. 0. 0?
     C1-D1   Skull

The occasion for this event is the birth of Shield-Jaguar II, the son of Bird-Jaguar. The scene shows both protagonists involved in blood-letting and vision rites, both of which are associated with the "fish-in-hand" event. In this text, however, the "fish-in-hand" appears as a verbal noun.

13. Yax L13   no date   Bird-Jaguar   9.16. 5. 0. 0?
     E1-E2

This verbal expression introduces the text accompanying the figure of Bird-Jaguar. I cannot detect T59 or an equivalent sign, so it is possible that this expression is an auxiliary verb + complement phrase rather than an auxiliary verb + *ti* + verbal noun construction. The event is surely blood-letting and is related to similar expressions at Yaxchilan and Pomona. See #14, 21:20, 52:6-9, and 76:2.

14. Yax L1   no date   Lady Zero-   9.16. 6. 0. 0
     E1-F1   Skull

No date appears with this expression, but the event occurred on the occasion of the accession of Bird-Jaguar on 9.16.1.0.0. The agent of the verb, Lady Zero-Skull, is shown holding a bundle, but the "hun uinic" and "na chan" glyphs relate this verb to other blood-letting expressions at

Chart 38   **171**

Yaxchilan and Pomona (see #13, 21:20, 52:6-9, and 76:2). The association
of blood-letting with accession rites is supported by the occurrence of
the "fish-in-hand" event on the day of the accession of Shield-Jaguar
(see 46:3 and 72:6-7). The identification of this event phrase as blood-
letting and its occurrence as the verb with a figure holding the bundle
supports Merle Robertson's (n.d.) suggestion that these bundles held
blood-letting regalia.

15. Yax L33   9.16.16. 1. 6   Bird-Jaguar   9.17. 0. 0. 0
    C1-E1

A comparison of this verbal phrase to related one on Lintel 9 and Stela
11 (secondary text on the front) identifies the "moon-double-comb-sky"
glyph as the element referring to the cloth staff held by the protagonists on each of these monuments. The "double-comb" (T563) part of the
expression appears as the office in an accession expression on Lacanja
Lintel 1 and El Cayo Lintel 1 on which the rulers are shown holding the
same staff (see 71:12-13 and 100:7).

16. LAm 1   ???? 6 Zac   local ruler   Late Classic
    B1-A3

This verbal phrase is very badly eroded and available to me only in the
form of a reproduced rubbing. I assume that the eroded element in front
of the second glyph is some sign equivalent to T59.

17. Tik T4   9.15.15. 2. 3   ????   9.16. 0. 0. 0
    L3; E3

This event occurred on the three-tun anniversary of an event that took
place one day after a "star-shell" event. It is followed by no recognizable personal name from the Tikal dynastic lists and may have no subject
or a supernatural subject. The first glyph does not appear in other texts
as an auxiliary verb; it is possible, therefore, that this expression is
composed of a verb + prepositional phrase. This verb, however, appears to
be a version of the chuen glyph. Chuen can occur as part of a count
expression on Tikal Stela 31 and other monuments, and since other main
signs of "count" glyphs can function as auxiliary verbs, the chuen glyph
may have the same function here. This verbal phrase is followed by two
additional ones, the first of which has GVI (of the Palenque deity list)
as its agent, and the second, Ruler B. Each of these clauses is introduced by a *hel* "succession" glyph (T3:4:573a:178). The three clauses are
followed by another pair of clauses, again with GVI and then Ruler B
named as subjects. All five clauses appear to record events occurring on
the same day, and at least two of the verbal phrases have been associated
with anniversary events in other texts (T174:565.181 on Tikal Temple 1,

Lintel 3, C2; and T79:178.181 in the texts of the Group of the Cross at
Palenque). See 52:4, 79:7, 80:6, and 87:11.

18. Chk BCt   no date   Chaan-Ahau   9. 8. 0. 0. 0
     2ndy

This verbal phrase occurs in the interior scene of the ballcourt marker,
usually attributed to Chinkultic, but given the provenience of Colonia la
Esperanza by Thompson (1962:405). The figure is shown engaged in the
ballgame.

19. Bon T1   9.18. 0. 3. 4   eroded   9.18. 5. 0. 0
     Rm1
     S2-T2

The verbal noun that follows the now-eroded auxiliary verb occurs as the
main verb in an heir-designation expression at Naranjo(see 128:3). This
verbal phrase and date appear to correspond to the presentation of the
child in the upper register of this frieze. The personal name glyph of
the subject is damaged, but the name phrase includes a reference by title
to Shield-Jaguar II of Yaxchilan. Since the left-hand woman on Stela 2 is
named as Lady Yax-T'ul of Yaxchilan and is apparently the wife of Chaan-
Muan, it seems likely that the Shield-Jaguar reference functions to
highlight a kinship relationship between the Bonampak heir and the Yaxchilan ruler. Lounsbury (n.d.) has demonstrated that this date is five
uinals after the total eclipse recorded on Poco Uinic Stela 1 and that it
would have been a predicted eclipse station.

20. Bon T1   no date   Chaan-Muan   9.18. 5. 0. 0
     Rm2
     Text 32

This text is located above the right central figure of the upper register
of the judgment scene. Unfortunately, the verbal noun is too badly eroded
to identify the specific event.

21. Bon T1   no date   local person   9.18. 5. 0. 0
     Rm2
     Text 31

This text is located above the left central figure on the upper register
of the judgment scene, and again the verbal noun cannot be identified
because of erosion.

Chart 38 **173**

22. Bon T1   no date   local person   9.18. 5. 0. 0   
    Rm1
    Text 21

This text is located adjacent to the central figure of the dressing
scene.

23. Bon T1   no date   local person   9.18. 5. 0. 0
    Rm1
    Text 42

24. Cop T18   1 Cib 10 (missing)   missing   9.18.10. 0. 0
    Pier   (New-Sky-at-
    pC1-pD1   Horizon)

This verbal phrase occurs on a pier, and although the name of the agent
is missing it can be identified by comparison to other similar piers as
New-Sky-at-Horizon. The pier show a single standing figure dressed in
warrior regalia and holding a very unusual skull scepter.

25. Cop T18   no date   New-Sky-at-   9.18.10. 0. 0   
    pier   Horizon
    pA1-B1

The L-shape and damaged state of this text make it difficult to determine the reading order. Since the second glyph is the T516:103 auxiliary
verb, I am assuming that it is to be read in the second position, but the
lack of a *ti* prefix with the third glyph makes it possible that it is a
phonetic complement for the T1.60:501 auxiliary verb and, therefore,
should be read before the T516:103 verb. In this example, T501 substitutes for T757 as it does in other contexts, such as the 18-Rabbit/God K
name on Naranjo Stela 32.

26. Cop T18   no date   New-Sky-at-   9.18.10. 0. 0
    pier   Horizon
    pA1-pA2

27. Cop T18   no date   New-Sky-at-   9.18.10. 0. 0   
    Pier   Horizon
    pA1-pA3

28. Yax L32   9.13. 5.12.13   Shield-   9.17. 0. 0. 0   
    C1-E1   Jaguar I

See 48:2 and 79:4 for other occurrences of the same verb and date as
this lintel.

| 29. | Ixk 1
C1-C2 | 9.18. 0. 0. 0 | | Shell-Hand | 9.18. 0. 0. 0 | 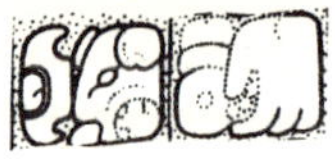 |

CHART 39   Affix T1   in Cluster 1.*.∅   with Main Sign T714

The "fish-in-hand" verbal expressions included here are associated with blood-letting rites.

#	LOCATION	DATE (EVENT)	PATIENT	AGENT	DEDICATION	
1.	CRic Jade	no date		Chaan	9. 0.11. 0. 0 or 9. 3.16. 0. 0	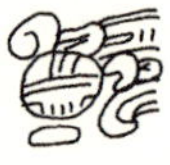

This verbal phrase is found on a reused jade published in Balser (1974: Plate XIV). The verb was damaged when the celt was cult in half during Pre-Columbian times so that its identification as T714 is not completely secure. It is followed by a "sky" glyph (T86:561:23?) and a glyph that looks suspiciously like the Early Classic version of the Tikal EG found on the Leiden Plaque and Stela 4. This clause is followed by a T684 "inaugural" statement, and the text closes with a PE on either 3 Ahau 17 Zac or 3 Ahau 17 Ch'en. The coefficient of the haab position is in error. The scene shows a standing figure remarkably similar in detail to those on the Leiden Plaque and Tikal Stela 31.

| 2. | PN L2
M1-N1 | no date | | Ruler 2
(by title) | 9.11.15. 0. 0 | 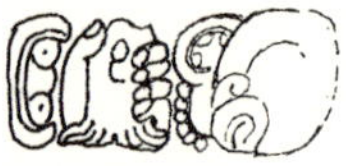 |

This expression occurs in the same passage as the IS date 9.11.6.2.1 and presumably on the same day. The "water-group" head (T41) included in the drawing occurs in other texts at Tikal and Palenque as part of the T714 compound, but if it is a part of this phrase, the agent is named only with the Piedras Negras EG and *ahau* (T1000a).

| 3. | Pal TFC
M10-M13 | 9.12.18. 5.19 | | deleted
(Chan-
Bahlum II) | 9.13. 0. 0. 0 | 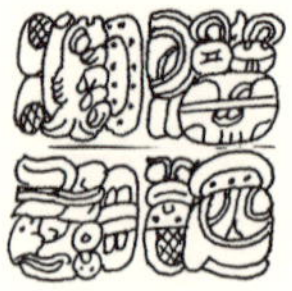 |

This expression is the first half of a verbal couplet and the third in a series of events celebrated on 9.12.18.5.16, 9.12.18.5.17, and 9.12.18. 5.19 in commemoration of the seventy-fifth tropical year anniversary of the accession of Pacal. Although the name of the agent is deleted here, it is clearly recorded in parallel clauses on the TC and TFC as Chan-Bahlum II. See 17:2-3, 23:3-6, 46:1-2, 56:5, and 59:6.

Chart 39   175

4. Pal TFC   2. 0. 0. 0. 0   ancestral   9.13. 0. 0. 0
   C9-D9   goddess

This "fish-in-hand" rite was conducted by the ancestral goddess who is
recorded as the mother of the gods of the Palenque Triad (Lounsbury 1980)
on the occasion of the end of the second baktun.

5. Yax L39   9.15.10. 0. 1   *u cab* Bird-Jaguar   9.16.15. 0. 0
   A2-B2

This event took place on the same CR date as the blood-letting rite shown
on Lintel 14 of which Lady Zero-Skull, the mother of Shield-Jaguar II,
was the agent. On Lintel 39, Bird-Jaguar is named as the agent, and the
scene portrays him in reclining position holding a double-headed serpent
bar. The God K head which consistently appears in "fish-in-hand" expressions at Yaxchilan, but not elsewhere, may not be part of the verbal
construction.

6. Yax L40   9.15.15. 6. 0   Lady Balam   9.16.15. 0. 0
   A2-B2

The name of the agent of this event is badly eroded, but I suspect it is
the same as the woman on Lintels 17 and 43.

7. Tik T1   9.13. 3. 9.18   Ruler A   9.15. 0. 0. 0
   L3; C3-C4

This expression is the second half of a verbal couplet of which Ruler A
is the subject (see 80:4). This blood-letting rite took place in celebration of the thirteenth-katun anniversary of the final date on Stela 31.
It is related structurally to similar expression on Yaxchilan Stela 18
and on the Orator from Palenque. See 35:4-5.

CHART 40   Affix T1   in Cluster 1.*.∅   with Miscellaneous Main Signs

#	LOCATION	DATE (EVENT)	PATIENT	AGENT	DEDICATION	
1.	Coll 8 pM1	9.10.10.15. 5		T'ul	9.11.10. 0. 0.	

AEI; this glyph may be a version of the T736 "death" event. See 24:3-9.

| 2. | Pal T18 Stc 437 | missing | | missing | 9.14.15. 0. 0 | |

The context of this glyph cannot be reconstructed, but its resemblance to a verb recording a posthumous event on Tonina M69 suggests that it functioned as a verb in the Temple 18 text. See 27:6.

| 3. | CRic Jade | no date | | missing | Early Classic | |

This fragmentary text is drawn after Balser (1974:Plate XV). The two glyphs are located in a circular cartouche on the upper half of a reused jade; presumably the agent of the verb was originally recorded on the missing lower half.

| 4. | Pal T18 Stc 444 | missing | | missing | 9.14.15. 0. 0 | |

| 5. | Nar 29 I1-H3 | 9.12.10. 9.12 | | Lady 6-Sky of Tikal | 9.14. 3. 0. 0 | |

The boundary of this verbal phrase is not clear from the context, so I have included all glyphs which precede the name phrase of the subject.

| 6. | Jon Pan A1-B2 | no date | | Manik | 9.15. 0. 0. 0? | |

The text on this panel is not complete, but from other fragments newly recognized as belonging to this panel, the general theme of the scene can now be identified as a "Tlaloc" complex associated with blood-letting rites. The first "skull" glyph functions at Palenque as a "death" expression, but the meaning and the grammatical function of the remaining three glyphs are not clear.

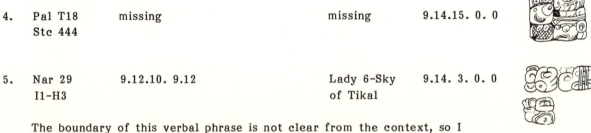

Chart 40 177

7. Bon A   9. 3. 0.14.13   6-Fishfin   9. 3.10. 0. 0
    F7

8. Mach 5   10. 0.10.17. 5   ????   10. 0.10. 0. 0
    A3-A4

The second glyph in this expression may record the patient or agent, but
if it is a party of the verbal phrase, the subject is deleted and this
clause is gapped to the succeeding one of which One-Fish-in-Hand is the
subject.

9. Altun   no date   Ruler 2   9.12. 0. 0. 0?
    Earplug

Mathews (1979:79) has tentatively identified this glyph as *u tup*, an
expression for "his earplug." I have included it and #10 because these
noun phrases occupy the structural position where a predicate is
expected.

10. CItz   no date   18-Rabbit   Late Classic
    Jade

This glyph is from a fragmentary jade which may have been an earplug. It
is drawn after Proskouriakoff (1974:118b).

11. Agua 1   9.15. 9.16. 1   Captor of   9.15. 0. 0. 0
    A5   Kin-Balam

12. Tam HS   unreadable   ????   missing   Late Classic

My source for the Tamarindito Hieroglyphic Stairs is the rubbings published by Merle Greene Robertson (Greene, Rands, and Graham 1972:Plate
94). The details of the text are difficult to see in the publication, but
the capture glyph clearly is prefixed by a third-person pronoun of Set A
(the ergative set). I have drawn the glyph as T13.515:25, but it might
well consist of T13.515[528]:130. In either case, T181 is not present.
The glyphs which follow the "capture" statement are badly eroded, but
there is enough room for the names of both the captive (patient) and
captor (agent) to have been recorded. The bound figure to the right is
named with the EG of Tikal, also known to have been used at Dos Pilas and
Aguateca.

13. NTun   9.16. 3.10. 4   Chaan-Cauac   9.16.10. 0. 0 
    GpIVe
    J1

CHART 41   Affix T1   in Cluster 1.*:130   with Main Sign T528.116:713

This glyph is a period ending term, such as "it ended, the tun" or "the end of the tun." T116, the phonetic complement -n(i), can be attached to the tun glyph (T528) or to the entire block.

#	LOCATION	DATE (EVENT)	PATIENT	AGENT	DEDICATION	
1.	Pal PTab F18	9.11. 0. 0. 0	tun	none	9.14.10. 0. 0	

This verb is followed by "scattering" and the name glyph of Pacal.

2.	Lac L1 C1	9.15.15. 0. 0		Knot-Eye-Jaguar of Bonampak	9.15.15. 0. 0	
3.	PN Alt2 G3	9.15. 0. 0. 0	tun	Ruler 4 (by title)	9.16. 0. 0. 0	
4.	Pom Wall Pan pI1	9.17. 0. 0. 0	tun	none	9.17. 0. 0. 0	

This expression is part of a long series of period ending statements which include sequentially the following elements: a variant of the "half period" glyph; 17 katuns; seating of the tun; scattering; end of the tun; a blood-letting expression; and the agent Jeweled-Jaguar. It is possible that the agent of the final verb is meant to be understood as the agent of all these verbal expressions. See 4:10, 43:7, 52:7, 66:9, and Fig. 39.

| 5. | Bon 1 G2 | 9.17.10. 0. 0 | tun | none | 9.17.10. 0. 0 |  |

This event is followed by "scattering" and the name glyph of Chaan-Muan.

| 6. | Pom PanX pD3 | 9.18. 0. 0. 0 | tun | none | 9.18. 0. 0. 0 | 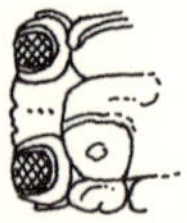 |

This glyph is followed by "scattering," but the remaining part of the text is missing.

| 7. | PN 12 Right | 9.18. 5. 0. 0 | tun | Ruler 7 | 9.18. 5. 0. 0 | 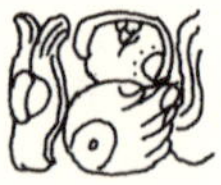 |

Chart 42 179

8.	LMar 3 B2	9.18. 5. 0. 0		Macaw-GI	9.18. 5. 0. 0	
9.	Nar 32 W8	9.19.10. 0. 0	tun	18 Rabbit-God K	9.19.10. 0. 0	
10.	Seib 8 A2	10. 1. 0. 0. 0	tun	local ruler	10. 1. 0. 0. 0	
11.	Ixlu Alt B3	10. 2.10. 0. 0	tun	Ah Kal	10. 2.10. 0. 0	

This verb is followed by "scattering" and the name of the subject.

12.	Coll 24 B1	9.18.10. 0. 0	tun	Ah Cauac	9.18.10. 0. 0	

CHART 42   Affix T1   in Cluster 1.*:130   with Main Sign T218

These glyphs record some period ending term, such as "completion of." It is usually accompanied b
the second glyph which marks the number and type of period in the period ending and/or annivers

#	LOCATION	DATE (EVENT)	PATIENT	AGENT	DEDICATION	
1.	Tik 31 C10-D10	8.14. 0. 0. 0	14 katuns *u cab* Jaguar-Paw I		9. 0.10. 0. 0	

This phrase records the completion of fourteenth katun in Cycle 8. The
katun notation is followed by a "chuen" count variant, two titles (T86:
528:178 and T1.21:573:18, *u cab* (T1.526:18), and the name phrase of
Jaguar-Paw I (see 125:1).

2.	Tik 31 D15-C16	8.17. 0. 0. 0	17th katun	????	9. 0.10. 0. 0	

The glyph immediately preceding this "completion of seventeen katuns"
expression is almost completely destroyed, but if this passage is parallel to that for Katun 14 (#1), the missing glyph was an "end of tun"
(T528:713:117) notation. The katun glyph is followed by a "chuen" count
variant and a glyph that includes kan-cross, sky, and a bone (T281:515:
23.561:571). This last glyph does not appear to name a person, but rather

to give some ritual information about the period. The records of Katuns 14 and 18 have parallel phrases (C11-C12 and F16-F17).

3.	Tik 31 E18-F18	8.18. 0. 0. 0	18 katuns *u cab*	Curl-Snout	9. 0.10. 0. 0	
4.	Tik 3 A8-B8	9. 2.13. 0. 0	13th tun	Jaguar-Paw- Skull I	9. 2.13. 0. 0	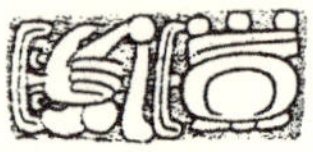
5.	Nar Alt1 I10-H11	9. 8. 0. 0. 0	8th katun	Ruler 1	9. 8. 0. 0. 0	

CHART 43   Affix T1   in Cluster 1.*:130   with Main Sign "scattering"

#	LOCATION	DATE (EVENT)	PATIENT	AGENT	DEDICATION	
1.	DPil 1 A4-A5	9.13.15. 0. 0		none?	9.13.15. 0. 0	
2.	DPil 8 I5-H6	9.14. 0. 0. 0		Shield-God K	9.15. 0. 0. 0	

Although this glyph has a mandible (T590) instead of the "scattering" hand, Mathews (n.d.b) has shown that it is clearly equivalent to the "scattering" expression as registered on Stela 1 (#1).

| 3. | Pal PTab
E19-F19 | 9.11. 0. 0. 0 | | Pacal II | 9.14.10. 0. 0 |  |

This glyph follows a T528.116:713 "end of the tun" expression.

| 4. | Ton M111
19 | 9.13. 0. 0. 0 | | Kuk | 9.13. 0. 0. 0 |  |

AEI.

| 5. | Ton M110
K | 9.14.10. 0. 0 | | Balam | 9.14.10. 0. 0 |  |

Chart 43   181

This expression follows a T528.116:713 "end of the tun" phrase. The name phrase of the subject is long and full of titles. A *mah kina* (T74:184) title precedes the head of GIII (the god of number 7), and I am assuming this title identifies the personal name of the protagonist. However, a Bird-Jaguar name glyph also appears later in this complex phrase.

6. Agua 1   eroded   Captor of   9.15.10. 0. 0
    A2   Kin-Balam

7. Pom Wall   9.17. 0. 0. 0   none   9.17. 0. 0. 0
    Pan pH1

This glyph occurs in the following sequence of period ending expressions: a "half period" variant that functions as a verb; 17 katuns; seating of the tun; scattering; end of the tun (T232.528:116:713:130); a blood-letting expression; and the name of the subject Jeweled-Jaguar. However, the subject of this final verb may have been intended to be understood as the subject of the other verbal expressions as well. See 4:10, 41:4, 52:7, and 66:9.

8. LPas L3   9.16.15. 0. 0   Bird-   9.16.15. 0. 0
    A3   Jaguar III

9. Quir Ee   9.17. 0. 0. 0   Two-Legged-   9.17. 0. 0. 0
    B19   Sky

10. Quir C   9.17. 5. 0. 0   Two-Legged-   9.17. 5. 0. 0
    C13   Sky

11. Quir P   9.18. 5. 0. 0   Two-Legged-   9.18. 5. 0. 0
    C4b-C5a   Sky

This verbal phrase follows an IS date clearly recorded as 9.18.5.0.0; however, Two-Legged-Sky, named thereafter, was surely dead on this date and another ruler was in office. Nevertheless, his name phrase, as well that of the closely associated 18-Rabbit of Copan, occurs in the text. Either the Quirigua scribes recorded this as a posthumous event, or these names should be considered the patients of the event and the current ruler named at E1 to F1 as the agent. Perhaps this "scattering" rite, now believed to be blood-letting, was conducted, not only in celebration of the PE, but also in commemoration of the previous ruler.

12. Ixt 4   9.17.10. 0. 0   Ah Yax-Kal   9.17.10 0. 0
    B2

#	LOCATION	DATE (EVENT)		AGENT	DEDICATION	
13.	Quir De B18	9.16.15. 0. 0		Two-Legged-Sky	9.16.15. 0. 0	
14.	Quir Dw A23b–A23c	9.15.15. 0. 0		Two-Legged-Sky	9.16.15. 0. 0	
15.	Quir Str1 Ctr Door	9.19. 0. 0. 0		Mul-Chaan	9.19. 0. 0. 0	
16.	Quir Str1 w Door	9.19. 0. 0. 0		Mul-Chaan	9.19. 0. 0. 0	
17.	Car Alt12 pH2–pH3	9.19.10. 0. 0		Ox-Cauac	9.19.10. 0. 0	
18.	Seib 10 A3	10. 1. 0. 0. 0		Ah Hun-Kin-God K	10. 1. 0. 0. 0	
19.	Ixlu 1 A3	10. 1. 0. 0. 0		local ruler	10. 1. 0. 0. 0	
20.	Uca 4 B2	10. 1. 0. 0. 0		local ruler	10. 1. 0. 0. 0	
21.	DPil 26 A7–B7	9.14.10. 0. 0		Shield-God K	9.14.10. 0. 0	

The third part of this glyph is phonetic *mal*, a phonetic complement that occurs with "scattering" in other examples (see 3:2,12–13).

CHART 44   Affix T1   in Cluster 1.*:130   with Miscellaneous Main Signs

All of these examples are associated with period ending dates.

#	LOCATION	DATE (EVENT)	PATIENT	AGENT	DEDICATION	
1.	Mach 11 A4b	9.15.10. 0. 0	tun	Etz'nab-GI	9.15.10. 0. 0	

Chart 44   183

| 2. | Quir J A14 | 9.16. 5. 0. 0 | | ???? | 9.16. 5. 0. 0 |  |

This verb follows "scattering."

| 3. | Ixt 4 A2 | 9.17.10. 0. 0 | tun | Ah Yax-Kal | 9.17.10. 0. 0 |  |

This verb follows "scattering."

| 4. | Quir C B7-A8a | 13. 0. 0. 0. 0 4 Ahau 8 Cumku | tun | GIII and Aged-Stingray-God | 9.17. 5. 0. 0 |  |

| 5. | Quir C A10 | (13. 0. 0. 0. 0 4 Ahau 8 Cumku) | tun | Black-Skull-God | 9.17. 5. 0. 0 |  |

| 6. | Quir C C7-D7a | 9. 1. 0. 0. 0 | tun | Maize Lord | 9.17. 5. 0. 0 |  |

| 7. | Itz 4 A2-A3 | 9.18.12. 0. 0 | tun | eroded | 9.18.12. 0. 0 |  |

| 8. | Pal TIw A7-B7 | 9.12. 0. 0. 0 | | ???? | 9.12.15. 0. 0 |  |

See 31:1-2.

| 9. | Car 17 A2-B2 | 10. 0.19. 4.15? | | Ox-Cauac | 10. 1. 0. 0. 0 |  |

The CR date as recorded in the text is in error.

| 10. | Quir Fe C11a | 9.16.10. 0. 0 | | Two-Legged-Sky | 9.17. 0. 0. 0 |  |

| 11. | LHig 1 D5 | 9.17.10. 0. 0 | | Ahau | 9.17.10. 0. 0 |  |

CHART 45   Affix T1   in Cluster 1.*:130   with Miscellaneous Main Signs

#	LOCATION	DATE (EVENT)	PATIENT	AGENT	DEDICATION	
1.	CRic Jade	none		????	9. 0.11. 0. 0 or 9. 3.16. 0. 0	

This T684 "inaugural" expression is from a Costa Rican jade celt
published by Balser (1974:Plate XIV). The glyphs following this verbal
phrase looks suspiciously like the T1.I:606 "child of mother" expression,
but the jaguar glyph occurring thereafter is not marked as a female name.
However, if this is a parentage statement, the subject of the verb is the
possessed noun "child of Balam." Another verbal expression precedes this
inaugural event, and the subject is named with a "sky" glyph and an EG
very similar to the early Tikal EG found on the Leiden Plaque and Stela
4. I suspect that the Chaan personage is also the subject of this "inaugural" verb and the "child of Balam." See 39:1.

#	LOCATION	DATE (EVENT)	PATIENT	AGENT	DEDICATION	
2.	Pal PTab H11-G12	9.11.13. 0. 0	????	Kan-Xul II	9.14.10. 0. 0	

The head variant that follows this "ahau-in-hand" glyph may record an
object, but on the tablet from Temple 14, the forehead mirror of God K is
adjoined to this verb as a semantic determinative specifying that the God
K scepter and no other is held (see 20:8 and 38:8-10). The head variant
may also specify the kind of scepter used in this particular rite.

#	LOCATION	DATE (EVENT)	PATIENT	AGENT	DEDICATION	
3.	Pal TIm C6	9.11. 0. 0. 0	his cycle	GI	9.12.15. 0. 0	

This helmet appears to be a variant of the drum-major headdress important
at Yaxchilan and Palenque, but it most closely resembles the head gear
worn by the kneeling visitors on Lintel 2 at Piedras Negras. In this
Palenque text, the helmet occurs in three passages each for Katuns 11 and
12. In the Katun 11 passages, the three gods of the Palenque Triad are
named as the agents of these verbs, which are followed by *hun kalal*
(TI.683:102) and "his baktun" in either geometric or zoomorphic form. The
baktun cannot refer to a cycle of 400 tuns since the subject of the
discussion is Katun 11. Fortunately, the baktun glyph appears as the sign
for the katun cycle on the Leiden Plaque and Tikal Stela 31, and, therefore, it must represent some concept, such as "cycle," which is appropriate to both the katun and the baktun, The "helmet" verb must record
some activity, such as "rule," that is appropriate for a deity to pursue
in a katun celebration. In the Katun 12 passages the *hun kalal* and "his
cycle" glyphs do not appear. See 109:7 for the remaining example of this
verb.

Chart 45 185

4.	Pal TIm F2	9.11. 0. 0. 0	his cycle	GIII	9.12.15. 0. 0	
5.	Pal TIm K8	9.12. 0. 0. 0		GI	9.12.15. 0. 0	
6.	Pal TIm I9	9.12. 0. 0. 0		GII	9.12.15. 0. 0	
7.	Pal TIm M4	9.12. 0. 0. 0		GIII	9.12.15. 0. 0	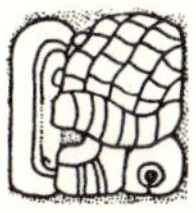
8.	DPil HSe C1-D1	9.11. 9.15.19	????	Flint-Sky-God K	9.12.12. 0. 0	

The meaning of this verbal phrase is not known, nor are the boundaries of
the verbal phrase easily identified. The first glyph carries the verbal
affixing, and either or both of the two following glyphs may record an
object or additional information pertinent to the verbal expression.

9.	Pal TFC E5-E6	no date	????	Kuk I	9.13. 0. 0. 0	

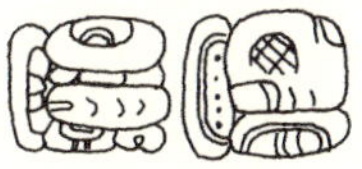

These two glyphs follow the name glyph of Chan-Bahlum and precede the
name of the ancestral ruler Bahlum-Kuk I. Either or both of these glyphs
may represent actions, or they may be possessed nouns in which case the
nouns refer to Chan-Bahlum and the possessive pronouns refer to Bahlum-
Kuk I.

10.	Mach 7 C1	10. 0. 0.13. 0		deleted?	10. 0. 5. 0. 0	

This verb follow the CR date and precedes a T528.116:713 "end of the tun"
expression and the agent One-Fish-in-Hand. The first verb is part of an
extended verbal phrase or it is the first part of a period ending couplet
and has, therefore, a deleted subject.

11.	Pal T14 B8	13 Oc 18 Uo		Bolon-Yocte	9.13.15. 0. 0	

See 20:8, 23:7, 82:4-5, 87:10, 121:4.

12. EZotz   no date   Rodent-Bone? Early Classic
    Lintel

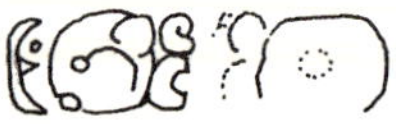

This wooden lintel is now in the Denver Art Museum. The second glyph in
this phrase is badly eroded, but it may be a locative + noun phrase as
found in auxiliary verb + *ti* + verbal noun phrases.

13. NimP 2   9.15. 6.17. 1   Fish-Face   9.15.10. 0. 0
    A2-B2

14. DPil 8   9.13. 6. 2. 0   Shield-God K   9.15. 0. 0. 0
    F15

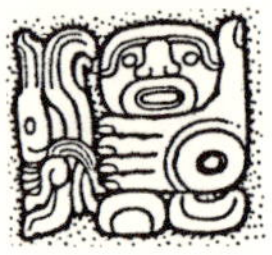

This is the second half of a couplet recording accession (see 112:18).

15. PN 1   9.13.14.11. 1   Ruler 3   9.13.15. 0. 0
    K15

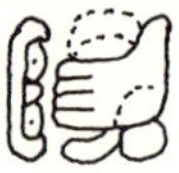

CHART 46   Affix T1   in Cluster 1.*:130   with Main Sign T714

These verbal phrases record a blood-letting rite.

#	LOCATION	DATE (EVENT)	PATIENT	AGENT	DEDICATION	
1.	Pal TC O9-O12	9.12.18. 5.19		deleted (Chan- Bahlum II)	9.13. 0. 0. 0	

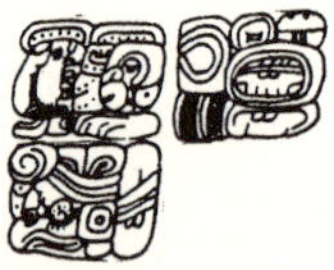

This passage is parallel to one on the TFC (39:3) and records one event
in a series of three which celebrated the seventy-fifth tropical year
anniversary of the accession of Pacal II (see 17:2-3 and 23:3-6). This
verbal phrase is followed by another verb (T204.60:713:18) and the subject of both verbs, Chan-Bahlum. See 56:5 and 59:6.

2.	Pal TS O13	9.12.18. 5.19		deleted	9.13. 0. 0. 0	

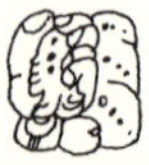

This single glyph records the same event as those discussed in #1, but
all complementary glyphs, the second part of the verbal couplet, and the
subject have been deleted--perhaps because the redundancy of the records
in these temples allowed the expression to be reduced to its most critical component.

Chart 47 187

3. Yax L25   9.12. 9. 8. 1   Shield-   9.15. 0. 0. 0
    B1-E1   Jaguar I

This event occurred on the same day as the accession of Shield-Jaguar
(recorded in the last clause of the center upper stair of Structure 44).
As at Palenque, a blood-letting rite seems to have been a part of accession ritual at Yaxchilan. The last three glyphs of this expression seem to
be equivalent to the *ti* + verbal noun construction which follows an
alternative expression for blood-letting on Lintel 24 at D1 (see 55:5).
Shield-Jaguar is named as the subject of both blood-letting events.

4. Cop 8   9.17.12. 6. 2   New-Sky-at   9.17.15. 0. 0
    B2-C2   Horizon

This blood-letting event was conducted by New-Sky-at-Horizon on the one-
katun + five-day anniversary of his accession.

CHART 47   Affix T1   in Cluster 1.*:136   with Main Sign "Scattering"

#	LOCATION	DATE (EVENT)	PATIENT	AGENT	DEDICATION
1.	Agua 5 C3	9.13. 0. 0. 0		missing	9.13. 0. 0. 0

This "scattering" expression is preceded by the CR date and "completion
of (T218) 13 katuns" and followed by a T516:103 auxiliary verb + *ti* +
verbal noun construction in which the verbal noun is the T502 expression
associated with period endings at Copan (see 31:10-14,16 and 79:3). The
name phrase of Flint-Sky-God K, the contemporary ruler of Dos Pilas,
follows the *ti* construction, and he may be presumed to be the deleted
agent of this "scattering" also. Dos Pilas rulers appear as the protagonists of Aguateca monuments in this example, on Stela 3 (#2), and on
Stela 2.

#	LOCATION	DATE (EVENT)	PATIENT	AGENT	DEDICATION
2.	Agua 3 C3b	9. 15. 0. 0. 0		Spangle-Head	9.15. 0. 0. 0

#	LOCATION	DATE (EVENT)	PATIENT	AGENT	DEDICATION
3.	Ton M104 G	3 Ahau 3 Zac		Ik-Skull Dragon	10. 0. 7. 9. 0

Peter Mathews (personal communication, 1980) has informed me that the
"half-period" event recorded on this monument must refer to the half-
period of either one tun (i.e. nine uinals) or fifteen tuns (i.e., seven

tuns and nine uinals). The existence of this usage and a similar one on
the east panel of the Temple of Inscriptions of Palenque where a "half-
period" glyph is used in reference to ten katuns as "half a baktun"
demonstrates that this glyph refers to "half" of all cycles, not just the
katun.

4.	Agua 1 D1	9.15.10. 0. 0		God K- Mah-Kina	9.15.10. 0. 0	
5.	Ton M7 H	9.16.10. 0. 0		deleted	9.16.10. 0. 0	

CHART 48	Affix T1	in Cluster 1.*:136	with Main Sign T757

#	LOCATION	DATE (EVENT)	PATIENT	AGENT	DEDICATION	
1.	Nar 21 A3-A5	9.13.14. 4. 2		Smoking- Squirrel	9.13.15. 0. 0	
2.	Yax L53 E1-F1	no date		Lady Ik- Skull-Sky	9.14. 0. 0. 0	

This phrase occurs in the text accompanying the woman on Lintel 53, and
although no date occurs with it, the event must have happened on the same
date, 9.13.5.12.13 7 Ben 16 Mac, as Shield-Jaguar's event. The verb
phrases characterizing the actions of both figures are the same, but
since they carry different objects, it must be assumed that this verbal
expression refers to some similarity of state or action that is shared by
the protagonists, rather that to something differentiated. The name of
this woman includes a skull followed by a sky sign, a series of names
recurring on Lintel 32, where the skull occurs with an Ik sign in the
forehead (see Maler 1903: Plate LXII). This identification associates
this scene as well as that on Lintel 32 (which has the same date and
event as Lintel 53) with the woman named as the mother of Bird-Jaguar on
Stelae 11 and 12. See 38:28.

Chart 48   189

3.   Yax L6   9.16. 1. 8. 6   Kan-Tah   9.16. 5. 0. 0
     B1-B2

This auxiliary verb construction occurs in the text accompanying the
secondary figure, and although the verb of the main text is eroded, it
can be assumed that it recorded some form of the same event. Since the
same verbal expression occurs on Lintel 43, on which the same basket-God
K staff is displayed, it can be assumed that the "zip" verbal noun refers
to the staff in some way.

4.   Yax L43   9.16. 1. 8. 6   Bird-   9.16. 5. 0. 0
     B2   Jaguar III

The first part of this verbal expression is lost, and it is not possible
to discern whether or not it was an auxiliary verb + *ti* construction.
However, since the date and the action shown are the same as those on
Lintel 6, and since the surviving section of the verb is clearly the
"zip" verbal noun in #3, I include it here to facilitate comparison of
these two examples.

5.   LPas L2   no date   Zac-Muluc   9.16.15. 0. 0
     A1-A2

Although no date accompanies this text it can be deduced that it occurred
on 9.16.15.0.0, the featured date of this lintel. The auxiliary verb
construction is a period ending expression related to similar ones at
Palenque, Copan, Aguateca, and perhaps Piedras Negras. See 5:8, 31:10-14,
15, 38:6, and 79:3.

6.   Yax L26   no date   Shield-   9.15. 0. 0. 0
     S1-U2   Jaguar I

Although the T684 "inaugural" glyph occurs as the verbal noun in this
construction, the event cannot be accession because of the late dates
(9.14.18.6.12 and 9.14.14.13.17) recorded in other passages on this
lintel. This text accompanies the main scene, which shows Shield-Jaguar
attended by a woman and in the process of dressing in battle gear. This
phrase is the first part of a verbal couplet of which the second part is
"scattering" + *ti* + nouns (see 3:16).

CHART 49   Affix T1   in Cluster 1.*:136   with Miscellaneous Main Signs

#	LOCATION	DATE (EVENT)	PATIENT	AGENT	DEDICATION	
1.	Pal 96G E4	9.14.10. 4. 2		????	9.17.15. 0. 0	

By structural comparison, it can be shown that this event is parallel to
passages at D5-C6 and G5-H5, both of which display a T644 "seating" sign
over a throne pillow covered with a jaguar pelt. This glyph must be a
phonetic or semantic substitution for these "seating" compounds (see 32:
8-9). This verb is followed by a glyph which may record the agent
(Chaacal III) by title or may be part of the verb. T126 may also be part
of the verbal affix pattern.

#	LOCATION	DATE (EVENT)	PATIENT	AGENT	DEDICATION	
2.	Cop P A8	9. 9.10. 0. 0		GI?	9. 9.10. 0. 0	

This period ending expression is the second of three components of a
verbal triplet. See 67:1 and 98:5.

CHART 50   Affix T1   in Cluster 1.*:24   with Miscellaneous Main Signs

#	LOCATION	DATE (EVENT)	PATIENT	AGENT	DEDICATION	
1.	Mach 3 F3b	9.19. 5. 0. 0		Split-Kin- God K	9.19. 5. 0. 0	
2.	Cop 6 A7	9.12.10. 0. 0		none	9.12.10. 0. 0	
3.	Pal TIw S12b	no date		Pacal II	9.12.15. 0. 0	

This "death" glyph, which is found in the closing statement of the west
tablet of the Temple of Inscriptions, may be a possessed noun, rather
than a verb, but I have included it here because its affixing configuration (T1.*:24) appears on known verbal glyphs. It follows a "God C-in-
elbow" glyph which functions as the verb in an early mythological passage
on the Tablet of the Cross (32:13). The function of this last passage
seems to be to link Chan-Bahlum, the succeeding ruler, to the dead ruler

Chart 51   191

Pacal, and to restate the death of Pacal as the dedication statement of the inscription.

#	Location	Date (event)		Agent	Dedication	
4.	Pal TFC E6	no date		Kuk I	9.13. 0. 0. 0	

See 45:9.

| 5. | Quir J
B13 | 9.16. 5. 0. 0 | | deleted
(Two-Legged-
Sky) | 9.16. 5. 0. 0 |  |

CHART 51   Affix T1   in Cluster 1.*:24   with Main Sign T757

In all of these examples, T757 functions as a general verb introducing name phrases in many different contexts. These verbal phrases cannot refer to any of the specific activities shown in accompanying scenes.

#	LOCATION	DATE (EVENT)	PATIENT	AGENT	DEDICATION	
1.	Yax L39 A4	9.15.10. 0. 1		Bird- Jaguar III	9.16.15. 0. 0	

This general verb is the last part of a verbal couplet or triplet which includes the following elements: (1) a "fish-in-hand/God K" expression (see 39:5); (2) u cab (T1.526:246?); (3) a cauac compound (T58:136. 528[hand?]:140); and (4) T204.757:24. The name phrase of Bird-Jaguar follows the T757 verb, which seems to function as a means of highlighting the subject.

| 2. | Yax L25
G1a | no date | | Lady Xoc | 9.15. 0. 0. 0 |  |

This verb accompanies a vision scene associated with blood-letting.

| 3. | Coll 5
A1 | no date | | Lady Ik-Skull | 9.15. 0. 0. 0?? |  |

The verb accompanies a scene of a woman seated in a moon sign.

| 4. | Yax L14
A1 | no date | | Lady of
Yaxchilan
Lady Yax-Kal | 9.16. 5. 0. 0 |  |

This verb introduces the name glyphs of the person emerging from the serpent in this vision scene. It should be noted that the CR date for this lintel is the same as for Lintel 39, which shows a reclining Bird-Jaguar holding a double-headed serpent bar. The featured events for both lintels are "fish-in-hand/God K" (see 39:5).

5.   Yax L15   no date   Lady 6-Tun   9.16.18. 0. 0
     C1   Lady of the
                                       Ik site.

This verb accompanies a vision scene associated with blood-letting.

6.   Yax L17   no date   Lady   9.16.18. 0. 0
     D1   Balam-Ix

No date is recorded on this lintel, but since the main text includes a reference to the birth of Shield-Jaguar II, I suggest that this blood-letting event took place is celebration of that event. The CR of this birth is badly damaged, but one of the likely LC positions for it is 9.16.0.14.5.

7.   Cop 1   9.11.15.14. 0   Knot-Skull   9.11.16. 0. 0
     C5

This verb follows a CR date and period ending verb and precedes the name of the subject as a means of highlighting the subject.

8.   Cop 4   9. 15. 0. 0. 0   18-Rabbit   9.15. 0. 0. 0
     B8

The verb follows a CR date and two period ending phrases.

9.   LMar 2   no date   missing   9.17. 0. 0. 0
     D1

10. Yax 11   no date   Lady Ik-   9.16. 5. 0. 0
     Rear A'1   Skull

Chart 52   193

CHART 52   Affix T1   in Cluster 1.*:24   with Main Sign T757

In all of these examples, T757 appears as an auxiliary verb accompanied by one or more complements that seem to specify the particular event. No locative signs occur between the T757 verb
and its complements.

#	LOCATION	DATE (EVENT)	PATIENT	AGENT	DEDICATION	
1.	Nar 24 E4-D4	9.13. 7. 3. 8		deleted	9.13.10. 0. 0	

This verbal phrase is part of a complicated series of expressions which
record rites occurring on the same day as the event on the front of Stela
24, recorded there as an auxiliary verb + *ti* + T1001 (see 38:5). This
phrase is the third part of a verbal series (see 9:4-5 and 80:1), the
subject of which is named as Lady 6-Sky of Tikal.

#	LOCATION	DATE (EVENT)	PATIENT	AGENT	DEDICATION	
2.	Coll 16 A1-B1	no date		Lady Chac- Mol	Late Classic	

This undate stela in the Dallas Museum of Fine Arts shows a single
standing female holding a double-headed serpent bar. This verbal phrase
includes the general tree sign and may be related to similar expressions
associated with period endings (see 68:3, 69:3, and 84:5-6).

#	LOCATION	DATE (EVENT)	PATIENT	AGENT	DEDICATION	
3.	Yax Str44 Ctr Low A2a-B2	9.11.18.15. 1		Shield-	9.15. 0. 0. 0	

This expression is identical to one from Lintel 3 of Temple 4 of Tikal
(#4). The Tikal example has a supernatural agent and is associated with
an anniversary event, but the historical context of the Yaxchilan example
is not as well understood. It took place nine years begore the accession
of Shield-Jaguar. This verbal phrase is the second half of a couplet; se
16:10 for the first half.

#	LOCATION	DATE (EVENT)	PATIENT	AGENT	DEDICATION
4.	Tik T4 L3 E3-F5	no date		GVI	9.16. 0. 0. 0

This expression is the second part of a series of event expressions
recording the three tun + one day anniversary of a "star-shell" event.
GVI of the Palenque deity list is named as the subject of this event. See
38:17, 79:7, 80:6, 87:11, and Fig. 38.

5. Tik 9   9. 2.19.12.19   Kan-Chitam   9. 3. 0. 0. 0?
    B1-B2

6. Yax L14   no date   Zero-Skull   9.16. 5. 0. 0
    G1-G2

This verb phrase accompanies the male figure in a vision scene. The "yax-muluc" (T16:580) of this phrase is part of the expression in ##7-9, but the presence of T712, a lancet, following it clearly associates this expression with blood-letting.

7. Pom Wall   9.17. 0. 0. 0   GI-Jaguar   9.17. 0. 0. 0
    Pan pJ1-
    pL1

This Pomona expression is the last part of a long series of period ending verb phrases that include the following: (1) a variant of the "half-period" glyph; (2) 17 katuns; (3) "seating of the tun"; (4) "scattering"; (5) "end of the tun" (T204.528.116:713:130); and (6) this auxiliary verb + complement expression. See 4:10, 41:4, 43:7, and 66:9

8. Pom X   9.18. 0. 0. 0   eroded   9.18. 0. 0. 0
    pB4-pC2

Although this expression is very badly damaged, it is clearly parallel to that in #7. This passage is found in the following series: (1) an "inverted bat" phrase for "expiration of the eighteenth katun"; (2) "seating of the tun"; (3) missing; (4) this auxiliary verb + complement phrase; (5) the agent, Ahpo-Ac; (6) "end of the tun" (T13:528.missing: 713:130); (7) "scattering"; and (8) missing. See 4:7, 41:6, and 64:3.

9. Yax Str33   9.15.13. 6. 9   Bird-   9.16. 6. 0. 0
    Step 7   Jaguar III
    Q3-R4

This is the last of three expressions (see 3:12 and 13:6) which accompany a ballgame scene. This expression is identical to those in ##7 and 8, both of which occur as period ending expressions at Pomona. These expressions are composed of the auxiliary verb (T1.737:24); "yax mul" (T16: 580); "hun uinic" (TI.521H); and "na chan" (T4.764). Several of these components occur as parts of verbal phrases recording an act of blood-letting (see Yaxchilan Lintels 13 [38:13], 14 [52:6], and 15 [76:2]), suggesting that the period ending expressions at Pomona and at Quirigua (21:20) as well as this Yaxchilan expression are related in some way to blood-letting rites. This identification also helps elucidate an anomalous parentage statement on the Palace Tablet at Palenque on which this

Chart 53 195

alternative expression for blood-letting replaces the more usual T757/712 expression (see Chart 132). Also see 15:6 and 38:14.

CHART 53   Affix T1   in Cluster 1.*:24   with Main Signs T757

All of these examples are auxiliary verb + *ti* + verbal noun constructions.

#	LOCATION	DATE (EVENT)	PATIENT	AGENT	DEDICATION	
1.	Nar 20 A3-A4	see note		Smoking-Squirrel	9.13.15. 0. 0	

The superfix of the month glyph is damaged in this text, and the date cannot be securely determined. Possible interpretations are as follows: 9.13.2.8.16 7 Cib 14 Yax; 9.13.10.9.16 8 Cib 14 Ch'en; 9.13.14.13.16 7 Cib 14 Ceh; and 9.14.2.12.16 7 Cib 14 Ch'en.

| 2. | Yax L17 A1-A2 | no date | | deleted | 9.16.18. 0. 0 |  |

Lintel 17 does not include a date in its inscription, but the initial auxiliary verb construction is followed by what seems to be an embedded clause recording the birth of Shield-Jaguar II. This same birth is recorded on Lintel 13 (also a blood-letting lintel) on a date that is damaged, but possibly 9.16.0.14.5 1 Chicchan 13 Pop. I suggest that Lintel 17 records a blood-letting rite celebrating the same event on the same day. A second verbal phrase (preceded by T59 *ti*) follows the embedded birth clause, and this featured text ends with the name phrase of the agent, Bird-Jaguar III. See 77:4 for the third part of this verbal series.

| 3. | Seib 7 A4-A5 | 9.18.10. 0. 0 | | Ah Ahpo-Tah | 9.18.10. 0. 0 |  |

This expression follows a CR and "half-period" glyph.

| 4. | Seib 9 A1b-C1 | 10. 1. 0. 0. 0 | | Ah Bolon-Tun/Ah Hun-Kin | 10. 1. 0. 0. 0 | |

This is a period ending expression.

CHART 54   Affix T1   in Cluster 1.*:24   with Main Sign T331

#	LOCATION	DATE (EVENT)	PATIENT	AGENT	DEDICATION	
1.	DPil 16 D3-C3	9.15. 4. 6. 5	????	*u cab* Spangle-Head	9.15. 5. 0. 0	

This text records the same series of events as Stela 2 from Aguateca
(#2). In both texts, the "axe" event occurs one day after a "star-over-
Seibal" event identified by Lounsbury (n.d.) as the first appearance of
Venus as Evening Star. It precedes by six days a third event enacted upon
Jaguar-Paw-Jaguar, a ruler recorded on the Seibal Hieroglyphic Stairs. In
the Aguateca text, the subject of the "axe" event is deleted, but in this
text, he is named in an elaborate phrase which includes two titles with
shield glyphs. The name phrase begins after an *u cab* glyph. In other
examples of the "axe" event (See Chart 14), the "axe" part of the compound is followed by T1.757, but in these two examples, it is followed by
T1:563:501:24, which is known to be substitutable for T1.757 in other
contexts. The T501 and T757 glyphs may be inflected verbs or possessed
nouns. See 10:12-13 and 95:11-12 for other events in this text.

#	LOCATION	DATE (EVENT)	PATIENT	AGENT	DEDICATION	
2.	Agua 2 D1-C2	9.15. 4. 6. 5	????	deleted	9.15. 5. 0. 0	

CHART 55   Affix T1   in Cluster 1.*:140   with Miscellaneous Main Signs

#	LOCATION	DATE (EVENT)	PATIENT	AGENT	DEDICATION	
1.	Cop AltQ A2-B2	9.15. 6.16.17	????	Yax-Kuk-Mo'	9.17. 5. 0. 0	

This "God K-in-hand" glyph is used at Quirigua to record the accession of
Two-Legged-Sky, but on the tablets of Temple 14 and the TFC at Palenque,
it refers to the "holding" or "display" of God K on occasions other than
the accession to the throne of a ruler. This Copan example, like those
from Palenque, cannot refer directly to the accession of this person to
the throne because his accession is recorded in other texts as having
occurred on a later date. This event may be the taking of some other
office, perhaps specified by the second glyph, or it may be the display
of a scepter. It should be noted that the "ahau-in-hand" glyphs, which
are semantically equivalent to "God K-in-hand," with both meaning to
display the God K scepter, occur on the tablet from Temple 14 at Palenque
with a God K mirror adjoined as a semantic determinative specifying the
type of scepter held; the crossed-torch glyph following this Copan exam-

Chart 55   197

ple may serve the same function. The agent is named with a conflation of a quetzal (*kuk*) and a macaw (*mo'*) prefixed by *yax*, and this name glyph appears prominently in the name phrase of New-Sky-at-Horizon, who is surely the agent of this event.

2.	Pal T18	missing		missing	9.14.15. 0. 0	
	Stc 409					

3.	Yax L38	9.16.12. 5.14	Lady 6-Tuns Lady of Ik site	9.16.15. 0. 0	
	A2-B2				

See 39:5-6 for related events.

4.	Coll 4	no date	Lady 6-Sky-Ahau	9.11.10. 0. 0	
	E1				

This glyph is from Site Q Panel 5. It introduces the name of a female who stands facing a male engaged in a "scattering" rite and holding a tri-lobe flint.

5.	Yax L24	9.13.17.15.12	Shield-Jaguar I	9.15. 0. 0. 0	
	B1a-D1				

The verbal noun which occurs in the first *ti* construction can be identified as a blood-letting lancet from its appearances as a replacement for a stingray spine in the bowls on Lintels 13 and 14. The second *ti* is followed by a verbal noun phrase that appears to give added information about the blood-letting event; this second phrase is parallel to information addended to the "fish-in-hand/God K" event on Lintel 25 (see 46:3). The verbal phrase for the female participant (#6) is identical to Shield-Jaguar's expression, except that the addended information is not included in her text.

6.	Yax L24	no date	Lady Xoc	9.15. 0. 0. 0	
	G1				

7.	Yax 12	no date	Shield-Jaguar I	9.16. 5. 0. 0	
	E1-F1				

Since no date is recorded with this text, it must be assumed that the event occurred on one of the dates recorded on the other side of the stela: i.e., on the day of the death of Shield-Jaguar (25:5) or the seating of Bird-Jaguar (112:19). And since the subject of this verb is

Shield-Jaguar, it can be assumed that it refers in some way to death or
to a posthumous event. The verbal noun is an ahau half covered with a
jaguar pelt. Balam is the term for "jaguar" and balan means "hidden
partially behind something," so the event may refer to "burial." However,
it should be noted that this ahau variant is a prominent component in the
name phrases of Underworld characters, and this verbal noun may refer,
therefore, to Shield-Jaguar's posthumous position in the Underworld.

8.	Cop Alt O' Frt A1-B1	no date	local person	Late Classic

9.	Pal TIw G6	1. 0. 0. 0. 0. 8	none	9.12.15. 0. 0

This glyph usually occurs with PEs divisible by five: i.e., with katuns,
hotuns, lahuntuns, holahuntuns. Here it occurs because this date is the
eightieth CR anniversary of Pacal's accession, and eighty is divisible by
five.

10.	Pal TIw G10	1. 0. 0. 0. 0. 8	none	9.12.15. 0. 0

This example appears to both T679 as an PEI and T1 as an inflectional
pronoun.

CHART 56	Affix T1	in Cluster 1.*:18	with Miscellaneous Main Signs

#	LOCATION	DATE (EVENT)	PATIENT	AGENT	DEDICATION	
1.	Cop B B7	9.15. 0. 0. 0		deleted	9.15. 0. 0. 0	

This "scattering" expression is the third of four parts in a series of
passages recording the end of the tun in alternative expressions. It is
followed by a T1.757:106 general verb, which seems to function as a means
of focusing on or highlighting the name phrase of 18-Rabbit, the subject
of this "scattering" and the other events.

#	LOCATION	DATE (EVENT)	PATIENT	AGENT	DEDICATION	
2.	Agua 1 A7	9.15. 9.16.15		God K- Mah Kina	9.15.10. 0. 0	

Chart 56   199

3. Cop 10   eroded   ????   9.11. 0. 0. 0
    D4b–D6

This verb is preceded by an eroded area and a tun glyph (T528:116) and
followed by two pairs of glyphs each of which contains a zoomorphic head
and the "water-group" head variant (T41). In the first pair, "sky" is
attached to the God C variant, and in the second, "earth" appears. This
pairing of the "sky–God C" and "earth–God C" is reminiscent of similar
pairings in the initial clause of Tikal Stela 31.

4. Cop AltD'   9.17. 0. 0. 0   New–Sky–at–   9.17. 0. 0. 0
    F1   Horizon

The texts of Late Classic Copan tend to use sequences of long, complicated verbal phrases which provide alternative information about the
featured event. In this case, the T757 general verb follows two phrases
containing together five glyphs. The function of the general verb, here
in its full-figure form, seems to be to highlight the subject, recorded
in this text as New–Sky–at–Horizon.

5. Pal TC   9.12.18. 5.19   Chan–   9.13. 0. 0. 0
    O12   Bahlum II

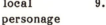

This T713 verb is the second part of a verbal couplet of which the first
part is a blood-letting event (see 17:2–3, 23:3–6, 39:3,46:1–2, and 59:6).

6. NTun   no date   local   9.16.10. 0. 0
    GpIVc   personage
    A1–A2

7. PN 40   9.15.15. 0. 0   Ruler 4   9.15.15. 0. 0
    C15

8. Quir Ew   9.17. 0. 0. 0   ????   9.17. 0. 0. 0
    A20b

CHART 57   Affix T1   in Cluster 1.*:106   with Main Sign T757

#	LOCATION	DATE (EVENT)	PATIENT	AGENT	DEDICATION	
1.	Yax 18 C2-C3	no date		Sky-God K?	9.15. 0. 0. 0	

This event apparently occurred on the day 9.14.15.17.11, on the occasion
of the capture of Chuen and in conjunction with a blood-letting rite (see
35:5). Those two events are recorded in the initial clauses of Stela 18,
but no date intervenes between them, this T1.757:106 expression, and two
others which follow. It is interesting to note that the rare serpent sign
in the second glyph also appears on the Dumbarton Oaks Tablet, which is
closely tied to GI of the Palenque Triad. The subject of this event
seems to be God K, GII of the Palenque Triad.

#	LOCATION	DATE (EVENT)	PATIENT	AGENT	DEDICATION	
2.	Cop A B9-C9	no date		18-Rabbit	9.15. 0. 0. 0	

This expression also appears on Stela N (#3) which it can be clearly
identified as a period ending expression. The calendric notation for this
Stela A phrase follows, rather than precedes it, and the reference seems
to be to the end of Katun 15 and not to previously recorded events. I
suspect these two expressions are related to others used with period
endings at Pomona and Quirigua (see 21:20 and 52:7-8).

#	LOCATION	DATE (EVENT)	PATIENT	AGENT	DEDICATION	
3.	Cop N A20-B4	9.16.10. 0. 0		New-Sky-at Horizon	9.16.10. 0. 0	

This expression is parallel to #2 and the second half of a couplet which
records the end of the tenth tun of Katun 16.

#	LOCATION	DATE (EVENT)	PATIENT	AGENT	DEDICATION	
4.	Cop AltO' Side C2-D3	missing		missing	Late Classic	

CHART 58   Affix T1   in Cluster 1.*:23 or 4   with Miscellaneous Main Signs

T23 is thought to have the phonetic value -na or -an because of the frequent appearance of this
affix on glyphs with a configuration of C-an, such as kan and chaan. T4 appears as a substitute
for T23 in the Group of the Cross at Palenque and in other contexts where a value of an or na is
favored.

Chart 58 201

#	LOCATION	DATE (EVENT)	PATIENT	AGENT	DEDICATION	
1.	Pal DO A5-B5	9.11. 4. 7. 0	????	GI	9.14.15. 0. 0	

This event occurred one day after the ninety-second tropical year anniversary of the death of Kan-Xul I, the ancestral ruler for whom the
protagonist of this monument was named. The main verb is the same as that
found on the jambs of the sanctuaries of the Group of the Cross, but the
context of the event there is the eighth tropical year anniversary of the
accession of Chan-Bahlum II. The identification of these events as ones
associated with anniversaries seems clear, and in all cases, a god of the
Palenque Triad is recorded as the agent. The version found on the Dumbarton Oaks
Tablet is followed by a prepositional phrase including *tu* (T89) and
balan-ahau, a combination that closely matches the anniversary phrase
for 2 Cib 14 Mol on the TS (see 23:6). The *balan-ahau* may well refer to
the dead Kan-Xul I, as this same glyph is used to refer to the dead
Shield-Jaguar on Yaxchilan Stela 12 (see 55:7). The DO verbal phrase is
followed by GI, *u cab*, and the name phrase of Pacal, the contemporary
ruler of Palenque. The agent of this event is GI of the Palenque Triad,
but the text make clear that the activity was conducted "under the
auspices" of the human ruler of the site. This clause is the first
half of a couplet of which Kan-Xul II is named as the agent of the
second half, and since Kan-Xul II is shown dancing as GI in the scene,
this couplet construction may indicate that Kan-Xul II impersonated GI in
the earlier ceremony. See 20:1, 81:6, and 27:4-5 for other events in
which both supernaturals and historical rulers are named.

#	LOCATION	DATE (EVENT)	PATIENT	AGENT	DEDICATION	
2.	Ton M7 L	9.16.10. 0. 0		Ah Imix	9.16.10. 0. 0	

This "half-period" glyph is a very rare notation in which the "half-
period" is held in the T713 hand of the "end of tun" expression. It is
preceded by a "scattering" event and the CR date in an unusual arrangement of period ending phrases.

#	LOCATION	DATE (EVENT)	PATIENT	AGENT	DEDICATION	
3.	Sach 2 C1-D2	no date		local ruler	10. 2.10. 0. 0	

No date survives on this stela fragment, but the presence of a tun glyph
No date survives on this stela fragment, but the presence of a tun glyph
at B1 and the "mandible" variant of the "scattering" event (see 43:2)
suggest that this was a period ending notation. The date of dedication is
taken from the front surface of the stela, but since the lower section is
missing, it is not possible to determine whether or not the verbal phrase
belongs to the IS date.

CHART 59   Affix T1   in Cluster 1.*.-*ah* or *lah*   with Miscellaneous Main Signs

All of these examples include T1 or an equivalent as prefix and some form of the affix -*ah* (T12, T181, or T228) or -*lah* (T178.181) as suffixed.

#	LOCATION	DATE (EVENT)	PATIENT	AGENT	DEDICATION	
1.	Cop 6 C1-C2	no date		Imix-God K	9.12.10. 0. 0	

Although no date precedes this phrase, it is part of a clause series recording an event series celebrating the date 9.12.10.0.0.

| 2. | Cop 2 D6-D7a | no date | | ???? | 9.10.15. 0. 0 | |

This passage is not marked by a CR notation and presumably records information about the IS date 9.10.15.0.0. The period ending passage includes a "new cycle" glyph (T86:16.528.528) which closely resembles a glyph associated with 4 Ahau 8 Cumku on the tablets of the Group of the Cross at Palenque; there is no evidence, however, that the Copan passage is referring to the era date. The "new cycle" glyph is followed by a God C "water-group" variant (T41) with an infixed "sky" glyph; by God C and an anthropomorphic "earth" glyph; and, finally, by kin and akbal signs. The remaining glyphs of the passage are destroyed, but the contrasting couplets recall other period ending passages at Copan (see 56:3) and the 9.0.10.0.0 period ending passage on Tikal Stela 31.

| 3. | Cop 4 B7a | 9.15. 0. 0. 0 | 15 katuns | none | 9.15. 0. 0. 0 | |

This "completion" glyph is followed by "15 katuns," by another period ending verb (T679.58?:586.181), by the T757 general verb, and by the name phrase of 18-Rabbit.

| 4. | Yax Str44 se A5a | no date | | none | 9.15. 0. 0. 0 | |

The DNIGs listed as #4 and #5 may not be verbal in construction, but I have included them because they carry the T181 *ah* suffix as well as T12 *ah*.

| 5. | Yax Str44 se D4c | no date | | none | 9.15. 0. 0. 0 | |

Chart 59   203

6. Pal TFC   9.12.18. 5.19   Chan-Bahlum   9.13. 0. 0. 0
    M13

    This T713 verb is the second part of a verbal couplet of which the first
    part is a blood-letting event (17:2-3, 23:3-6, 39:3, 46:1-2, and 56:5).

7. PN 8   9.12.14.11. 1   Ruler 2   9.13. 0. 0. 0
    F2

    According to the date, this event must be posthumous because it occurred
    seven days after death after Ruler 2's death as recorded on Stela 7 (see
    25:18) (D. Stuart, personal communication, 1981).

8. Pal T18   9.13. 0. 7. 0   Chaacal III   9.14.15. 0. 0
    Jamb B17

    This event, which occurred to Chaacal at age 14.1.2, is related to a
    similar event recorded on the Palace Tablet as occurring to Kan-Xul II at
    age 7.0.19 (see 33:3 and 92:6).

9. Altun   9. 7.11. 2.17   local ruler   9. 8. 0. 0. 0
    Jade

    This event records an accession (Mathews and Pendergast 1979).

10. Cop 7   9. 9. 0. 0. 0   Smoking-Head 9. 9. 0. 0. 0
    B7

11. Yax L14   9.15.10. 0. 1   Lady Great- 9.16. 5. 0. 0
    E4   Skull

    This verbal glyph is the second part of a verbal couplet of which the
    first part is the "fish-in-hand" expression associated with blood-let-
    ting. This *balan-ahau* glyph also occurs in the blood-letting expression
    on Lintel 15 (see 76:2).

12. Tort 1   9.10.13. 0. 0   tun   none   9.11. 0. 0. 0
    A3c-A3d

    This verb is the second part of a verbal couplet of which the first part
    is a period ending expression (see 28:10).

13. Pal TC   9.11. 9.14. 9   Batz'   9.12.10. 0. 0
    Cens1 E2

CHART 60   Affix T1   in Cluster 1.*:82   with Miscellaneous Main Signs

#	LOCATION	DATE (EVENT)	PATIENT	AGENT	DEDICATION	
1.	Mach 6 A2	10. 0. 5. 0. 0		none	10. 0. 5. 0. 0	
2.	Quir Ee A16	13 Ahau 13 Uo	????	????	9.17. 0. 0. 0	

This event follows an ADI which seems to refer to a previous CR date 13
Ahau 13 Cumku, noted as being six very long, but unknown, cycles in the
past. The boundary of this verbal phrase and, therefore, its subject
cannot be identified at present.

#	LOCATION	DATE (EVENT)	PATIENT	AGENT	DEDICATION	
3.	Pal PTab O10-P10	no date	????	Kan-Xul II (by title)	9.14.10. 0. 0	

This verbal phrase is the second part of a verbal couplet (or third part
of a triplet) which records the accession of Kan-Xul II on 9.13.10.6.8 5
Lamat 6 Xul. Kan-Xul II is named by a maize title (T177.507:178); by a
damaged anthropomorphic head of either *kan* maize or *balan-ahau*; and by
the bird and skull variants of the Palenque EG. The second glyph of the
verbal phrase seems not to refer to Kan-Xul individually, since it occurs
in a parallel phrase for Chan-Bahlum (#4); instead it seems to be equivalent to the T757 glyph that records "succession" in the T713/757
"accession" expression.

#	LOCATION	DATE (EVENT)	PATIENT	AGENT	DEDICATION	
4.	Pal PTab K10-L10	no date	????	Chan-Bahlum (by EG)	9.14.10. 0. 0	

This phrase is parallel to #3, but the subject is named as "Lord of
Palenque" by the skull variant of the Palenque EG. The fact that it is
the second half of a couplet structure recording Chan-Bahlum's accession
clearly identifies him as the subject of this verbal phrase. Since the
verbal suffix is missing, it cannot be identified as T82, but I have
listed this example here for the purpose of comparison to #3. The main sign
of the second glyph, "God C-in-elbow" (T187:1016:228), may be related to
an event that occurred to GI of the Palenque Triad at 13.0.1.9.2 (see
17:1, 20:1, and 32:12-13).

#	LOCATION	DATE (EVENT)	PATIENT	AGENT	DEDICATION	
5.	Mach 2 B2	9.18.10. 0. 0	tun	none	9.18.10. 0. 0	

This glyph precedes the CR date and a "half-period" glyph.

Chart 61   205

| 6. | Tort 6
D7-C8 | 9.10.17. 2.14 | | Ahpo-Balam | 9.12. 0. 0. 0 | |

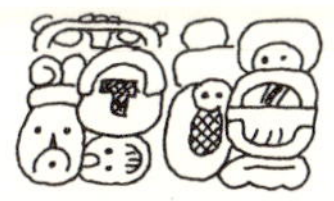

This phrase is part of the second half of a clause in which the first
part displays a "star-over-earth" as the verb (see 116:11). This phrase
follows three other verbal glyphs in the second clause, and all three
have the verbal suffix T181. Although the "zac-ahau-ik" appears in the
"wing-shell" death expression, I do not think it records death in this
context.

CHART 61		Affix T1		in Cluster 1.*:various		with Miscellaneous Main Signs
#	LOCATION	DATE (EVENT)	PATIENT	AGENT	DEDICATION	
1.	Ton M113 M	9.12. 0. 0. 0		deleted	9.12. 0. 0. 0	

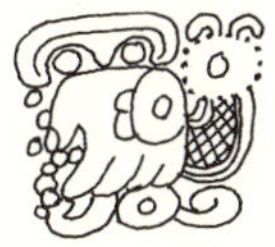

This "scattering" is followed by a verbal phrase in which a "house"
variant (T79:614:126.181) is the main sign. The appearance of T61 as a
verbal affix or as a suffix to the "scattering" glyph is unique to my
knowledge. See 87:1.

| 2. | PN L3
P1-O2 | 9.15.18. 3.16 | | Ruler 4 | 9.16.10. 0. 0 | |

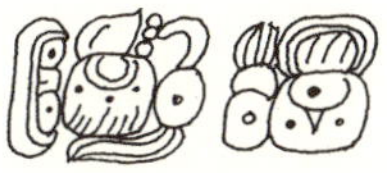

This event phrase appears after a glyph which includes *ti* (T59) and a
half-darkened kin sign, a combination which functions as a DN of one day
on the TFC at Palenque. T116 may function as a phonetic complement,
rather than as a verbal affix.

| 3. | Jimb 2
D7 | 10. 3. 0. 0. 0 | | local ruler | 10. 3. 0. 0. 0 | |

| 4. | Yax L46
F9 | no date | Etz'nab-
Bat | Knot-Eye-
Jaguar | 9.15. 0. 0. 0 | |

This "capture" variant, and presumably ones on Lintels 44 and 45, is very
unusual, and apparently it is a part of a passage which related a historic capture by Shield-Jaguar to an earlier capture by a previous ruler.
The earlier captures are recorded in detail on the stairs below each
lintel. Although only the passage from Lintel 46 survives intact, the
first glyph of the passage can be seen on Lintel 45, suggesting that all
these lintels recorded parallel information. The first glyph of the

passage contains a *ka* fist and a *pa-ca-l(a)* phonetic compound (T1:44:
669b.586:25:178 or T1:44:669b:314.1:586P:25:178). The second glyph records Knot-Eye-Jaguar, the person named as the subject of this capture on
the southeast stair below. The "capture" glyph follows, but this is one
of only two examples in which the third person pronoun of Set A is found
prefixed to the capture glyph. T126 is the verbal suffix. The last glyph
is damaged, but enough remains to identify it as Etz'nab-Bat, the person
recorded as the captive on the southeast stair. The syntactical order
seems to be VSVO [deleted subject]. See 32:10-11 for the first verbal
expression in the Lintel 45 and 46 passages.

CHART 62   Affix T126   in Cluster T126.*:130   with Main Sign T669b

The values for the components of this verbal expression are not completely understood, but
since T126 appears as a prefixed sign, I have tentatively identified it as verbal on the chance
that T126 functions as an inflectional prefix, rather than as a phonetic complement of the
verbal stem. The semantic context in which these verbs appears is better understood and provides some evidence that it is a transitive construction. The first two and one-third of the
panels of the Temple of Inscriptions at Palenque record katun histories in a highly repetitive
fashion by utilizing formulistic expressions. This verb begins a passage found in all of the
katun records, usually following a passage which links the katun (or lahuntun or oxlahuntun, as
appropriate) to the "seating" of the ruler in power at the time of the period ending. The T669b
verb is followed in each case by a "baktun" glyph in geometric or zoomorphic form. However, the
baktun notation in this context cannot refer to a cycle of 400 tuns, since the katun is the
focus of this text. Fortunately, the geometric variant of the baktun glyph is now known to
stand for the katun on Tikal Stela 31 in the Early Classic period and for the tun on Naranjo
Stela 29. In addition, the zoomorphic versions of the baktun and katun glyphs are known to be
in exchanged positions on several monuments. The "baktun" glyph must stand, therefore, for some
concept, such as "cycle," appropriate to units of 360 days, 20 tuns, and 400 tuns. In the
context of the Temple of Inscriptions, it must stand for a cycle of 20 tuns or a katun, and
since it is prefixed by a third person pronoun of Set A, it can be identified as a possessed
noun. The T669b formula continues with a God C-"water group" (T41) glyph (also prefixed by a
pronoun) and the name phrase of the contemporary ruler or one or all of the gods of the
Palenque Triad. The T41 God C glyph can be shown to function as a nominal introducing glyph
throughout the texts of Palenque, so it can be classified as part of the name phrase. The
entire clause consists of the following parts: T669b verb, "his cycle," nominal Introductory
Glyph, ruler. Syntactically, these components can be interpreted in a number of different ways,
such as "something happened to the cycle of the king (or Triad god)"; however, in the texts of
Katuns 11 and 12, the T669b verb is not followed by a cycle glyph, but rather by other glyphs
related to the Triad. Therefore, a better interpretation seems to be "the ruler (or Triad god)
did something to to his cycle," with the "something" posited as some action, such as "received"
or "ended." Examples of the various kinds of clauses are given below. See 45:3-7 for other
verbs used in the formulas for Katuns 11 and 12, and see Chart 129 for other verbs prefixed by
T126.

Chart 62   207

126.669b:130		his cycle	God C IG	Name Phrase	
					Palenque Triad
					Pacal
					GI

#	LOCATION	DATE (EVENT)	PATIENT	AGENT	DEDICATION	
1.	Pal TIe A7	9. 4. 0. 0. 0	his cycle	Pal Triad	9.12.15. 0. 0	
2.	Pal TIe D10	9. 5. 0. 0. 0	his cycle	Pal Triad	9.12.15. 0. 0	
3.	Pal TIe E11	9. 6.10. 0. 0	his cycle	eroded	9.12.15. 0. 0	
4.	Pal TIe J6	9. 7. 0. 0. 0	his cycle	Chan-Bahlum I (by title)	9.12.15. 0. 0	
5.	Pal TIe K7	9. 8. 0. 0. 0	her cycle	Lady Kanal-Ikal	9.12.15. 0. 0	
6.	Pal TIe O4	9. 9. 0. 0. 0	her cycle	Lady Zac-Kuk	9.12.15. 0. 0	

The subjects of #6-8 are recorded with the variant of the Palenque EG bird that appears as the name of the ancestral goddess whose birth is recorded on the TC and who was the mother of the Palenque Triad. The identification of this TI name phrase as Pacal's mother, Lady Zac-Kuk, can be made on structural grounds. Lounsbury (1976) has shown that the birth date of the ancestral goddess was arithmetically contrived to be "like-in-kind" to the birth date of Pacal, and the use of this deity name for his biological mother seems a natural outcome of the numerological identity established between Pacal and the goddess. However, Lounsbury (personal communication, 1979) has accumulated evidence that the variant of the EG bird used in both names was homophonous to the quetzal bird used in the more normal version of Lady Zac-Kuk's name glyph, and the use of the goddess' name in the TI may have been a phonetic as well as semantic usage.

7. Pal TIe   9. 9. 0. 0. 0   her ????   Lady Zac-Kuk 9.12.15. 0. 0
    R4

8. Pal TIe   9. 9. 0. 0. 0   her cycle   Lady Zac-Kuk 9.12.15. 0. 0
    Q7

9. Pal TIe   9.10. 0. 0. 0   his cycle   Pacal II   9.12.15. 0. 0
    S10

10. Pal TIm   9.11. 0. 0. 0   deleted (GI) 9.12.15. 0. 0
    C5

In ##10-12, I am tentatively assuming that the glyphs following the T669b verb are not alternative names for the three gods of the Triad because, although the gods may be associated with these objects, they seem to act independently of or upon them in pottery scenes. For example, GI and GIII can be shown carrying the Quadripartite Sun Monster in a back pack, but there is no evidence that either GI or GIII was considered to be the same as that entity.

11. Pal TIm   9.11. 0. 0. 0   deleted (GII) 9.12.15. 0. 0
    C8

12. Pal TIm   9.11. 0. 0. 0   deleted (GIII) 9.12.15. 0. 0
    F1

13. Pal TIm   9.12. 0. 0. 0   ????   ????   9.12.15. 0. 0
    I4

The glyphs following this verb are not yet understood.

14. Pal TIm   9.12. 0. 0. 0   Pacal II   9.12.15. 0. 0
    J10

The object following this verb is not a "cycle" glyph as in the passages from the east panel; rather it is a katun glyph, qualified as a katun of

Chart 62 209

reign by the T93.672:140 title. This passage marks Katun 12 as a katun of this title (or rule?) for Pacal.

15.	Pal TIm K3	9.12. 0. 0. 0	his cycle+	????	9.12.15. 0. 0

16.	Pal TIm L9	9.12. 0. 0. 0	his cycle+	????	9.12.15. 0. 0

17.	Pal TIw S11a	no date	????	????	9.12.15. 0. 0

This verb appears in the final passage of the west panel which relates Pacal, the dead ruler, to his son and successor, Chan-Bahlum. The verb is followed by the TI.606:23 glyph, which as a reference to Chan-Bahlum may be the object of the verb. The subject would then be the TIX.78:514:4 glyph that follows.

18.	Pal TIe Q4-Q5	9. 9. 0. 0. 0	????	Lady Zac-Kuk	9.12.15. 0. 0

In this expression, the T669b verb is preceded by a *mac* glyph (T74: 743:140), which also appears as a part of a similar phrase on the wooden box from Tortuguero (M.D. Coe 1974) (see 5:6). This clause seems to represent a redundant expression of this part of the katun history formula since it does not appear in the history of any other katun.

19.	Pal TIe P11-O12	9. 9. 0. 0. 0	????	????	9.12.15. 0. 0

This expression is the verbal phrase of an entirely different part of the katun history than the previous eighteen examples. It is followed by a "9-16-9" expression found with different, but presumably parallel, verbal expression in the histories of Katuns 9, 10, 11, and 12, but not in the histories of the earlier katuns. See 70:1-3.

20.	Nar 32 A'1-Z2	9.19. 4.15. 1		none	9.19.10. 0. 0

This Naranjo example is included in this chart because the verb is identical to those above, although the context is quite different. These two examples appear on the throne under the seating ruler. This verb is the first part of a verbal couplet in which neither part is recorded with an agent. See 26:11.

21.	Nar 32 Y5-Z5	9.19. 5. 9.12		none	9.19.10. 0. 0	

This expression is the second part of a verbal couplet which appears to
be parallel to the couplet in #20, although these two couplets record
events occurring 251 days apart. Both event expressions are located in a
secondary text incised on the stairs of the central throne of the scene,
and since none of the four verbal phrases of this text are recorded with
an agent, these events may have been intended to be cosmological, or the
protagonist of the monument (18-Rabbit) may have been understood as the
agent. See 26:12.

CHART 63   Affix T4   in Cluster T4.*:181   with Miscellaneous Main Signs

#	LOCATION	DATE (EVENT)	PATIENT	AGENT	DEDICATION	
1.	Pal AD Jamb	5 ???? 5 Kayab		Pal Triad	9.14.10. 0. 0	

This verb is found on fragments of what was originally a tablet mounted
on the inside of the center piers on the north side of House AD. T4 *na*
appears as a prefix to this glyph, although its function here is not
entirely clear. *Na* is a term for an unpossessed house, and T4 may function, therefore, as a phonetic complement altering the *otoch* glyph into
na.

2.	Yax 11 Frt C4-E1	9.16. 1. 0. 0		Bird-Jaguar	9.16. 5. 0. 0	

CHART 64   Affix T181 or T228   in Cluster *.181 or 228   with Miscellaneous Main Signs

All of these examples are period ending expressions.

#	LOCATION	DATE (EVENT)	PATIENT	AGENT	DEDICATION	
1.	CRic Jade	9. 0.11. 0. 0	tun	eroded	9. 0.11. 0. 0	

T228, the suffix to this "end of tun" glyph, has the phonetic value *ah*
and is found along with T181 as the prefixed male article. Here it is a
phonetic substitute for T181 *ah* as a verbal suffix.

Chart 65   211

| 2. | Tort Box B2 | 9.12. 7. 0. 0 | tun | none | 9.12.10. 0. 0 |  |

See 5:6.

| 3. | Pom PanX pB3 | 9.18. 0. 0. 0 | 18 katuns | none | 9.18. 0. 0. 0 |   |

Thompson (in Aulie and Aulie 1978:9) associated the Chol phrase *suts'atax i wut* with this "inverted bat" glyph. The Chol expression, which means "face of the bat," is used to describe a very tired person, perhaps as Thompson says because "his head looks like a bat resting with the head downward." In the context of this PE expression, the bat seems to be used as a metaphor for "expired." See 4:7, 41:6, and 52:8 for other verbal expressions in this text.

| 4. | Yax L2 C2-E1 | 9.16. 6. 0. 0 | 5th tun as *ahau* | none | 9.16. 6. 0. 0 | |

| 5. | DPil 13 B4 | no date | | Flint-Sky-God K | 9.13. 0. 0. 0 |  |

This verb appears with period endings at other sites, but here it functions to link this Dos Pilas ruler to Great-Jaguar-Paw of Site Q, whose accession is recorded in the immediately preceding clause (see 71:4). T229 seems to function as a phonetic substitute for T181 *ah*, as it does in #1.

| CHART 65 | Affix T181 | in Cluster *.181 | with Main Sign "Scattering" |

#	LOCATION	DATE (EVENT)	PATIENT	AGENT	DEDICATION	
1.	Coll 9 B4	9.11. 6. 3. 4		missing	9.12. 0. 0. 0	

This verb is from Site Q Glyphic Panel 8. Note that this "scattering" is not associated with a PE date.

| 2. | Quir Fe A9-B9a | 9.16.10. 0. 0 | | none | 9.17. 0. 0. 0 |  |

3.   Car 17   10. 1. 0. 0. 0   Ox-Cauac   10. 1. 0. 0. 0
     C5

CHART 66   Affix T181   in Cluster *:181   with Main Sign "Half-Period"

Peter Mathews (personal communication, 1979) has informed me that he has found this glyph associated, not only with a half-period of a katun, but also with a half-period of a uinal, a tun,
fifteen tuns, and a baktun. Note that some of these examples function as period ending rather than
half-period expressions.

#	LOCATION	DATE (EVENT)	PATIENT	AGENT	DEDICATION	
1.	Tik 31 A13-B13	9. 0.10. 0. 0	1 cycle	Stormy-Sky	9. 0.10. 0. 0	
2.	Tik 31 H7-G8	8.19.10. 0. 0	1 cycle	none	9. 0.10. 0. 0	
3.	Coll 7 pA19	9. 8. 0. 0. 0	see note	none	9. 8. 0. 0. 0	

The date on this stela in Brussels in not a half-period, but a katun
ending; and the center of this glyph is not T606 as expected, but rather
T617. This distinction may mark the two different kinds of period ending
phrases.

4.	Ton M111 K	9.13. 0. 0. 0	13 katuns	none	9.13. 0. 0. 0	

This phrase is associated with a katun ending like that on the Brussels
stela; however, my source does not reveal enough detail to determine if
the center of the glyph is like the Brussels example.

5.	Coll 8 pC1	9.11.10. 0. 0	none	Rodent-Turtle	9.11.10. 0. 0	
6.	Bon D D1	9.14. 3. 8. 3	13 tuns	Flint-Mandible	9.14. 5. 0. 0	

This example from the Bonampak Column in the St. Louis Museum does not
occur on a PE date of any sort. The text cannot be analyzed within a

Chart 67   213

historical context, so it is not possible to determine whether the event might be a thirteen-tun anniversary of some earlier event, or a half-period of thirteen tuns.

| 7. | Quir Fw A16b | 9.16.10. 0. 0 | none | none | 9.17. 0. 0. 0 |  |

This is the second part of a couplet; see 5:4 for the first part.

| 8. | Tik 31 F24 | 8.18.10. 0. 0 | 1 cycle | none | 9. 0.10. 0. 0 |  |

| 9. | Pom Wall Pan pE1 | 9.17. 0. 0. 0 | 17 katuns | deleted | 9.17. 0. 0. 0 |  |

This example is similar in detail to #8, but an additional element is superposed to the main sign. The PE glyph is followed by "17 katuns" and a long series of additional phrases including the following: (1) this phrase; (2) "seating of the tun"; (3) "scattering"; (4) "end of the tun"; (5) a T757 + complement phrase; and (6) the subject of all these verbs, GI-Jaguar. See 4:10, 41:4, 43:7, and 52:6.

CHART 67   Affix T181   in Cluster *.181   with Main Sign T218

#	LOCATION	DATE (EVENT)	PATIENT	AGENT	DEDICATION	
1.	Cop P A6-A6b	9. 9.10. 0. 0	half-period	*u cab* ????	9. 9.10. 0. 0	
2.	Yax 3 pA1-pA3	no date	1 katun of ruler	6-Tun-Bird-Jaguar II	9.12. 5. 0. 0?	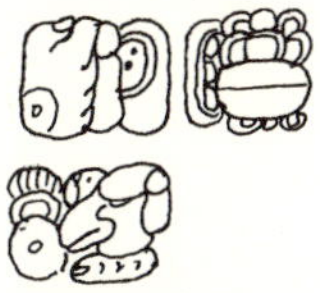
3.	Pal TC C7-D7	2. 0. 0. 0. 0	2 baktuns	deleted	9.13. 0. 0. 0	

PEI. This phrase is followed by a "fish-in-hand" blood-letting verb (39:4) of which the ancestral goddess, whose birth is recorded on the TC, is recorded as the agent. Presumably she let blood on the occasion of this baktun ending and is to be understood as the agent of the "completion" verb.

4. ArP 3   9.15. 0. 0. 0   15 katuns   deleted   9.15. 0. 0. 0
    C1-D1

This glyph is followed by another period ending expression (109:4),
"scattering" (68:3), and the name of the agent.

5. Cop B   9.15. 0. 0. 0   15 katuns   deleted   9.15. 0. 0. 0
    B5-B6

This phrase is followed by a T586 PE expression, "scattering," a T757
verb, and the name phrase of the agent.

6. Yax 6   9.11.16.10.13   ???? as   Bird-   9.12. 0. 0. 0
    C7b-C8   *ahpo*   Jaguar II

This phrase records an anniversary of accession, but the period glyph is
eroded.

7. Cop Alt   9.11.15. 0. 0   none   9.11.15. 0. 0
    of 5; S1-
    T1

CHART 68   Affix T181   in Cluster *.181   with Miscellaneous Main Signs

All of these expressions are associated with period endings.

#	LOCATION	DATE (EVENT)	PATIENT	AGENT	DEDICATION	
1.	PN L3 F2-H1	9.15.18. 3.13	1 katun of reign	Ruler 4	9.16.10. 0. 0	
2.	Pom Wall Pan pL5	9.17. 0. 0. 3	missing	missing	9.17. 0. 0. 0	

The glyphs which followed this verb are now missing, but the text from
Piedras Negras Lintel 3 (#1) suggests that this Pomona example recorded
some sort of period ending expression. Since the date of the event is
after a katun ending, it seems likely that the period was something like
a period of reign. See 98:4.

Chart 69   215

3.	ArP 3 C2-D2	9.15. 0. 0. 0	tun?	deleted	9.15. 0. 0. 0

This expression is the second part of a verbal triplet (see 67:4). It is followed by a "scattering" glyph (109:4) and the name of the agent, Ah Chac-Be/ Ah Cauac. The second glyph in this expression is prefixed by a third person pronoun of Set A, marking it as a possessed noun. The main sign is a general tree sign, found in anniversary and dedication phrases at Palenque. A T528 glyph occupies the lower right corner of the block, perhaps marking the period ended as a tun. The occurrence of this general tree sign in a period ending expression suggests that the verbal phrase on the Dallas Stela (see 52:2) may also be a period ending expression. See 26:13-14, 67:1, 69:3, 84:6, and 131:2-3.

4.	Quir C B6	13. 0. 0. 0. 0	????	none	9.17. 5. 0. 0

See #5, 5:15, and 104:3-4 for other examples of this era expression.

5.	Coba 1 A18-B19	13. 0. 0. 0. 0		none	9.15. 0. 0. 0

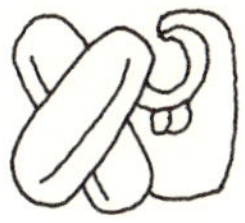

The Initial Series date of this stela is clearly 4 Ahau 8 Cumku, but the LC includes nineteen periods above 13.0.0.0.0, the more common designation for 4 Ahau 8 Cumku. However, since this expression is very similar to the era expression used at Palenque (104:3-4), I believe that this Coba date also records the era event, and that all cycles above the katun were (at least at Coba) considered had a numerical coefficient of 13 on the day the current era began.

CHART 69	Affix 181	in Cluster *.181	with Main Signs Tnn[586] or Tnn:586

#	LOCATION	DATE (EVENT)	PATIENT	AGENT	DEDICATION	
1.	Coll 7 pA20	9. 8. 0. 0. 0		5-Kix-Chan	9. 8. 0. 0. 0	

This PE expression follows 66:3.

#	LOCATION	DATE (EVENT)	PATIENT	AGENT	DEDICATION	
2.	Cop E Alt; G	missing	missing	missing	9. 9. 5. 0. 0?	

PEI.

3. Cop 6   9.12.10. 0. 0   ????   eroded   9.12.10. 0. 0
    C6-C7

This seems to be a standard expression for a period ending event which
reappears on Stela M and perhaps elsewhere. The last glyph is the general
tree sign with a cauac (tun) glyph adjoined to it. This part of the
expression seems to be related to the verbal expression on the Dallas
Stela (52:2) and Arroyo de Piedra Stela 3 (68:3).

4. Cop 4   9.15. 0. 0. 0   deleted   9.15. 0. 0. 0
    A8   (18-Rabbit)

PEI. This example is preceded by a "completion of fifteen katuns" expression and followed by a T204.757 general verb and the name of the subject,
18-Rabbit.

5. Cop B   9.15. 0. 0. 0   ????   deleted   9.15. 0. 0. 0
    B1

6. Cop M   9.16. 5. 0. 0   deleted or   9.16. 5. 0. 0
    B4b-B5   none

7. Cop N   9.16.10. 0. 0   New-Sky-at-   9.16.10. 0. 0
    A16   Horizon

This verb is the first part of a couplet; see 57:3 for the second half.

8. Quir Ee   9.17. 0. 0. 0   13 Ahau   *u cab* Two-Legged-   9.17. 0. 0. 0
    A9   tun   Sky (by
                                                        title)

These three glyphs seem to be a verbal triplet recording the end of Katun
17, with the last glyph specifying the event as a "death." "13 Ahau tun"
follows the verbal expression and the agent is named only with the
"shell-fist" title, but surely the agent is meant to be understood as
Two-Legged Sky, the protagonist of the monument.

9. Quir De   9.16.15. 0. 0   ????   ????   9.16.15. 0. 0

This expression seems to be related to ones recorded at Dos Pilas (43:1-
2) and may be related to the Copan examples under #3-6.

Chart 70 217

10.	Car 1 C2	9. 8. 0. 0. 0		Ruler 2	9. 8. 0. 0. 0	

CHART 70   Affix T181   in Cluster T*.181   with Miscellaneous Main Signs

#	LOCATION	DATE (EVENT)	PATIENT	AGENT	DEDICATION	
1.	Pal TIe T5	9.10. 0. 0. 0		9-16-9	9.12.15. 0. 0	

This verbal stem is composed of two signs for which the phonetic values are known; T89 is *tu* and T586 is *pa*, which together form the stem *tup*. The meaning of the verb is not known, but it begins a clause repeated in the histories of Katuns 9, 11, and 12. In all three clauses, the verb is followed by three glyphs: 9-sky-kin animal (TIX.561:23/115.756c:116); 16-kin animal (TXVI.756c:116); and 9-*hel* (TIX.168:573:21 or 130). The meaning of this series of glyphs is not understood. See 62:17 for the Katun 9 version of this expression. See 31:7-9 for the same verb in an alternative context in these same katun histories.

2.	Pal TIm A9	9.11. 0. 0. 0		9-16-9	9.12.15. 0. 0	
3.	Pal TIm H9	9.12. 0. 0. 0		9-16-9	9.12.15. 0. 0	

This glyph is found in a position clearly parallel to those of #1 and #2, but it is not known whether or how this glyph is equivalent to the first two.

4.	Pal TIe M3-N4	9. 8.13. 0. 0	tun-seating	Ac-Kan	9.12.15. 0. 0	

This verb is parallel to those list on Chart 62.

5.	Cop 2 B6b	9.11. 0. 0. 0	11 katuns	Bat-Uinal?	9.11. 0. 0. 0	

This drawing is very suspect.

6.   Pal Tabs   9.11. 1.12. 6   his haab   Pacal II   9.11. 5. 0. 0
      E2-F2

The date of this clause occurs on the thirteenth haab (365-day year)
anniversary of 9.10.8.9.3 9 Akbal 6 Xul, the day on which Chan-Bahlum II
was made heir-designate. The verbal glyph is composed of T534 *la* and T181
ah, which together form *lah*, a term documented in several Maya languages,
including Yucatec and Tzotzil, for "end" or "finish." Since the date is a
known haab anniversary, and since the verb is *lah* "end" or "finish," the
second glyph must record haab in some manner or some special term for a
cycle of "13 haabs." Note that its configuration is markedly in contrast
to T528 as tun (T528:116).

7.   Pal T18   no date   local person   9.14.15. 0. 0
      Stc e1

This verb and the one in #8 once occurred in secondary texts that
accompanied now-missing figures.

8.   Pal T18   no date   local person   9.14.15. 0. 0
      Stc g1

9.   Cop A   9.14.19. 8. 0   missing or   9.15. 0. 0. 0
      A12b   none

CHART 71   Affix T181   in Cluster *.181   with Main Sign T684

All these examples are accession expressions. When T683, the full version of T181, is infixed into
the T684 "bundle" glyph, I assume that this sign functions as a verbal suffix.

#	LOCATION	DATE (EVENT)	PATIENT	AGENT	DEDICATION	
1.	Tik 4 A5-B5	8.17. 2.16.17		Curl-Snout	8.17. 5. 0. 0	

This expression follows T51.1:788 (37:4).

2.	Ton F34 pB3-pB4	missing		missing	9.10. 0. 0. 0?	
3.	Coll 1 A2-D2	9. 9.12.10. 6		Zac-Mac	9.10. 0. 0. 0	

Chart 71   219

4.	DPil 13 B2b-A3a	9.12.13.17. 7	Great- Jaguar-Paw of Site Q	9.13. 0. 0. 0 
5.	PN 8 G3-H3	9.12.14.13. 1	missing (Ruler 3)	9.13. 0. 0. 0 
6.	Agua 1 B12	9.15. 9.17.17	God K/ Mah Kina	9.15.10. 0. 0 
7.	PN Alt2 E2	9.14.18. 3.13	Ruler 4	9.16. 0. 0. 0 
8.	PN 14 B11	9.16. 6.17. 1	Ruler 5	9.18.10. 0. 0 
9.	Yax L30 H4	9.16. 1. 0. 0	Bird-Jaguar	9.17. 0. 0. 0 
10.	PN 16 C5	9.16.12.10. 8	Ruler 6	9.16.15. 0. 0 
11.	ECayo L3 J4	9.14.18. 5. 7	eroded	9.15. 5. 0. 0 
12.	ECayo L1 E1-F1	9.16.12.14.10	Ah Chac-Zotz'	9.17. 5. 0. 0 
13.	ECayo L1 K15-L15	9.17. 1. 5. 9	4-Pa-na-ca/ Ahau	9.17. 5. 0. 0 
14.	PN 15 C5	9.17.10. 9. 4	Ruler 7	9.17. 15. 0. 0 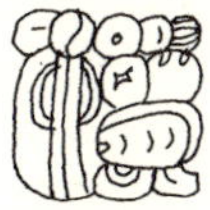
15.	Bon 2 C1-C2	9.17. 5. 8. 9	Chaan-Muan	9.17.15. 0. 0 

16.	Nar 6 A3	9.16.17.14.3		Ruler IIIa	9.17. 0. 0. 0	
17.	Nar 14 D9-C10	9.17.13. 4. 3		Ruler IIIb	9.18. 0. 0. 0	
18.	PN 11 E7	9.14.18. 3.13		Ruler 4	9.15. 0. 0. 0	

This same accession is recorded as #7.

19.	PN Thr1 G'3	9.17.10. 9. 4		Ruler 7	9.17.15. 0. 0	
20.	Yax 11Frt pC4-pE1	9.16. 1. 0. 0		Bird- Jaguar III	9.16. 5. 0. 0	
21.	DPil 8 C18b-D18	9.14.15. 5.15		Spangle-Head	9.15. 0. 0. 0	
22.	MJos 2 A8-A9	9. 8. 9. 1.17		eroded	9.14. 0. 0. 0	
23.	Res HS3 B10	missing		missing	9. 4. 0. 0. 0?	

CHART 72	**Affix T181**		**in Cluster *.181**		**with Main Signs T713 or T670**

#	LOCATION	DATE (EVENT)	PATIENT	AGENT	DEDICATION	
1.	Coll 10 B2-C1	????		Uinal-Ahau	????	

This text is on a small bone which shows an accession scene in which a
ruler sits upon a "world" throne (marked by waterlilies and sky signs;
see Naranjo Stela 32 for another example) holding a quadripartite badge,
while an Aged God holds a proto-typical headdress above his head and in
front of the ruler. The CR date, 5 Cib 20 Yaxkin, of this event is in
error because the day Cib cannot go with the haab coefficient 20. In

Chart 72   221

working with this date, I assumed that the day 5 Eb, the possibility graphically closest to Cib, was intended and calculated the following set of LC positions:

	Date of Event	Dedication
1.	9. 3. 1.14.12	9. 3. 5. 0. 0
2.	9. 6.10. 9.12	9. 6.15. 0. 0
3.	9. 9. 3. 4.12	9. 9. 5. 0. 0
4.	9.11.15.17.12	9.12. 0. 0. 0
5.	9.14.18.12.12	9.15. 0. 0. 0
6.	9.17. 1. 7.12	9.17. 5. 0. 0

A provenience of Palenque has been suggested for this bone, and in terms of both style and iconography, this assumption is fitting; however, the style of drawing is deliberately archaic, so that it does not help in assigning the time period. If the bone is from Palenque, the second and fifth possibilities are the least in conflict with the known dynastic history. And it is also a possibility that this bone records the accession of a mythological personage or of a ruler of a subordinate site in the Palenque region and not of the main center.

2.	Pal HS A11-B11	9. 9. 2. 4. 8	Pacal II	9.11.10. 0. 0	
3.	Pal TC M3-N1	9.12.11.12.10	Chan-Bahlum II	9.13. 0. 0. 0	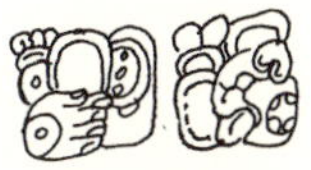
4.	Pal Slav A5	9.14.10. 4. 2	Chaacal III	9.15. 0. 0. 0	

PEI.

5.	Pal PTab O1-P4	9.13.10. 6. 8	Kan-Xul II	9.14.10. 0. 0	
6.	Yax Str44 Ctr Up D11-C13	9.12. 9. 8. 1	deleted (Shield-Jaguar I)	9.15. 0. 0. 0	

PEI. No subject is recorded for this verbal phrase, but since it is in the final clause of a text in which only Shield-Jaguar is named as protagonist, it can be assumed that he is the intended subject here. Either his name phrase is deleted as redundant, or as Mathews (personal communication, 1980) suggests, his name may be recorded on the front part (riser) of this stair, which apparently has never been photographed.

#	LOCATION	DATE (EVENT)	PATIENT	AGENT	DEDICATION	
7.	Quir J F4-F6	9.14.13. 4.17		Two-Legged- Sky	9.16. 5. 0. 0	
8.	Pal ISpot G1-H1	9.18. 9. 4. 4		6-Cimi/Pacal	9.18.10. 0. 0	
9.	LMar 3 B2-A3	9.17.18. 6.19		local ruler	9.18. 5. 0. 0	

See 37:20; this verbal phrase follows a T757 auxiliary verb.

10.	Tik 31 H8	8.19.10. 0. 0		Stormy-Sky	9. 0. 10. 0. 0	
11.	EPeru B	9.15.10. 0. 0?		local ruler	9.15.10. 0. 0	

CHART 73	Affix T181	in Cluster *.181	with Miscellaneous Main Signs

#	LOCATION	DATE (EVENT)	PATIENT	AGENT	DEDICATION	
1.	Cop AltY A2	9. 7. 1. 7. 6?		local ruler	9. 7. 5. 0. 0?	
2.	Chin Thr pD2	9.13. 5.16. 4		Feather- Shield	9.14. 0. 0. 0	

A drawing of this monument is published in Maler (1901:12 and Pl. II). This "death" verb follows a "seating" expression and a DN that establishes the time between the accession and death of this lord. Another "seating" event follows immediately after, but its agent is not recorded in Maler's drawing. The date may be one CR earlier or later. See Chart 19.

3.	Pal PTab N7	9.13.10. 1. 5		deleted (Chan- Bahlum II)	9.14.10. 0. 0	

Chart 73   223

PEI. The DN which precedes the verb is the length of time between the date of Chan-Bahlum's accession and this event, his death. Although the subject of this verb is not named, this passage is the first part of a couplet in which the subject of the second part is named as Chan-Bahlum II. See Chart 19 for other examples of this verb.

4. DPil 8   9.14.15. 2. 3   Shield-God K   deleted   9.15. 0. 0. 0
    C14

Mathews (n.d.b) has identified this event and the one listed as #5 as burial rites conducted respectively three and four days after the death of the patients of each verb. His analysis includes a reading of the verbal stem as *muc*, a word for "burial" widely distributed in the Mayan languages. His analysis of this Dos Pilas example identifies the parts of the glyph as *tu.mu:ca.ah*, and he points out the difference between this example and that from Piedras Negras (#5), which utilizes a different *mu* sign and is without the *tu* prefix. He posited that this construction is transitive, with *tu* recording a preposed tense-aspect particle and the third person pronoun of Set A; that the name of the agent is deleted; and that this clause is gapped to the next one, where the agents of both events are named. A paraphrase is as follows: ". . . On 11 Cauac 17 Mac, he died, Shield-God K, Lord of Dos Pilas; three days later, he [Spangle-Head] buried Shield-God K; in twelve days and three uinals, he was inaugurated as Ahau, Spangle-Head, Lord of Dos Pilas." I accept Mathews' suggestion is a viable hypothesis, but there are some problems which should be noted. It is possible that the *tu* sign is part of the main graph and not intended to be read as a separate sign at all. The most normal environment for this sign combination is as an infix in the upper part of the seating glyph. In a "seating of the tun" expression on the Pomona Wall Panel, this compound sign is taken out of the main sign and placed below it, apparently without changing the meaning of the expression. A comparative example from Pomona Panel X shows this sign in its normal infixed position, and although the example from the Wall Panel has the infix below the main sign, rather than infixed into it, there is no apparent difference in meaning, and both examples occur in identical contexts. The compound identified as *tu-mu* by Mathews may function, therefore, as a single, rather than multiple, sign, in which case no agent is named in this burial clause. See Chart 27 for other examples of verbs with *tu* prefixes.

Pomona   Panel X   Wall Panel

5. PN L3   9.16. 6.12. 0   Ruler 4   none   9.16.10. 0. 0
    V5

The second occurrence of the "burial" glyph is on Lintel 3 at Piedras

Negras. The burial was three days after the death of Ruler 4, and the verb is followed by a titular reference to him, by a series of eroded glyphs which may have contained a DN, and finally, by the name phrase of Ruler 7 preceded by *u cab*. This structure may be parallel to the deleted structure of Dos Pilas Stela 8, but it seems more likely that Ruler 4 was buried by his successor, not the ruler who came to the throne after two intervening reigns.

6. Pal T18   missing   missing   9.14.15. 0. 0
    Stc 471

This glyph is composed of the same signs as the "burial" glyph under #5, but since it was not in its original location, its meaning cannot be confirmed. However, it should be noted Blom (Blom and LaFarge 1926:175) recorded a "death" event in place on the rear wall of Temple 18, and a DN ("the second day after") was found among the glyphs detached from the rear wall.

7. Pal T18   missing   missing   9.14.15. 0. 0
    Stc 462

8. Pal T18   missing   missing   9.14.15. 0. 0
    Stc 485

PEI. Both this example and #7 are glyphs recording "death"; see Chart 19 and ##2-3.

9. Ton F71   missing   missing   Late Classic
    B

10. Pal Frag   ???? 1 Kayab   missing   Late Classic

This fragment is in the bodega at Palenque, but it was found at the Palenque railroad station where looters left it and is from an unknown site in the general region of Palenque.

11. Pal TC   eroded   Lady Ahpo-?? 9.12.10. 0. 0
    Cens1 G4

12. Quir Dw   9.16.15. 0. 0   missing   9.16.15. 0. 0
    B22a

Chart 74   225

CHART 74   Affix T181   in Cluster *.181   with Main Sign T515

#	LOCATION	DATE (EVENT)	PATIENT	AGENT	DEDICATION	
1.	Tort Sarc 36	9.10.17. 1. 2	deleted?	deleted (Ahpo-Balam)	9.12.10. 0. 0	

This "capture" glyph is part of a series of events including two "star-over-earth" events (see 10:7). This "capture" event is followed by *u mul* (T1:513) and the tzolkin position 1 Muluc. Arithmetically, it can be determined that 1 Muluc occurred seven days after the CR of the "capture" event, and it seems likely that the *u mul* preceding 1 Muluc is a "count" glyph, rather than the object of the capture. It is somewhat shorter than the glyphs around it, and I suspect the expected *ti* (T59) is eroded. The "capture" verb seems to occur without patient or agent, and the 1 Muluc event (an "axe" war event) is followed by a partially eroded glyph which contains *chac* (T109), *ik* (T503), and T126. These two events are followed 25 days later by a "star-over-earth" and another "capture" event (see #2).

| 2. | Tort Sarc 44 | 9.10.17. 2.14 | 4-Chuen | *u cab* Ahpo-Balam | 9.12.10. 0. 0 |  |

This event follows the two events described above and a "star-over-earth/ bundled sky" event (see 10:7). It is followed by a long name phrase, which seems to name the patient, and then by *u cab* and the name glyph of Ahpo-Balam, presumably the agent of all three events. The same "star-over earth/bundle" events are recorded on the Tortuguero earplugs, but without the "capture" notation (see 10:5).

| 3. | DPil HSe G4 | 9.11.11. 9.17 | Tah-Mo' | deleted | 9.12.12. 0. 0 |  |

The name of the agent is deleted from this clause, but it follows a second verb which seems to be a variation of the proposed agency expression found in other capture statements (see 34:2, 12-17). The normal form of this *u mal* expression is T1.501:102, but here it is *ma:la.ah* (T501:178.181). The name Flint-Sky-God K, the protagonist of this monument and presumably the agent of the both verbs, concludes the text.

4.   Pal HS   9.11. 6.16. 3   deleted   deleted   9.11.10. 0. 0
     E7

This event occurs in a very difficult passage from the Hieroglyphic
Stairs of House C in the Palace. The passage seems to consist of a series
of clauses recording different events occurring on the same day (there
are no intervening dates), or else these clauses record the same event in
a triplet form. The verb of the first section is an "axe" event (14:1)
associated with a personage named with the Site Q EG and all three
members of the Palenque Triad. The second verb is of unknown meaning, but
it is followed by several glyphs: a name (?) Crossed-Bands-Jaguar/GI; a
possible relationship glyph (T575[565]:18); the name Shield-Jaguar of
Yaxchilan (but this event occurred when he was approximately six,
1.7.9.17 before his accession [Proskouriakoff 1963: Table 1]); and a
T87.515 *chu* sign without either the *cu* (T528) or *ca* (T25) required to
complete the verbal stem for "capture" *chuc* (see #5). The third section
is composed of another verb and name phrase followed by the "capture"
glyph *chu:ca.ah*, T515:25.181), but the name of neither patient nor agent
is included in the text. I do not believe that the structure of this
text is understood well enough to conclude that a six-year-old Shield-
Jaguar was capture by a Palenque ruler, but the context appears to be one
of war.

5.   Pal HS   9.11. 1.16. 3?   ????   ????   9.11.10. 0. 0
     F6

As discussed above, this example does not include the *cu* (T528) or *ca*
(T25) required to form the verbal stem for "capture" (*chuc*).

6.   Yax 20   9.13. 9.14.14   Ah Kan   *u cab* Shield-   9.13.10. 0. 0?
     A3   Jaguar II

Proskouriakoff (1963:160-161) noted a difficulty with this date and
capture event. A capture involving a captive of the same name occurs on
Lintel 46 where the date twelve years later is recorded. Because of the
similarity of the two CRs (5 Ix 17 Kankin and 6 Ix 16 Kankin) and the
repeated names, Proskouriakoff suggested that the captures are the same,
and that the earlier of the two monuments, Stela 20, recorded an error
in the CR date.

7.   Yax 18   9.14.15.17.11   Ah Chuen   deleted   9.15. 0. 0. 0
     A4   (Shield-
                                                 Jaguar I)

See 35:5.

Chart 74   227

8.	Yax 19 A3	9.12. 8.14. 0	Death or Ah Ahaual	*u mal* Shield-Jaguar I	9.15. 0. 0. 0 
9.	Yax Str44 nw low A2a	9.10.14.13. 0	Cauac-Bat	6-Tun/Bird-Jaguar II	9.15. 0. 0. 0 
10.	Yax Str44 nw Up A2a	9. 8. 0.15.11	eroded	eroded	9.15. 0. 0. 0 
11.	Yax Str44 se Up D6b	9.14.17.15.11	Ah Chuen	Shield-Jaguar I	9.15. 0. 0. 0 
12.	Yax Str44 se Low A2	eroded	eroded	eroded	9.15. 0. 0. 0 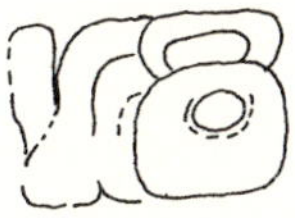
13.	Yax Str44 Ctr Up C3	9.12. 8.14. 1	Ah Ahaual	Shield-Jaguar I	9.15. 0. 0. 0 

This "capture" construction is unusual in that the *u mal* (T1.T501:102), which usually stands between the captive and captor, is found immediately following the verb with the locative *ti* preceding the name of the captive (patient). The construction seems to read *chucah u mal ti Ah Ahaual*.

| 14. | Yax L44 A3 | 9.12.17.12. 0 | Ah Zac-Manik | Shield-Jaguar I | 9.15. 0. 0. 0  |
| 15. | Yax L45 pB1b | 9.12. 8.14. 1 | Ah Ahaual | *u mal* Shield-Jaguar I | 9.15. 0. 0. 0  |

Although the verb has been entirely destroyed on Lintel 45, I have listed it as an example because the text can be reconstructed with some security.

| 16. | Yax L46 F3 | 9.14. 1.17.14 | Ah Kan | *u mal* Shield-Jaguar I | 9.15. 0. 0. 0  |
| 17. | Pal Slav E1a | 9.14.11.17. 6 | Knot-Manik | deleted (Chac-Zutz') | 9.15. 0. 0. 0  |

This "capture" verb is followed by the name Knot-Manik (T12:60?:671) which appears on the Jonuta Panel in the Museo Nacional de Antropologia y

Historia in Mexico City. Two additional glyphs follow this name, but it is not certain whether they record additional names or titles of this individual, or name additional captives. This capture is preceded by an "axe" event (1.12.16 earlier) of which the agent is recorded as "u cab Chac-Zutz'," and it is followed by a second "axe" verb (5.13.13. later) recorded with the same agent phrase. If the agent of the "capture" event is deleted, then he is named as Chac-Zutz' in the following clause.

18.	Yax L8 A3	9.16. 4. 1. 1	Jeweled-Skull	u mal	Bird-Jaguar III	9.16. 5. 0. 0
19.	Yax L41 C1	no date	Jeweled-Skull	u mal	Bird-Jaguar	9.16. 5. 0. 0

The main text of this lintel records a "star-shell" event as the featured occasion, and the date is the same as on Lintel 8, 9.16.4.1.1. This "capture" event is recorded in the secondary text and without a date.

20.	LPas L1 A3	no date	Manik-Cauac		Bird-Jaguar III	9.16.15. 0. 0
21.	Coll 2 A2	9.17.12.13.14	Balam-Ahau	u cab	Ah Chac-Ma-??	9.17.15. 0. 0

This "capture" event from the Kimbell Museum panel is followed three days later by a second event (T23.130:180 na.wa:ah) which appears to record the public disposition and perhaps sacrifice of the captive. The main figure in the scene is seated on a throne marked by the name phrase of Shield-Jaguar II of Yaxchilan, but the agent of this capture seem to be a different person. The prominent display of the name of a Yaxchilan ruler may signal that the site from which this panel comes was aligned in some way with the Yaxchilan dynasty. The name of the captive also occurs in the frame adjacent to the principal figure in the lower part of the composition.

22.	Bon L1 A3	9.17.16. 3.12	Ah 5-Skull		Chaan-Muan	9.18. 5. 0. 0
23.	Bon L2 A3	9.17.16. 3. 8	Zotz'		Shield-Jaguar II of Yaxchilan	9.18. 5. 0. 0

Chart 74   229

| 24. | Bon L3
A3 | 9.15. 9. 3.14 | eroded | Knot-Eye-
Jaguar | 9.18. 5. 0. 0 |  |

| 25. | LMar 3
C1 | no date | Ah Bone-
Chu | deleted | 9.18. 5. 0. 0 |  |

This glyph occurs in the secondary text associated with a captive figure.
The "capture" event proper is recorded in the main text as having occurred on 9.18.4.2.19.

| 26. | Yax 5
A2 | 9.18. 6. 5.11 | deleted | deleted | 9.18.10. 0. 0 |  |

This "capture" glyph is followed immediately by the "captor" glyph (T1.
108:764), which appears on Lintel 8 (32:14), where it occurs as a verb in
a clearly transitive construction. Because of the syntactical order--
"captor," patient, agent--this glyph must be verbal in this text also,
and it is, therefore, the second half of a verbal couplet.

| 27. | Yax L10
B7 | 9.18.17.12. 6 | Turtle-
Bat | deleted | 9.19. 0. 0. 0 |  |

The "capture" statement is found within a long series of clauses which do
not have intervening dates. Among the preceding events are "ahau-in-hand"
(129:6) and a "star-shell" event (10:20). The "capture" is followed by
the name "Turtle-Bat," but without the agent being named; however, the
agent of the capture, who is named with a skull glyph, follows in the
next clause after a repetition of the initial "ahau-in-hand" verb (27:4).

| 28. | Yxh 31
A2 | 9.15.13. 4.14 | Zotz' | *u cab* Yax-God K/
Ek-GIII | 9.16. 0. 0. 0? |  |

| 29. | Coll 25
A4a | ???? | Star-Parrot | Ah Kan | Late Classic |  |

The calendric information for this date is written as 2 Kan 3 Chicchan
(or Ahau) with no haab position given. The presence of the two tzolkin
days, rather than a CR is unexplained. T17:565:18 occurs between the name
glyphs of the patient and the agent.

| 30. | Cop AltR
L1a | 9.18. 2. 8. 0 | | New-Sky-at
Horizon | 9.18. 5. 0. 0 |  |

This example is surely not "capture," as can be seen by the sign pene-

trating the *chuc* (T515[528]) glyph. In the "capture" glyph, this sign
should be T87, but here is is a "torch" (*tah*) sign. It is doubtful
whether the glyph retains the same reading when this phonetic complement
is changed.

31.	DPil HSe B5	9.11.17. 8.19	????	????	9.12.12. 0. 0	

This example is graphically equivalent to the Copan example above, but
there is some evidence that it is associated with "capture" or "war"
events in this context. It appears in a text in which the initial event
is "star-shell" with the main sign of the Tikal (Dos Pilas?) EG adjoined;
and this pseudo-"capture" glyph is followed by the same Tikal main sign,
by *ah kin* (T584:544), and by two eroded signs. But more importantly, the
pseudo-"capture" glyph is adjoined to a glyph which replaces the normal
"captor" (T1.108:764) glyph on the Forth Worth panel so that the adjoined
sign may function as a semantic determinative specifying "capture." (The
text below is read right to left in reverse order).

1 personal name (Chel Te')
2 "sky" (Chaan)
3 "west" (a substitute for the expected Mah Kina title)
4 "the captor of" 5 Tah-Mo'
6-7 Lord of Yaxchilan

32.	Yax 15 A2	9.12. 8.14. 1	Ah Ahaualu *mal*	Shield-Jaguar I	9.12.10. 0. 0	
33.	Yax Str44 nw Low C8b	9.15. 0.12. 0	Na-Cauac-Manik	eroded	9.15. 0. 0. 0	
34.	Yax Str44 nw Low D4	9.15. 0.12. 0	Na-Cauac-Manik	deleted	9.15. 0. 0. 0	
35.	Yax Str44 se Up D1b	9.14. 1.17.14	Ah Kan	Shield-Jaguar I	9.15. 0. 0. 0	
36.	Yax Str20 HS 58	9.18. 6. 4.19	eroded	Shield-Jaguar-II	9.18.10. 0. 0	

Chart 74   231

The verb is preceded by the CR date, a verb, three eroded blocks, and two names. Since no additional date occurs between the initial clause and this verb, it is either an alternative expression for the first verb and, therefore, the second part of a couplet construction, or it records a second event, "capture," that occurred on the same day.

37. Yax Str20   9.18. 6. 5.11   Inverted-Ahau Shield-   9.18.10. 0. 0
     HS 72   Jaguar II

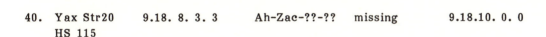The glyph to the left occurs between the names of the captive (patient) and captor (agent) in all "capture" clauses in this inscription. Although it seems to occur only in this inscription, its structural position makes it another candidate for an agentive expression.

38. Yax Str20   9.18. 7. 6. 0   missing   missing   9.18.10. 0. 0
     HS 94

39. Yax Str20   9.18. 7.16. 9   missing   missing   9.18.10. 0. 0
     HS 105

The main sign of this verb is the head of a brocket deer, pronounced *chih* in the Cholan languages. The presence of the head here is not understood, but since the majority of verbs in this texts record capture event, I have placed it here for the purpose of comparison.

40. Yax Str20   9.18. 8. 3. 3   Ah-Zac-??-??   missing   9.18.10. 0. 0
     HS 115

41. Yax Str20   9.18. 9. 6. 6   God K-   Shield-   9.18.10. 0. 0
     HS 137   Cleft-Sky   Jaguar II

The name glyph of this captive is the same as that of the protagonist of the Early Classic Stela 31 of Tikal. It is unlikely that these names refer to the same person because of the time differential, but this Yaxchilan inscription is a good example of the preservation and reuse of important Classic Maya names.

42. Yax Str20   9.18. 9. 7.18   eroded   Shield-   9.18.10. 0. 0
     HS 148   Jaguar II

Shield-Jaguar is recorded by the "captor of Tah-Mo'" expression that often occurs in his name phrase, but his personal name glyph does not appear. The use of this phrase to record Shield-Jaguar also occurs on

Lintel 10 and on Bonampak Lintel 2 (Mathews 1980:67). In this example of the "captor" glyph the number four (*chan*) replaces the more usual snake glyph (also *chan*).

43. Yax Str20   9.18. 9. 9.14   captor of   ????   9.18.10. 0. 0
     HS 160   ????

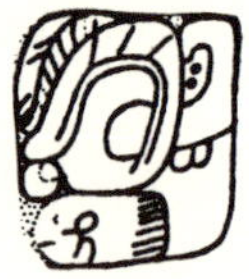

The T515 *chu* glyph has a feather-like sign in the position usually held by the T87 sign, but its possible equivalence to T87 and its function is not presently known. Since this verb has the same affixing (T25.181) as the other "capture" verbs in this text, and since it is followed by the same structure as other clauses in this inscription (i.e., name, agency?? [see #37], name), the event recorded is likely to be capture. The name glyph of the agent is eroded.

CHART 75   Affix T181   in Cluster *.181   with Miscellaneous Main Signs

Many of these examples are associated with war or "star" events.

#	LOCATION	DATE (EVENT)	PATIENT	AGENT	DEDICATION
1.	Tik 31 G28	9. 0. 3. 9.18		Spear- Thrower-Cauac	9. 0.10. 0. 0 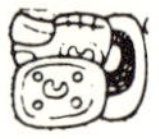

The thirteen-katun anniversary of this event in one of the final clauses of Stela 31 is celebrated on Lintel 3 of Temple 1. The object held in the hand may not be an axe, and the identity of the agent is difficult to establish because the same "spear-thrower-cauac" glyph appears in a phrase which seems to name the father of Curl-Snout, the father of the protagonist of Stela 31. However, it seems unlikely that the grandfather of Stormy-Sky would still be active during this later reign, and, therefore, the glyph may represent something other than an individual person. It may record a person who reused an ancestral name, or it may be part of the verb.

2. Tik 31   8.17. 1. 4.12   Jaguar-Paw I 9. 0.10. 0. 0
    D23

This verbal phrase occurs in a long series of glyph not yet understood.

Chart 75 233

3. Altun   9. 6.15. 6. 4   *u cab* Chac-Pax   9. 8. 0. 0. 0
    Jade

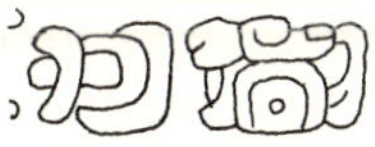

This "axe" event is the initial verb recorded in this text. It is followed by *u cab*; by "west" (possibly as a substitute for the *mah kina*
title); and by a name glyph consisting of *chac* (T109) and the *pax* glyph
(T299:548:178). This clause is followed by an "accession" phrase (59:9)
and another name, which I assume is an alternative name for the subject
of this first clause.

4. Tort 6   9.10.12. 3.10   destroyed   9.12. 0. 0. 0
    B14

This "axe" event occurred 244 days after a "star-shell" event (10:4), and
is followed by another "axe" (#5) and several "star" events.

5. Tort 6   9.10.16.13. 6   none   9.12. 0. 0. 0
    C1-D1

Lounsbury (n.d.) has identified the occasion of this "axe" event as the
first appearance of Venus as Evening Star. It precedes a "star" event by
148 days.

6. Tort Sarc   9.10.17. 1. 9   Chac-Ik-   deleted 9.12.10. 0. 0
    38   missing

This "axe" event follows a "capture" by seven days and precedes a "star-
over-earth/capture" event by twenty-five days. The second glyph may
record the object or be a part of the verbal phrase, but the subject of
the event is apparently deleted. Ahpo-Balam is named as the subject of
the succeeding event, and presumably he is to be understood as the agent
of this event also. See 74:1-2.

7. Tort 6   9.10.11. 9. 6   none   9.12. 0. 0. 0
    A10-B10

This "inverted-sky" glyph is part of a verbal series and seems to be a
verb itself because of the presence of the T181 suffix. It is the second
part of a verbal triplet of which the first part features the *oc* (T765)
glyph and the third a "star-over-earth" glyph. The lower part of this
glyph includes the locative T565 *ta* and a head identified by Mathews as
the front head of the Celestial Monster. See 10:4 and 21.22.

8. Ixk 2   9.17. 9. 0.14   *u cab* local ruler 9.17.10. 0. 0
    C4-D5

9. Yax 18   9.14.15.17.11   Shield-   9.15. 0. 0. 0
    A8-C5   Jaguar

This verbal phrase is at the end of a series of events beginning with the
capture of Chuen (74:7) and continuing with a blood-letting rite (35:5)
and an unknown event (57:1). The subject is named as Shield-Jaguar, and
all of the event phrases seem related to the capture or to the blood-
letting rites.

10. Quir Fw   9.15. 6.14. 6   18-   *u cab* Two-Legged-   9.17. 0. 0. 0
    A12b   Rabbit   Sky
                                     of Copan

CHART 76   Affix T181   in Cluster *.181   with Miscellaneous Main Signs

Most of these examples can be associated with blood-letting rites.

#	LOCATION	DATE (EVENT)	PATIENT	AGENT	DEDICATION
1.	Yax L14 D2-E2	9.15.10. 0. 1		deleted	9.16. 5. 0. 0

The three glyphs following the "fish-in-hand/God K" glyphs seem to record
additional information about this blood-letting rite, rather than a
patient or agent. The full phrase is followed by a *balan-ahau* verb
(T1:539:178.181; see 59:11) and the name of the agent, Lady Great-Skull.
The same *balan-ahau* glyph occurs in the text on Lintel 15 (#2), but it
occurs there without the T181 suffix.

2. Yax L15   9.16.17. 2. 4   deleted   9.16.18. 0. 0
    A2-G1

This phrase is the first half of a verbal couplet recorded without an
agent or patient being named (see 15:6). It is an example of a newly
identified blood-letting expression which usually occurs with the T757
verb as the main verb rather than with the "fish-in-hand" glyph (see
21:20, 38:13-14, and 52:6-9). The second glyph in this phrase consists of
yax (T16) and a sign that can now be identified as the personified
version of T580.

Chart 76 235

3. Bon 2   9.17.18.15.18   Lady Cauac-   9.18. 0. 0. 0
    D5-D6   Skull

This event is the later of two events recorded in this text, and must
correspond, therefore, to the scene of blood-letting shown on the front
of the monument. The agent of this verb is recorded here and on Stela 1
as the mother of Chaan-Muan, the center male. Since the woman behind
Chaan-Muan is named as a "woman of Yaxchilan," the woman to his front is
the protagonist and his mother. The name phrase of the Yaxchilan woman
includes the "hun uinic" and "na-chan" components of the verbal phrase
discussed in #2.

4. DPil 26   9.14.10. 0. 0   ????   Smoking-GI   9.14.10. 0. 0
    C5

This is the third part of an event series that occurred on 9.14.10.0.0.
Smoking-GI may be the patient rather than the agent. See 43:21, 47:6,
95:18, and 109:4 for other verbs in this event series.

5. Cop E   9. 9. 2.17. 0?   local person   9. 9. 5. 0. 0
    B10

This phrase may record blood-letting.

6. Yax Str20   9.18.6.4.19   ????   ????   9.18.10. 0. 0
    HS 52

The three glyph blocks following the verb are entirely eroded, but there
does not seem to have been another date between this verb and the
following "capture" verb. If text lacks a second date, the verb occurs in
the first part of couplet clauses, or it records an event that took place
on the same day as a capture. The following capture verb is preceded by
two glyphs prefixed by T228 and T12, both having the value *ah* and functioning as male articles. The presence of the affixes mark both glyphs as
nouns, but it is not possible to identify them as patient or agent.

7. Tik 10   9. 5. 4. 5.16   Curl-Head   9. 5. 5. 0. 0
    D11

This blood-letting verb is identical to one found on the Late Pre-Classic
Hauberg Stela (3:20) and on Caracol Stela 3 (128:5).

CHART 77   Affix T181   in Cluster *.181   with Main Sign T501:178

I am assuming that T501:178, *ma:l(a)*, forms the same verbal stem as T501:102, *ma:al*, and that both forms represent the same verb as it carries different inflectional or derivational affixes. See Chart 34.

#	LOCATION	DATE (EVENT)	PATIENT	AGENT	DEDICATION	
1.	DPil HSw F2b	9.12.12.11.2		Flint-Sky-God K	9.12.12. 0. 0	

This verbal phrase includes a "completion" hand, two "successions" (TII or III.676?:178), and "his katun" (T11.28:548), but since the date is not a tun ending, the phrase seems to record an anniversary of some dynastic event such as "accession."

| 2. | DPil HSe G5 | 9.11.11. 9.17 | | Flint-Sky-God K | 9.12.12. 0. 0 |  |

This verb follows "capture" and Tah-Mo' (the name of the captive). In turn, the captor, or agent of the capture, follows this *ma:la.ah* verb in this order: "he was captured, Tah-Mo', *malah*, Flint-Sky-God K." This structure is parallel to the capture constructions at Yaxchilan in which T1.501:102 (*u mal*) stands between the name of the captive (patient) and captor (agent). See 34:2,12-17, and Chart 74.

| 3. | DPil 17 A3 | 9.12.10. 0. 0? | | eroded | 9.12.10. 0. 0 |  |

This verb follows a date which is written only with 9 Ahau, but since the name Flint-Sky-God K seems to appear as the last glyph on the monument, I have placed the LC at a PE within his lifetime.

| 4. | Yax L17 A4-B4 | no date | | Bird-Jaguar III | 9.16.18. 0. 0 | |

This phrase is the last of a series of verbs in which the middle names the occasion as the birth of Shield-Jaguar II. The first verbal phrase is too damaged to be readable, but the scene is clearly one of blood-letting. This phrase seems to be constructed of an auxiliary verb (T501:178?.181) and the "yax-muluc" part of a blood-letting expression (see 21:20, 38:13-14, 52:6-9, and 76:2). The function of the prefixed *ti* sign is not known. See 53:2 for the first part of this verbal series.

Chart 78   237

CHART 78   Affix T181   in Cluster *.181   with Main Sign T757

#	LOCATION	DATE (EVENT)	PATIENT	AGENT	DEDICATION	
1.	Coll 9 pA1	9.11. 5.12. 2		Chaan-Muan	9.12. 0. 0. 0	

This phrase is from Glyphic Panel 8 of Site Q. See 52:2.

| 2. | DPil HSe C4 | missing | | Great- Jaguar-Paw of Site Q | 9.12.12. 0. 0 | |

The Jaguar-Paw name glyph is followed by another name phrase, Flint-Sky-God K, the protagonist of the monument. Two glyphs are found between these two names, but unfortunately the first is destroyed. The second of the two intervening glyphs is composed of a crossed-bands motif which seems to have been derived from a belt motif, and a skull. This glyph is associated with "star" events on these stairs and with an "axe" event on the Palenque Hieroglyphic Stairs. It is possible that Flint-Sky-God K is the agent of this event and that Great-Jaguar-Paw is the patient, but with the first of the two intervening glyphs destroyed, it is not possible to give a secure analysis of the syntax.

| 3. | Tik T4 L3; G5 | 9.15.15. 2. 3 | child of mother | | 9.16. 0. 0. 0 | |

This example of T757 is one of the most important ones known because it exists in an environment which can be shown to be exactly parallel to ones in which T757 appears with the prefix T1 *u* or an equivalent. The comparison of these two forms demonstrates that T757 is the verbal stem, and that both T1 and T181 function as verbal inflections. The context is one of genealogy in which the protagonist of the monument includes the names of his parents within his own name phrase; T60.757:181 is part of the expression recording the relationship between the child and his mother. The glyph following T757 is a possessed noun in which the noun refers to the child, Ruler B, and the pronominal prefix T3 refers to the mother. The syntax is then verb (T60:757.181), child of mother, name of the mother; and the subject of the verb is the noun "child," not the mother of the child. Here T757 seems to function as a means of highlighting the glyph for "child" and the name of the mother in much the same manner as it serves as a highlighter in other contexts. A comparative summary of the forms of T757 and equivalents that occur in genealogical statements is given in Charts 132 and 133.

| 4. | Cop HS Step G | missing | | missing | 9.17.10. 0. 0 | |

CHART 79   Affix T181   in Cluster *.181   with Main Sign T516:103

All of these examples are auxiliary verb + *ti* (or an equivalent) + verbal noun constructions, although the verbal nouns in some examples have been lost.

#	LOCATION	DATE (EVENT)	PATIENT	AGENT	DEDICATION	
1.	Coll 11 pD3	9. 9.16. 0. 0?		missing	9.12. 0. 0. 0	 

This glyph follows the CR and an ordinal construction for "second." It is from Site Q Panel 3.

| 2. | DPil HSw F2-E3 | 9.12.10. 0. 0 | | Personage of Site Q | 9.12.12. 0. 0 |  |

T103 is replaced by the sign of an ocote torch. Since T103 is known to function as a locative preposition, and since the word for "torch" in most Mayan languages is *tah* (or its cognate *chah*), T103 seems to represent the phonetic value *ta*, which is a locative in Tzeltal and Tzotzil.

| 3. | Agua 5 D4-E1 | 9.13. 0. 0. 0 | | Flint-Sky-God K | 9.13. 0. 0. 0 |  |

This is the third part of a triplet of which the first part is "completion of thirteen katuns" and the second is "scattering." This auxiliary verb phrase is equivalent to PE expressions from other sites (see 5:7, 31:10-13, 38:6, and 48:5).

| 4. | Yax L53 B2-C1 | 9.13. 5.12.13 | | Shield-Jaguar I | 9.16. 5. 0. 0 | |

Proskouriakoff (1964:164-165) discussed the problems of placing the CR 7 Ben 16 Mac into the LC. A position one CR later places the date after Shield-Jaguar's death. However, assuming an error in the day sign coefficient yields LC positions (9.13.17.15.13 6 Ben 16 Mac and 9.15.10.5.13 12 Ben 16 Mac) that are closely associated with other important events in his life, and Lintel 32, which records the same event, seems to have a day sign coefficient with at least two bars, supporting the 12 Ben 16 Mac reading. However, I have tentatively used the clearly preserved 7 Ben 16 Mac of the Lintel 53 text and placed it at its latest possible LC position within Shield-Jaguar's life. Proskouriakoff also pointed out that this lintel and Lintel 32 were found in buildings housing much later Bird-Jaguar lintels, and Peter Mathews (personal communication, 1982) has suggested that Bird-Jaguar had them carved in order to show his mother

Chart 79   239

of his claim to the throne. All lintels in buildings contemporary to Shield-Jaguar's buildings have scenes showing him with a woman who is not recorded as Bird-Jaguar's mother.

5.   DPil 26   9.14.10. 4. 0   Shield-God K   9.14.10. 0. 0
     E5-F5   (by title)

This phrase is the second half of a couplet of which the first half is clearly a period ending expression; however, the CR as recorded does not correspond to any PE near 9.14.10. 0. 0. It does occur, however, four uinals after the IS date 9.14.10. 0. 0, implying that the lahuntun ceremonies may have extended over a period of 80 days.

6.   ECayo L3   9.12.17.13. 1   *u cab* Turtle-Shell   9.15. 5. 0. 0
     E1

This El Cayo event occurred on the three-tun anniversary of the accession of Ruler 3 of Piedras Negras. The verbal phrase is followed by the name phrase of the contemporary ruler of El Cayo (F1); a glyph including a *u* prefix and a T236 suffix which are characteristic of the *u cab* glyph; another name glyph (Ruler 3?) and the Piedras Negras EG; and "ti three tuns," the glyph which apparently records the anniversary. Note that the El Cayo ruler named as the agent of this event is the father of the protagonist of Lintel 3.

7.   Tik T4   9.15.15. 3. 2   GVI   9.16. 0. 0. 0
     L3   G2-H2

This phrase is the fourth part of a series of clause that record, in alternative forms, the three-tun anniversary of an important event that occurred one day after a "shell-star" event. See 10:14, 38:17, 52:4, 80:6-7, and 87:11.

8.   Yax L7   9.16. 1. 8. 8   Bird-   9.16. 5. 0. 0
     B2-C2   Jaguar III

9.   Yax 11Frt   9.15. 9.17.16   Shield-   9.16. 5. 0. 0
     T1b-T2a   Jaguar I

This verb occurs as the secondary text in a scene showing Shield-Jaguar and Bird-Jaguar holding cloth staffs. See 38:15.

10. Yax L54   9.16. 5. 0. 0   Bird-   9.16. 5. 0. 0
     A2-B2   Jaguar III

The verbal phrase accompanies a scene in which Bird-Jaguar holds a God K scepter.

11. Yax L2   9.16. 6. 0. 0   Bird-   9.16. 6. 0. 0
     K1-L1   Jaguar III

This verb refers in some way to the holding or display of a bird-scepter.

12. Yax L5   9.16. 1. 2. 0   Bird-   9.16. 5. 0. 0
     B2-C2   Jaguar III

This verb refers in some way to the holding or display of a bird-scepter.

13. PN L3   9.15.18. 3.15   Ruler 4   9.16.10. 0. 0
     M1-N1

This event occurred two days after the one-katun anniversary of the accession of Ruler 4, in celebration of which a Yaxchilan lord apparently visited Piedras Negras. See 68:1 and 99:6.

14. Yax L9   9.16.17. 6.12   Bird-   9.16.18. 0. 0
     A4-B2   Jaguar III

This event (the display of a cloth staff) took place on the twenty-fifth tun anniversary of a date on Lintel 26. See #6 and 38:15 for other examples of this verbal noun.

15. Cop HS   missing   missing   9.17.10. 0. 0
     Step K3

16. Cop HS   missing   New-Sky-at-   9.17.10. 0. 0
     Step L5   Horizon

Chart 80 241

CHART 80   Affix T181   in Cluster *.181   with Miscellaneous Main Signs

The meaning of many of these examples is not known, but each is followed by a prepositional phrase.

#	LOCATION	DATE (EVENT)	PATIENT	AGENT	DEDICATION	
1.	Nar 24 E4-E5	9.13. 7. 3. 8		Lady 6-Sky of Tikal	9.13.10. 0. 0	

This verb + prepositional phrase represents the fourth part of a series of verbal phrases which records in alternative form the event (the taking of the T1001 title) occurring on the front of this monument. See 9:4-5, 38:5, 52:1, and for another office-taking event including the same prepositional phrase, see 118:4.

#	LOCATION	DATE (EVENT)	PATIENT	AGENT	DEDICATION
2.	Pal DO C3-D4	9.11. 4. 7. 0		Kan-Xul II	9.14.15. 0. 0

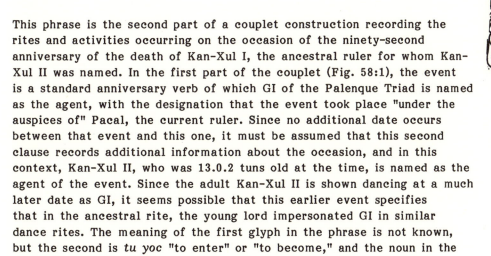

This phrase is the second part of a couplet construction recording the rites and activities occurring on the occasion of the ninety-second anniversary of the death of Kan-Xul I, the ancestral ruler for whom Kan-Xul II was named. In the first part of the couplet (Fig. 58:1), the event is a standard anniversary verb of which GI of the Palenque Triad is named as the agent, with the designation that the event took place "under the auspices of" Pacal, the current ruler. Since no additional date occurs between that event and this one, it must be assumed that this second clause records additional information about the occasion, and in this context, Kan-Xul II, who was 13.0.2 tuns old at the time, is named as the agent of the event. Since the adult Kan-Xul II is shown dancing at a much later date as GI, it seems possible that this earlier event specifies that in the ancestral rite, the young lord impersonated GI in similar dance rites. The meaning of the first glyph in the phrase is not known, but the second is *tu yoc* "to enter" or "to become," and the noun in the prepositional phrase may be a personified eccentric flint. See 108:4.

#	LOCATION	DATE (EVENT)	PATIENT	AGENT	DEDICATION	
3.	Tik Alt5 15-18	9.13.11. 5. 7	*u cab* ????		9.14. 0. 0. 0	

These two event phrase seem to compose a verbal couplet which is followed by *u cab* and a name phrase (Crossed-Bands-Cauac-Jaguar) not found elsewhere in the inscriptions of Tikal.

4. Tik T1   9.13. 3. 9.18   Ruler A   9.15. 0. 0. 0
    L3; C2-D2

This verbal phrase records the thirteenth-katun anniversary of the last
event surviving on Stela 31 (75:1). It is immediately followed by a
blood-letting verbal phrase (39:7) and a long elaborate name phrase that
includes not only the personal name and titles of Ruler A, but his
genealogy as well.

5. Tik T1   9.13. 3. 9.18   deleted   9.15. 0. 0. 0
    L3; E12-   (Ruler A)
    F12

This final clause of the Lintel 3 text links the anniversary event above
to the seating of Ruler A, but since he has already been named as the
agent of the anniversary event in its first occurrence, and since he is
clearly the protagonist of this monument, his name is deleted after this
redundant statement of the event. A full paraphrase of this last clause
is as follows: "It was 13.10.2 since 5 Cib 14 Zotz' since he was seated
as lord of the succession, Ruler A, until the anniversary event." #4 and
#5 are alternative forms of the same verbal phrase, and note that T565,
known to be *ta/ti*, is replaced in the second example by T671, known at
least in the codices to have the value *chi*. This substitution suggests
that T671 does not represent the *k/ch* correspondence between Yucatecan
and Cholan languages, but rather the *ch/t* correspondence.

6. Tik T4   9.15.15. 2. 3   Ruler B   9.16. 0. 0. 0
    L3; E8-
    F8b

This verbal phrase seems to be related to examples #4 and #5 in form as
well as meaning. This phrase is part of a series of clauses recording the
three-tun anniversary of the event in #7, which took place on the day
after a "star-shell" event. See 10:14, 38:17, 52:4, 79:7, 80:6, and 87:11.

7. Tik T4   9.15.12. 2. 3   GVI?   9.16. 0. 0. 0
    L3; D5-D6

This event occurred one day after a "star-shell" event associated with
the EG of Yaxha. GVI of the Palenque deity series seems to be named as
the agent of this verb.

8. Tik T4   9.15.15.14. 0   Ruler B   9.16. 0. 0. 0
    L2; C1-D1

Chart 81 243

9. Yax L52   9.16.15. 0. 0   Bird-   9.16.15. 0. 0
    A2-C1   Jaguar III

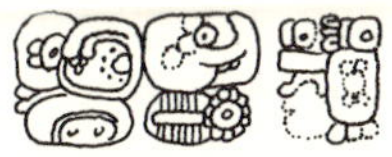

Bird-Jaguar is shown holding a God K scepter.

CHART 81   Affix T181   in Cluster *.181   with Miscellaneous Main Signs

All of these examples includes some form of the human hand as the main sign.

#	LOCATION	DATE (EVENT)	PATIENT	AGENT	DEDICATION	
1.	Bon B D2-C3	9. 4. 8.14. 9		Kan-Chuen & Fishfin of Bonampak	9. 4.10. 0. 0	

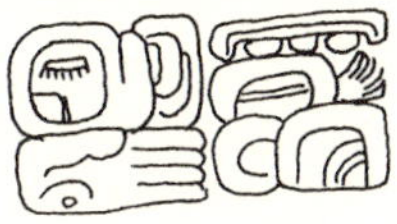

The scene on the Early Classic lintel shows two figures, each facing the
other, and seated on either side of the main text. Both figures are drawn
at the same scale and in the same posture, making the same gesture. The
equivalence of these two figures leads me to suspect that the subject of
this verb is compound, and that the two names do not record a patient and
agent. Clearly, in a pictorial sense, neither of these persons acts upon
the other.

#	LOCATION	DATE (EVENT)	PATIENT	AGENT	DEDICATION	
2.	Coll 12 F7	9. 3. 19. 3. 8		Skull	9. 4. 0. 0. 0	
3.	Car 14 B7	9. 6. 0. 0. 0		Ruler 2	9. 6. 0. 0. 0	
4.	ASac 4 A10-B10	unreadable		local ruler	9. 10.10. 0. 0	

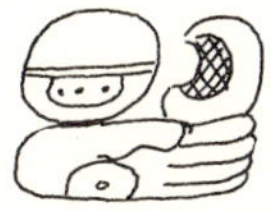

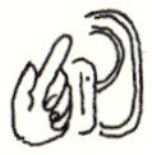

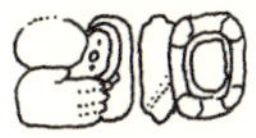

This event follows the death of a prior ruler, but the DN connecting the
two events is eroded.

#	LOCATION	DATE (EVENT)	PATIENT	AGENT	DEDICATION	
5.	Pal HS G3	9.11. 1.16. 3		Crossed- Bands-Jaguar	9.11.10. 0. 0	

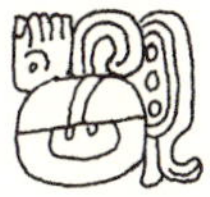

This verb is the second in a series of clauses beginning with an "axe"
event and including possible "capture" events. See 14:1 and 74:4-5.

6. Pal TFC   9.12.19.14.12   GII   9.13. 0. 0. 0
    Alf G1

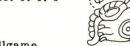

This is an event celebrated on the eighth tropical year anniversary of
Chan-Bahlum II's accession. See 58:1 and 127:4-6.

7. Coll 23   no date   none or   9.15. 0. 0. 0
    pA2   missing

This is the second part of a verbal couplet that accompanies a ballgame
scene. See 82:25 for the first part of the couplet.

CHART 82   Affix T181   in Cluster *.181   with Miscellaneous Main Signs

#	LOCATION	DATE (EVENT)	PATIENT	AGENT	DEDICATION
1.	PN Bur5 Shell E3	9.12.14.10.11		Lady Ahpo- Katun	9.15. 0. 0. 0

The events in ##1-3 occur in parallel texts found on the monuments listed, as well as on Stelae 3 and 7 (Stuart n.d.). This event series consists of the following sequence: (1) the birth of Lady Ahpo-Katun; (2)
this event 12.9.15 after her birth; (3) the death of Ruler 2 three days
later; and (4) two sacrificial events conducted by Lady Ahpo-Katun, two
and three days respectively after the death of Ruler 2. The components of
the second event are identical to both phonetic and logographic configurations of the month glyph Mac, and surely the reading of this event is
mac.ah, but no meaning has been proposed for the verb. Lady Ahpo-Katun's
name is followed by *u cab* and the name phrase of Ruler 2, who was three
days from his death. If *u cab* records a phrase such as "under the auspices of," its presence here may indicate that the action was conducted
by Lady Ahpo-Katun "under the auspices of" or "during the reign of" Ruler
2.

#	LOCATION	DATE (EVENT)	PATIENT	AGENT	DEDICATION
2.	PN 1 F2	9.12.14.10.11		Lady Ahpo- Katun	9.13.15. 0. 0

#	LOCATION	DATE (EVENT)	PATIENT	AGENT	DEDICATION
3.	PN 8 B19	9.12.14.10.11		Lady Ahpo- Katun	9.13.15. 0. 0

#	LOCATION	DATE (EVENT)	PATIENT	AGENT	DEDICATION
4.	Pal T14 A6	13 Oc 18 Uo		supernaturals	9.13.15. 0. 0

Chart 82   245

The verbs listed as #4 and #5 are found in parallel passages on the
tablet from Temple 14 at Palenque. Although it is structurally clear that
this 13 Oc 18 Uo event is associated with the mythological "ahau-in-hand"
event that took place on 9 Ik 10 Mol, the exact calendric relationship
cannot be established because no DN expresses the relationship between
the two events. One of the supernatural agents is identified as God K,
but it is not clear if the *balan-ahau* (T1.539:178) is intended as a
title for God K or as a reference to GIII. See 20:8 and 45:11.

5.   Pal T14   13 Oc 18 Uo   supernaturals 9.13.15. 0. 0
     F2

6.   Pal TFC   9.12.18. 5.16   Chan-   9.13. 0. 0. 0
     O12   Bahlum II

This verb seems to be the second part of a couplet which records an event
associated with the seventy-fifth tropical year anniversary of Pacal's
accession. It follows an "inverted-sky" event (23:3-6), a possessed noun,
and the names of seven supernaturals, including the Palenque Triad. This
passage seems related to a similar structure on the Dumbarton Oaks Tablet
in which the first part of a couplet records GI as the agent, and the
second half, the young Kan-Xul II. In that context, I suggested that the
couplet implied that the actual act was conducted by Kan-Xul in the guise
of GI (80:2). I suspect that the same information is implied in this
passage: i.e., that the agents of the "inverted-sky" event were the seven
supernaturals, but that the historical rites were conducted by Chan-
Bahlum in the guise of the Triad.

7.   Pal TS   9.10. 8. 9. 3   deleted   9.13. 0. 0. 0
     Q13   (Chan-Bahlum)

This verb repeats redundant information and links Chan-Bahlum's heir-
designation (recorded twice in the preceding clauses) to his birth, and
because the subject of both the birth and the heir-designation can be
easily deduced from previously given information, the subjects of both
verbs are deleted. The main sign of this verb is a variant of the *oc*
glyph, which functions as the noun of office in two instances (12:3 and
113:3), and as the verb in one instance (21:5).

8.   Tik 31   8.17. 0. 0. 0   missing   9. 0.10. 0. 0
     D27

This "house" variant is found in a passage celebrating the end of 8.18.
10.0.0. It is followed by a "tun-sky-over-earth" glyph and an eroded
block, but since a DN immediately follows these two glyphs, the name of a
recognized person is missing and may have once been in the eroded block.

See 23:2, 23:10, 49:2, 87, 94:6, 114, and 128:6 for related "house" events.

9. Pal AD   5 ???? 5 Kayab   Pal Triad   9.14.10. 0. 0
    Jamb

This "house" event is found on a fragment of a stone panel once mounted on the inner side of one of the center piers of the outer gallery of House AD. The Palenque Triad may be recorded as the patient of the verb since the text following their names is now missing. The prefix (*na*) may be a phonetic complement, since *na* is a word for "house," or it may be a verbal affix.

10. Car 6   9. 8.10. 0. 0   ????   9. 8.10. 0. 0
     F23

11. Tik 12   9. 4.13. 0. 0?   ????   9. 4.13. 0. 0
     D2

The glyphs following this verb seem to be titular, but I recognize no personal names in the surviving text.

12. DPil 1   9.13.15. 0. 0   missing   9.13.15. 0. 0
     B1

This verb following a "scattering" verb; see 43:1.

13. Pal T18   missing   missing   9.14.15. 0. 0
     Stc 478

This verb may record a PE event; see Charts 44 and 69.

14. Nar 23   9.13.18. 9.15   Person of   Smoking-   9.14.10. 0. 0
     F18   Yaxha?   Squirrel

This verb is followed by a possible "captive" glyph (*u bac*-??, T1.570: ??), another possessed noun with a skull as the main sign, and two additional glyphs, one of which seems to be the Yaxha EG. The clause is closed by a very elaborate version of the name phrase of Smoking-Squirrel. The suffix may not be T181.

15. Tik Alt5   9.13.19.16. 6   deleted   9.14. 0. 0. 0
     26

Chart 82 247

| 16. | Yax 7 2ndy | 9.17. 0. 0. 0 | | Shield-Jaguar II | 9.17. 0. 0. 0? | |

| 17. | Cop 2 B7a | eroded | | Bat-Uinal | 9.12. 0. 0. 0 | |

| 18. | Cop HS | missing | | missing | 9.17.10. 0. 0 | |

| 19. | Cal 43 B9-B10 | 9. 4. 0. 0. 0 | | eroded | 9. 4. 0. 0. 0 | |

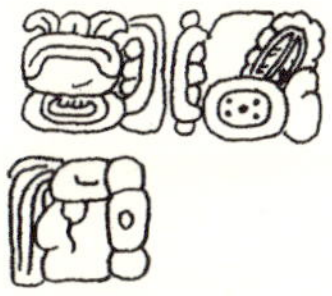

This phrase is the second half of a couplet recording the katun ending (see 6:1). The agent appears to be the local ruler, but the glyphs are too eroded to identify a personal name.

| 20. | Tort 6 C6-C7 | 9.10.17. 2.14 | | deleted? (Ahpo-Balam) | 9.12. 0. 0. 0 | |

This event phrase immediately follows a "star-shell" verb (116:11) and precedes a third phrase (60:6) in which the "zac-ahau-ik" glyph of the "death" expression is the main sign. Ahpo-Balam is named as the agent of the succeeding verb, and presumably he is also the agent of this verb. The second glyph may represent a ballcourt (see 13:6), and the skull under it may be Venus as Evening Star.

| 21. | Tort 6 E6-F6 | 9.11.16. 8.18 | | deleted | 9.12. 0. 0. 0 | |

This verbal phrase is linked by DN to the seating of Ahpo-Balam in the following manner: "It was 1.5.6.8 since he was seated as Ahau of the succession, Ahpo-Balam, until [this event]." The second verbal phrase appears without a agent so either it is a neutral event without an agent, or the agent is deleted and to be understood as Ahpo-Balam. See 21:4.

| 22. | Quir C base G1 | 9.17. 4.10.12 | | deleted | 9.17. 5. 0. 0 | |

| 23. | DPil HSw D4 | 9.12. 6.16.17 | 13-Gourd | Flint-Sky-God K | 9.12.12. 0. 0 | |

This "eccentric-flint" event is followed by the same "u-skull" glyph as in the Naranjo expression in example #14. The name following the verb is 13-Gourd (or Jaguar-Caller), a glyph related to the name of the captive on

Tikal Altar 8 and Column Altar 1 (see 36:9). The two glyphs following this name glyph are eroded so that it cannot be determined if another event glyph or a relationship glyph stood between it and Flint-Sky-God K. I am assuming that the first name records the patient and the second the agent, but this conclusion must remain tentative.

24.	Coll 22 pB4	9.15. 1. 1. 7	missing	9.15. 5. 0. 0	

25.	Coll 23 pA1-pA2	no date	none or missing	9.15. 0. 0. 0	

This phrase from Ballplayer Panel 3 of Site Q accompanies a ballgame scene in which a person dressed as GI of the Palenque Triad confronts another dressed as God L.

26.	Coll 20 pA1	no date	Jaguar-Paw of Site Q	9.15. 5. 0. 0	

27.	Pus D F14	9. 8. 1.12.17	eroded	9.10.15. 0. 0	

28.	NTun GpI H4	9.15. 8. 9. 4	eroded	9.16.10. 0. 0	

29.	NTun GpIVf A3-A5	eroded	Chaan- Ah Cauac	9.16.10. 0. 0	

See #31, 26:18, 98:12, and 116:20-21.

30.	NTun GpVIb B1	9.16.11.12. 4	Chaan- Ah Cauac	9.16.10. 0. 0	

See 26:23.

31.	NTun GpVIe B1-D1	9.16. 3.10. 4	Chaan- Ah Cauac	9.16.10. 0. 0	

See #29, 26:18, 98:12, and 116:20-21.

Chart 83 249

32. PN Thr1   missing   Ruler 7   9.17.15. 0. 0
     H1-I1

The date of this event is missing, but it appears to be followed by a PE
expression recording some tun in the fifteenth katun and by the birth
record of Ruler 7.

33. PN Thr 1   9.17.10. 6. 1   deleted   9.17.15. 0. 0
     F'4-F'6   (Ruler 7)

This verbal phrase is a redundant record of an event which occurred
shortly before the accession of Ruler 7 (see 21:15 for a detailed comparison of the two forms of this event phrase). Since this phrase is the
second occurrence of the event, the agent (Ruler 7) is deleted. The
verbal phrase is introduced by the locative *ta* (T103) and a half-
darkened kin which stands for a DN of one day on the TFC (L5) at Palenque. In the Piedras Negras passage, however, the DN is 1.0.10, and the
half-darkened kin must represent some phrase such as "on the day."

34. Cop AltH'   9.12. 8. 3. 9   Smoke-Head   9.12.10. 0. 0
     M2

35. PN L4   9.11. 6. 1. 8   Ruler 2?   9.16.10. 0. 0
     O4

This event took place 19.17.7 after the death of Ruler I. The verb is the
last glyph of the main text, and since the immediately preceding event is
death, it seems unlikely that the subject is deleted and to be reconstructed as the dead Ruler 1. I suggest, therefore, that the clause continues to the secondary text next to the protagonist, and tentatively
identify the agent as Ruler 2.

CHART 83	Affix T181	in Cluster *.181	with Main Sign T759

#	LOCATION	DATE (EVENT)	PATIENT	AGENT	DEDICATION
1.	Coll 25	4 Cimi		Ah Kan	Late Classic
	B5b				

This verb occurs with only the tzolkin day 4 Cim i recorded as a date, but
it immediately follows a "capture" event occurring on 2 Kan and 3 Chicchan, the two previous days. The captive in the earlier event is recorded
as Star-Parrot of Bonampak and the agent by the same Ah Kan name as in

this clause. This event should represent,therefore, some action appropriate to the day after a "capture" event. The main sign is T759, the head of a rabbit (*t'ul* in western Mayan languages). It is not known if the suffix T25 *ca* is part of the verbal stem or of the verbal affixing, but it should be noted that in the only other occurrences of this verb (Dresden 3a-20a), T759 occurs with the same affixing, and that this affix combination occurs with no other verbal main signs in the Classic inscriptions.

| 2. | Coll 25 | no date | | Cab-Chaan- | Late Classic |
| | A8 | | | Te' | |

This is a repetition of the event above, but the agent recorded is different. The same name phrase, however, occurs in the first five glyphs of this monument fragment in a passage that seems to record the agent of a now missing verb. The parallel structure of the final passages seem to be a mechanism of showing that both the agent of the capture and the protagonist of the monument participated in this *t'ulcah* event.

CHART 84   Affix T181   in Cluster *:178.181   with Main Sign T520H

T178 has the phonetic value -*la* and T181 that of -*ah*, forming together a verbal suffix -*lah*, reconstructed as the perfective suffix for positional verbs in Yucatec. In Cholan, the suffix might well consist of the inchoative suffix -*l*- plus a perfective -*ah*.

#	LOCATION	DATE (EVENT)	PATIENT	AGENT	DEDICATION	
1.	AgC 1 B2	missing		Chac-Tun	9.18. 0. 0. 0?	

See #2, 5:6, 59:1, 98:5-9,11-12, 103:3-4.

2.	Uax 13 A4	10. 0. 0. 0. 0		local ruler	10. 3. 0. 0. 0	
3.	Cop 9 A9-B10	9. 6.10. 0. 0		missing	9. 6.10. 0. 0	

This expression seems to be related to other period ending expressions at Copan and elsewhere. See #6 and 52:2, 57:2-3, 68:3, and 69:3.

4.	Ton M95 D1-E1	9.16. 1.12. 0		Dragon	9.16. 5. 0. 0	

Chart 85   251

This verbal phrase does not record an 819 Day Count.

5. Ton M74   2 ???? 11 Zac?   local ruler   Early Classic
    A3-A4

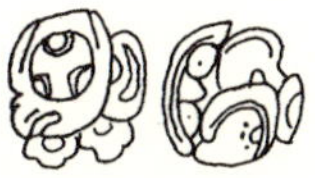

This verbal phrase does not record an 819 Day Count.

6. Ton M30   missing   Dragon?   Late Classic
    A4-A6

Although the date is missing on the fragment, I suspect that the verbal
phrase is related to a category of period ending expression utilizing
this "tree-tun" combination. See 52:2, 68:3, 69:3, and 131:3.

7. Yax 11   9.15.19.14.14   God K   9.16. 5. 0. 0
    C'6

This example is from an 819 Day Count.

8. Quir K   9.18.14. 7.10   God K   9.18.15. 0. 0
    A7a

This example is from an 819 Day Count.

9. Quir K   9.18. 5. 0. 0   Ruler 2   9.18.15. 0. 0
    B11

This verbal phrase does not record an 819 Day Count.

CHART 85   Affix 181   in Cluster *:178.181   with Main Sign T644

All of these examples record "accession" events.

#	LOCATION	DATE (EVENT)	PATIENT	AGENT	DEDICATION	
1.	Yax L47 A4-B4	9. 4.11. 8.16		Ta-??-Skull	9. 8. 0. 0. 0?	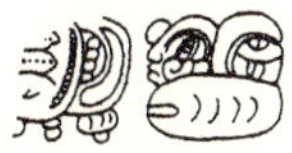
2.	Car 6 E3-F3	9. 5.19. 1. 2		Ruler 2	9. 8.10. 0. 0	

3.   Car 6   9. 5.19. 1. 2   deleted   9. 8.10. 0. 0
       E6-F7   (Ruler 7)

AEI. This expression is recorded as the event from which a DN is counted, and since the subject of the verb is named in an earlier clause, it is deleted from this redundant passage, but it can be reconstructed as Ruler 2. The lower affix is now missing from the glyph, but the presence of T181 almost certainly argues for the original presence of T178 (see #2 and #4).

4.   Car 6   9. 8. 5.16.12   Ruler 3   9. 8.10. 0. 0
       F14-E15   (by title)

5.   Coll 1   9. 8. 9.12.14   Ahpo-Kuk   9.10. 0. 0. 0
       C2

6.   Coll 1   9. 8.12.12. 9   Ah Naab-   9.10. 0. 0. 0
       E1-F1   Chaan

7.   Tik 21   9.15. 3. 6. 8   deleted   9.16. 0. 0. 0
       B10-A11   (Ruler B)

This "seating" verb occurs in the last clause of the text. It functions to link the period ending event, "scattering," to the earlier accession of Ruler B. Since Ruler B was named as the subject of the first clause, and since no other person is named as the subject of a verb (Ruler A's name occurs in a genealogical statement), the subjects of both the "seating" and "scattering" verbs are deleted, but understood as Ruler B. This same pattern of syntax can be seen on Temple 1 Lintel 3 and Stelae 19 and 22.

8.   Pal 96G   9.13.10. 6. 8   Kan-Xul II   9.17.15. 0. 0
       D4-C5a

9.   Pal 96G   9.14.10. 4. 2   Chaacal III   9.17.15. 0. 0
       F3

10.   Pal 96G   9.16.13. 0. 7   Kuk II   9.17.15. 0. 0
       H2

11.   Cop HS   missing   missing   9.17.10. 0. 0

Chart 86 253

CHART 86   Affix T181   in Cluster *:178.181   with Miscellaneous Main Signs

#	LOCATION	DATE (EVENT)	PATIENT	AGENT	DEDICATION	
1.	Pal PTab U4	9.13.14. 8. 0		Xoc	9.14.10. 0. 0	

This verb is located in the secondary text of the Palace Tablet. This
verb with a different affix pattern (see 113:3-4) is used to record heir-
designation on the Tablet of the Sun, but it records accession as ruler
on other tablets at Palenque, at Quirigua, and at Yaxchilan (see 72:5-7).
In this context, however, the event is more likely to be associated with
an heir-designation, since it takes place some four years after the
accession of Kan-Xul II, and fourteen years before Xoc's accession (as
recorded at R13-Q14 on the Palace Tablet).

#	LOCATION	DATE (EVENT)	PATIENT	AGENT	DEDICATION	
2.	Ton F37 pA2	missing		missing	Late Classic	

AEI.

#	LOCATION	DATE (EVENT)	PATIENT	AGENT	DEDICATION	
3.	Pal TIm B4	9.11. 0. 0. 0		Evening Star	9.12.15. 0. 0	

This verb and #4 are part of the katun history of Katun 11. A similar
passage from the history of Katun 12 has been identified by Closs (1979)
as the maximum western extension of Venus. Recently, Lounsbury (n.d.) has
identified 9.11.0.0.0 as the day on which Venus first appeared as Evening
Star. This verb, therefore, appears to represent logographically the
emergence of Venus from the earth, and the glyph naming the subject, an
Ik-Skull, can be identified as Venus as Evening Star. This identification
is supported by the appearance of this skull with a Venus sign attached
on the headdress of Ruler A on Tikal Stela 14, the date of which Lounsbury has also identified as the first appearance of Venus as Evening
Star.

#	LOCATION	DATE (EVENT)	PATIENT	AGENT	DEDICATION	
4.	Pal TIm B5	9.11. 0. 0. 0		Evening Star	9.12.15. 0. 0	
5.	Pal T18 Stc 439	missing		missing	9.13.15. 0. 0	

6. Yax L21   9.16. 1. 0. 9   Bird-   9.16. 5. 0. 0
    C6   Jaguar III

This verb is linked to a similar event which occurred to an early ruler of Yaxchilan. See 127:13 for the Early Classic event and 16:11 for a related event.

7. Sac 1   9.16.10. 0. 0   Ahau-Kin?   9.16.10. 0. 0
    C3

This verb occurs between Glyph B and the haab position; it seems to be a part of the addended information about the date.

8. Ton MNAH   9 Ahau   ????   Late Classic
    Disk B1

This occurs in a couplet construction with a "death" verb (see 25:11).

9. Yax Str44   no date   ????   9.15. 0. 0. 0
    Ctr Low
    E1

10. Coll 13   9.18. 9. 7.10   deleted   9.18.10. 0. 0
    C5b-D5

This verbal phrase seems to be the second part of a couplet structure of which the first verbal phrase is now missing. The glyphs immediately before the verbal phrase are the name of a woman (Lady Be [T1000a.672: 585]), *u cab,* and the name of a male. The deleted subject may have referred to either of these persons.

11. Cop 23   9.10.18.12. 8   missing   9.11. 0. 0. 0
    F5

This is the second half of a verbal couplet (see 3:19).

Chart 87   255

CHART 87   Affix T181   in Cluster *:178.181   with Main Sign T79

#	LOCATION	DATE (EVENT)	PATIENT	AGENT	DEDICATION	
1.	Ton M113 N-O	9.12. 0. 0. 0		eroded	9.12. 0. 0. 0	

This verb follows "scattering"; see 61:1.

#	LOCATION	DATE (EVENT)	PATIENT	AGENT	DEDICATION	
2.	Pal PasTr B3	no date		relative of GI	9.12.15. 0. 0	

The published fragment of the Pasadena Tracing includes the haab position
of the date 8 Ahau 13 Pop, a birth verb, and the name of Pacal II of
Palenque. The name is followed by "4 tun seatings" (a conflation that
almost always refers to katun endings), and "4-katun-ahau," a phrase
known to have been used on the Tableritos, the subterranean throne, and
the Palace Tablet as a reference to katun of reign, rather than to katuns
of life. The birth date of Pacal is known to have been 9.8.9.13.0, and
assuming that the katun notations refer to katun endings between his
birth and this "house" event, they must refer to 9.9.0.0.0, 9.10.0.0.0,
9.11.0.0.0, and 9.12.0.0.0. The "house" event occurred sometime after the
end of Katun 12, but since this particular kind of DN, a count of katun
endings, is characteristic of the sarcophagus inscription, I suspect that
the "house" event was near to or after Pacal's death. The subject of the
event is named with a glyph (T86:325var[575(671)]) which is almost surely
some kind of relationship (though probably not of kinship) glyph. The
names which follow the relationship glyph include GI of the Palenque
Triad, but I suspect that Pacal is understood as the subject. A similar
kind of relationship statement is found in the name phrase of Chan-Bahlum
on the Tablet of the Sun, P9-Q10.

#	LOCATION	DATE (EVENT)	PATIENT	AGENT	DEDICATION	
3.	Pal Tabs L2	9.11. 1.12. 8		none	9.11. 5. 0. 0	

The phrases listed as #3 and #5-11 are anniversary phrases associated
with the following cycles:
    #3 the thirteen haab (13 x 365) anniversary of 9 Akbal 6 Xul,
        the heir-designation of Chan-Bahlum II.
    #5-7 the seventy-fifth tropical year (75 x 365 + 13) anniversary
        of 5 Lamat 1 Mol, the accession of Pacal II.
    #8-9 the eighth tropical year (8 x 365 +2) anniversary of 8 Oc
        3 Kayab, the accession of Chan-Bahlum II.
All of these examples utilize T79 as the main sign of a verb, but several
are followed by a couplet construction consisting of two glyphs: (1) a
general tree sign and *naab* the glyph for "waterlily" and "ocean" or
"lake";and (2) a glyph for "sky" plus a glyph that may imply "center."

This pair of phrases contrasts metaphors for earth based on water with
sky in a couplet implying the "world" or "cosmos." Similar kinds of
couplet constructions are characteristic of modern Mayan languages; for
example, in Chuh the couplet for "world" is "mountains and grass," while
in Achi it is "mountains and valleys." And in terms of iconography, this
couplet can be seen in the "world" throne which has alternating bands of
"waterlily" and "sky" motifs (see Naranjo Stela 32). When the main verb
(T79) of these phrases is followed by different expression, such as
"house" (see #4), the agent can be a historical person, but when the *te'-
naab-chaan* phrase follows it, the agent is recorded as a supernatural,
such as one of the gods of the Palenque Triad, or no agent is named. The
frequent lack of an agent implies that the T79/*te'-naab-chaan* event is
neutral, like tun ending or era events, so that it cannot be enacted by a
human agent.

tree sign + waterlily   sky + center

| 4. | Tort Box M'2-M'3 | 9.12. 9. 7.12 | | Ah Ka-?- Balam by title | 9.12.10. 0. 0 | |

This event occurred 1.11.5 after the accession of this ruler.

| 5. | Pal TC Alf K2-L2 | 9.12.19.14.12 | | none | 9.13. 0. 0. 0 | |

| 6. | Pal TFC Alf K2-L2 | 9.12.19.14.12 | | none | 9.13. 0. 0. 0 | |

| 7. | Pal TFC Jmb B12 | 9.12.19.14.12 | | none | 9.13. 0. 0. 0 | |

| 8. | Pal TS N14-N15 | 9.12.18. 5.16 | | GIII | 9.13. 0. 0. 0 | |

| 9. | Pal TFC O16 | 9.12.18. 5.16 | | child of Chan-Bahlum | 9.13. 0. 0. 0 | |

PEI. This example of the T79 anniversary event occurs without the *te'-
naab-chaan* expression in the final passage of the TFC as part of temporal
directions for the last DN, which leads from the previous event on 2 Cib
14 Mol (recorded at N8-N13) to the katun ending 9.13.0.0.0 8 Ahau 8 Uo.

Chart 87   257

This verb is preceded by 2 Cib and followed by T1:I:606:23 "child of mother" and by the name glyph of Chan-Bahlum. The referents of the possessed noun "child of mother" are not named, but they can be reconstructed by a comparison of this passage to other 2 Cib 14 Mol clauses (TFC, M14-L17 [21:8] and TS, N14-N15 [#8]). The latter clauses are used to insure that a DN of three days is counted, not from the previous CR 3 Caban 15 Mol, but from 2 Cib 14 Mol, and in both cases, the subjects of the 2 Cib verbs (one written with the same T79 verb) are named respectively as GI and GIII of the Palenque Triad. In a similar anniversary context on the doorjamb panels of the TC and TFC, the appropriate member of the Triad is named as as the agent of the 9.12.19.14.12 5 Eb 5 Kayab event, which occurred in celebration the eighth tropical year anniversary of Chan-Bahlum's accession. In both of these texts, the name phrase of the Triad god is followed by the T1.I:606:23 "child of mother" glyph and the name of Chan-Bahlum. In the histories of Katuns 11 and 12 (TIm, F4-E9; TIm, M6; and TIw, A3), one or more of the Triad gods are named as the agents of verbs, and their name phrases are followed by the same "child of mother" glyph and the name of Pacal, the contemporary ruler of Palenque. In these unusual contexts, the Triad gods are named as "children" of a historical person, who as current male ruler is characterized as a "mother." Clearly, the final passage of the TFC is intended to be a similar reference, but the names of the Triad gods are deleted, perhaps because of the need to conserve space at the end of the text, and because the identities of the children were known from redundant information and contemporary cultural tradition. The agent of the final verb of the TFC is paraphrased as "the children of (mother) Kina Chan-Bahlum, Lord of Palenque." It should be noted that these unusual relationship statements are probably echoed in the *Popol Vuh* and other sources where human sacrifice and blood-letting rituals are characterized as the nourishment and "nursing" (an exclusively female activity) of the gods.

10. Pal T18   9.13.13.15. 0   none   9.13.15. 0. 0
     B10-A11

PEI. This verb is part of the temporal directions for the count of a DN (5.18.4.7.8.13.18) leading from 9 Ik 10 Mol to 9 Ahau 3 Kankin. The first clause of the text records the 9 Ik 10 Mol event as "chicchan (ahau)-in-hand/God K," and a later occurrence of the same verb at the other end of the DN is recorded as the "first (T204.4:565:178) ahau-in-hand/God K" (see 20:8). This verb occurs in a passage immediately preceding the DN with the first two glyphs being an ADI and an alternative form of the 9 Ik 10 Mol event (see 21:9), thus establishing the base event of the count. This T79 anniversary verb is prefixed by a PEI and followed by "yax ahau-in-hand." Here *yax*, meaning "first" in Yucatec, is in direct substitution for T204.4:565:178, a form of "first" which seems to be based on the Cholan term *nahil*. The T79 verb is marked as the anniversary of the "first" holding of the God K scepter 945,608 tuns before the historical date celebrated by this tablet.

11.	Tik T4	9.15.15. 2. 3		Ruler B	9.16. 0. 0. 0
	L3; H3				

This T79 verb is in the fifth of a series of five clauses recording the three-tun anniversary of an event which took place one day after a "star" event (see 80:7). In this final clause, Ruler B is named as the agent and his genealogy is recorded in his name phrase. See 38:17, 52:4, 79:7, and 80:6.

CHART 88   Affix T181   in Cluster *.181:126   with Main Sign T741

T126 appears with T181 as a verbal suffix configuration in two forms: (1) T181:126, and (2) T126.181. Although I am cataloging these two configurations on separate charts, I am not sure that they were intended as contrasting and differentiated affix patterns (see Chart 89). Proskouriakoff (1960) identified this verb as equivalent to some initial event in a ruler's life, but now it is generally accepted as birth.

#	LOCATION	DATE (EVENT)	PATIENT	AGENT	DEDICATION	
1.	Tik 23 B4	9. 3. 9.13. 3		Lady of Tikal	9. 4. 0. 0. 0+?	
2.	Cop 3 B7a	9.10.19. 3.11		local person	9.11. 0. 0. 0	
3.	Pal HS A9	9. 8. 9.13. 0		Pacal II	9.11.10. 0. 0	
4.	PN 36 C5	9. 9.13. 4. 1		Ruler 2	9.11.15. 0. 0	
5.	Cop 7 B12	9. 9. 0. 0. 0		Smoking-Head	9. 9. 0. 0. 0	

This "birth" glyph seems to be the verb in the second part of a couplet in which the first verb is perhaps related to the "hand-over-earth" metaphor for birth used at Palenque. See 32:1-4 and 59:10.

| 6. | Pal TC A17 | 12.19.13. 4. 0 | | ancestral goddess | 9.13. 0. 0. 0 |  |

Chart 88 259

7.	Pal TC E7	12.19.13. 4. 0		deleted (ancestral goddess)	9.13. 0. 0. 0

Paraphrase: ". . . since she was born until she acceded, the ancestral goddess."

8.	Pal TC P5	5 Cimi 14 Kayab		Kuk I	9.13. 0. 0. 0
9.	Pal TFC B16	1.18. 5. 4. 0		GII	9.13. 0. 0. 0

This verb is preceded by an ordinal construction for "third" (T204.III: 565:178), perhaps in reference to the fact that GII was the third born of the Palenque Triad gods.

10.	Pal TS C1	1.18. 5. 3. 6		GIII	9.13. 0. 0. 0
11.	Pal TS P13	9.10. 2. 6. 6		deleted (Chan-Bahlum)	9.13. 0. 0. 0
12.	Car 3 A8b	9. 6.12. 4. 6		Ruler 3	9.10. 5. 0. 0
13.	Car 3 B17a	9. 7.14.10. 8		Ruler 4	9.10. 5. 0. 0
14.	Tort 6 B5	9. 8.19.10. 5		deleted (Ahpo-Balam)	9.12. 0. 0. 0

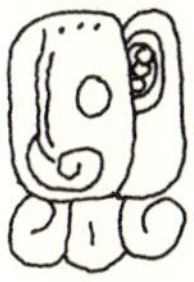

Although the date of this event was recorded on a now-missing part of this monument and the subject is deleted, the verb occurs in a context from which both may be reconstructed. A paraphrase of the passage is as follows: "It was 1.11.11.5 since he was born, count (GI variant) until 1 Oc 3 Cumku (9.10.11.3.10), he was seated as ahau of the succession, Ahpo-Balam."

15. Pal D   missing   ancestral   9.14.10. 0. 0
     Pier g   goddess

The date of this birth is missing, but it is the same event as that as
the initial event on the TC (see ##6-7).

16. Pal T18   missing   missing   9.13.15. 0. 0
     Stc 501

17. Yax L17   no date   Shield-   9.16.18. 0. 0
     C3   Jaguar II

This "birth" phrase is embedded in the verbal phrase beginning with a
phrase for blood-letting which has a deleted subject. The birth glyph
with its subject Shield-Jaguar II occurs between that initial verbal
phrase and another which frame the birth, presumably because it was the
occasion for the blood-letting rites. Bird-Jaguar is named as the agent
of the framing events.

CHART 89   Affix T181   in Cluster *:126.181   with Main Sign T741

This affix pattern may or may not be in contrast to the *.181:126 pattern listed in Chart 88.

#	LOCATION	DATE (EVENT)	PATIENT	AGENT	DEDICATION	
1.	Coll 14 D1	9. 9. 2. 0. 8		Chac-Naab-Be	9.10.15. 0. 0	
2.	Coll 14 F8	9.10.12. 4. 8		Puma	9.10.15. 0. 0	
3.	PN 8 A9	9.11.12. 7. 2		Ruler 2	9.13.15. 0. 0	
4.	Coll 15 B2	9.10.16.16.19		Jaguar Paw of Site Q	9.12. 0. 0. 0	
5.	Cop 6 C8c-C8d	no date		18-Rabbit	9.12.10. 0. 0	

Chart 89 261

6.	Nar 24 B13	9.12.15.13. 7	Smoking-Squirrel	9.13.10. 0. 0	
7.	Nar 29 H8	9.12.15.13. 7	Smoking-Squirrel	9.14. 3. 0. 0	
8.	PN 3 A8	9.12. 2. 0.16	Lady Ahpo-Katun	9.14. 0. 0. 0	
9.	PN 3 D6	9.13.16. 4. 6	Lady Ahpo-Kin	9.14. 0. 0. 0	
10.	DPil 25 H1	no date	????	9.14. 0. 0. 0	

This "birth" is found in the secondary text and is not likely to record the birth of a historic person. It is followed by *u ahau* (T11.168:1000e. 130) and an "akbal-kin" couplet similar to period ending expressions found at Naranjo and elsewhere (see Chart 35). The text closes with *u cab* (T11:526:136?) and Shield-God K, the contemporary ruler of Dos Pilas.

11.	Pal PTab C4	9.10.11.17. 0	Kan-Xul II	9.14.10. 0. 0	
12.	Pal PTab S3	9.10.17. 6. 0	Xoc	9.14.10. 0. 0	
13.	ECayo L3 A10	9.10.16. 8.14	Carapace-Shell	9.15. 5. 0. 0	
14.	PN Alt2 A2	9.13. 9.14.15	Ruler 4	9.16. 0. 0. 0	
15.	Yax L13 A3	9.16. 0.14. 5?	Shield-Jaguar II	9.16. 5. 0. 0	
16.	Yax L31 H1	9.12.17.12.10	Bird-Jaguar III	9.17. 0. 0. 0	

#	LOCATION	DATE		AGENT	DEDICATION	
17.	ECayo L1 A10	9.16. 4. 3.15		4-Pa-Na-Ka	9.17. 5. 0. 0	
18.	Cop HS	missing		Chac-Muluc	9.17.10. 0. 0	
19.	PN Thr1 Q1	9.15.18.16. 7		Ruler 7	9.17.15. 0. 0	
20.	Nar 12 B2	9.17. 0. 2.12		Ruler IIIb	9.18.10. 0. 0	
21.	Nar 10 A2	9.17. 0. 2.12		Ruler IIIb	9.19. 0. 0. 0	
22.	Uax 7 pC2	missing		missing	9.19. 0. 0. 0	
23.	PN Bur5 Shell B1	9.12. 2. 0.16		Lady Ahpo-Katun	9.15. 0. 0. 0	
24.	Pal TC Cens1 J2	missing		Cauac	9.12.10. 0. 0	
25.	Pal TC Cens2 C3	9.10. 5. 8. 4		Chac-Cauac	9.13.10. 0. 0	

CHART 90		Affix T181		in Cluster *:126.181		with Miscellaneous Main Signs

#	LOCATION	DATE (EVENT)	PATIENT	AGENT	DEDICATION	
1.	Cop AltG2 A2b-B2	9.18. 5. 0. 0	eroded?	none	9.18. 5. 0. 0	
2.	Smj Shell B1	10 Ahau ????		local person	9.13. 0. 0. 0?	

Chart 91   263

3. Pal TFC   1.18. 4. 7. 1   God K   9.13. 0. 0. 0
    B14

This is a verb from an 819 Day Count passage, although it does not record
the station for the Initial Series date. Rather it appears to be related
to the CR implied by the recorded DN by a number of Jupiter cycles
(Lounsbury, personal communication, 1980).

CHART 91   Affix T181   in Cluster *:136.126.181   with Main Sign T741

Thompson (1962:450) listed the first two affixes of this cluster as a single sign; however, since
either sign can appear independently of the other, and since T126 may function as an AEI in this
context, I have transcribed each affix separately.

#	LOCATION	DATE (EVENT)	PATIENT	AGENT	DEDICATION	
1.	Pal TC D2	12.19.11.13. 0		deleted (GI the First)	9.13. 0. 0. 0	

The date is implied by a DN, and the subject has been identified through
syntactical analysis (Lounsbury 1980) as GI the First, the god who was
father of the Palenque Triad.

| 2. | Pal TC P7 | 5 Cimi 14 Kayab | | deleted (Kuk I) | 9.13. 0. 0. 0 |  |

The DN recorded does not work arithmetically with the two CRs, and no
adequate explanation for the error has been posited. This passage in
which this verb occurs is paraphrased as follows: "It was 1.2.5.14 since
he was born until he acceded, Kuk I."

| 3. | Pal TC P11 | 8.19. 6. 8. 8 | | Ruler 3 | 9.13. 0. 0. 0 |  |

| 4. | Pal TC P13 | 8.19. 6. 8. 8 | | Ruler 3 | 9.13. 0. 0. 0 |  |

Paraphrase: "It was 13.3.9 since he was born, Ruler 3, until 3 Caban 10
Xul; it was 6.3 until he acceded, Ruler 3."

5. Pal TC   9. 1. 4. 5. 0   Manik   9.13. 0. 0. 0

    S4

    Paraphrase: It was 1.8.1.18 since he was born, Manik, until he acceded,
    Manik."

6. Pal TC   9. 1.10. 0. 0   Chaacal I   9.13. 0. 0. 0

    S9

    Paraphrase: "It was 1.16.7.17 since he was born on 5 Ahau 3 Zec, Chaacal
    I, until he acceded on 5 Caban 0 Zotz'."

7. Pal TC   9. 4. 9. 0. 4   Chaacal II   9.13. 0. 0. 0

    U7

    Paraphrase: "It was 1.0.1 since he was born, Chaacal II, until he was
    born, Chan-Bahlum I, on 7 Kan 17 Mol."

8. Pal TIw   9. 8. 9.13. 0   Pacal II   9.12.15. 0. 0

    E2

    Paraphrase: "It was 12.9.8 since he was born, Pacal, on 8 Ahau 13 Pop,
    until he acceded, Pacal, on 5 Lamat 1 Mol."

9. PN 1   9.12. 2. 0.16   Lady Ahpo-   9.13.15. 0. 0

    B3   Katun

    This is not an anterior event.

10. Ton   eroded   Dragon-   Late Classic

    Pestac St   Jaguar

11. Tik 24   missing   missing   9.19. 0. 0. 0

    yA16

12. Ton M20   missing   eroded   Late Classic

    pC4

13. Izt Pan1   missing   local person   Late Classic

    VIII 2

Chart 92 265

CHART 92   Affix T181   in Cluster *:136.126.181   with Miscellaneous Main Signs

#	LOCATION	DATE (EVENT)	PATIENT	AGENT	DEDICATION	
1.	Ton M111 O	9.12.16. 3.12		deleted (Mah Kina Kuk)	9.13. 0. 0. 0	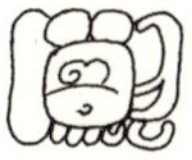

This "seating" is linked by DN to a period ending and a "scattering" event, where the agent of both verbs is named as Mah Kina Kuk.

2.	Ton F34b pA6	missing		missing	Late Classic	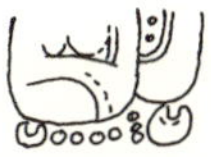
3.	Yax L30 E3	9.13.16.10. 3		God K	9.17. 0. 0. 0	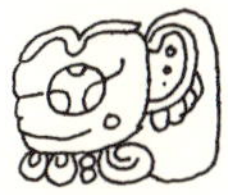

This is the verb in an 819 Day Count passage.

4.	Car 3 D12b	9. 9. 9.10. 5		Ruler 4	9.10. 5. 0. 0	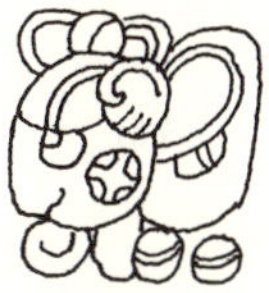
5.	Pal T18 Stc 420	missing		missing	9.14.15. 0. 0	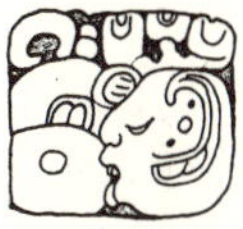
6.	Pal PTab E8	9.10.18.17.19		Kan-Xul II	9.14.10. 0. 0	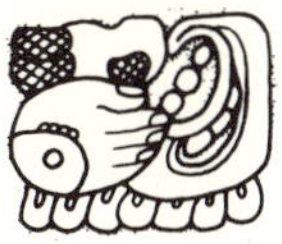

This "deer-hoof-in-hand" glyph is the second part of a verbal couplet (see 20:12) recording an event that occurred to Kan-Xul II at age 7.0.19. Since the same event occurred to Chaacal III at age 14.1.2 (see 59:8), it seems to be one involving young future rulers, but it is a rite distinct from heir-designation. The only other occurrence of this verb is on the TC, where it is associated with 4 Ahau 8 Cumku either as an event that took place 8.5.0 after the birth of the first GI or as an era event that has no expressed agent (see 33:3).

CHART 93   Affix T181   in Cluster *:82.181   with Main Sign T218

#	LOCATION	DATE (EVENT)	PATIENT	AGENT	DEDICATION	
1.	Car 3 C11b	9. 9. 9.10. 5		Ruler 3	9.10. 5. 0. 0	

This is the first verb in a couplet; see 92:4 for the second verb.

#	LOCATION	DATE (EVENT)	PATIENT	AGENT	DEDICATION	
2.	Tik Alt 5 29	9.13.19.16. 9		relation of the batab	9.14. 0. 0. 0	

CHART 94   Affix T181   in Cluster *:24.181   with Miscellaneous Main Signs

#	LOCATION	DATE (EVENT)	PATIENT	AGENT	DEDICATION	
1.	Car 3 B14b	9. 7.10.16. 8		Ruler 3	9.10. 5. 0. 0	

The event occurred when the ruler was age 12.4.8; see 93.1.

#	LOCATION	DATE (EVENT)	PATIENT	AGENT	DEDICATION	
2.	Nar 24 C7-C9	9.12.10. 5.12		Lady 6-Sky of Tikal	9.13.10. 0. 0	
3.	Nar 29 F8-F10	9.12.10. 5.12		Lady 6-Sky of Tikal	9.14. 3. 0. 0	
4.	Cop I C1	9.12. 3.14. 0		*u cab* Knot-Skull	9.12. 5. 0. 0	
5.	DPil 1 B2	9.13.15. 0. 0		missing	9.13.15. 0. 0	

This verb follows the CR, "scattering," and an unknown verb.

#	LOCATION	DATE (EVENT)	PATIENT	AGENT	DEDICATION	
6.	Cop Alt of St13	no date		local ruler	9.11. 0. 0. 0	

Chart 95   267

CHART 95   Affix T181   in Cluster *:130.181   with Miscellaneous Main Signs

#	LOCATION	DATE (EVENT)	PATIENT	AGENT	DEDICATION	
1.	Bon C A3	9.10. 3. 2. 0		Chul	9.13.15. 0. 0	
2.	PN 1 G5	9.12.14.10.16		deleted	9.13.15. 0. 0	

The following signs are components in the verb listed in ##2-13: one of several signs (T23, T1000a, and T537var) with the phonetic value *na*; the phonetic sign *wa* (T130); and the suffix *-ah* (T181). This combination of signs renders the term *na.wa:ah*, of which *na* or *naw* may be the verbal stem. In researching this particular glyph and its contexts, I have found that the verbal stem *naw* is rare and exists only in a few Mayan languages, such as Yucatec, where it is the term for "walking drunkenly (for various reasons)," a meaning not appropriate to the context of this verb. However, as a verb, *na* is widely distributed and has many different meanings appropriate to the contexts of war and sacrifice in which this verb is found (Schele n.d.b). For this reason, I have cataloged T130 as a verbal suffix, not as part of the verbal stem. David Stuart (n.d.) has shown that the *na* event in #2 and #3 occurred two days after the death of Ruler 2 and was conducted by Lady Ahpo-Katun, the wife of Ruler 3. The actor is clearly an elite person of the royal family, not a captive of war, as in later examples, and the rite occurred in the context of funerary rites. *Na* means both the gaining of honor by righteous public acts and commemorations for the dead, and here it very likely implies sacrificial rites undertaken by the wife of the succeeding ruler in commemoration of the death of the preceding one.

#	LOCATION	DATE (EVENT)	PATIENT	AGENT	DEDICATION	
3.	PN 3 D3b	9.12.14.10.16		Lady Ahpo- Katun	9.14. 0. 0. 0	
4.	PN Bur5 Shell I2	9.12.14.10.17		Lady Ah-Be	9.15. 0. 0. 0	

The *na* event in #4 and #5 occurred on the day following the rite above (##2-3) and three days following the death of Ruler 2. Although the name of the agent in this event seems to be recorded solely by a title glyph, she can be clearly identified as Lady Ahpo-Katun because of the recurrence of the same date and verb with Lady Ahpo-Katun clearly recorded as agent in #5.

| 5. | PN 8
E1 | 9.12.14.10.17 | | Lady Ahpo-
Katun | 9.13.15. 0. 0 | |

| 6. | Pal A
sAlf A3 | 9.14. 2. 5.13 | | ???? | 9.14.10. 0. 0 | |

The verbs in #6 and #7 are found on the loincloths of the figures flanking the west stairs of House A. The stones are thought to have been reused and, therefore, the LC positions of the dates may be one or two CRs earlier. In both cases, the verb is followed by a "knot-skull" glyph (T126:60.1042:24) which may be part of the verbal phrase or the subject of the verb. In this text, the "knot-skull" glyph is followed by the T24: 528.515 title glyph. It should noted that while these two figures do not seem to be bound, the seven figures flanking them are clearly marked with sacrificial iconography.

| 7. | Pal A
nAlf A3 | 9.14. 2. 5.14 | | Lord of
Palenque | 9.14.10. 0. 0 | |

In this text, the "knot-skull" is followed by the Palenque EG.

| 8. | Pal T18
Stc 446 | missing | | missing | 9.14.15. 0. 0 |  |

| 9. | Pal Scb
A3 | ???? 7? Zec | | Chac-Zutz' | 9.15. 0. 0. 0 |  |

In the texts of the Scribe and the Orator (#10), the *na* verb is followed by a prepositional phrase consisting of T116.59:25:501:126 (*ni.ti:ca:ba: ??*). The protagonists of both monuments are shown in sacrificial regalia, and blood is shown flowing from the ear of the Scribe, identified as the ruler Chac-Zutz' (Schele n.d.b). The name of the agent follows a glyph that Mathews (personal communication, 1980) has tentatively identified as an expression of agency. The variant of this same glyph precedes the name of the agent in the texts of #4 and #11. In this example, however, the "agency" glyph is preceded by a "scattering" hand, which very likely refers to the scattering of blood in sacrificial rites.

| 10. | Pal Ora
E3-E4 | missing | | Chaacal III | 9.15. 0. 0. 0 | |

| 11. | Agua 2
E2 | 9.15. 4. 6.11 | Jaguar-Paw-
Jaguar of
Seibal | Captor of
Kin-Balam | 9.15. 5. 0. 0 | |

Chart 95   269

12. DPil 16   9.15. 4. 6.11   Jaguar-Paw-   Ruler 3   9.15. 5. 0. 0
     E1a   Jaguar of
                                   Seibal

The texts of Dos Pilas Stela 16 and Aguateca Stela 2 record the same
series of events. This *na* event occurred eight days after a "star-over-
Seibal" event and seven days after an "axe" event (see 10:12-13 and 54:1-
2). The patient of this verb is recorded as Jaguar-Paw-Jaguar of Seibal,
a name phrase that appears in the contemporary text of the Seibal HS, as
well as adjacent to the captive on the base of this stela. In the Aguateca text, the agent is named as the "captor of Kin-Balam," a title also
appearing on Aguateca Stela 1. However, in the Dos Pilas text, the agent
is recorded "Spangle-Head," the name of the contemporary ruler of Dos
Pilas that occurs on several other monuments. He is the agent of both the
na and the "axe" events. Finally, it should be noted that in both texts,
the name of the agent follows a possible agency expression (T17.86:671 or
575[671]).

13. Coll 2   9.17.12.13.17   ????   9.17.15. 0. 0
     B4

The text of the Fort Worth panel records that a *na* event took place three
days after a "capture" event; however, neither the captive's name nor the
the captor's follows the verb. Instead, there is a two-glyph phrase which
seems to name the patient (the captive) as *u bac-al* (T1.570:102, a glyph
perhaps meaning "his captive") and *ti* followed by the T518 title, a glyph
known to refer to rulers. The agent is apparently deleted, and the patient named as "the captive of the ruler." It should be noted that this
designation also occurs following Great-Jaguar-Paw's name phrase on
Lintel 3 of Temple 1 at Tikal. See 12:5.

Coll 2   Tikal T1, L3

14. Tik Str   9.13. 3. 8.11   Uuc-Bolon-   missing   9.15. 0. 0. 0
     5D-57   Imix

This *na* event occurred thirteen days after a war event (12:5) in which
Great-Jaguar-Paw of Site Q was apparently captured and twenty-seven days
before the blood-letting rites held in celebration of the thirteen-katun
anniversary of the last date on Stela 31. Although the name of the victim
of this *na* event does not correspond to that of Great-Jaguar-Paw, the
proximity of the dates and the tendency of *na* events to occur several
days after capture and war events suggest that the victim was in fact
Great-Jaguar-Paw. The standing ruler (presumably Ruler A) wears a costume
that shares the same "Tlaloc" iconography as Aguateca Stela 2 and Dos

Pilas Stela 16. This "Tlaloc" complex is especially associated with the sacrificial rituals recorded by both the *na* and the "star-shell" verbs.

15. PN Bur5   9.14.17.14.17   Lady Ma-Ta-   9.15. 0. 0. 0
     Shl L2a   La-Zotz'

This *na* event occurs on the last of four shells from Burial 5 at Piedras Negras; it is linked by a DN of 2.3.4.0 to an earlier *na* event of which Lady Ahpo-Katun was the actor (#4). The verbal phrase is followed by "scattering," perhaps specifying blood-letting, and a *ka* fist (T669b: :24), which may be part of the verb. The name of the agent Lady Ma-Ta-La-Zotz' (T1000a:74:565.178:756b) is followed by *u cab* and the name Lady Ahpo-Katun, a relationship glyph (T575.86:575?), and the name of Ruler 3. The text, therefore, ends with the names of three persons, but I suspect the first woman named is intended to be the subject of the verb. The sequence of names possibly should be paraphrased as follows: "she *na*-ed, Lady Ma-Ta-La-Zotz', *u cab* ("under the auspices of"?) Lady Ahpo-Katun, who was related to Ruler 3, Lord of Piedras Negras, a four-katun lord, Ahpo Kin."

16. Tik T4   9.15.12.11.13   Kin-Balam?   9.16. 0. 0. 0
     L2; B10-
     B11

See 80:5 and 80:8 for other verbs with some of the same glyphs.

17. Tik T4   9.15.12. 2. 2   GVI   9.16. 0. 0. 0
     L3; B5

This verbal phrase is followed by GVI of the Palenque list of gods, by *u cab*, and by Ruler B's name. See 58:1 for another example of a text in which the name of a god is followed *u cab* and the name of a current ruler.

18. DPil 26   9.14.10. 0. 0   ????   Smoking-GI   9.14.10. 0. 0
     C2

Smoking-GI may be the patient rather than the agent. See 76:4.

CHART 96   Affix T181   in Cluster *:23 or 4.181   with Miscellaneous Main Signs

T23 and T4 are known to have the phonetic value *na*; when they appear with T181, the resulting affix pattern should be *-nah*.

Chart 96 271

#	LOCATION	DATE (EVENT)	PATIENT	AGENT	DEDICATION	
1.	Ton F35 B-D	6 Etz'nab 1 Yaxkin		none	Late Classic	

Peter Mathews (personal communication, 1980) has pointed out to me that this phrase must represent an elaborate way of recording the number 1. It is preceded by 6 Etz'nab and followed by Yaxkin. The *te'* sign is known to function as a numerical classifier for month positions, and, therefore, the phrase must mean something like "the completion of its succession" as day 1 of the month in contrast to the "seating" of the month which occurs on the last day of the preceding month.

#	LOCATION	DATE (EVENT)	PATIENT	AGENT	DEDICATION	
2.	Pal T18 Fer44	missing		missing	9.14.15. 0. 0	

This glyph was published by Miguel Angel Fernandez (1954) as Number 44. See 74:30-31 for other examples with the torch infix.

#	LOCATION	DATE (EVENT)	PATIENT	AGENT	DEDICATION	
3.	Coll 14 E5	9.10.12. 0. 9		Chac-Naab-Be	9.10.15. 0. 0	

This verb records an accession event.

#	LOCATION	DATE (EVENT)	PATIENT	AGENT	DEDICATION	
4.	Yax Str33 Step 7 Q1	9.15.13. 6. 9	3-Knot-Skull	deleted	9.16. 6. 0. 0	

This verb is the first in a series that includes a ballcourt event (13:6), a "scattering" expression (3:12), and a "blood-letting" phrase (52:9). It is followed by a name glyph (TIII.12:60.1042:24?), which also appears in the first half of the text as the agent of three events that occurred in the ancient mythological past. I assume that the same supernatural is named as the patient of this event, and the Bird-Jaguar is to be understood as the deleted agent. However, it is possible that the supernatural is the intended agent.

#	LOCATION	DATE (EVENT)	PATIENT	AGENT	DEDICATION	
5.	Yax Str44 nw Up D7a	9.15. 0.15. 3		Captor of Ix-Tun-Ahau	9.15. 0. 0. 0	

CHART 97   Affix T181   in Cluster *:18.181   with Miscellaneous Main Signs

#	LOCATION	DATE (EVENT)	PATIENT	AGENT	DEDICATION	
1.	Tik LP B9	8.14. 3. 1.12		Bone-Head	8.14. 5. 0. 0	
2.	Pal Sarc 3	9. 8. 9.13. 0		deleted (Pacal II)	9.12.15. 0. 0	

AEI. This "birth" verb is linked by a DN "four katun seatings" to "death," and Pacal II is named as the subject of both.

#	LOCATION	DATE (EVENT)	PATIENT	AGENT	DEDICATION	
3.	RAz Tomb A9	8.19. 1. 9.13		Cauac-Waterlily	8.19. 5. 0. 0	

This glyph is the verb in a painted inscription on the walls of a looted tomb at Rio Azul. The iconography of these murals features water symbolism, and the date presumably corresponds to the birth of the buried person.

CHART 98   Affix T18   in Cluster *:18   with Miscellaneous Main Signs

These examples are associated with period ending or "era" (4 Ahau 8 Cumku) events.

#	LOCATION	DATE (EVENT)	PATIENT	AGENT	DEDICATION	
1.	Quir Ew B17b	9.17. 0. 0. 0		Two-Legged-Sky	9.17. 0. 0. 0	
2.	Pal TS C9-D9	13. 0. 0. 0. 0		none	9.13. 0. 0. 0	

AEI.

#	LOCATION	DATE (EVENT)	PATIENT	AGENT	DEDICATION	
3.	Pal TC D15	13. 0. 1. 9. 2		GI the First	9.13. 0. 0. 0	

AEI. This "era" expression is apparently used erroneously. The verb functions to reiterate an earlier event as part of temporal instructions leading to a later event, but the earlier event occurs in a triplet in which the event is repeated in three varying forms (17:1, 20:1, and

Chart 98 273

32:13). The sky sign (T561) or a phonetic substitute occurs as a featured part of each of these previous expressions, and it is clear from the structure of this clause that one of those three "sky" expressions or a fourth variant was intended here. GI the First is named or implied as the agent of all four versions of this event. However, it seems an error was made in the selection of this fourth version because the identical expression occurs on the TS (#2) in reference to 4 Ahau 8 Cumku, and that context misunderstanding or error is less likely. Because of the possibility of confusion is very much higher in the TC text, I am assuming that it is erroneous.

4.   Pom F12   9.12.10. 0. 0   eroded   9.14. 0. 0. 0?
       pA2-pA3

This verb is preceded only by 9 Ahau without a haab position; however, since the period ending 9.13.0.0.0 follows this clause, and since this verb is known to function as a period ending verb (see 68:1-2), I have placed the 9 Ahau date at 9.12.10. 0. 0.

5.   Cop P   9. 9.10. 0. 0   *u cab* local ruler   9. 9.10. 0. 0
       A9-B9a

This expression is the third verbal passage to record the period ending 9.9.10.0.0 (see 49:2 and 67:1).

6.   Cop 6   9.12.10. 0. 0   Imix-God K   9.12.10. 0. 0   
       C1-C2a

This expression is the third of four clauses recording this period-ending (see 50:2, 69:3, and 103:5).

7.   Tort Box   9.12. 6.17.18   Ahpo-Balam   9.12.10. 0. 0
       C2-D2

See 5:6.

8.   Quir De   9.16.15. 0. 0   Two-Legged   9.16.15. 0. 0
       A22d   Sky

9.   Pal Scb   no date   Chac-Zutz'   9.15. 0. 0. 0
       B1-C1   (by title)

This is not a period ending expression, but rather seems to record a blood-letting event.

#	LOCATION	DATE (EVENT)	PATIENT	AGENT	DEDICATION	
10.	Ton M110 P-Q	9.14.10. 0. 0		none	9.14.10. 0. 0	
11.	Coll 21 B4	9.11.10.16.15		Lord of Site Q	9.12. 0. 0. 0	
12.	NTun GpIVh A3-A4	9.16. 4. 1. 5		Chaan-Ah Cauac	9.16.10. 0. 0	

See 26:18, 82:29,31 and 116:20-21.

| 13. | PN 40 B14 | 9.15.15. 0. 0 | | ???? | 9.15.15. 0. 0 | |
| 14. | PN 11 F5a | 9.13. 9.14.15 | | Ruler 4 | 9.15. 0. 0. 0 | |

CHART 99	Affix T18		in Cluster *.18		with Miscellaneous Main Signs

#	LOCATION	DATE (EVENT)	PATIENT	AGENT	DEDICATION	
1.	PN Bur5 Shell E1	9.12. 2. 0.16		deleted (Lady Ahpo-Katun)	9.15. 0. 0. 0	

AEI. This verb is the base from which a DN is counted and is redundant, repeating information from the preceding clause. The subject can, therefore, be reconstructed as Lady Ahpo-Katun.

| 2. | Pal T18 Jamb C7 | 9.12. 6. 5. 8 | | deleted (Chaacal III) | 9.14.15. 0. 0 | |

AEI. The subject of the "birth" verb is deleted, and the clause is gapped to a T700var "accession" event from which the subject is also deleted. An embedded clause relating an ancient mythological "accession" to the historical one follows the event glyphs and precedes the name phrase of the subject (of both events), Chaacal III. It is possible that a "death" event follows the mythological "accession" clause while preceding the name phrase, in which case the single name phrase would be recorded as the subject of three events. *U cab* precedes the name phrase.

Chart 99 275

3. PN L2   9.10. 6. 5. 9   Ruler 2   9.11.15. 0. 0 
    X9-W10

    AEI.

4. Car 6   9. 5.19. 1. 2   Ruler 2   9. 8. 10. 0. 0 
    E11-F11

    AEI.

5. Bon A   9. 3. 0.14.13   none   9. 3.10. 0. 0 
    F6

This glyph phrase occurs between the tzolkin and haab positions where one
would expect a notation of the appropriate "Lord of the Night," but Glyph
F is missing, and G4, not G5, is the proper station for this date. This
glyph, should represent, therefore, some kind of event. The haab position
is followed by a glyph with the prefixes *u* and *tu* (see 40:7) and the name
phrase "Fishfin of Bonampak." The glyph preceding the name phrase may be
part of a verbal phrase of which this verb is the first part.

6. PN L3   9.15.18. 3.13   Jaguar of   9.16.10. 0. 0 
    J1-I2   Yaxchilan

This verbal phrase may record a visit by canoe of a Yaxchilan lord in
celebration of the first katun anniversary of the accession of Ruler 3 of
Piedras Negras.

7. Ixk 2   9.17. 9. 0.13   *u cab* local ruler   9.17.10. 0. 0 
    B11

This event occurred one day before an "axe" event (see 75:8). The name of
the agent of both events is the same, but in this clause, the name glyph
is followed by *u cab* and two eroded glyphs. At other sites, the events in
7 and #8 are associated with "star," "axe," and other kinds of war
events (see Chart 11).

8. Ixk 2   9.17. 9. 3. 4   deleted   9.17.10. 0. 0 
    C9

CHART 100   Affix T18   in Cluster *:178:18   with Main Sign T644

#	LOCATION	DATE (EVENT)	PATIENT	AGENT	DEDICATION	

1. Car 6   9. 8. 5.16.12   deleted   9. 8.10. 0. 0
    D17-E17   (Ruler 3)

This is a redundant expression which functions as the base for the count of a DN. The deleted subject can be reconstructed as Ruler 3.

2. Coll 1   9. 9.12.10. 6   Zac-Ma-??   9.10. 0. 0. 0
    B5-A6

AEI. This "seating" verb follows a DN and appears in a context where the expected structure is "it was some much time since event 1 until event 2." However, the event following this clause is the earlier of the two events. Either the AEI (T126) is used incorrectly, or there is some property of both the AEI and the PEI not yet understood which would allow for an atypical usage in this context. See 87:9 for a similar "misuse" of the PEI.

3. Coll 1   9. 8. 9.12.14   Ahpo-Kuk   9.10. 0. 0. 0
    D4-C5

AEI.

4. Pal TFC   9.12.11.12.10   deleted   9.13. 0. 0. 0
    N7-N8   (Chan-Bahlum II)

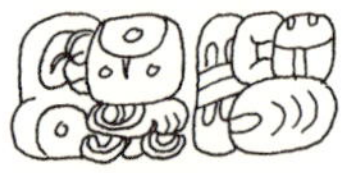

AEI. This is a redundant expression which functions as the base for the count of a DN. The deleted subject can be reconstructed as Chan-Bahlum II.

5. Tik T1   9.12. 9.17.16   Ruler A   9.15. 0. 0. 0
    L3; F9-E10

AEI.

6. Tik 22   9.16.17.16. 4   deleted   9.17. 0. 0. 0
    B11-A12   (Ruler C)

AEI. This "seating" phrase occurs in the final passage of the text, the purpose of which is to relate the period ending to the accession of Ruler C. Since only Ruler C is named as the subject of the initial verb (Ruler

Chart 101   277

B occurs in a genealogical statement for Ruler C), the subjects of both
the "seating" and the "scattering" verbs of this final clause are
deleted, but clearly understood to be Ruler C.

| 7. | Lac L1 L3-K4 | 9.15.12.17.13 | | Knot-Eye-Jaguar of Bonampak | 9.15.15. 0. 0 |  |

AEI.

| 8. | Cop HS | missing | | Ahpo-Kankin-Kin | 9.17.10. 0. 0 |  |

CHART 101   Affix T18   in Cluster *.18:126   with Miscellaneous Main Signs

#	LOCATION	DATE (EVENT)	PATIENT	AGENT	DEDICATION	
1.	DPil 8 A12	9.12. 0. 10.11		deleted (Shield-God K)	9.15. 0. 0. 0	

This "birth" glyph functions as the base of a DN and, therefore, repeats
information from the initial clause of the text. The subject can be
reconstructed as Shield-God K, and T126 may function as an AEI.

| 2. | Cop 6 D8-D9 | 9.12.10. 0. 0 | | deleted | 9.12.10. 0. 0 |  |

The reference of this passage is problematic because the monument displays only one date to which all of the recorded events may or may not
refer. This passage closes the text and has a deleted subject, but it can
be shown to be related either to an event recorded in the immediately
preceding clause (a blood-letting of which 18-Rabbit is the agent) or to
an earlier period ending expression on Stela 6 (see 98:6). This T757
expression is also related to a body of similar phrases directly associated with blood-letting events (see Chart 35 and 39:7) and to another
period ending at Copan (see 35:2). It should be noted that period ending
scenes at Yaxchilan (the local version of the "scattering" rite) are full
of blood-letting iconography, so that the association of a blood-letting
rite with a period ending has precedence elsewhere. If this event is
accepted as blood-letting, then it would be the coupleted repetition of
the previous "fish-in-hand" verb, and the deleted subject would be identified as 18-Rabbit, who at the time was still a katun from his
accession.

3. Pal ISpot   9.18. 7.10.13   God K   9.18.10. 0. 0
    E2

This glyph is the verb of an 819 Day Count clause.

4. Pal TS   1. 6.14.11. 2   God K   9.13. 0. 0. 0
    A14

This is the verb is an 819 Day Count passage, and T126 may function as an AEI.

5. Chin Thr1   9. 7. 0. 1. 0   ??-Ah-Kan   none?   9.10. 0. 0. 0
    pS

AEI? This "capture" verb is followed by a single glyph, but since it is an earlier event from which a DN is counted, the agent's name may have been deleted and the clause gapped to the succeeding one, which did not survive or was not reproduced by Maler.

6. Yax Str44   9. 6.10.14.15   Etz'nab   Knot-Eye-   9.15. 0. 0. 0
    sw Up A2   Jaguar

The first half of this "capture" glyph has been damaged so that it is possible that it carried a pronominal prefix as does its counterpart on Lintel 46 (see 61:4).

7. Quir Fe   ????   none   9.17. 0. 0. 0
    C14

CHART 102   Affix T18   in Cluster *.18:136   with Miscellaneous Main Signs

#	LOCATION	DATE (EVENT)	PATIENT	AGENT	DEDICATION	
1.	Cop AltF' B3a	9.16. 0. 1.11?		deleted	9.17. 5. 0. 0	

This "bundle" expression follows a DN of 1.4.0.0 and an unknown glyph, and it precedes a possible "death" verb (with a PEI adjoined) in which the main sign is T585 (see 127:2) and which appears to reiterate the initial event recorded in the text, a death occurring on 2 Chuen 4 Pop (9.17.4.1.11). The subject of the second "death" event is listed as

Chart 103   279

T575:86:671 (possibly a relationship glyph or an expression of agency) and the name phrase of New-Sky-at-Horizon, who is recorded as a "two-katun lord." However, it seems unlikely that New-Sky-at Horizon was intended as the subject of this "death" verb because of the relationship glyph preceding his name and because of the 1.4.0.0 DN, which would yield 9.17.16.5.17 if added to his accession date, 9.16.12.5.17. If the initial date of Altar F' (9.17.4.1.11) is subtracted from this calculated 9.17. 16.5.17 anniversary date, the resulting DN is 12.4.6. The DN at the beginning of the text included tuns, uinals, and days, but unfortunately only the coefficient for ten days has survived. Ten days does not match the DN required between the hypothetical anniversary date and the recorded CR. Either the two "death" events recorded on this monument are not the same event (an unlikely eventuality because of the lack of additional calendric information), or the subject of the "death" verb is not New-Sky-at-Horizon. It is interesting to note that the noun in the prepositional phrase following the "bundle" verb is not known to record the office of ruler in any other text from Copan or elsewhere, so that the office assumed in this event may not have been that of the ruler.

2. Tort Box   9.12. 7. 1.19   Ahpo-Balam   9.12.10. 0. 0
    F2

Michael Coe (1974:52) identified this T585 glyph as a means of recording two uinals "less one day" for a DN of thirty-nine days. His identification may be partially correct because T585 appears in an earlier DN of two days (glyphically, *ca bix*-?? or in Chol *cha bix*-?? and linguistically *chab-ix*-??). However, the T585 glyph identified as "one day less" has superfixes identical to those of the T585 "death" glyph prominent at Palenque (see Chart 19, 59:7, 73:2-3,7-8 and 106:1-2,8-9). Furthermore, this glyph is followed by the name Ahpo-Balam without the intervention of a verbal glyph, and while Mayan grammar allows the subjects of verbs to be deleted in phrases such as "it was thirty-nine days since event 1 until event 2, subject", it is not possible to delete a verb and leave a free-standing subject. The T585 glyph must record, therefore, a verbal expression, and since 9.12.7.0.0 (the date from which the DN is counted) is the latest date associated with Ahpo-Balam, a "death" event seems appropriate to the context. However, since thirty-nine days, not forty, are required between 9.12.7.0.0 and 9.12.7.1.19, it is possible that the T585 glyph functions both as a "death" verb and as "less one day."

CHART 103   Affix T136   in Cluster *:136   with Miscellaneous Main Signs

All of these examples are associated with period ending dates.

#	LOCATION	DATE (EVENT)	PATIENT	AGENT	DEDICATION	
1.	Pom PanY pD2	9. 9. 0. 0. 0		none	9.18. 0. 0. 0	

AEI?

#	LOCATION	DATE (EVENT)	PATIENT	AGENT	DEDICATION	
2.	Agua 5 C2-D2	9.13. 0. 0. 0	13 katuns	none or deleted	9.13. 0. 0. 0	

If the subject of this verb is deleted, it is recorded after two additional verbal phrases as Flint-Sky-God K.

#	LOCATION	DATE (EVENT)	PATIENT	AGENT	DEDICATION	
3.	Pom PanY A2-B3	9. 8. 0. 0. 0		GI-Jaguar	9.18. 0. 0. 0	
4.	Pom PanY pD1	9. 9. 0. 0. 0		5-Jaguar	9.18. 0. 0. 0	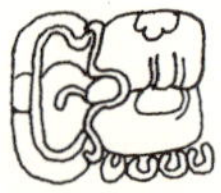
5.	Cop 6 B7c-A8	9.12.10. 0. 0		local ruler (by title)	9.12.10. 0. 0	
6.	Pal 96G K6-L6	9.17.13. 0. 7		deleted (Kuk II)	9.17.15. 0. 0	
7.	Yax L23 M2b-L3a	9.14.14. 8. 1	5th tun in Katun 3	Shield-Jaguar I	9.15. 0. 0. 0	

This period ending appears to refer to the "completion of the fifth tun in the third katun" (or the twenty-fifth tun) in the reign of Shield-Jaguar (Mathews, personal communication, 1981).

CHART 104   Affix T136   in Cluster *:136   with Miscellaneous Main Signs

All of these examples are in either 819 Day Count passages or 4 Ahau 8 Cumku "era" expressions.

#	LOCATION	DATE (EVENT)	PATIENT	AGENT	DEDICATION	
1.	Coll 6 B7	10. 1.13.17.19		God K	10. 1.15. 0. 0	

Chart 105   281

AEI. This is the verb of an 819 Day Count passage.

2. Pal TFC   9.12.18. 7. 1   God K   9.13. 0. 0. 0
    Jamb A6a

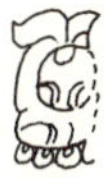

This is the verb in an 819 Day Count passage.

3. Pal TC   13. 0. 0. 0. 0   new cycle?   none   9.13. 0. 0. 0
    C6b–C7

AEI? This verb occurs in an "era" expression.

4. Pal TS   13. 0. 0. 0. 0   new cycle?   none   9.13. 0. 0. 0
    D17–N2

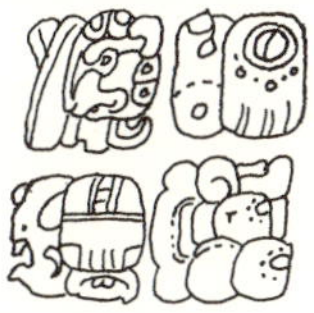

See 5:15–16 and 68:4–5 for other examples of this "era" expression.

CHART 105   Affix T136   in Cluster *:136   with Main Sign T741

In any of these examples, the suppressed T126 may function as an AEI, rather than as a verbal affix.

#	LOCATION	DATE (EVENT)	PATIENT	AGENT	DEDICATION	
1.	Pal TC E13	5. 7.11. 8. 4		U-Kix-Chan	9.13. 0. 0. 0	

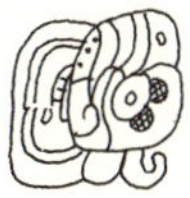

PEI. Paraphrase: "It was 3.6.10.12.2 count since 9 Ik until he was born, U-Kix-Chan."

| 2. | Pal TC E17 | 9. 7.11. 8. 4 | | U-Kix-Chan | 9.13. 0. 0. 0 | |

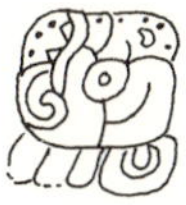

AEI? Paraphrase: " It was 1.6.7.13 since? he was born, U-Kix-Chan, until he acceded, U-Kix-Chan, on 11 Caban O Pop, Lord of Palenque."

| 3. | Pal TC U2 | 9. 4. 9. 0. 4 | | deleted | 9.13. 0. 0. 0 | |

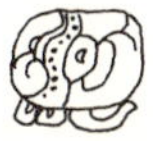

Paraphrase: "It was 2.2.4.17 since(?) he was born until he acceded, Chaacal III, on 1 Imix 4 Zip."

4. Pal TC   9. 4.10. 1. 5   Chan-   9.13. 0. 0. 0
   U9   Bahlum I

PEI. Paraphrase: "It was 1.0.1 since(?) he was born, Chaacal II, until he was born, Chan-Bahlum I, on 7 Kan 17 Mol." The recorded date does not correspond to the birth date of Chan-Bahlum as the syntax suggests, but rather it is the birth date of Chaacal II. The short time between these births and their structural linkage in this passages suggests that the two rulers were brothers.

5. Pal TC   9. 4.10. 1. 5   Chan-   9.13. 0. 0. 0
   T13   Bahlum I

Paraphrase: "It was 2.8.4.7 since? he was born, Chan-Bahlum I on 11 Chicchan 13 Uo . . ." In this passage the date of Chan-Bahlum's birth is explicitly stated, while in #4, it is implied.

6. Pal TC   9. 4.10. 1. 5   Chan-   9.13. 0. 0. 0
   T16   Bahlum I

This birth verb follows the example above and a DN or 16, 17, 18, or 19.8.2 and precedes the phrase "until he acceded." The earlier DN is confirmed as the correct one by the records of Chan-Bahlum I's accession on the east panel of the TI, so this second DN must lead from his birth to some unspecified event.

7. Pal Slav   9.11.18. 9.17   Chac-Zutz'   9.15. 0. 0. 0
   A4a

8. PN 7   9.11.12. 7. 2   Ruler 3   9.14.10. 0. 0
   B10a

CHART 106   Affix T136   in Cluster *:136   with Miscellaneous Main Signs

#	LOCATION	DATE (EVENT)	PATIENT	AGENT	DEDICATION	
1.	ASac 4 A11	9.10. 3.17. 0		deleted	9.10.10. 0. 0	

This "death" glyph is part of the temporal instructions of a DN leading

Chart 106   283

from it to a later event. The text opens with an IS date and a "wing-shell/zac-ahau-ik" death expression, which this T585 "death" glyph reiterates as follows: "On 9.10.3.17.0 4 Ahau . . . 8 Muan, he died (wing-shell), Personage A; it was so much time since he died (T585) . . ." This is one of two occurrences where the T585 "death" glyph directly substitutes for the "wing-shell" variant (see #2).

2. Pal TIw   9.12. 0. 6.18   deleted   9.12.15. 0. 0
   Q11b   (Lady Ahpo-
                                     Hel)

The second substitution of T585 "death" for the "wing-shell" variant occurs in the following context: "It was 2.7.6.1 since she was seated until she died (wing-shell), Lady Ahpo-Hel, on 5 Etz'nab 6 Kankin; it was 9.11.2 since she died (T585) until 9 Ahau 18 Zotz', the lahuntun." The "wing-shell" death variant and the T585 "death" glyph must be semantically equivalent in examples #1 and #2 because they record the same event.

3. Pal TIw   13. 4.12. 3. 6   GI the First   9.12.15. 0. 0
   O11-P11

The verbs in #3 and #4 are parallel expressions appearing in the following couplet structure: "It was 9.7.11.3.0 [since] verb #4 Ahpo-Skull; on 1 Cimi 19 Pax verb #3, GI, count until 7 Cimi 19 Ceh . . ." Although the syntax seems to be scrambled, the arithmetical relationship between the dates and the DN clearly shows the two verbs and their subjects to be structurally equivalent.

4. Pal TIw   13. 4.12. 3. 6   Ahpo-Skull   9.12.15. 0. 0
   O9

5. Pal PTab   9.13.10. 6. 8   Kan-Xul II   9.14.10. 0. 0
   R5-Q6

   AEI?

6. Pal PTab   9. 9. 2. 4. 8   Pacal II   9.14.10. 0. 0
   P18-O19

AE1. This passage functions to link Pacal's accession to that of Kan-Xul II.

7. PN Thr1   9.17. 9. 5.11   Ruler 7   9.17.15. 0. 0
   Z5-Z6

These glyphs may be part of a name phrase, rather than a verbal phrase.

8.	PN L4 M2	9.10. 6. 2. 1	Ruler 1	9.11.10. 0. 0	
9.	Cop A B8a	9.14.19.11. 0	????	9.15. 0. 0. 0	
10.	Pal TC Cens2 H6	9.13. 2. 4.13	deleted	9.13.10. 0. 0	 

This event is followed by another 3.14.18 later, but the second verb is too badly eroded to be identified.

11.	Agua 5 A9	missing	deleted or missing	9.13. 0. 0. 0	

This verb appears to function as a base for the count of a DN, but the damaged condition of the monument makes it presently impossible to determine whether a subject was present or not. However, Flint-Sky-God K, a ruler who appears in contemporary records at Dos Pilas, is recorded as subject of the next verbal series, and it is probable that he was also the subject of this verb.

CHART 107   Affix T136   in Cluster *:136   with Miscellaneous Main Signs

#	LOCATION	DATE (EVENT)	PATIENT	AGENT	DEDICATION	
1.	Tik T4 L2 B9-A11	9.15.12.11.13		none?	9.16. 0. 0. 0	

The three glyphs following this "star" verb may record an agent, perhaps a supernatural, or they may be part of the verbal expression.

2.	Ton F43 pB	missing	Zac-Balam	Rodent-Bone?	Late Classic	

This text occurs with a captive figure.

3.	Ton M84 pD	missing	eroded	????	Late Classic 

Chart 107 285

4.	Yax Str44 Ctr Up C9b	9.12. 8.14. 1	Ah Ahaual	deleted	9.15. 0. 0. 0 

5.	PN 12 pA17a	9.17.16.14.19	Ah Nabe Ah ??-Kin	Ruler 7?	9.18. 5. 0. 0 

6.	Yax Str33 Step7 A1- B3	13 Manik 5 Pax		The First Ah Knot-Skull	9.16. 6. 0. 0 

The event phrases in ##6-8 record events (perhaps of an astronomical
nature) which took place at an immense distance in the past. The verb in
all of these clauses is an "axe" glyph, but each phrase has a different
supernatural subject named with a personal name; a "succession" glyph
qualified with an ordinal or cardinal number ("first," second," and
"three"); and a glyph "Ah Knot-Skull," which also occurs as a part of
GII's name phrase in his birth record on the TFC (C1) at Palenque (D.
Stuart, personal communication, 1981). In this clause the agent is named
as follows:

7.	Yax Str33 Step7 C1- C3	9 Kan 12 Xul		The Second Ah Knot-Skull	9.16.10. 0. 0 

The second "axe" event took place 5.19.0.17 after the first, and the
agent is named as follows:

8.	Yax Str33 Step7 E1- F1	1 Ahau 13 Xul		3-Ah Knot- Skull	9.16.10. 0. 0 

The third "axe" event took place 3.8.10.14.11 after the second and
13.13.13.13.13.13.13.13.9.15.13.6.9 before the historical event recorded
on this step. The agent is recorded as follows (see 96:4):

9.	Quir J H3	9.15. 6.14. 6	18-Rabbit of Copan	Two-Legged- Sky	9.16. 5. 0. 0 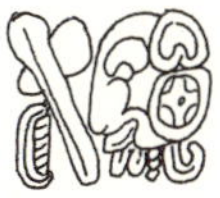

This verb follows a DN of 18.3.13, leading from this event to the PE
9.16.5.0.0, the date that opens the inscription. This clause is followed
by a second one with an eroded T670 verb of which Two-Legged-Sky is named
as the subject. I am assuming that the subject of this "axe" verb is
deleted and named in the second clause. See 129.13.

| 10. | Quir Ew
B12b | 9.15. 6.14. 6 | 18-Rabbit
of Copan | deleted
(Two-Legged-
Sky) | 9.17. 0. 0. 0 | 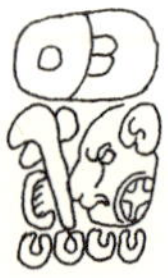 |

This "axe" verb is one of the few occurrences at Quirigua in which the
name phrase of Two-Legged-Sky does not follow that of 18-Rabbit. I am
assuming that the Two-Legged-Sky name is deleted, and the clause gapped
to the following one where the subject is named with *u cab* and a title
which presumably refers to Two-Legged-Sky.

CHART 108   Affix T136   in Cluster *:136   with Miscellaneous Main Signs

#	LOCATION	DATE (EVENT)	PATIENT	AGENT	DEDICATION	
1.	Cop AltF' A2 AEI.	9.17. 4. 1.11		deleted	9.17. 5. 0. 0	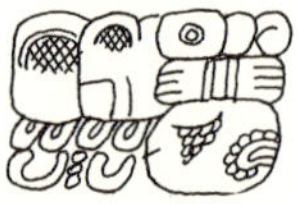
2.	Pal TIm C3	9.11. 0. 0. 0		Pacal II	9.12.15. 0. 0	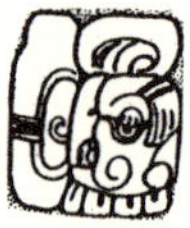

This verb is associated with period ending records.

| 3. | Pal TIm
H2 | 9.12. 0. 0. 0 | | Pacal II | 9.12.15. 0. 0 | 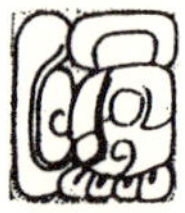 |
| 4. | Pal D
L1 | 9.14.11. 2. 7 | | GI | 9.14.15. 0. 0 | 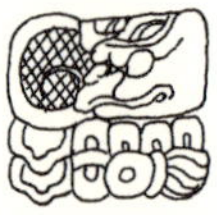 |

This is the final verb in the text, and I am placing it at the late LC
position because the iconography of this tablet and that of Temple 14
have been identified as posthumous (Schele n.d.c). The glyph which follows the verb is the version of GI that has the numbers 3 and 9 adjoined
to the head. See Chart 16, 23:7-8, 40:5, and 110:4 for other examples of
the main sign.

| 5. | Pal Slav
F5b | 9.14.18. 1. 1 | | Chac-Zutz' | 9.15. 0. 0. 0 | 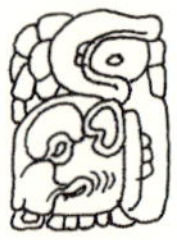 |
| 6. | Quir Ee
A14a | ???? | | Ek-Mac | 9.17. 0. 0. 0 | |

Chart 109   287

This verb follows a calendric notation that includes a period sign of unknown length in the following statement: "were completed nineteen periods (of unknown length) count since 13 Ahau 18 Zac, event phrase, subject." The month sign appears in a very unusual form, now identified by Mathews (n.d.b) as the month Zac, on Tonina M69, where the arithmetical context is not open to question.

CHART 109   Affix T130   in Cluster *:130   with Miscellaneous Main Signs

T130 has the phonetic value *wa.*

#	LOCATION	DATE (EVENT)	PATIENT	AGENT	DEDICATION	
1.	Car 3 D15	9. 9.10. 0. 0		Ruler 4	9.10. 5. 0. 0	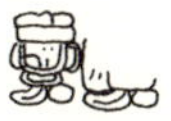
2.	DPil 26 B6	9.14.10. 0. 0		none	9.14.10. 0. 0	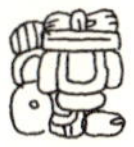

This verb is followed by a "scattering" expression and Shield-God K's name glyph. See 43:21.

| 3. | Pom Pan1 pA3-pB3 | 9.13. 0. 0. 0 | | eroded | 9.18. 0. 0. 0? | 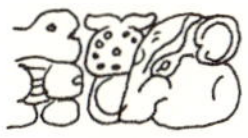 |

The verb follows a "tun-seating" glyph.

| 4. | ArP 3 C3 | 9.15. 0. 0. 0 | | Chac-Be-?? | 9.15. 0. 0. 0 | 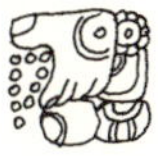 *to scatter* |

This verb follows a "completion of fifteen katuns" expression (67:4) and and a *te'-tun* period ending expression (68:3).

| 5. | Cop Str11 eDoor s B1a | 9.17. 2.10. 4 | | God K | 9.17. 0. 0. 0 | 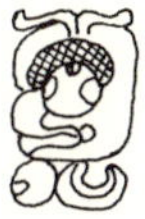 |

This verb is from an 819 Day Count passage.

| 6. | Cop Str11 eDoor n C3 | 9.15.15.12.16 | | Ahau Chac-Ek | 9.17. 0. 0. 0 | 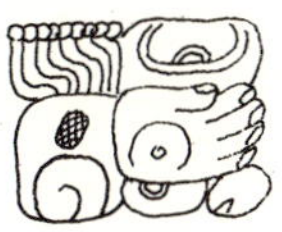 |

Lounsbury (n.d.) has identified this date as that of the first appearance of Venus as Evening Star. The main verb (the text is written in mirror image, so it is on the right) occurs as the featured verb in the Venus passages of the Dresden Codex.

7.   Pal TIm   9.11. 0. 0. 0   his cycle   GII   9.12.15. 0. 0
     D9

This helmet verb is part of a series of passages associated with the histories of Katuns 11 and 12. In five of the six examples of this verb, it is preceded by T1 or an equivalent and carries the T130 -*wa* suffix, but this single example carries only the -*wa*. This difference in affix pattern (which occurs in a context identical to the other five examples) must be accepted as a difference in inflectional pattern, or some other explanation must be found for it. The three passages for Katun 11 record ritual information about the katun in terms of the three members of the Palenque Triad, and the text is repeated, therefore in three parallel passages, each consisting of a couplet. The first half of the couplet is composed of the T669b verb (see Chart 62) and a variable dependent of the particular Triad god named in the passage. The second half consists of the helmet verb, an object composed of the glyph *hun kalal* (possibly meaning "all of something") and a baktun glyph which in this context must refer to the katun, and the subject (the appropriate Triad god). Since the helmet glyph corresponds to headgear worn by lords, I suggest that the second part of the couplet should be paraphrased as "he ruled all of the katun, GI, etc." The variable in the passages for GI and GIII consists of one glyph block, as do all of the variables in similar passages in the history of Katun 12. However, the variable for GII consists of two glyphs, the second of which is the zoomorphic version of GI. It seems unlikely that GI would appear as a semantic determinative or phonetic complement of a variable which depends on GI, and it is possible, therefore, that the GI head functions as the missing pronominal sign for the helmet verb. If this analysis is correct, then this example of the helmet verb, like the other five, appears with a third person singular ergative pronoun. See 45:3-7. A comparative analysis is as follows:

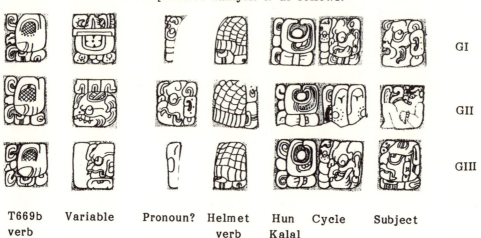

T669b verb	Variable	Pronoun?	Helmet verb	Hun Kalal	Cycle	Subject	
							GI
							GII
							GIII

Chart 110   289

I suspect that the variable in Part 1 of the comparison above is the object, and that the subject in each passage is deleted. If this analysis is correct, the Triad gods would be the subjects of both parts of the couplet.

CHART 110   Affix T130   in Cluster *:130   with Miscellaneous Main Signs

#	LOCATION	DATE (EVENT)	PATIENT	AGENT	DEDICATION	
1.	PN L2 H1-G2	9.11. 6. 2. 1		Ruler 2	9.11.15. 0. 0	
2.	PN L2 W4-X4	9.11. 6. 2. 1?		Ruler 2	9.11.15. 0. 0	
3.	Quir O M1	9.17.14.16.18		Ruler 2	9.18.10. 0. 0	
4.	Yax L10 D8b-E1a	9.18.17.13.10		*u cab* Captor of Turtle-Macaw	9.19. 0. 0. 0	

This event happened twenty-four days after a date on which an "ahau-in-hand" event (see 27:4 and 129:6), a "star" event (see 10:20), and a "capture" event (see 74:27) occurred. Ten glyphs stand between the verbal expression as drawn and the *u cab* which precedes the name phrase of the agent, but I do not know if these intervening glyphs are part of the verbal phrase or record a patient. See Chart 16 for other event phrases including the same glyphic signs.

#	LOCATION	DATE (EVENT)	PATIENT	AGENT	DEDICATION	
5.	Pal TC wSanc D1	9.12.11.13. 0	U-Kix-Chan	Chan-Bahlum II	9.13. 0. 0. 0	

PEI. Although no CR is recorded in this text, it opens with a DN of ten days which must have been counted from some major and publicly known event. Because the major pictorial event celebrated in the three temples of the Group of the Cross is the accession of Chan-Bahlum II, I am assuming that this event is the unnamed calendric base of the DN. This T671 verb is the event that occurred ten days after the accession. It is followed by the name glyph U-Kix-Chan, an ancestral personage whose birth and accession in Baktun 5 are recorded on the inner tablet. Since U-Kix-Chan is the first personage to be recorded after the gods of the Palenque Triad in the ancestral list of the main tablet, this event must have involved some rite honoring or recalling him. Chan-Bahlum is named as the agent of the verb. It should be noted that stingray spines are a prominent part of the headdress of Chan-Bahlum as he is pictured on this panel; perhaps the event was blood-letting conducted in the context of ancestral recall.

6. Pal Slav   9.14.13.11. 2   *u cab* Chac-Zutz'   9.15. 0. 0. 0
    D3

7. PN L12   9. 3.19.12.12   Kin-Ma-Cu-?? 9. 4. 5. 0. 0
    I1

The name glyph following this verb may also occur as the subject of the verb in the secondary text (38:1).

CHART 111   Affix T130   in Cluster *:130.136   with Main Sign "Scattering"

#	LOCATION	DATE (EVENT)	PATIENT	AGENT	DEDICATION	
1.	Tik 21 B11	9.16. 0. 0. 0		deleted (Ruler B)	9.16. 0. 0. 0	

PEI. This "scattering" verb occurs in the final clause of this text and links the rite celebrating the PE to the accession of Ruler B as follows: "It was 1.11.12 [since] 3 Lamat 6 Pax since he was seated as *batab* of the succession until he scattered." Although the first part of the text is missing, the same 3 Lamat 6 Pax date is recorded as Ruler B's accession date on Stela 5, confirming the missing PE date and the identify of the deleted subject as Ruler B. This text is structurally parallel to those on Stelae 19 and 22.

| 2. | Tik 22 B12 | 9.17. 0. 0. 0 | | deleted (Ruler C) | 9.17. 0. 0. 0 |  |

PEI. This "scattering" verb occurs in a structure parallel to #1 as follows: "It was 2.1.16 [since] 11 Kan 12 Kayab since he was seated as *batab* of the succession until he scattered." Since Ruler C is the only person named as a subject of a verb (Ruler B occurs in the genealogical information about Ruler C), he can be reconstructed as the subject of both the seating and scattering, and in fact he is shown in the act of scattering.

Chart 112   291

3.   Tik 19   9.18. 0. 0. 0   deleted   9.18. 0. 0. 0
     B13   (Ruler C)

PEI. The "scattering" verb in ##1-3 occur in contexts characteristic of
the Late Classic katun monuments of Tikal. All begin with a PE clause,
marking the occasion as the end of a katun and recording the agent and
his genealogy. The PE rite, specifically recorded as the "scattering"
action shown on all three monuments, is then linked to the seating as
ruler of the protagonist, or in this case with the "completion of the
first katun as *batab* of the succession." Since only one protagonist is
named on each of these three monuments, the name of the subject is
deleted after both of the final verbal phrases. This Stela 19 clause may
be paraphrased as follows: "It was 1.14.19 [since] 2 Imix 9 Kayab since
he completed the first katun as *batab* of the succession until he scattered [on 9.18.0.0.0]." Jones (1977:56) noted that the one-katun anniversary of accession recorded on this monument is one katun and 97 days
later than the accession date recorded on Stela 22.

4.   Ixlu Alt   10. 0. 0. 0. 0   Ah Kal   10. 2.10. 0. 0
     A4

This verb follows "half-period" and "tenth tun" and precedes the name of
the agent.

CHART 112   Affix T130   in Cluster *130:116   with Main Sign T644 "Seating"

#	LOCATION	DATE (EVENT)	PATIENT	AGENT	DEDICATION	
1.	Tort 6 A7-B8	9.10.11. 3.10		Ahpo-Balam	9.12. 0. 0. 0	
2.	Tort 6 D10-C11	9.10.11. 3.10		deleted (Ahpo-Balam)	9.12. 0. 0. 0	

AEI. Paraphrase: "It was 3.16.1 since he was seated as ahau of the
succession until an event on 11 Chuen 4 Muan." This verb reiterates the
information in #1 as the base of DN.

#	LOCATION	DATE (EVENT)	PATIENT	AGENT	DEDICATION	
3.	Tort 6 E4-F5	9.10.11. 3.10		Ahpo-Balam	9.12. 0. 0. 0	

AEI. Paraphrase: "It was 1.5.5.8 since he was seated as ahau of the
succession, Ahpo-Balam, until an event on 9 Etz'nab 6 Kayab."

| 4. | Tort Sarc 63-64 | 9.10.11. 3.10 | | missing | 9.12.10. 0. 0 | |

AEI.

| 5. | Tort Box H1-I1 | 9.12. 7. 1.19 | | Black-Scroll-Shell | 9.12.10. 0. 0 | |

This "seating" expression is preceded by a "on tun" glyph, but as a DN, one tun is not related arithmetically to any of the adjacent dates, which record "seating" events on 9.12.7.1.19 and 9.12.7.14.7. The first date also corresponds to the "death" date of Ahpo-Balam, the previous ruler.

| 6. | Tort Box L2-M1 | ???? | | Ah Nen | 9.12.10. 0. 0 | |

| 7. | Tort Box O1-P1 | 9.12. 7.14. 7 | | Ah-Ka-??-Balam | 9.12.10. 0. 0 | |

| 8. | Tort Box R2-S1 | 9.12. 7.14. 7 | | deleted (Ah-Ka-??-Balam) | 9.12.10. 0. 0 | |

| 9. | Pal TIe A11-B11 | 9. 3. 6. 7.17 | | Chaacal I | 9.12.15. 0. 0 | |

AEI? Because this verb appears in the initial clause of this inscription, it occurs in a structure reversing that of later passages by placing the PE before the "seating" record, as follows: 9.4.0.0.0 13 Ahau 18 Yax . . . was 13.10. 3. since he was seated as lord, Chaacal I." The date of this accession is implied by the DN.

| 10. | Pal TIe G6-H6 | 9. 6.11. 5. 1 | | Chaacal II | 9.12.15. 0. 0 | |

AEI. Paraphrase: "It was 1.12.19 since he was seated as lord, Chaacal II, until the end of the tun 9 Ahau 18 Muan."

| 11. | Pal TIe I8-J8 | 9.6.18. 5.12 | | Chan-Bahlum I | 9.12.15. 0. 0 | |

AEI.

Chart 112   293

12. Pal TIe   9. 7.10. 3. 8   Lady Kanal-   9.12.15. 0. 0
    L3-K4   Ikal

AEI. Paraphrase: "It was 9.14.12 since she was seated as lord, Lady Kanal-Ikal, until the end of the tun 5 Ahau 3 Ch'en."

13. Pal TIe   9. 8.11. 9.10   Ahc-Kan   9.12.15. 0. 0
    L10-K11

AEI. Paraphrase: "It was 1.8.10 since he was seated as *ahpo* of ????, Ahc-Kan, until the end of the tun 5 Ahau 18 Zec, the oxlahuntun."

14. Pal TIe   9. 9. 2. 4. 8   Pacal II   9.12.15. 0. 0
    R10-Q11

AEI. Paraphrase: "It was 19.13.12 since he was seated as *ahpo* and T518 title of the succession, Pacal II, until the end of the tun 1 Ahau 8 Kayab, the seating of 10 katuns, the half-period of the baktun."

15. Chin Thr   missing   Mah Kina   9.14. 0. 0. 0?   
    pA2-pB2   Rabbit-Flint

AEI? The verbs in ##15-16 are found on the top of a throne published in a drawing by Maler (1901:12). A DN of 8.7.8 precedes this verb, and it is followed by a T585 "death" glyph (73:2) and a different name. In turn, this clause is followed by DN of 3?.3?.9.16, the CR date 1 Cib 19 Zac, and another "seating" expression, but the remainder of the text is missing, and, therefore, it is not possible to determine if the second "seating" is the same event as the first.

16. Chin Thr   9.12.17. 8.16   missing   9.14. 0. 0. 0?
    pG1-pH1

The PE date, 9.7.0.0.0 7 Ahau 3 Kankin, recorded on the side of this throne, may indicate that the dates of these "seating" events should be placed 3 CRs earlier. The graphic style of the carving, however, suggests later positions in the LC.

17. Pal PTab   9.13.10. 0. 0   Kan-Xul II   9.14.10. 0. 0
    K12-L12

The lower affix on this "seating" glyph is now missing, but because T116 is clearly visible to the right of the main sign, I am classifying the verbal suffixing as -130.116. This passage is found between the accession and death records of Chan-Bahlum, but two reasons, I believe it is designed to associate the accession of Kan-Xul II to that of Chan-Bahlum

II. First, the "vulture-piercing-jaguar-eye" and "III-axe-over-earth" glyphs that appears in the name phrase occur exclusively in Kan-Xul's name. In addition, this "seating" passage is introduced by a DN of "one katun of the maize title," and the length of Chan-Bahlum's reign plus the interregnum was 18.11.18, which would be rounded off to one katun.

| 18. | DPil 8
F14-G14 | 9.13. 6. 2. 0 | | deleted
(Shield-
God K) | 9.15. 0. 0. 0 |

This verb is followed by an "ahau-in-hand" (45:14), a glyph found on Yaxchilan Lintel 1 as a term for an "accession" event. Although "ahau-in-hand" may occur in association with other kinds of rites, I am assuming that it functions here as the second half of a verb couplet referring to accession.

19.	Yax 12 C2-D2	9.16. 1. 0. 0		Bird- Jaguar III	9.16. 5. 0. 0
20.	Cop HS	missing		missing	9.17.10. 0. 0
21.	Cop Str11 nDoor s AEI.	9.16.12. 5.17		New-Sky-at- Horizon (by title)	9.17.10. 0. 0
22.	Cop Str11 wDoor s A2	9.16.12. 5.17		deleted (New-Sky-at- Horizon)	9.17.10. 0. 0
23.	Cop HS AEI.	missing		missing	9.17.10. 0. 0
24.	Cop HS	missing		missing	9.17.10. 0. 0
25.	Cop AltU K2-L2 AEI.	9.16.12. 5.17		New-Sky-At- Horizon	9.18. 5. 0. 0

Chart 113 295

26.	Cop AltU O4-P4	9.17. 9. 2.12		Yax-Zotz'	9.18. 5. 0. 0	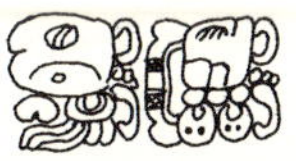

27.	PUin 3 A18-B18	9.17.14.15.16		Chac-Balam	9.18.10. 0. 0	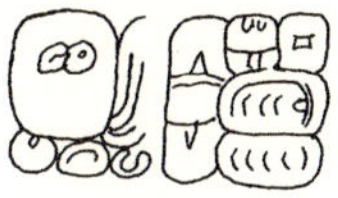

28.	Tort 1 A4a-A4b	9.10.11. 3.10		deleted (Ahpo-Balam)	9.11. 0. 0. 0	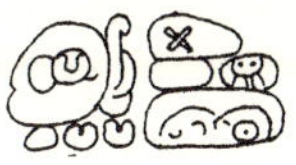

27.	PUin 3 A18-B18	9.17.14.15.16		Chac-Balam	9.18.10. 0. 0	

28.	Tort 1 A4a-A4b	9.10.11. 3.10		deleted (Ahpo-Balam)	9.11. 0. 0. 0	

AEI. This text begins with the record of the date 9.10.13.0.0, which is linked by DN to this "seating." Ahpo-Balam is named as the subject of the PE verbs, and he is understood to be the subject of this event also.

29.	Tort 6 D9	9.10.11. 3.10		deleted (Ahpo-Balam)	9.12. 0. 0. 0	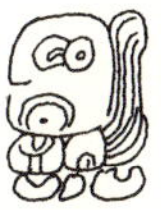

AEI.

30.	Cop AltL A3	2 Chicchan 3 Uo		missing	Late Classic	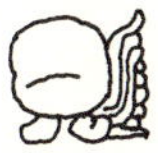

31.	Cop AltH' V1-V2	9. 9.14.17. 5		deleted	9.12.10. 0. 0	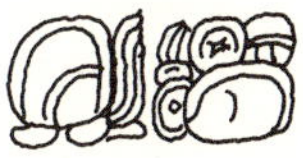

CHART 113   Affix T130   in Cluster *.130.116   with Miscellaneous Main Signs

#	LOCATION	DATE (EVENT)	PATIENT	AGENT	DEDICATION	
1.	Pal TIw F12	1 Manik 10 Zec		supernatural	9.12.15. 0. 0	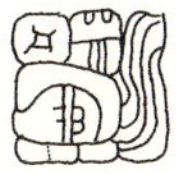

The intention of this passage is to link the accession of Pacal II to an earlier mythological accession which occurred 7.18.2.9.2.12.1 before the historical rite (see #2).

2. Pal TIw   9. 9. 2. 4. 8   Pacal II   9.12.15. 0. 0
   H2

3. Pal TS   9. 3. 1.15. 0   Kan-Xul I   9.13. 0. 0. 0
   P2-Q3

AEI. The verbal phrase records the designation as heir of Kan-Xul I, which is linked by DN to the same event as it occurred to Chan-Bahlum II. The main verb can occur with any office taking, and the particular office which is linked by DN to the same event as it occurred to Chan-Bahlum II. The main verb can occur with any office taking, and the particular office is specified by the *oc* variant in the second glyph. *Oc* means "to enter" or "to become" and is found in many different Maya languages in expressions for the taking of office (Schele n.d.a.).

4. Pal TS   9.10. 8. 9. 3   deleted   9.13. 0. 0. 0
   P7   (Chan-Bahlum)

This "mirror-in-hand" glyph records the heir-designation of Chan-Bahlum II in association with the same event in the life of the ancestral ruler, Kan-Xul I (see #3). The full passage (TS O16-Q10) is paraphrased as follows: "It was 7.6.17.3 since 12 Ahau 8 Ceh since he took office as enterer of the succession (#3), Kan-Xul I; count since the heir-designation (21:6) count until 9 Akbal 6 Xul, he took office; five days later, he became (*oc te*) the sun (*kin-kin*) (21:5), Mah Kina Chan-Bahlum . . ." The prepositional phrase recording the office and the subject of the 9 Akbal 6 Xul event are deleted, and this clause is gapped to the following one, where Chan-Bahlum is named as the subject of both events. His name, however, is followed by T86:325var.575[671], a glyph tentatively identified by Mathews (personal communication, 1980) as an expression of agency, and the name glyph of GI of the Palenque Triad. If the intervening glyph proves to be an agency expression rather than one of relationship, the agent would be GI and the patient of the verb would be Chan-Bahlum II.

5. Pal T18   missing   missing   9.14.15. 0. 0
   Stc J1

The front surface of all the T18 stucco glyphs were painted blue except for the stingray spine in the upper left corner of this glyph.

6. Yax L23   9.14.16.13. 9   Lady Xoc   9.15. 0. 0. 0
   E2-G1

Chart 114   297

#		DATE (EVENT)			
7.	Pal TC Cens1 J7-I8	9.13. 0. 4.12		Cauac	9.12.10. 0. 0 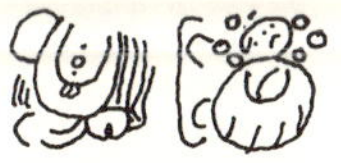
8.	TFC Cens A6-A7	9.13. 0. 4.12		Lady ????	9.13. 5. 0. 0 

CHART 114   Affix T130   in Cluster *:130.116   with Main Sign T79:614

#	LOCATION	DATE (EVENT)	PATIENT	AGENT	DEDICATION
1.	Pal PTab V1-X1	????		none or deleted	9.14.10. 0. 0 

This is the final clause in the secondary text and seems to function as a dedicatory passage of some kind. Either the "9-hel" glyph is the subject; the subject is deleted and to be understood as Xoc; or there is no subject.

2.	Coll 21 pA2-pB1	9.11. 9.17.16		deleted	9.12. 0. 0. 0 

The agent of the next verb is Smoking-Jaguar, and he is presumably the agent of this event.

3.	Cop AltG1 A2-A3	9.15.17. 5. 0		*u cab* New-Sky-at-Horizon	9.18. 5. 0. 0 
4.	Cop AltU N1	9.18. 1.13. 2		????	9.18. 5. 0. 0 
5.	Cop AltU N5	4 Ahau 13 Ceh		????	9.18. 5. 0. 0 

CHART 115   Affix T130   in Cluster *:130.18   with Main Sign T644

#	LOCATION	DATE (EVENT)	PATIENT	AGENT	DEDICATION	
1.	Pal TIe M12-N12	9. 8.19. 7.18		Lady Zac-Kuk	9.12.15. 0. 0	

AEI. Paraphrase: "It was 10.3 since she was seated as *ahpo* of the succession, until the end of the tun 3 Ahau 3 Zotz', the ninth katun."

#	LOCATION	DATE (EVENT)	PATIENT	AGENT	DEDICATION	
2.	NimP 15 O2	12 Ahau of Katun 14		local person	9.14.15. 0. 0	

The suffix is a verb difficult to read in available photographs and drawings; it could be either T130 or T126. The LC should be 9.14.10.1.0.

CHART 116   Affix T126   in Cluster *:126   with Miscellaneous Main Signs

T126 occurs on several of these examples in contexts where the verb is the earlier of two events linked by a DN. In some of these examples, T126 may function as an AEI, rather than as a verbal affix.

#	LOCATION	DATE (EVENT)	PATIENT	AGENT	DEDICATION	
1.	Tik 9 A1	9. 3. 0. 0. 0	3? katuns	none	9. 3. 0. 0. 0	

See the not to 37:8 for a discussion of the date of Stela 9.

#	LOCATION	DATE (EVENT)	PATIENT	AGENT	DEDICATION	
2.	Cop I D3a	8. 6. 0. 0. 0	the 6th katun	none	9.12. 5. 0. 0	
3.	Pal PTab D19	9.10.11.17. 0		deleted (Kan-Xul)	9.14. 0. 0. 0	

AEI?

#	LOCATION	DATE (EVENT)	PATIENT	AGENT	DEDICATION	
4.	Pal T18 Jamb B13	9.12. 6. 5. 8		Chaacal III	9.14.15. 0. 0	

Chart 116   299

| 5. | Pal TC U9 | 9. 4.10. 1. 5 | Chan-Bahlum I | 9.13. 0. 0. 0 |  |

PEI.

| 6. | Cop J 37a | 9.13.10. 0. 0 | 18-Rabbit | 9.13.10. 0. 0 |  |

| 7. | Pal Sarc 13 | none | ancestral goddess? | 9.12.15. 0. 0 |  |

The first two glyphs are the verbal phrase introducing the ancestral list
of death dates comprising the remainder of the sarcophagus text (see
Chart 19). The agent is named by the third glyph, a female head which may
refer to the ancestral goddess who is prominent in the inscriptions of
the Group of the Cross. T79 and the "seating" infix are the main signs of
the verb, and the second glyph is related to anniversary statements from
Tikal (80:4-5), and is found in PE phrases on the upper Tablet of the
Temple of Inscriptions (33:1-2 and 129:2) and at Copan (13:5).

| 8. | Cop A B4a | 9.14.19.11. 0 | ???? | 9.15. 0. 0. 0 |  |

| 9. | Tik Alt5 12 | 9.13.11. 6. 7 | Lady Ca-wa-c(a) (Cauac) | 9.14. 0. 0. 0 |  |

| 10. | Tik MT28 A3 | 9.14. 9. 0.12 | Mandible-Fist? | 9.15. 0. 0. 0 |  |

| 11. | Tort 6 C4-D4 | 9.10.17. 2.14 | 3-Jaguar-Sky-Bundle | 9.12. 0. 0. 0 | |

This is the first half of a couplet (see 60:6 and 82:20). The agent of
this verb seems to be recorded with two glyphs: (1) the number 3 and a
waterlily-jaguar and (2) "lord of the sky-bundle" (T168:684[561]:130).
The second half of the couplet records Ahpo-Balam as the agent, so that
the first half seems to record the activities of a supernatural and the
second half those of the local ruler.

| 12. | DPil HSw A1b-B2a | 9.12. 0. 8. 3 | none | 9.12.12. 0. 0 |  |

This "star" event is in the introductory passage which gives the time

elapsed between this event and another, later "star" event. T126 may
function, therefore, as an AEI.

13. LMar 3   9.18. 4. 2.19   Zac-Zotz'   Macaw-GI   9.18. 5. 0. 0
     B11

The EG following the name of the agent is also found on the monuments of
Pomona.

14. Cop 6   9.12.10. 0. 0?   18-Rabbit   9.12.10. 0. 0
     D6

15. PN L2   9. 4. 1. 0. 5   none   9.11.15. 0. 0
     C19

This verb records an earlier event from which a DN is counted to a later
recurrence of the same rite (110:2), and although the DN follows this
clause, instead of preceding it, T126 may be functioning as an AEI. In
addition, the suffix has been damaged, and it may originally have been
T130, the suffix found on the other verbal glyphs on this monument (see
110:1-2).

16. Tik 31   8.17. 0. 0. 0   none   9. 0.10. 0. 0
     C19

This "mirror" glyph is found following a DN and an "end of tun" expression, but preceding the date to which the DN is counted. The same glyph
is often found between calendric data and a verb, and seems to function
as a means of highlighting the verb or in this case a date. See 130:4-12.

17. Pal PTab   9.12.11. 5.18   Pacal II   9.14.10. 0. 0
     J10-I11

     PEI.

18. PN L12   9. 4. 0. 0. 0   none   9. 4. 5. 0. 0
     D1-F1

This verbal expression occurs between the tzolkin and haab components of
a CR date. The third glyph may record the subject of the phrase.

19. NTun   9.15. 8. 8. 5   ????   9.16.10. 0. 0
     GpIa G5

Chart 117   301

#	LOCATION	DATE (EVENT)		AGENT	DEDICATION	
20.	NTun GpIVd A3–A5	9.15. 6. 5.12	local person		9.16.10. 0. 0	
21.	NTun GpIVe A3–A5	9.16.10. 5. 2	local person		9.16.10. 0. 0	

CHART 117   Affix T126   in Cluster *:126.116   with Miscellaneous Main Signs

#	LOCATION	DATE (EVENT)	PATIENT	AGENT	DEDICATION	
1.	Pal PTab K7	9.12.11.12.10		Chan-Bahlum II	9.14.10. 0. 0	
2.	Pal T18 Jamb C11 AEI?	2. 0. 0.14. 2		ancestral goddess	9.14.10. 0. 0	
3.	Nar 1 E12	9.10.10. 0. 0		missing	9.13.10. 0. 0	
4.	Pal TIm F12	1 Manik 10 Zec		supernatural	9.12.15. 0. 0	

See the note to 113:1. The verbal suffixes are eroded and may be T130.116.

#	LOCATION	DATE (EVENT)	PATIENT	AGENT	DEDICATION	
5.	Pal del Rio Thr pB1	9. 9. 2. 4. 8		Pacal II	9.14.10. 0. 0	
6.	Pal del Rio Thr pE1	9.12.11.12.10		missing (Chan-(Bahlum II)	9.14.10. 0. 0	
7.	Pal del Rio Thr pL1	9.13.10. 6. 8		Kan-Xul II	9.14.10. 0. 0	

CHART 118   Affix T126   in Cluster *:24.126   with Miscellaneous Main Signs

#	LOCATION	DATE (EVENT)	PATIENT	AGENT	DEDICATION	
1.	Pal TFC C5	1.18. 5. 4. 0		GII	9.13. 0. 0. 0	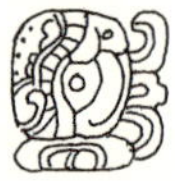

T126 may function as an AEI.

2.	Pal TIw R8-Q9	9. 9.13. 0. 7		deleted (Lady Ahpo -Hel)	9.12.15. 0. 0	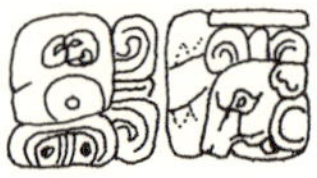

AEI? It is difficult to determine the function of T126 in examples ##1-2 because each verb is found in a context where the appearance of an AEI would be appropriate. In each context, a DN is counted from that event to a later one, and in both cases, the verbal stems are found in other contexts with the T24, not T24.126, as a suffix. I am classifying the affixing pattern of #1 and #2 as distinct from T24 with an AEI, because the verb in #3 is later event to which a DN is counted, and T126 must be verbal in that context. I strongly suspect, however, that T126 functions as an AEI in the first two examples.

3.	Pal TIw T7-S8	9.12.11. 5.18		deleted (Pacal II)	9.12.15. 0. 0	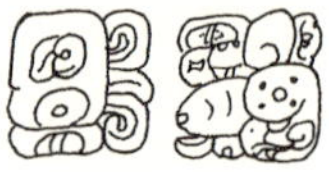

This "seating" phrase follows the record of the death of Pacal II and a DN equal to the time between his recorded birth and death dates. Since this "seating" phrase appears with the context of a "death" record, and since the preceding DN equals the lifetime of the dead person, the event cannot record the accession of Pacal II. And in fact, this phrase is marked as concerning a death by the presence of the T585H "death" glyph after the prepositional phrase *ta ahau le*. The phrase records that Pacal was "seated as an ahau of the succession in death" or "of the succession of the ancestral dead." Pacal's name is deleted from the passage, but the context is clear; he is the subject of the immediately preceding "death" verb, and he is the protagonist of the monument.

4.	Pal PTab O7-P7	9.13.10. 6. 8		Kan-Xul II	9.14.10. 0. 0	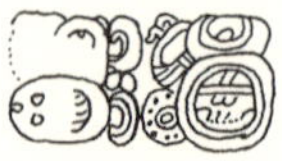

This phrase records an accession event.

CHART 119   Affix T24   in Cluster *:24   with Main Sign T741

#	LOCATION	DATE (EVENT)	PATIENT	AGENT	DEDICATION	
1.	Pal TIw K9b PEI.	9.11. 6.16.17		Skull-GI	9.12.15. 0. 0	
2.	Pal TIw K12	9.11. 6.16.17		missing	9.12.15. 0. 0	

This verb repeats #1 in a couplet structure.

#	LOCATION	DATE (EVENT)	PATIENT	AGENT	DEDICATION	
3.	Pal TIw O6b PEI.	9.12. 3. 6. 6.		Ti-??-Kin	9.12.15. 0. 0	
4.	Pal TC C17 PEI.	1.18. 5. 3. 2		GI (by title)	9.13. 0. 0. 0	
5.	Pal TS C10 PEI.	1.18. 5. 2. 6		GIII	9.13. 0. 0. 0	
6.	Sac 6 A3	9.14.16. 9. 9? + 1 CR?		missing	9.15. 0. 0. 0	

CHART 120   Affix T24   in Cluster *:24   with Miscellaneous Main Signs

#	LOCATION	DATE (EVENT)	PATIENT	AGENT	DEDICATION	
1.	CRic Jade	missing		Bone	Early Classic	

This verb is found on a split jade celt from Costa Rica (Balser 1974:Pl.

18). The right column of glyphs is missing so that the date and full name of the subject are not recoverable, but the name phrase of the protagonist seems to have included a genealogical statement from which the name of the fater has survived. It is interesting to note that this name glyph resembles the name of the father on MT 217 from Tikal Burial 195.

Costa Rican Jade   Tikal MT 217

2.   Pal T18   missing   missing   9.14.15. 0. 0
     Stc 435

3.   Pal TFC   1.18. 5. 4. 0   GII   9.14.15. 0. 0
     D13-C14

This event phrase is preceded by an ADI and followed by the CR date 1 Ahau 13 Mac, which is recorded earlier on this tablet as the birth date of GII of the Palenque Triad. Although this "knot-skull" glyph is recorded elsewhere as a "death" glyph, structurally it must refer (perhaps metaphorically) to birth.

4.   Pal PTab   9.12.11. 5.18   the lord   9.14.10. 0. 0
     I15   (Pacal II)

The verbs in ##4-5 are part of temporal instructions detailing that a DN is to be counted from the last recorded event until a later event, and in each context, the previous event is "death." Both #4 and #5 are marked with the AEI and the subjects of both are recorded as the T1030o title (the glyphic version of the Jester God) which may function as a semantic determinative for personified versions of ahau. Each passage is paraphrased as follows: "It was so much time since he died, the lord, until . . ."

Jester God

Palace Tablet, D11   Tablet of 96 Glyphs, J1

5.   Pal PTab   9.13.10. 1. 5   the lord   9.14.10. 0. 0
     N13   (Chan-Bahlum)

Chart 121   305

6.	Cop HS	missing		missing	9.17.10. 0. 0	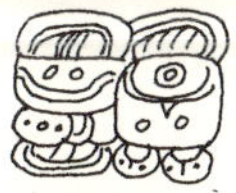
7.	Cop AltQ C2-D2	9.15. 7. 6.12		New-Sky-at- Horizon	9.17. 5. 0. 0	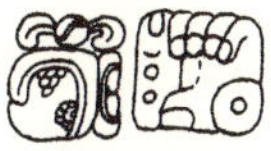
8.	ArP 3 E2	9.14. 0. 3. 5		Chac-Be-?? (by title)	9.15. 0. 0. 0	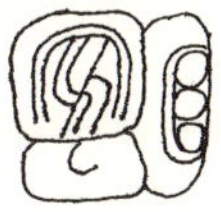

CHART 121   Affix T142   in Cluster *:142   with Miscellaneous Main Signs

#	LOCATION	DATE (EVENT)	PATIENT	AGENT	DEDICATION	
1.	Car 3 F3	9. 9.18.16. 3	????	Ruler 4 of Caracol?	9.10. 5. 0. 0	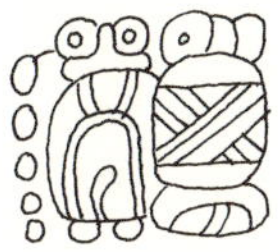

This "star" event occurred on the day after the fourteenth tun anniversary of the accession of Ruler 4 of Caracol. It also occurs on the HS at Naranjo (10:2), where the main sign of the Naranjo EG is part of the verbal expression.

| 2. | Tort 6
E2-F2 | 8.15.16. 0. 5 | | none | 9.12. 0. 0. 0 | 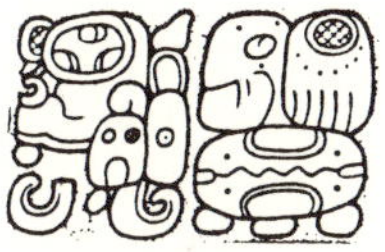 |

The first of the two glyphs is the "chuen" count glyph.

| 3. | Tik T1
L3; B2 | 9.13. 3. 0. 0 | | none | 9.15. 0. 0. 0 | 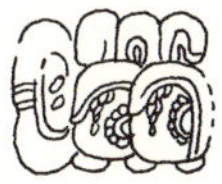 |

| 4. | Pal T14
B2 | 9 Ik 10 Mol | | *u cab* Moon Goddess | 9.13.15. 0. 0 | 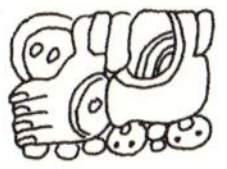 |

This "ahau-in-hand" event took place 5.18.4.7.8.13.18 before a historical event occurring 3.13.15 after the death of Chan-Bahlum. This event is recorded four times in the text, with the third example being "*yax* (first) God K-in-hand" (87:10) and the fourth being the "first ahau-in-hand" (20:8). In this first occurrence the "chicchan" glyph replaces "ahau", and the forehead mirror of God K is adjoined to the main verb as a semantic determinative specifying that the reference is to the God K scepter. The agent is recorded with four glyphs of which the first is the personified variant of *u cab* and the second is the T1000a female head with T181 attached. Since the syntactical position of this glyph is that of the subject, T181 cannot signal a verb, especially after *u cab*. There-fore, it must be part of a name (Lady Moon), or it functions as a seman-tic determinative specifying that the female agent really is the Moon Goddess. Her name is followed by two aged heads as yet unidentified.

#				
5.	Cop HS	missing	missing	9.17.10. 0. 0

6.	PUin 3 B21	9.18. 2.14. 6	none	9.18. 5. 0. 0

The verb records a total eclipse which is known to have occurred in this region on this date (July 19, 790 in the Gregorian calendar).

7.	NTun GpIIa A4	9.15.10. 0. 0	local person	9.16.10. 0. 0

See 26:20 for another example of this verb.

8.	Res HS1 A16b-A17a	missing	Ox-Ahau	9. 4. 0. 0. 0?

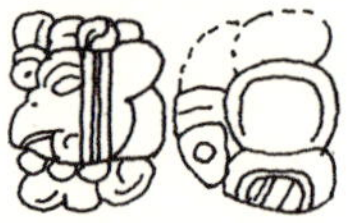

This accession verb follows a DN consisting of a katun glyph with a numerical superfix of one and a prefix of twelve or thirteen, and perhaps a one. This DN presumably linked this event to that following the IS date, but unfortunately the IS cannot be reconstructed and its verb is badly damaged. There are three stairways at Resbalon of which many of the stone were reset in Pre-Columbian times. A fragmentary IS date on another of these stairs records a date in Katun 4, and since this period fits the style of all three stairways, I am tentatively assigning a dedication date of 9.4.0.0.0.

9.	LHig 1 D1-D4	9.17.10. 0. 0	????	9.17.10. 0. 0

CHART 122   Affix T178   in Cluster *:178   with Miscellaneous Main Signs

#	LOCATION	DATE (EVENT)	PATIENT	AGENT	DEDICATION
1.	Pom PanY pA4b	9. 8. 0. 0. 0		none	9.18. 0. 0. 0 

Chart 123   307

This verb follows an ADI and precedes a DN of one katun, which leads from
9.8.0.0.0 to 9.9.0.0.0. The verb should refer to a rite on the earlier
PE.

2.   Ton M113   9.12. 4. 0. 1   Muluc-Jaguar   9.12. 0. 0. 0
     E

3.   Pal TFC   no date   the child of   9.13. 0. 0. 0
     G9   Pacal II

This "God K-in-hand" glyph is the second verb is a couplet recording the
heir-designation of Chan-Bahlum II. Here he is named only as the "child
of the five-katun *ahau*, Pacal, Lord of Palenque." The verb appears to
refer directly to the scenes on the piers of the Temple of Inscriptions,
which show a child, the size of a six-year-old, who displays the six toes
known in Chan-Bahlum's adult portraits and the "smoking celt" and other
characteristics of God K. The sign adjoined to the rear of the T670 hand
is a rare form of "ahau" which functions here as a semantic determinative
referring to the usual "ahau-in-hand" version of this verb. The same sign
can be seen replacing "ahau" in an "ahau-in-hand" glyph on the tablet of
Temple 14 (121:4), and it appears as the day sign Ahau on Piedras Negras
Lintel 12. It should be noted that this sign can also appear as the day
Chicchan and that "chicchan" and "ahau" are somehow interrelated. In a
seating expression from the HS at Copan, the personified form of "ahau"
appears with characteristics of both "chicchan" and "ahau".

4.   Pal Slav   9.14.17.12.18   *u cab* Chac-Zutz'   9.15. 0. 0. 0
     F3

This is one of two "axe" events that occurred before and after a capture
event. See 110:6.

CHART 123   Affix T17   in Cluster *:17   with Main Sign T218

#	LOCATION	DATE (EVENT)	PATIENT	AGENT	DEDICATION	
1.	Tik 31 H26	9. 0. 0. 0. 0	9 baktuns	deleted	9. 0.10. 0. 0	

This verb is followed by TIX:528.528, the geometric form of the baktun
cycle. In this example "baktun" is an appropriate interpretation, but
elsewhere on Stela 31 this doubled cauac sign stands for "katun." It must
refer, therefore, to "cycle" in general rather than to a specific period.

This example is recorded as an earlier event from which a DN is counted to a later, featured event.

2. Tik 31   8.17. 1. 4.12   Jaguar-Paw I 9. 0. 10. 0. 0
    C20

This event is not a PE, but the first half of the phrase seems identical to T218:575.

3. Tik 1   9. 1.10. 0. 0?   2 katuns   Stormy-Sky   9. 1. 10. 0. 0?
    B5

This text is badly damaged, but it seems likely that this clause records the second katun anniversary of the accession of Stormy-Sky. If this is a correct interpretation, the "death" date generally accepted for Stormy-Sky is called into question.

4. Tik 7   9. 3. 0. 0. 0   none   9. 3. 0. 0. 0
    A7

This verb precedes the CR.

5. Tik 8   9. 3. 2. 0. 0   none   9. 3. 2. 0. 0
    A6

This verb precedes the CR.

6. Pal Tbs   9.11. 0. 0. 0   11 katuns   none   9.11. 5. 0. 0
    L1b

7. PN 3   9.13.19.13. 1   25 tuns   Ruler 3   9.14. 0. 0. 0
    F4a

This "completion" glyph is followed by T1.V:89.528/I.28:548/59.168:188 or "fifth tun, one katun as *ahpo* (lord) of the succession."

8. PN 3   9.14. 0. 0. 0   14th katun   none   9.14. 0. 0. 0
    F9

9. Tik 16   9.14. 0. 0. 0   14th katun   none   9.14. 0. 0. 0
    A3

Chart 123   309

Lounsbury (n.d.) has identified this date as one on which Venus first appeared as Evening Star. The headdress worn by Ruler A is very likely the god of the Evening Star.

10.	Nar 23 G18	9.14. 0. 0. 0	14th katun	Smoking- Squirrel	9.14.10. 0. 0	
11.	EPeru Alt	2 Imix? 4 Pop	67 tuns of maize title	Ah Cauac	Late Classic	

This expression records an anniversary of some sort, but it is not possible to determine whether it is the anniversary of birth or accession. At both Palenque and Yaxchilan, this maize title is used to record "katuns of reign" in contrast to "katuns of life."

12.	PN 9 C11-C12	9.15. 5. 3.18	7th tun as *ahau*	Ruler 4	9.15.15. 0. 0	
13.	PN Alt2 J3	9.16. 0. 0. 0	16 katuns	Ruler 4	9.16. 0. 0. 0	
14.	Quir Dw B17	9.16.13. 4.17	2 katuns as *ahpo*	Two-Legged- Sky	9.16.15. 0. 0	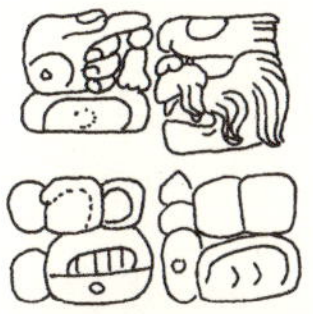
15.	Pal 96G H6	9.17.13. 0. 7	1st katun as *ahau*	Kuk II	9.17.15. 0. 0	
16.	Pal 96G K2	9.17.13. 0. 7	1st katun as *ahau*	Kuk (by title)	9.17.15. 0. 0	
17.	Quir Str1 Corn	9.19. 0. 0. 0	19th katun	missing	9.19. 0. 0. 0	
18.	CItz Jade 140	5 Imix 19 Zac	1 katun as *ahau*	????	Late Classic	

This expression is followed by a number of glyphs, any of which may record the subject.

19. Tik 19   9.17.18. 2. 1   1st katun   deleted   9.18. 0. 0. 0
     A12   as *batab*

The date of this anniversary is ninety-seven days later than the one-
katun anniversary required for the accession date recorded on Stela 22.
The discrepency is not understood.

20. DPil 25   9.14. 0. 0. 0   14 katuns   deleted   9.14. 0. 0. 0
     D2

This phrase is followed by a T713 "end of tun" glyph and the name of the
subject Shield-God K.

21. MJos 2   9.14. 0. 0. 0   14 katuns   local ruler 9.14. 0. 0. 0
     D6-C7

22. PN 30   9. 5. 0. 0. 0   ?? katuns   missing   9. 5. 0. 0. 0
     pA5

23. PN 8   9.13. 0. 0. 0   13th katun   none   9.13. 0. 0. 0
     M5-N5

24. Cop Alt   9.12. 0. 0. 0   12th katun   paddlers   9.12. 0. 0. 0
     of I pS7

David Stuart (personal communication, 1981) has identified the glyphs
following this phrase as the names of the paddlers in the canoe scenes
on the bones from Tikal Burial 116. The portrait heads of these gods are
shown emerging from the serpent bar on this monument. See 35:1,7-8 and
129:9,11.

CHART 124	Affix T17	in Cluster *:17	with Miscellaneous Main Signs

#	LOCATION	DATE (EVENT)	PATIENT	AGENT	DEDICATION	
1.	Pal 96G A2	9.11. 0. 0. 0	11th katun	*u cab* Pacal II	9.17.15. 0. 0	
2.	Ton M91 pA-pB	missing		????	Late Classic	

Chart 125   311

3. Pal Cr   missing   ????   *u cab* Chac-Rodent-   9.16. 0. 0. 0?
    J1-J2   Bone

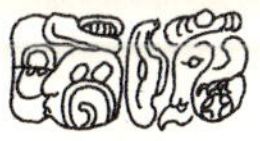

PEI. See the note to 14:4; ##3 and 4 are repeated here because of the
possibility that T17 functions as a verbal affix in these two examples.

4. Yax L25   9.14.11.15. 1   Lady Xoc   9.15. 0. 0. 0
    O2-Q1

See the note to 17:4.

5. Yax L26   9.14.18. 6.12   GI?   9.15. 0. 0. 0
    O1-P1

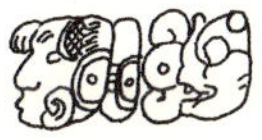

CHART 125   Affix T117   in Cluster *.117   with Main Sign T528.116:713

T23 and T4 have the phonetic value *-na* or *-an*.

#	LOCATION	DATE (EVENT)	PATIENT	AGENT	DEDICATION	
1.	Tik 31 D9	8.14. 0. 0. 0	tun	none	9. 0.10. 0. 0	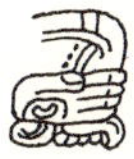

This verb is followed by "completion of" (T1.218:130), fourteen katuns,
the "chuen" count variant, two titles (?), *u cab*, and the name phrase of
Jaguar-Paw I. See 42:1.

| 2. | Tik 31 D15 | 8.17. 0. 0. 0 | tun | none | 9. 0.10. 0. 0 | 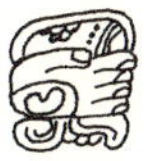 |

This verb is recorded as an earlier event from which a DN is counted to a
later and featured event. It appears without a CR notation, but repeats
information on the date recorded in the immediately preceding passage. It
is followed by T617:126.

| 3. | Tik 31 E17 | 8.18. 0. 0. 0 | tun | 7-Ek-Kan- Eccentric- Cauac | 9. 0.10. 0. 0 | 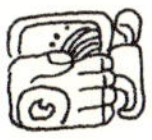 |

This verb is follows by a pair of glyphs 7-Ek-Kan (TVII.86:95[281]) and
Eccentric-Cauac (T122:529), which are the Early Classic versions of a
pair of deities known to play an important role on the TS at Palenque and

on other Late Classic monuments. These two glyphs follow the "end of tun" expression, but precedes a "completion of eighteen katuns" notation. They either record supernatural actors for the tun ending or express some kind of cosmological dedication for the katun.

| 4. | Car 16 B16 | 9. 5. 0. 0. 0 | tun | Nen-Oc | 9. 5. 0. 0. 0 |  |

| 5. | DPil 25 E1 | 9.14. 0. 0. 0 | tun | Shield-God K | 9.14. 0. 0. 0 |  |

| 6. | DPil 26 E3-F3 | 9.14.10. 4. 0 | tun | Shield-God K | 9.14.10. 0. 0 |  |

Either the CR is in error or it is intended to record that the PE rites either lasted for eighty days or were held eighty days apart.

CHART 126   Affix T117   in Cluster *.117   with Miscellaneous Main Signs

#	LOCATION	DATE (EVENT)	PATIENT	AGENT	DEDICATION	
1.	Pal PTab M7	9.12.11.12.10		deleted (Chan-Bahlum)	9.14.10. 0. 0	

This verb is in a context where it can be shown arithmetically to have occurred on the day of Chan-Bahlum II's accession so that it is semantically parallel to T700var and T1:60:713, the accession verbs of an earlier passage recording this accession. It is linked by DN to a T585 death event (see 73:3).

2.	Pal T18 Stc 431	missing		missing	9.14.15. 0. 0	
3.	Yax L31 J5-K1	9.16.13. 0. 0		Bird-Jaguar III	9.17. 0. 0. 0	
4.	Quir Fw B6	9.14.13. 4.17		Two-Legged-Sky	9.17. 0. 0. 0	

This verb records an accession event.

Chart 127   313

#	LOCATION	DATE (EVENT)	PATIENT	AGENT	DEDICATION	
5.	PN Thr1 Z2	9.17. 9. 5.11		Ruler 7	9.17.15. 0. 0	
6.	Pal T18 Stc 448	missing		missing	9.14.15. 0. 0	

CHART 127   Affix T23 or T4   in Cluster *:23 or 4   with Miscellaneous Main Signs

Both T23 and T4 have the phonetic value *-na* or *-an*.

#	LOCATION	DATE (EVENT)	PATIENT	AGENT	DEDICATION	
1.	Pal Slav H5b	9.14.18. 9.17		deleted	9.15. 0. 0. 0	

This "birth" verb follows "were completed three katuns" and the CR notation for the date. It specifies that the three katuns were completed since the birth of Chac-Zutz', recorded earlier in the text.

2.	Cop AltF' B3b	????		deleted	9.17. 5. 0. 0	

This verb may record a "death."

3.	Pal C Eave K2	9. 9. 6.10.19		deleted	9.11.10. 0. 0	

This verb is the last recorded on the eaves of House C, and although no agent is expressed, it follows the only date in the inscription. The verb immediately preceding this one is composed of the second half of the "wing-shell" death expression (see 25:14), but the event is unlikely to be death in this calendric context. Pacal II is named as the agent of the "zac-ahau-ik" event, and presumably he is intended to be understood as the agent of this last event. Since this event is associated with anniversaries in other contexts, I tested this example as a possible anniversary rite and found that it occurred 7.14.8 or 2,808 days (or 2 x 2 x 2 x 3 x 3 x 3 x 13) after the death of Pacal I, the ancestor for whom Pacal II was named, but these numbers do not seem to match any important calendric cycles.

4.	Pal TC Alf GI	9.12.19.14.12		GI	9.13. 0. 0. 0	

The events listed as ##4-6 occurred on the occasion of the eighth tropical year anniversary of the accession of Chan-Bahlum II. In #4, the verb is followed by the "6-ah-chaan (sky)" title found often in GI's name phrase, by a possessed noun (or second verb), and by the name phrase of Chan-Bahlum. With this structure, it would not be possible to identify the subject as GI or Chan-Bahlum, but in the parallel clauses in ##5-6, Chan-Bahlum's name appears following the "child of (mother)" glyph. GI is the subject, therefore, of #4, if it is parallel to #5 and #6. See 20:7, 58:1, and 81:6 for additional examples.

5.	Pal TC Jamb A3	9.12.19.14.12	GI	9.13. 0. 0. 0	
6.	Pal TFC Jamb A7b	9.12.19.14.12	GII	9.13. 0. 0. 0	
7.	Pal PTab R13-Q14	9.14. 8.14.15	Xoc	9.14.10. 0. 0	

This is an accession event.

8.	Pal Slav G4b-H4a	9.14.18. 9. 8	deleted? (Chac-Zutz')	9.15. 0. 0. 0	

Because of the presence of "dynasty"-associated signs (the te' general "tree" sign and T188 le, the glyph for "succession"), and because of the 5 Lamat day position, I tested the date of this event as a possible anniversary day and found that it was 5.16.5.0 or 41,860 days after the accession of Pacal II. This length of time is 114 years and 222 days, and it seems to be one of Lounsbury's (1976) "contrived numbers." The factors of the DN are as follows: 2 x 2 x 5 x 7 x 13 x 23; however, the cycles within this contrived number seem to have no particular importance. This event may have involved some sort of dynastic numerology based on the date of accession of Pacal II, but at the present time we do not understand it. No agent is named in the passage, so that this event may not have required one, but if the subject is deleted, it would have been understood as Chac-Zutz', the protagonist of the monument and subject of all of the events in the last two-thirds of the text.

9.	Mach 3 A2	9.19.14.15. 1	Split-Kin-GI	9.19. 5. 0. 0	
10.	Pal TFC L6-L8	9.12. 18. 5.17	Chan-Bahlum II	9.13. 0. 0. 0	

Chart 128 315

See 17:2-3 for commentary on this event. The God N glyph appears to function as an auxiliary verb, so the following glyphs are the semantically critical part of the verbal expression. Note that T23 and T4 appear as equivalent suffixes in this parallel context.

#					
11.	Pal TS O8-N10	9.12.18. 5.17	Chan-Bahlum II	9.13. 0. 0. 0	
12.	PN Thr1 K'3-K'5	9.17.15. 0. 0	Ruler 7	9.17.15. 0. 0	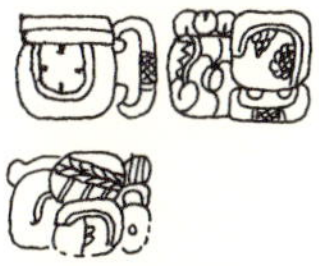
13.	Yax L21 A7b-B7	9. 0.19. 2. 4	Moon-Skull	9.16. 5. 0. 0	

This event is linked to a historical reenactment of it by Bird-Jaguar III. See 86:6 for the later event.

14.	PN L12 L1-N1	9. 4. 3.10. 1	local ruler	9. 4. 5. 0. 0
15.	Smj Shell B9	4 Cauac? 12 Mol	Pacal of Palenque	9.13. 0. 0. 0?

CHART 128 | Affix T116 | in Cluster *.116 | with Miscellaneous Main Signs

#	LOCATION	DATE (EVENT)	PATIENT	AGENT	DEDICATION	
1.	Pal Slav B1a	9. 9. 2. 4. 8		Pacal II	9.15. 0. 0. 0	
2.	Pal T18 Jamb D	9.14.10. 4. 2		deleted (Chaacal III)	9.14.15. 0. 0	
	PEI.					
3.	Nar 21 E10	9.13. 1. 4.16		Smoking-Squirrel	9.13.15. 0. 0	

This event occurred to Smoking-Squirrel at age 5.

4.	Nar 23 G9	9.13.19. 6. 3		*u cab* Smoking- Squirrel	9.14.10. 0. 0 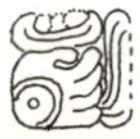
5.	Car 3 B19	9. 7.19.13.12		*u cab* Ruler 4	9.10. 5. 0. 0 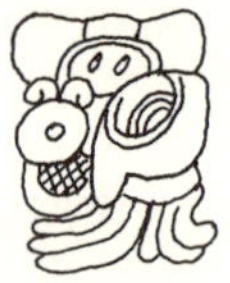

This event occurred to Ruler 4 at age 5.

6.	Cop AltS I1b-J1	10. 0. 0. 0. 0		none	9.15. 0. 0. 0 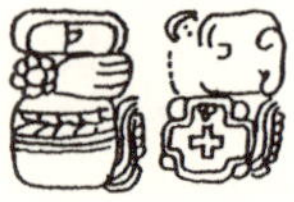

CHART 129   Affix T126   in Cluster 126.*:variable   with Miscellaneous Main Signs

All of these examples have T126 as a prefix, and a number of different of different suffixes. See Chart 62 for additional examples.

#	LOCATION	DATE (EVENT)	PATIENT	AGENT	DEDICATION
1.	Pal TI All Panels	various		various	9.12.15. 0. 0 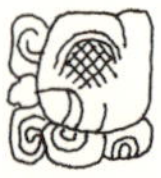

See Chart 62 for individual listings of these examples.

#	LOCATION	DATE (EVENT)	PATIENT	AGENT	DEDICATION
2.	Pal TIm I2-I3	9.12. 0. 0. 0		deleted (Pal Triad)	9.12.15. 0. 0 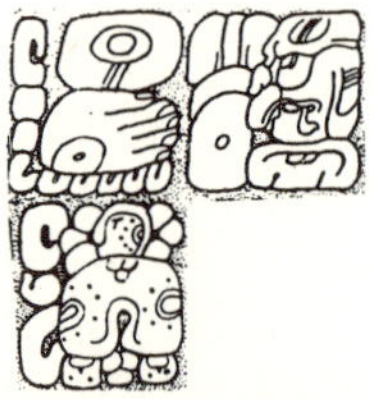

See 33:1-2.

#	LOCATION	DATE (EVENT)	PATIENT	AGENT	DEDICATION
3.	Pal T18 Stc 420	missing		missing	9.14.15. 0. 0 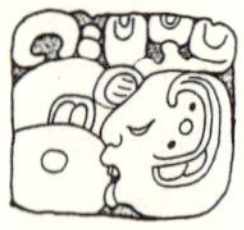
4.	Pal T18 Stc 478	missing		missing	9.14.15. 0. 0 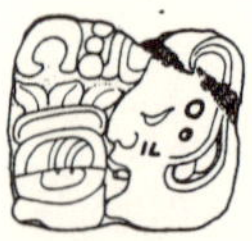
5.	Pal TIw O11-P11	13. 4.12. 3. 6		GI the First	9.12.15. 0. 0 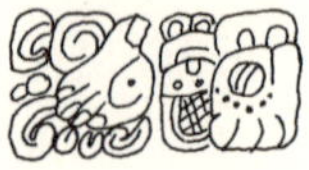
6.	Yax L10 A2b-B2	9.18.17.12. 6		Captor of Turtle-Macaw	9.19. 0. 0. 0 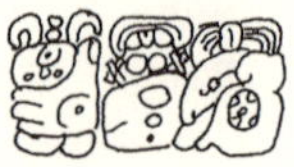

Chart 130 317

This expression is the first component of a long, complex statement
including (1) this verb, (2) a "star-shell" event (10:20), (3) a "capture" (74:27), and (4) a final verbal expression identical (except for
inflectional affixes) to this one (see 27:4). The repetition of the same
verbal phrase at the beginning and end of the passage functions to en-
frame it and to highlight both its beginning and end.

7. Yax L10   9.18.17.13.14   Great-Skull   9.19. 0. 0. 0
   F5

This event occurred twenty-eight days after #6. The glyphs following the
"ahau-in-hand" appear to differentiate this event from the earlier event,
also "ahau-in-hand."

8. Ton M110   9.14.10. 0. 0   5 Ahau?   none   9.14.10. 0. 0
   P-Q

9. PN L12   9. 4. 0. 0. 0   Kin-Ma-Cu-??   9. 4. 5. 0. 0
   I1

10. PN Thr1   9.17. 9. 5.11   deleted   9.17.15. 0. 0
    Z5-Z6   (Ruler 7)

11. Nar 23   9.14. 0. 0. 0   paddlers   9.14. 0. 0. 0
    G21-H22

David Stuart (personal communication, 1981) has identified the two latter
glyphs as names of the paddlers in the canoe scenes on the bones from
Tikal Burial 116. This clause is parallel to one on Tonina M110 (#8). See
35:1,7-8, and 123:24.

CHART 130   Affix T229   in Cluster T229.*:various   with Miscellaneous Main Signs

All of these examples have T229 *ah* as a prefix and various different suffixes.

#	LOCATION	DATE (EVENT)	PATIENT	AGENT	DEDICATION	
1.	Car 14 E3	9. 5.19. 1. 2		Ruler 2	9. 6. 0. 0. 0	 

2. Nar 21   9.13. 1. 4.16   Smoking-   9.13.15. 0. 0
    E10   Squirrel

This event occurred to Smoking-Squirrel at age 5.

3. Pal T18   2. 0. 0.14. 2   ancestral   9. 14.15. 0. 0
    Jamb C11   goddess

4. Tik 31   9. 0.10. 0. 0   none   9. 0.10. 0. 0
    A12

This "mirror" compound compound functions not only in the contexts listed
here, but also as the IG of the Primary Standard Sequence in pottery
texts (M.D. Coe 1973). In all of the examples from monumental texts, this
glyph stands between calendric information and verbal glyphs in manner
suggesting that it functions to highlight the verb or a CR. In this
example, it follow the IS date and lunar data and precedes a "chuen"
count variant, the event phrase, and the extended name of the agent. In
the two other examples from Stela 31, it stands between a DN and "end of
tun" phrase and the date to which the DN is counted, or between a DN and
"end of tun" phrase and the event occurring on that date; and in both
cases, T229 *ah-* is not included as a prefix (see 116:16). In both cases,
the date or event phrase following the "mirror" glyph might be considered
the patient of the verb.

5. Cal 43   9. 4. 0. 0. 0   none   9. 4. 0. 0. 0
    pA8

The sequence of components is as follows: IS date + lunar data + "mirror"
+ verbal phrase + agent.

6. Cop Alt   no date   ????   9.11. 0. 0. 0
    of St13

7. Tort 1   9.10.13. 0. 0   none   9.11. 0. 0. 0
    A3b

The sequence of components is as follows: CR + "end of tun" + agent
(Ahpo-Balam) + "mirror" + event 1 (redundant) + DN + event 2 + agent
(deleted).

8. Tort 1   9.10.13. 0. 0   none   9.11. 0. 0. 0
    A4c

Chart 130 319

The sequence of components is as follows: event 2 (#7) + "mirror" + PDI + DN (from event 1) + CR + event 3.

9. Tort Box   9.12. 7. 1.19   none   9.12.10. 0. 0
    N1

This "mirror" glyph follows a DN of one tun (which does not appear related to any of the recorded dates) and a "seating" expression, and precedes a second "seating" expression. In this context, the "mirror" glyph may record the subject of the first "seating" event.

10. Pal TS   1.18. 5. 3. 6   none   9.13. 0. 0. 0
    B16

The sequence of components is as follows: IS date + lunar data + 819 Day Count clause + "mirror" + verbal phrase ("birth") + subject (GIII).

11. Quir J   9.15. 0. 0. 0?   none   9.16. 5. 0. 0
    E1

The sequence of components is as follows: "mirror" + DN (leading to a katun ending) + ADI + event (earlier) + subject. The "mirror" glyph may refer to the katun ending, which is implied, but not explicitly stated in the text.

12. Pal ISpot   9.18. 9. 4. 4   none   9.18.10. 0. 0
    F4

The sequence of components is as follows: IS date + lunar data + 819 Day Count clause + "mirror" + event with PEI + subject.

13. Quir J   9.14.13. 4.17   none   9.16. 5. 0. 0
    G1

This glyph appears in contexts parallel to the "mirror" glyph above, and it includes the the same affix pattern, T229.*:126, but the main sign is GI of the Palenque Triad, rather than T617, the "mirror" sign. It also occurs as the IS of the Primary Standard Sequence. This example occurs in the following sequence of components: GI "count" + DN + CR + event + patient + agent.

14. Tort 6   9.10.11. 9. 6   none   9.12. 0. 0. 0
    A6

The sequence of components is as follows: DN + "birth" + GI "count" + CR with locative + "seating" + subject.

15. Tort 6   9.10.12. 3.10   none   9.12. 0. 0. 0
    A13

The sequence of components is as follows: DN + GI "count" + CR + event.

16. Tort 6   9.10.16.13. 6   none   9.12. 0. 0. 0
    B16

The sequence of components is as follows: DN + GI "count" + CR + event.

17. Tort 6   9.10.17. 2.14   none   9.12. 0. 0. 0
    D2

The sequence of components is as follows: DN + GI "count" + CR + event + subject.

18. Tort 6   9.11.16. 8.18   none   9.12. 0. 0. 0
    E11

The sequence of components is as follows: DN + CR with ADI + "five tuns lacking" + GI "count" + event.

CHART 131   Affix T236 or T126   in Cluster *:236 or 126   with Main Signs T586

Although these verbs from Copan have different affix patterns, they have been included on this chart in order to facilitate comparison because they seem to be interrelated and are spaced three uinals apart in the LC. The meaning of these events is not known, but the iconography of Stela H is full of blood-letting symbolism, and Stela A, its paired monument, includes a long section of mythological/ cosmological information.

#	LOCATION	DATE (EVENT)	PATIENT	AGENT	DEDICATION
1.	Cop H B1-A3	9.14.19. 5. 0		18-Rabbit	9.15. 0. 0. 0

Although Stela H has been identified as a female, no female name glyph appears on the monument. The agent is clearly identified as 18-Rabbit, the local ruler.

Chart 132   321

2.   Cop A   9.14.19. 8. 0   deleted?   9.15. 0. 0. 0
      A10-C1?

This event phrase accompanies the IS date, but no agent is named. The
full event phrase seem to contain two verbal phases in couplet form; both
of the verbs seem related to PE expressions, but the date is clearly not
a PE. See 5:1-2, 31:10-14, 44, and 69.

3.   Cop A   9.14.19. 11. 0   deleted?   9.15. 0. 0. 0
      B3-B4a

This expression records an event which took place three uinals after #2
and six uinals after #1. It is followed by a T736 "death" glyph and a
series of glyphs in which I recognize no personal name glyphs. The death
glyph in turn seems to be the verb in a couplet construction in which the
second verb is T585 "death," but again I cannot detect a name glyph in
the passage which follows the second death glyph. See Chart 19 and 24:3-
11 for other examples of these death glyphs.

      T736 "death"   T585 "death"

CHART 132   Affix T1   in Cluster 1*:various   with Main Sign T757/712

These examples are found in genealogical statements which record the relationship between child
and parent. Although this "child of parent" expression probably functions as a noun in the context
of genealogy, it is clearly derived from the T712 expression for the act of "blood-letting," a
verbal phrase. Because of the obvious morphological similarity between the "child of parent"
expression and the verbal phrase for "blood-letting," I have included these examples for comparative purposes. Since the genealogical contexts do not include dates, patients, or agents, I have
changed the format of this chart to reflect the nature of the useful information associated with
each example. Brackets signal that information is reconstructed.

#	LOCATION	DEDICATION	CHILD	PARENT	
1.	ASac 4 D5-C6	9.10.10. 0. 0	local ruler	prior ruler	
2.	Tort 6 E16-E17	9.12. 0. 0. 0	[Ahpo-Balam]	Lady of Palenque	

3.	Pal TC E3	9.13. 0. 0. 0	GI (by title)	ancestral goddess	
4.	Pal TS C11-D11	9.13. 0. 0. 0	GIII (by title)	ancestral goddess	
5.	Pal PTab C10	9.14.10. 0. 0	Kan-Xul II	Pacal II	

This phrase is based on the "na-chan" variant of blood-letting. See 38:13, 52:6-9, and #14 below.

6.	Pul E C10	9.15. 0. 0. 0	local ruler	Sky-God K	
7.	Mach 11 A6	9.15.10. 0. 0	Etz'nab-GI	Split-Kin-GI	
8.	Lac L1 C6-D6	9.15.15. 0. 0	Knot-Eye-Jaguar of Bonampak	Tu-Yoc-Balam	

This example includes the T60:501 version of the T60:757 auxiliary verb. See Chart 38.

9.	Yax 11Frt H3-pG4	9.16. 5. 0. 0	Bird-Jaguar III	Shield-Jaguar I	

This example uses both the T757 and T580 auxiliary verbs.

10.	Yax 10 pD2	9.16. 5. 0. 0	[Bird-Jaguar III]	Shield-Jaguar I	
11.	Yax 7 pC6	9.17. 0. 0. 0?	Shield-Jaguar II	Lady Zero-Skull	
12.	Yax 7 pD8	9.17. 0. 0. 0?	Shield-Jaguar II	Bird-Jaguar III	
13.	Yax L10 D6	9.19. 0. 0. 0	Skull	Shield-Jaguar II	

Chart 133   323

14.	Nar 8	9.18.10. 0. 0	Ruler IIIb	Ruler IIIa
	E7-F8			

The second glyph is the "yax-mul" (T16:580) glyph of the "na-chan" blood-letting expression (see 52:6-9), and the last glyph is the forehead motif of the personified perforator which here replaces the T712 lancet.

15.	Mach 6	10. 0. 5. 0. 0	One-Fish-in-Hand	captor of
	B1b			??-lu

16.	Tik T1	9.15. 0. 0. 0	Ruler A	Shield-Skull
	L3; F4			

17.	Tik T4	9.16. 0. 0. 0	Ruler B	Ruler A
	L3; G8			

#15-17 use the T580 version of the auxiliary verb.

18.	Coba Sarc	Early Classic	????	Smoke-Head
	pU-pV			

19.	Ixk 1	9.18. 0. 0. 0	local ruler	father
	K1-J2			

The verb is probably T1.60.501.

CHART 133   Affix T1 in Cluster 1.*   or Affix T181 in Cluster *.181   with Main Sign T757

All of these examples are found within the context of genealogical statements in which T757 is followed by a term (T1.I:606:23) recording the relationship between a child and his or her mother. Syntactically, the relationship glyph, a possessed noun, is the subject of the verb, which appears to have a function similar to T757 in other contexts in that it highlights the relationship glyph "child of (mother)."

#	LOCATION	DEDICATION	SUBJECT	
1.	ASac 4	9.10.10. 0. 0	child of Lady Deer	
	C6			

2.	Tort Sarc M	9.12.10. 0. 0	child of Lady Cauac of Palenque	
3.	Nar 24 E7	9.13.10. 0. 0	child of Lady Muluc	
4.	Pal PTab C14	9.14.10. 0. 0	child of Lady Ahpo-Hel	
5.	Pus E D3	9.15. 0. 0. 0	child of Lady ????	
6.	Mach 11 B5a	9.15.10. 0. 0	child of Lady Pach-Kuk	
7.	Tik T4 L3; G5	9.16. 0. 0. 0	child of Lady Macaw	
8.	Yax 10 pA1	9.16. 5. 0. 0	child of Lady Ik-Skull	
9.	Nar 13 G1	9.17.10. 0. 0	child of Lady Scroll	
10.	Pal 96G J6	9.17.15. 0. 0	child of Lady Ahau-????	
11.	Yax L10 D4	9.19. 0. 0. 0	child of Lady Crossed-Bands	
12.	Ixk 1 K1-J2	9.18. 0. 0. 0	child of Lady Ik	

Appendix 1

The Patterns of Affixation in the Writing System

The data presented in this appendix summarize the material collected in the verb catalog (Chapter 9), but here the affix patterns are presented without provenience, dates, agents, or the other additional information included in the catalog. This summary is intended as a means of quick reference and as an entry into the main catalog. It should be used in conjunction with Appendix 2, which lists the same examples organized by the glyph numbers of the Thompson (1962) catalog system, and Appendix 3, which lists them by site and monument designations.

The forty-nine affix patterns (several of which are repeated in the last sections dealing with parentage statements) detected in the writing system are listed in the order in which they occur in the catalog. Each affix category lists with a general illustration those verbs occurring with it. Individual examples of verbal glyphs are noted by the appropriate catalog designations, which are recorded as 1:3, 27:3-5, 107:2, etc., with the first number referring to the major chart number and the second to the individual example on the chart. I have noted those phonetic values that I accept, and where possible, I have included information on the relationship of glyph affix patterns to linguistic ones. All affix patterns are listed by frequency of occurrence at the end of the appendix.

Each affix pattern is transcribed according to the system used by Thompson (1962) in his *Catalog of Maya Hieroglyphs*. In this system, "." indicates that the following sign is to the right of the previous one; ":" indicates it is below; "*" or "main sign" indicates the location of the verbal stem; and "nn" indicates that a sign does not have a T-number. At the end of the appendix, each affix pattern is listed by frequency of occurrence.

1. Zero affixing

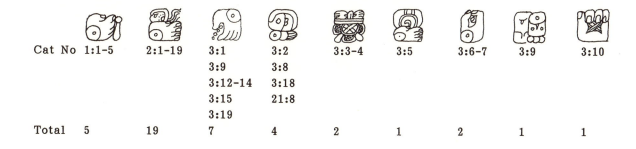

Cat No	1:1-5	2:1-19	3:1	3:2	3:3-4	3:5	3:6-7	3:9	3:10
			3:9	3:8					
			3:12-14	3:18					
			3:15	21:8					
			3:19						
Total	5	19	7	4	2	1	2	1	1

1. Zero affixing (continued)

Cat No	3:11	3:15	3:17	3:20	3:21 20:3 26:19	4:1-18	5:1-3 5:11	5:4	5:5 5:13
Total	1	1	1	1	3	18	4	1	2

Cat No	5:6	5:7	5:8 26:21	5:9-10	5:12	5:14	6:1	6:2	7:1-13
Total	1	1	2	2	1	1	1	1	13

Cat No	8:1-18 9:4 20:12	9:1	9:2 9:6 9:13	9:3	9:5	9:7-12	10:1-25	11:1-7	12:1-11
Total	20	1	3	1	1	6	25	7	11

Cat No	13:1-5 13:7-9	13:6	14:1-4	15:1-6	16:1-11 23:7-8	17:1-9	18:1-6	19:1-11	20:1 21:5 21:22
Total	8	1	4	6	13	9	6	11	3

Cat No	20:2	20:4	20:5 20:15	20:6	20:7	20:8-10 20:13-14	20:11	21:1	21:2
Total	1	1	2	1	1	4	1	1	1

Cat No	21:3	21:4	21:6	21:7	21:9	21:10 21:25	21:11	21:12	21:13-15
Total	1	1	1	1	1	2	1	1	3

Cat No	21:16	21:17-18	21:19	21:20	21:21	21:23-24	21:26	21:27	21:28
Total	1	2	1	1	1	2	1	1	1

1. Zero affixing (continued)

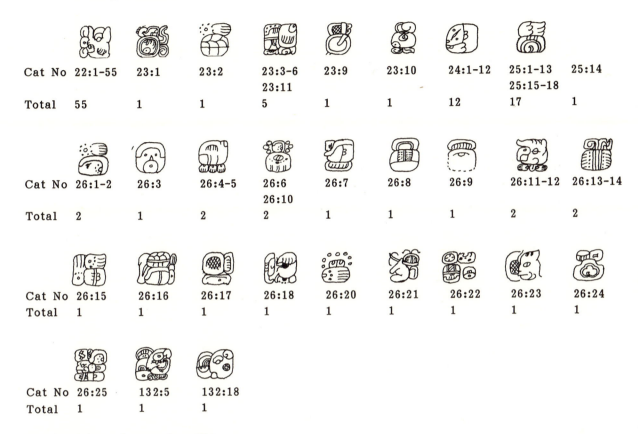

Cat No	22:1-55	23:1	23:2	23:3-6 23:11	23:9	23:10	24:1-12	25:1-13 25:15-18	25:14
Total	55	1	1	5	1	1	12	17	1

Cat No	26:1-2	26:3	26:4-5	26:6 26:10	26:7	26:8	26:9	26:11-12	26:13-14
Total	2	1	2	2	1	1	1	2	2

Cat No	26:15	26:16	26:17	26:18	26:20	26:21	26:22	26:23	26:24
Total	1	1	1	1	1	1	1	1	1

Cat No	26:25	132:5	132:18
Total	1	1	1

Total number of examples: 390

2. *tu*.main sign with *tu* being either T89  or T115

Both T89 and T115 are found as locative prepositions with the value *tu* derived from a contraction of the locative *ti* and the pronoun *u*. This value as a contraction may explain the function of this affix pattern, but Lounsbury (personal communication, 1980) has suggested that this prefixed *tu* possibly represents a contraction of the tense-aspect particle *t-* and the *u* pronoun.

Cat No	27:1	27:2	27:3	27:4	27:5	27:6
Total	1	1	1	1	1	1

Total number of examples: 6

3. T1.main sign(s).∅

T1 is the sign identified as equivalent to Landa's *u* sign. *U* is the third person pronoun of the ergative set in Yucatec, and although the modern equivalent in Chol is *i*, the pronoun of the Classic writing system was surely *u*. Verbs (or glyphs found in the syntactical position where a verb is expected) are most likely to be inflected as transitive forms; as imperfective intransitives (?); as statives; or as possessed nouns. An examination of all catalog examples with this inflection pattern will identify those signs functionally equivalent to T1.

Cat No	28:1-26	29:1-13	30:1-6	31:1-2	31:3-6	31:7-9	31:10-14 31:16	31:15	31:16
Total	26	13	6	2	4	3	6	1	1

Cat No	32:1-4	32:5	32:6-9	32:10 32:11	32:12 32:13	32:14 32:15	32:16	32:17	32:18
Total	4	1	4	2	2	2	1	1	1

Cat No	33:1-3 33:10	33:4	33:5-9	34:1-17	35:4 +cm	35:5 +ti	36:1-16	35:1-2 35:6-8 37:1-26 +cm	35:3 38:1-16 38:18-24 38:26-29 +ti
Total	4	1	5	17	1	1	16	31	29

Cat No	38:25 +ti	39:1-7	40:1	40:2	40:3	40:4	40:5	40:6	40:7
Total	1	1	1	1	1	1	1	1	1

Cat No	40:8	40:9-10	40:11	40:12	40:13
Total	1	2	1	1	1

Total number of examples: 200

4. T1.main sign(s):130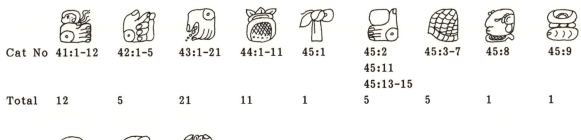

T130 appears as part of the *cacau* glyph in the Dresden Codex, and it functions as a phonetic complement for the *ahau* glyph, especially when *ahau* occurs in an anthropomorphic or zoomorphic form. In these contexts and others, T130 has the phonetic value *-wa* or *-w(a)*.

Cat No	41:1-12	42:1-5	43:1-21	44:1-11	45:1	45:2 45:11 45:13-15	45:3-7	45:8	45:9
Total	12	5	21	11	1	5	5	1	1

Cat No	45:10	45:12	46:1-4
Total	1	1	4

Total number of examples: 68.

5. T1.main sign(s):136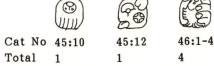

Cat No	47:1-5	48:1-6	49:1	49:2
Total	5	6	1	1

Total number of examples: 13

6. T1.main sign(s):24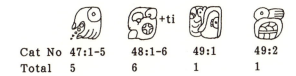

Because of its frequent appearance on nouns, T24 seems most likely to be a *-vl* suffix.

Cat No	50:1	50:2 50:5	50:3	50:4	51:1-10	52:1-9	53:1-4	54:1-2
Total	1	2	1	1	10	9	4	2

Total number of examples: 29

7. T1.main sign(s):140

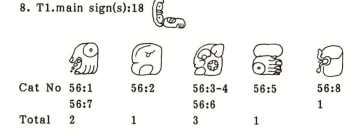

Cat No	55:1-2	55:3	55:4	55:5-8	55:9-10
Total	2	1	1	4	2

Total number of examples: 10

8. T1.main sign(s):18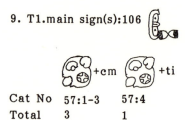

Cat No	56:1	56:2	56:3-4	56:5	56:8
	56:7		56:6		
Total	2	1	3	1	1

Total number of examples: 8

9. T1.main sign(s):106

Cat No	57:1-3	57:4
Total	3	1

Total number of examples: 4

10. T1.main sign(s):23 or 4

T23 appears as a phonetic complement on glyphs (such as *chaan* and *kan*) that take the phonetic complement *na*. This proposed phonetic value for both T23 and T4 is supported by substitution patterns discovered by Lounsbury (personal communication, 1978) which confirm the value *na* for T23, and T4 is found in free substitution with T23.

Cat No	58:1	58:2-3
Total	1	2

Total Number of examples: 3

11. T1.main sign(s):181 or 12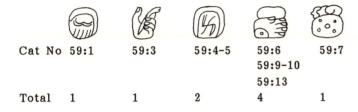

T181 appears in Landa's *ha* example with the value *-a*. The phonetic value for T181 is confirmed by the appearance of both T181 and T12 as the male article *ah* (Fig. 1).

Cat No 59:1	59:3	59:4-5	59:6 59:9-10 59:13	59:7
Total 1	1	2	4	1

Total number of examples: 9

12. T1.main sign:178.181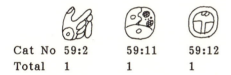

T178 has the phonetic value *-la*; combined with T181, the reading is *-lah*.

Cat No 59:2	59:11	59:12
Total 1	1	1

Total number of examples: 3

13. T1.main sign(s):82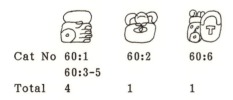

T82 is freely interchangeable with T24, and may, therefore, have a *-vl* value.

Cat No 60:1 60:3-5	60:2	60:6
Total 4	1	1

Total number of examples: 6

14. T1.main sign(s):misc.

Cat No 61:1   61:2   61:3   61:4   59:8
Total   1   1   1   1   1

Total number of examples: 5

15. T126.main sign:130   T130 is phonetic -wa.

Cat No 62:1-21   129:6   129:10
Total   21   1   1

Total number of examples: 23

16. T4 or 23.main sign(s).181   T4 and T23 are phonetic na, and T181 is phonetic ah.

Cat No 63:1   63:2
Total   1   1

Total number of examples: 2

17. main sign(s).181 or 228

T228 occurs as -ah in 64:1 and 64:5; all other examples are suffixed by T181 -ah.

Cat No 64:1   64:2   64:3-4   64:5   65:1-3   66:1-2   66:3-6   67:1-7   68:1-2
                                               66:7-8   66:9
Total   1   1   2   1   3   4   5   7   2

Cat No 68:3   68:4-5   69:1-10   70:1-2   70:3   70:4   70:5   70:6   70:7
Total   1   2   10   2   1   1   1   1   1

17. main sign(s).181 or 228 (continued)

Cat No	70:8	70:9	71:1-23	72:1-10 81:1-2 81:5	72:11 81:7	73:1 73:9 73:12	73:2-3 73:7-8	73:4-6	73:10
Total	1	1	23	13	2	3	4	3	1

Cat No	73:11	74:1-29 74:32-38 74:40-43	74:30-31	74:39	75:1	75:2	75:3-6 75:8 75:10	75:7	75:9
Total	1	40	2	1	1	1	6	1	1

Cat No	76:1-2	76:3-5	76:6	76:7	77:1-4	78:1-4	79:1-16 +ti	80:1	80:2
Total	2	3	1	1	4	4	16	1	1

Cat No	80:3	80:4 80:6	80:5	80:7	80:8	80:9	81:3	81:5	81:6
Total	1	2	1	1	1	1	1	1	1

Cat No	82:1-3	82:4-5	82:6	82:7	82:8	82:9	82:10	82:11-12	82:13
Total	3	2	1	1	1	1	1	2	1

Cat No	82:14-15	82:16	82:17	82:18	82:19	82:20	82:21	82:22-23	82:24-26
Total	2	1	1	1	1	1	1	2	3

Cat No	82:27	82:28	82:29-31	82:32-33	82:34	82:35	83:1-2
Total	1	1	3	2	1	1	2

Total number of examples: 231

18. main sign(s):178.181

In combination, T178 (*-la*) and T181 (*-ah*) produce the suffix *-lah*, which is documented as the completive suffix for positional verbs in Yucatec. In Cholan, the suffix may be a combination of the inchoative suffix *-l-* and the perfective *-ah*. It should be noted that this affix pattern appears prominently with the T644 "seating" glyph, a positional verb.

Cat No	84:1-2	84:3-9	85:1-11	86:1-2	86:3-4	86:5	86:6	86:7	86:8
Total	2	7	11	2	2	1	1	1	1

Cat No	86:9-10	87:1-2	87:3-11
Total	2	2	9

Total number of examples: 41

19. main sign(s):126.181

Cat No	86:11	88:1-17	89:1-27	90:1-2	90:3
Total	1	17	27	2	1

Total number of examples: 48

20. main sign(s):136.126.181   In some of these examples, T126 may function as an AEI.

Cat No	91:1-12	92:1-2	92:3	92:4	92:5	92:6
Total	12	2	1	1	1	1

Total number of examples: 18

21. main sign(s):82.181   T82 is possibly a –*vl* suffix, and T181 is –*ah*.

Cat No 93:1-2
Total   2

Total number of examples: 2

22. main sign(s):24.181

T24 is possibly a –*vl* suffix and interchangeable with T82; T181 is –*ah*.

Cat No 94:1-3   94:4   94:5   94:6
Total   3   1   1   1

Total number of examples: 6

23. main sign(s):130.181   T130 is –*wa* and T181 is –*ah*.

Cat No 95:1   95:2-15   95:16-   95:18
                95:18   17
Total   1   15   2   1

Total number of examples: 19

24. main sign(s):23 or 4.181   T23 and T4 are phonetic *na*, and T181 is –*ah*.

Cat No 96:1   96:2   96:3   96:4   96:5
Total   1   1   1   1   1

Total number of examples: 5

25. main sign(s).181:18

In most other contexts, T181 and T18 seem to be interchangeable; these are the only examples in which the two affixes appear on one verb. Number 98:7 includes T228, rather than T181, as the suffix.

25. Main sign(s).181:18 (continued)

Cat No 97:1   97:2-3   98:7?
Total   1   2   1

Total number of examples: 4

26. main sign(s):18

Cat No 98:1   98:2-3   98:4   98:5-9   98:10   98:14   99:3   99:4   99:5
        98:13   98:11-12   99:1-2
Total   2   2   1   7   1   3   1   1   1

        99:6   99:7-8
Total   1   2

Total number of examples: 22

27. main sign(s):18.178 or :178.18

Cat No 100:1-8
Total   8

Total number of examples: 8

28. main sign(s):126.18

Cat No 101:1   101:2   101:3-4   101:5-6   101:7   102:1   102:2
Total   1   1   2   2   1   1   1

Total number of examples: 9

29. main sign(s):136 (or 246)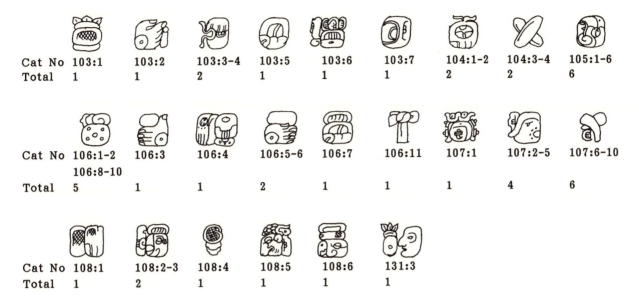

Cat No 103:1   103:2   103:3-4   103:5   103:6   103:7   104:1-2   104:3-4   105:1-6
Total   1   1   2   1   1   1   2   2   6

Cat No 106:1-2   106:3   106:4   106:5-6   106:7   106:11   107:1   107:2-5   107:6-10
       106:8-10
Total   5   1   1   2   1   1   1   4   6

Cat No 108:1   108:2-3   108:4   108:5   108:6   131:3
Total   1   2   1   1   1   1

Total number of examples: 44

30. main sign(s):130    T130 is phonetic *wa*.

Cat No 109:1-2   109:3-4   109:5   109:6   109:7   110:1-2   110:3   110:4   110:5
Total   2   2   1   1   1   2   1   1   1

Cat No 110:6   110:7
Total   1   1

Total number of examples: 14

31. main sign(s):130.136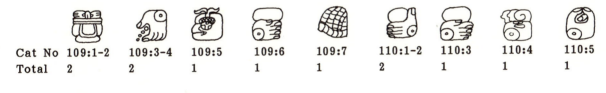

Cat No 111:1-6
Total   6

Total number of examples: 6

32. main sign(s):130.116

In combination, T130 (*wa*) and T116 (*ni*) produce the suffix -*wan*, which is reconstructed as the completive suffix for positionals in proto-Cholan (Kaufman and Norman n.d.). It should be noted that this affix is particularly prominent on the T644 "seating" glyph, a positional verb, and that it is found in complementary distribution with -*lah* (T178.181) in the Classic inscriptions.

Cat No	112:1-31	113:1-2	113:3-4 113:6	113:5	113:6	113:7	113:8	114:1 114:3	114:2
Total	31	2	3	1	1	1	1	2	1

Cat No	114:4-5
Total	2

Total number of examples: 45

33. main sign(s):130.18

Cat No	115:1	115:2
Total	1	1

Total number of examples: 2

34. main sign(s):126

In some of these examples, T126 may function as a Anterior Event Indicator, but a number of them are posterior events and therefore should not apppear with an AEI.

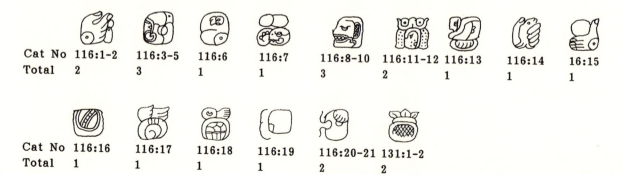

Cat No	116:1-2	116:3-5	116:6	116:7	116:8-10	116:11-12	116:13	116:14	16:15
Total	2	3	1	1	3	2	1	1	1

Cat No	116:16	116:17	116:18	116:19	116:20-21	131:1-2
Total	1	1	1	1	2	2

Total number of examples: 24

35. main sign(s):126.116

Cat No 117:1-2   117:3-4
        117:5-7
Total   5   2

Total number of examples: 7

36. main sign(s): 24(or 82).126

Cat No 118:1   118:2-3   118:4
Total   1   2   1

Total number of examples: 4

37. main sign(s):24   T24 is possibly a -vl suffix.

Cat No 119:1-6 120:1 120:2 120:3-5 120:6 120:7 120:8
Total   6   1   1   3   1   1   1

Total number of examples: 14

38. main sign(s):140

Cat No 121:1 121:2 121:3 121:4 121:5 121:6 121:7 121:8 121:9
Total   1   1   1   1   1   1   1   1   1

Total number of examples: 9

39. main sign(s):178   T178 is phonetic -la.

Cat No 122:1 122:2 122:3 122:4
Total   1   1   1   1

Total number of examples: 4

40. main sign(s):17(or 575)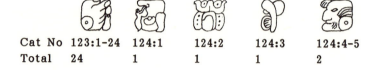

Cat No 123:1-24   124:1   124:2   124:3   124:4-5
Total   24   1   1   1   2

Total number of examples: 29

41. main sign(s):117

Cat No 125:1-6   126:1   126:2,6   126:3   126:4   126:5
Total   6   1   2   1   1   1

Total number of examples: 12

42. main sign(s).23 or 4

T23 and T4 are both phonetic *na*, but in this context, both signs may record an *-an* or *-vn* suffix.

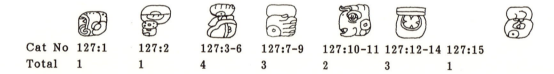

Cat No 127:1   127:2   127:3-6   127:7-9   127:10-11   127:12-14   127:15
Total   1   1   4   3   2   3   1

Total number of examples: 15

43. main sign(s).116

T116 appears as a phonetic complement on glyphs, such as *kin* and *muan*, which end in *-n*. Since T116 is quite possibly the Classic equivalent of Landa's *n* sign, it most likely has the phonetic value *-n* or *-n(i)*.

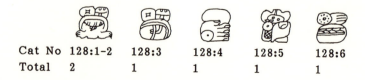

Cat No 128:1-2   128:3   128:4   128:5   128:6
Total   2   1   1   1   1

Total number of examples: 6

44. T126.main sign(s)

Cat No   18:8   129:7
Total   1   1

Total number of examples: 2

45. T126.main sign(s):136

Cat No   129:2   129:5   129:10
Total   1   1   1

Total number of examples: 3

46. T126.main sign(s):136.181

Cat No   129:3
Total   1

Total number of examples: 1

47. T126.main sign(s).181

Cat No   129:4
Total   1

Total number of examples: 1

48. T126.main sign(s):18

Cat No   129:9   129:11
Total   1   1

Total number of examples: 2

49. T228.main sign(s):misc.   T228 is phonetic *a* or *ah*.

Cat No   18:3   79:8   130:1-2   130:3   130:4-12   130:13-18
                   79:12

Total   1   2   2   1   9   6

Total number of examples: 21

The following affix patterns are found with verbs in the T712 "child of parent" and T606 "child of mother" expressions. See Charts 132 and 133.

50. T1.main sign(s)

+cm +cm +cm +cm +cm

Cat No   132:1-4   133:1-6   132:9   132:8   132:7   132:19
         132:6   133:8-11   132:15-17   132:10
         132:9
         132:11

Total   7   10   4   1   2   1

Total number of examples: 25

51. T1.main sign(s):136

Cat No 132:13
Total   1

Total number of examples: 1

52. T1.main sign(s):24?

Cat No 132:14
Total   1

Total number of examples: 1

53. main sign.181

54. 679.main sign

Cat No 133:7
Total   1

Cat No 132:18
Total   1

Total number of examples: 1

The following chart lists the frequency of occurrence of each affix pattern detected in the writing system. Numbers marked with parentheses may appear instead of the preceding number.

Pattern	zero	*.181	1.*	1.*:130	*:126.181	*:130.116
Total	390	231	225	68	48	45

Pattern	*:136(246)	*:178.181	1.*:24	*:17(575)	*:126	126.*:130
Total	44	41	29	29 or 60	24	23

Pattern	*.18	*130.181	*:136.126.181	*:23(4)	*:130	*:24
Total	22	19	18	15	14	14

Pattern	1.*:136	*.117	1.*:140	1.*.181(12)	*:140	228.*:178
Total	13	12	10	9	9	9

Pattern	*:126.18	*:178.18	1.*:18	*:126.116	89(115).*	*:24.181
Total	9	8	8	7	6	6

Pattern	1.*:82	*:130.126	*:116	228.*:126	*:23(4).181	1.*:106
Total	6	6	6	6	5	4

Pattern	*:18.181	*:24.126	*:178	1.*:23(4)	1.*:178.181	126.*:136
Total	4	4	4	3	3	3

Pattern	23(4).*:181	*:82.181	126.*	*:130.18	228.*:181	228.*:116
Total	2	2	2	2	2	2

Pattern	1.*:136.181	126.*:136:181	126.*:181	126.*:18	1.*:126	1.*:61
Total	1	1	1	1	1	1

Pattern	1.*:116	228:*	228.*:1	679.*
Total	1	1	1	1

Total number of examples in the sample: 1,478

The total number of examples for affix pattern *:17 (575) is listed as either 29 or 60 because I am not sure whether T575 should be considered as part of the main sign or as a verbal affix on the "wing-shell" death, "star-shell," and other expressions. If T575 functions as a verbal suffix in these expressions, the count for the *:17(575) should be 60, and the "zero" pattern should be reduced by 32.

The frequencies as they occur in this chart should be used with caution. For example, the pattern T126.*:130 appears primarily with one sign (T669b); if it is later determined that either T126 or T130 functions as part of the verbal stem, the frequency of this pattern will greatly change. However, it is interesting to note that the largest category is the "zero" pattern in which no affixes appears with the verb. The T1.*:∅ pattern is the third largest category, but if all the patterns with the T1 prefix are treated as one group, the resulting number (381) rivals the size of the "zero" category. Since the T1 prefix is indicative of transitive, imperfective intransitive(?), and stative constructions, the high number of examples of this pattern reflects the frequent use of these constructions in the writing system.

The second largest category is that which is suffixed by T181. It should be noted that to some degree the presence of T181 seems to exclude the T1 prefix, but I have found eight examples (including some dubious ones) which appear to violate this pattern of exclusion.

Two patterns (*:130.116 and *:178.181) can be associated with positional verbs in the writing system and with linguistic affix patterns on positional verbs in spoken Mayan languages. These two affix patterns are documented in 85 examples. Finally, the "birth" verb (T741) seems to be particularly associated with the affix pattern *:126.181 (or *.181:126); it occurs in a total of 48 examples.

Appendix 2

Verbs and Affix Patterns According to T-Numbers

Since the verb catalog is organized according to affix patterns, rather than by Thompson numbers, it is difficult to compare all of the examples of any one verb contained in the catalog. The list included in this appendix is designed to provide an entry in the verb catalog through T-numbers, and to allow comparative analysis of the kinds of affix patterns that appear with any one verb or verbal phrase. The list is organized into major categories by the T-number of the main sign of a verbal glyph, but since a particular sign can appear in more than one verbal glyph, and since not all people can manipulate T-numbers with ease, a generalized drawing of each verb and its affix patterns is included. Furthermore, the use of T-numbers is restricted throughout this publication because they require the elimination of distinct differences that may be important, and a great many signs simply are not listed in the Thompson catalog or cannot be distinguished by its use. For example, T501 must be used for *naab* "waterlily" or "lake"; for the day sign Imix; and for the phonetic sign *ba/ma*.

The Thompson system also causes difficulties in the transcription of affix patterns because there are many graphically distinct signs that can stand for the third person singular pronoun of the ergative set (Set A). At present, it is not possible to determine if these signs are phonetically equivalent, but they are surely semantically equivalent. All of them are illustrated under T1, the most frequently occurring of

these pronominal signs. Other affixes can appear in more than one graphic configuration without change in value; for example, the T181 suffix can appear in suppressed form as a postfix or in full form as a subfix (listed as T180) without change in meaning. And most interestingly. the head of a rabbit, a skull, or the face of the young moon goddess can appear in the center of the "lunar" glyph as a pictorial pun, without affecting its function as a verbal suffix. The suffix *-lah* can appear in all of the following graphic configurations without change in value:

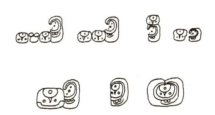

For information on the precise configuration of each individual example, consult the verb catalog (Chapter 9), where each is accurately illustrated.

The entries in this appendix are organized to record not only the inflectional patterns with which each verb occurs, but also complex patterns of syntax. The first line includes a generalized drawing of each verbal main sign with complex construction marked as follows:

*+cm   signals that the listed verb is followed by a complement.

*+ti   signals that the listed verb is followed by a *ti* + verbal noun construction.

The second line includes a generalized drawing of each affix pattern with which the verb may occur. If it occurs without affixes "zero" is recorded, and other complex constructions are marked as follows:

vb+*   signals that the recorded examples follow another verb.

aux+*   signals that the recorded examples follow an auxiliary verb.

ti+*   signals that the recorded examples occur as a verbal noun within an auxiliary verb + *ti* construction.

The third line records the catalog designations of all occurrences of the verb and affix pattern, and the fourth line lists the total number of occurrences. If the verbal glyph includes more than one sign, it is recorded under both signs, so a single verb may be recorded in more than one location.

T21

zero	zero		
12:1	19:1-11	59:7	73:2-3
12:3-4	118:3		73:7-8
12:6-11			73:11
9	12	1	5

102:2	106:1-2
	106:8-10
1	5

Other occurrences: 5:9-10, 24:1

T23

 aux+*

aux+*

17:6	95:2-15	37:21
	95:18	
1	15	1

Other occurrences: 21:26

T41

 aux+*

46:1-2	57:2-3	39:2,4
2	2	2

Other occurrences: 3:20, 46:3, 131:2

T44

zero	vb+*	zero	
3:10	5:8	21:6	31:10-14
1	1	1	5

ti+*		
79:3	131:2	32:10-11
1	1	2

Other occurrences: 16:3

T45

zero	zero	
11:7	26:20	121:7
1	1	1

Other occurrences: 90:1

T57

132:7
1

132:10
1

132:12
1

T59

70:8
1

T68

31:15
44:1-7
44:10-11
10

69:1-11

11

103:1

1

131:2-3

2

76:5
1

82:13
1

82:19
1

86:7
1

T74

zero

3:13
1

zero

5:6
1

70:8
1

82:3
1

T77

zero

25:1-12
25:15-18
16

116:17

1

zero

20:11

1

zero

25:13

1

zero

26:15
1

T78

zero

21:3
1

82:20
1

T79

zero

23:2
1

49:2

1

82:8

1

87:1-2

2

94:6

1

114:1
114:3
2

128:6

1

116:18
23:2

1

87:3-11

9

zero

26:1-2
26:15
3

114:2

1

114:4
114:5
2

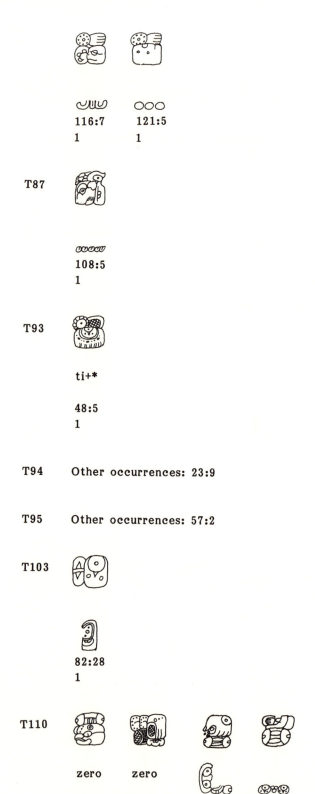

116:7   121:5
1   1

T87

108:5
1

T93

ti+*

48:5
1

T94   Other occurrences: 23:9

T95   Other occurrences: 57:2

T103

82:28
1

T110

zero   zero

5:14   21:6   43:12,19   122:6
1   1   43:14-16   1
                6

Other occurrences: 21:3, 82:18,
110:2, 116:15

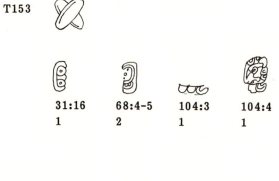

T121

aux+*

52:3-4
2

T148

82:10
1

T151

zero

5:9-10   70:4
2   1

Other occurrences: 23:9, 39:3, 46:1

T153

31:16   68:4-5   104:3   104:4
1   2   1   1

T173

zero   vb+*

3:3-4   43:17   66:1-2   109:1-2
                  55:5
                  66:7-8
2   1   5   2

         zero   zero   zero

13:7   21:1   21:16   24:10
1   1   1   1

vb+*   ti+*

45:8   38:6
1   1

Other occurrences: 40:2, 67:1

T173var

66:3-7
66:9
6

T174

zero   zero

5:2   26:6   80:4   80:5
         26:10?   80:6
1   2   2   1

vb+*   vb+*   vb+*

33:1-2   33:7   87:1
129:3   113:7-8
                  116:7
3   1   4

Other occurrences: 13:5

T177

82:5
1

T182

zero   ti+*

21:7   38:5
1   1

T187

vb+*

3:14   32:12-13   33:4   121:6
1   2   1   1

Other occurrences: 13:9, 16:3-6,
16:11, 60:3-4, 69:3, 76:3, 84:3,
103:5, 114:1, 131:1, 131:3

T200

82:24-
25
3

T203

82:10
1

T207var

zero   zero

16:1   16:2   40:5   108:4
16:3-11   23:7
23:8   23:10
11   3   1   1

zero

19:1-11   59:7   102:2   106:1-2
            73:2-3   106:8-9
            72:7-8   4
11   5   1

T218

zero

1:1-5   42:1-5   59:2   59:3
5   5   1   1

67:1-7   96:1   103:2   123:1-24
7   1   1   24

116:1-2   79:5
2   1

Other occurrences: 15:2, 37:19

T221

zero

20:7   58:1   81:6   127:3-6
127:14
2   1   1   4

T226

ti+*

70:3
1

79:13
1

T257

78:1
1

Other occurrences: 10:3-4, 10:17, 11:2, 12:2, 12:5, 12:9, 75:9, 81:4, 82:18, 116:11, 124:2

T266

zero

12:1-11
11

Other occurrences: 46:3, 55:5

T280

zero   ti+*

5:7   38:6
1   1

T281

ti+*   ti+*

18:3   79:10
1   1

Other occurrences: 84:4, 131:1, 131:3

T294

33:3   59:8   92:6
1   1   1

Other occurrences: 70:6

T333

zero

14:1-3 14:4   75:3-6 107:6-
54:1-2   75:8   10
                75:10

3   1   6   5

110:6   122:6
1   1

T348

82:6

1

T356

82:11

1

T358   Other occurrences: 75:2

T361

zero

75:1   75:2

1   1

T367   Other occurrences: 98:2-3

T501   *+cm   *+cm   *+cm   *+cm

zero

3:9   35:4   59:1   37:22
16:3   132:22
2   1   1   2

*+ti   *+cm   T333+

38:24?   21:10   68:4   14:1
38:25
132:8
2   1   1   1

T333+

54:1-2   40:13   zero   77:1-4
                    3:12
                    3:15
                    43:21
2   1   3   4

ti+*   vb+*   *+ti

38:24   3:12   34:1-17   35:5
          11:1   74:13
          116:19
1   3   18   1

113:8   ti+*   ti+*

          38:6   38:26   40:4
1   1   1   1

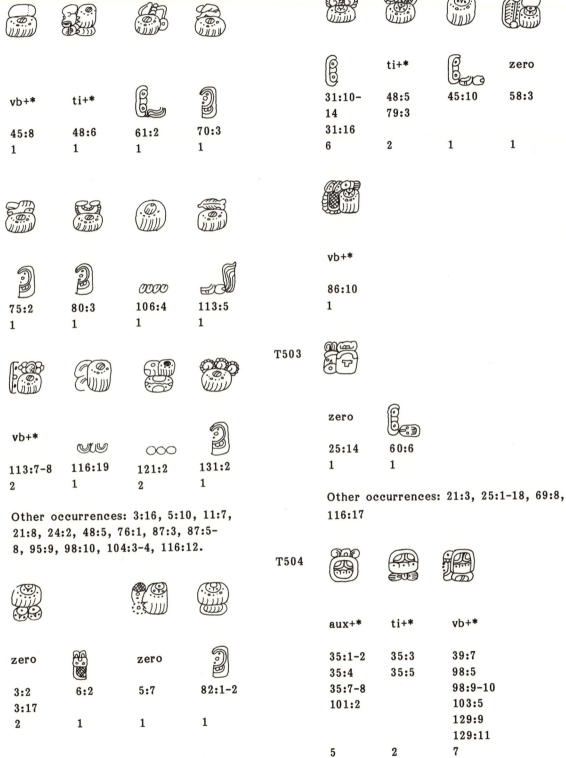

vb+*

45:8
1

ti+*

48:6
1

61:2
1

70:3
1

75:2
1

80:3
1

106:4
1

113:5
1

vb+*

113:7-8
2

116:19
1

121:2
2

131:2
1

Other occurrences: 3:16, 5:10, 11:7, 21:8, 24:2, 48:5, 76:1, 87:3, 87:5-8, 95:9, 98:10, 104:3-4, 116:12.

T502

zero

3:2
3:17
2

6:2
1

zero

5:7
1

82:1-2
1

31:10-14
31:16
6

ti+*

48:5
79:3
2

45:10
1

zero

58:3
1

vb+*

86:10
1

T503

zero

25:14
1

60:6
1

Other occurrences: 21:3, 25:1-18, 69:8, 116:17

T504

aux+*

35:1-2
35:4
35:7-8
101:2

5

ti+*

35:3
35:5

2

vb+*

39:7
98:5
98:9-10
103:5
129:9
129:11

7

T506

	vb+*
40:8	106:4
	123:11
1	2

T507

vb+*	zero		ti+*
3:2	21:10	122:1	53:4
	21:26		
1	2	1	1

vb+*
120:3
1

T509H

50:3
1

T510b
510af

zero	zero		
10:8-9	10:15	10:1	10:19
10:12		21:16	
10:14			
10:16			
10:20			
10:21-23			
10:25			
9	1	2	1

zero			zero
10:4-7	10:17	10:18	10:2-3
10:11			10:13
10:24			
6	1	2	3

zero	vb+*	vb+*	
10:10	21:16	22:27	107:1
1	1	1	1

star

116:11	121:1	124:2
116:12		
2	1	1

T510d

aux+*   vb+*

37:18   43:21
1   1

Other occurrences: 114:3, 128:6

T511

vb+*

75:3   79:16   98:2-3   126:3
1   1   2   1

T513

*+vb   *+ti   *+cm   *+cm
        zero   zero

5:11   3:2   3:8   126:2
        3:18   107:10   126:6
        21:8
1   3   2   2

Other occurrences: 69:3, 103:5, 131:1, 131:3

Note: ADI and PDI glyphs (which may well be verbal) are not included in the catalog.

T515

zero

20:7   58:1   81:6   127:3-6
127:14
2   1   1   4

zero

26:7   61:4   74:1-29   101:5-6
26:25   74:32-38
                  74:40-43
2   1   42   2

107:2-5   116:13   74:30   ti+*
                     74:31   79:6
4   1   2   1

96:2   49:1   zero
                21:28
1   1   1

Other occurrences: 21:26, 40:5, 113:6

T516   *+ti   *+ti

        zero   ti+*

        18:1-6   38:11   79:1-16   79:8
                  38:15   79:12
                  38:22-25
                  38:27-28
                  48:3
        6   7   16   2

T518

zero   ti+*

9:14   38:1   110:7   113:1-2
            38:19   129:9
1   2   2   2

117:3-4   120:1   130:1   128:3
                                     130:2
2   1   1   2

Other occurrences: 12:4, 13:1, 33:9,
37:5, 45:2, 99:4, 100:8, 112:14

T520

ti+*   zero   zero   zero

18:1   21:11   23:1   38:17
1   1   1   1

ti+*

38:27   59:12   73:10   84:3
1   1   1   1

84:5   90:2   101:3-4   121:2
1   1   2   1

vb+*

103:5
1

T526

zero

10:4-7   59:10   86:3-4   32:1-4
10:11
10:18
10:24
7   1   2   4

Other occurrences: 21:14, 26:3,
75:9, 86:5, 107:1

T528

zero   ti+*   zero

21:16   21:4   79:7   21:26
            82:21
1   2   1   1

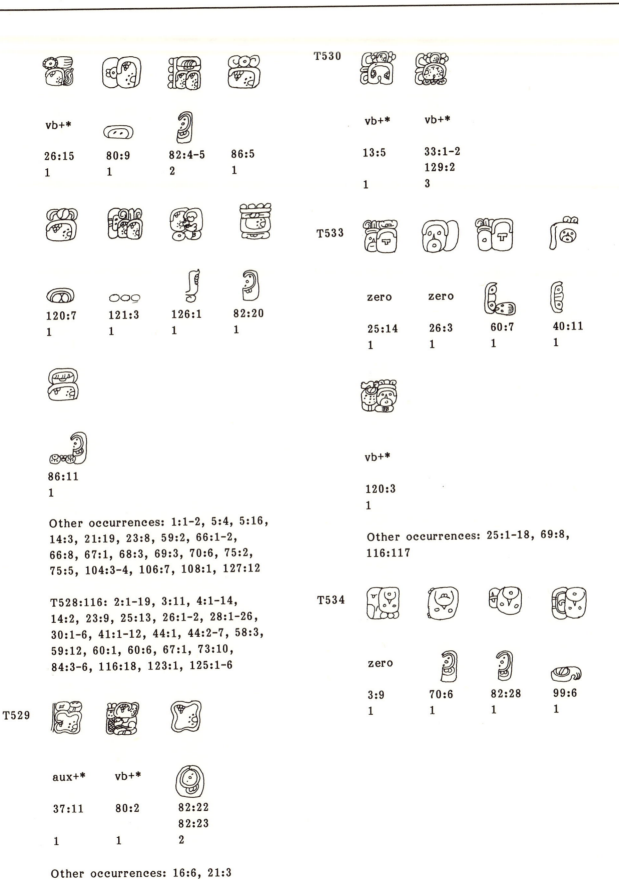

vb+*

26:15   80:9   82:4-5   86:5
1   1   2   1

120:7   121:3   126:1   82:20
1   1   1   1

86:11
1

Other occurrences: 1:1-2, 5:4, 5:16,
14:3, 21:19, 23:8, 59:2, 66:1-2,
66:8, 67:1, 68:3, 69:3, 70:6, 75:2,
75:5, 104:3-4, 106:7, 108:1, 127:12

T528:116: 2:1-19, 3:11, 4:1-14,
14:2, 23:9, 25:13, 26:1-2, 28:1-26,
30:1-6, 41:1-12, 44:1, 44:2-7, 58:3,
59:12, 60:1, 60:6, 67:1, 73:10,
84:3-6, 116:18, 123:1, 125:1-6

T529

aux+*   vb+*
37:11   80:2   82:22
                82:23
1   1   2

Other occurrences: 16:6, 21:3

T530

vb+*   vb+*
13:5   33:1-2
        129:2
1   3

T533

zero   zero
25:14   26:3   60:7   40:11
1   1   1   1

vb+*
120:3
1

Other occurrences: 25:1-18, 69:8,
116:117

T534

zero
3:9   70:6   82:28   99:6
1   1   1   1

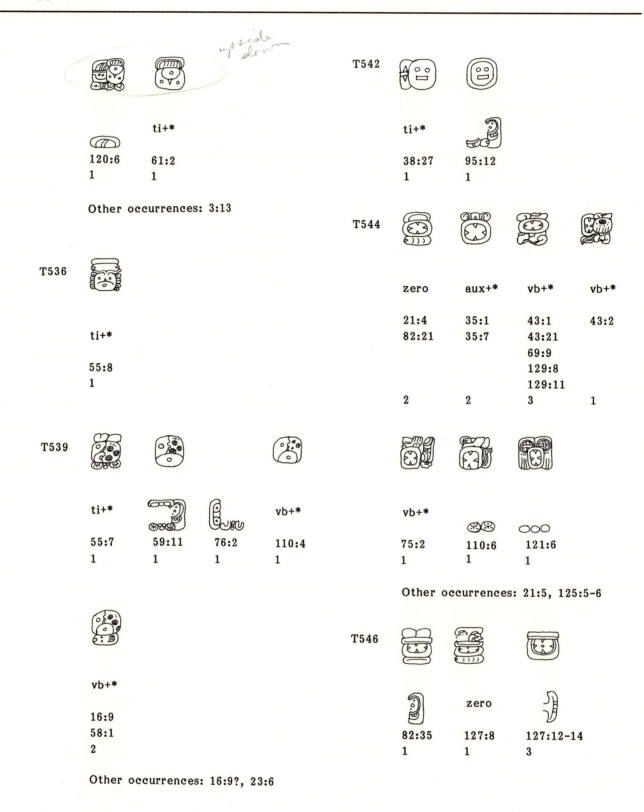

upside down

ti+*

120:6   61:2
1   1

Other occurrences: 3:13

T536

ti+*

55:8
1

T539

ti+*   vb+*

55:7   59:11   76:2   110:4
1   1   1   1

vb+*

16:9
58:1
2

Other occurrences: 16:9?, 23:6

T542

ti+*

38:27   95:12
1   1

T544

zero   aux+*   vb+*   vb+*

21:4   35:1   43:1   43:2
82:21   35:7   43:21
                  69:9
                  129:8
                  129:11
2   2   3   1

vb+*

75:2   110:6   121:6
1   1   1

Other occurrences: 21:5, 125:5-6

T546

82:35   zero   127:12-14

         127:8
1   1   3

T548

zero

6:1
1

82:27
1

103:6
1

T550

zero

21:13-15
3

82:32-33
2

T552

ti+*

48:3
1

zero

48:4
1

T554

aux+*

57:1
1

75:9
1

T556   Other occurrences: 32:13

T559var

66:9
1

68:1-2
2

98:4
1

103:7?
1

T561

aux+*

17:1

1

vb+*

20:1
38:17

2

ti+*

38:14

1

ti+*

38:17
79:9
79:14
3

vb+*

75:9

1

vb+*

80:1
118:4

2

82:18

1

aux+*

37:19

1

Other occurrences: 5:9, 10:7, 21:3,
23:9, 39:1, 39:3, 46:1, 57:1, 76:1,
87:3, 87:3, 87:6, 87:8. 98:3-4,
104:3-4

T561inv

10:4
75:7
1

vb+*

23:2

1

zero

23:2-6
23:11
5

T563

zero

3:10

1

zero

16:1
16:3-10
23:8
10

zero

16:2

1

zero

26:13

1

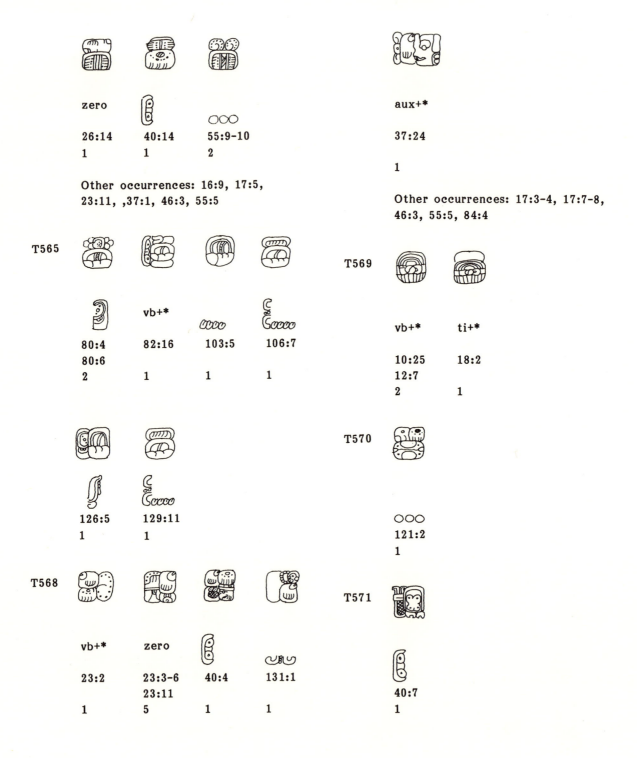

zero

26:14
1

40:14
1

55:9-10
2

Other occurrences: 16:9, 17:5, 23:11, ,37:1, 46:3, 55:5

aux+*

37:24

1

Other occurrences: 17:3-4, 17:7-8, 46:3, 55:5, 84:4

T565

80:4
80:6
2

vb+*

82:16
1

103:5
1

106:7
1

T569

vb+*

10:25
12:7
2

ti+*

18:2

1

126:5
1

129:11
1

T570

121:2
1

T568

vb+*

23:2
1

zero

23:3-6
23:11
5

40:4
1

131:1
1

T571

40:7
1

T573

59:4-5   70:7   120:8   32:17
2   1   1

123:1-23
23

Other occurrences: 96:1, 114:1

T575

T578

zero

5:8   10:8-9   10:1   10:17
       10:12
       10:14
       10:16
       10:20-23
       10:25
1   10   1   1

73:5-6   26:24
2   1

T580

zero   zero   zero   vb+*

3:9   9:5   20:3   33:5
          132:15-17
1   3   1   1

zero   zero

10:19   121:2   12:1   25:1-13
                  12:3-4   25:15-18
                  12:6-11
1   1   9   17

aux+*   ti+*   vb+*   *+cm

52:6-9   53:3?   76:2   132:5
77:4?
132:14
5   1   1   1

vb+*

116:17   99:6   109:6   108:2-3
1   1   1   2

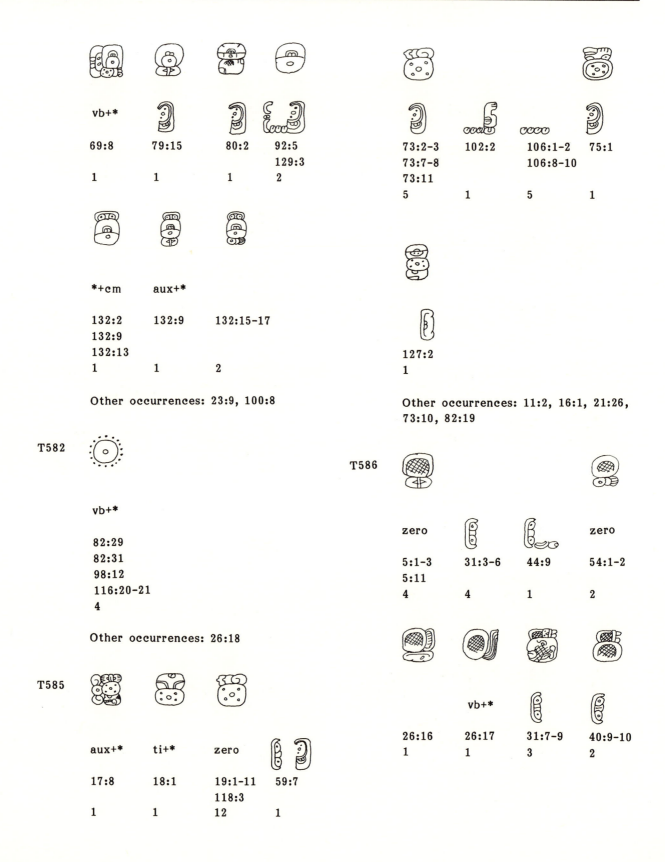

vb+*

69:8   79:15   80:2   92:5
                         129:3
1   1   1   2

+cm   aux+

132:2   132:9   132:15-17
132:9
132:13
1   1   2

Other occurrences: 23:9, 100:8

T582

vb+*

82:29
82:31
98:12
116:20-21
4

Other occurrences: 26:18

T585

aux+*   ti+*   zero

17:8   18:1   19:1-11   59:7
                 118:3
1   1   12   1

73:2-3   102:2   106:1-2   75:1
73:7-8   106:8-10
73:11
5   1   5   1

127:2
1

Other occurrences: 11:2, 16:1, 21:26,
73:10, 82:19

T586

zero   zero

5:1-3   31:3-6   44:9   54:1-2
5:11
4   4   1   2

vb+*

26:16   26:17   31:7-9   40:9-10
1   1   3   2

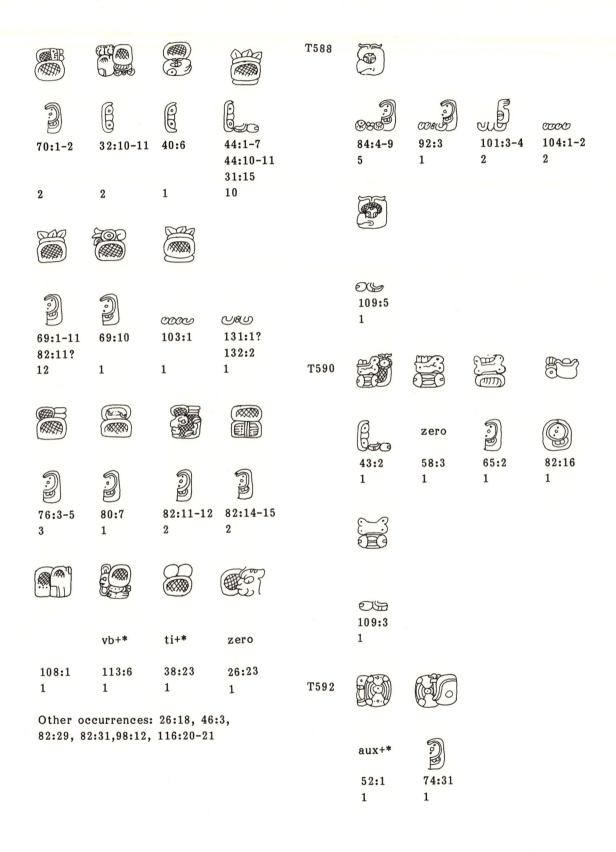

T588

70:1-2
2

32:10-11
2

40:6
1

44:1-7
44:10-11
31:15
10

84:4-9
5

92:3
1

101:3-4
2

104:1-2
2

109:5
1

69:1-11
82:11?
12

69:10
1

103:1
1

131:1?
132:2
1

T590

43:2
1

zero
58:3
1

65:2
1

82:16
1

109:3
1

76:3-5
3

80:7
1

82:11-12
2

82:14-15
2

T592

vb+*
108:1
1

113:6
1

ti+*
38:23
1

zero
26:23
1

aux+*
52:1
1

74:31
1

Other occurrences: 26:18, 46:3,
82:29, 82:31, 98:12, 116:20-21

T598 Other occurrences: 21:14, 21:15, 23:7, 75:9, 87:3, 87:5, 87:6, 87:8

T600

zero	aux+*	vb+*
9:3	37:13-14	55:1
1	2	1

T604

zero			vb+*
26:12	40:4	80:3	86:10
1	1	1	1

T606

82:6	121:2
1	1

Other occurrences: 21:6, 21:16, 133:1-13

T609

96:3
1

Other occurrences: 9:6, 32:8-9, 48:6

T610

vb+*

17:2-4
3

Other occurrences: 16:3?, 127:10-11

T614

zero			
23:2	49:2	82:8	87:1-2
1	1	1	2

	ti+*		
27:5	48:1	63:1	82:9
1	1	1	1

94:6	114:1	116:18	128:6
	114:3		
1	2	1	1

ti+*

79:5
1

Other occurrences: 16:5, 16:10,
23:1, 23:8-10, 32:13, 87:4, 92:7,
113:6, 26:3, 127:12-13

T617

45:9	58:3	59:9	72:1
			72:5-7
1	1	1	4

= became lord

86:1	109:5	99:5	vb+*
			116:18
1	1	1	1

129:2	116:16	130:4	130:5
			130:8
1	1	1	2

130:6	94:6
130:9-11	
4	1

T624

vb+T1.*	vb+*
10:3-4	11:2
10:17	75:7
12:2	81:4
12:5	82:18
12:9	
12:11	
116:11	
124:2	
7	4

Other occurrences: 46:3, 75:9

T626

82:3
1

T628

zero	zero	
20:12	21:3	82:20
1	1	1

T630

ti+*   vb+*

38:17   58:3
79:14
2   1

T639

zero

3:16
1

T644

zero   zero

4:1-18   30:1-6   9:2   32:6-9
                    9:6
                    9:13
18   6   3   4

85:1-11   92:1-2   97:1   99:4
11   2   1   1

100:1-8   112:1-31 115:1   116:6
8   31   1   1

116:19   118:2-3   122:2   126:3
1   1   1   1

92:7   121:9
4   1

Other occurrences: 75:2?

T645

                        vb+*

98:10   127:14
129:8
2   1

T646

aux+*   vb+*

57:2-3   84:3
2   1

T653

23:9
27:1
2

T669

aux+*

17:7	26:4-5	32:10-11	45:9 50:4
1	2	2	2

aux+*

57:1	62:1-21 129:1	70:4	80:2
1	22	1	1

81:1

1

Other occurrences: 26:12, 46:3, 106:3

T670

ti+*   zero

5:12	20:8-9	27:4	33:5 33:7
1	2	1	2

ti+*

38:8-10	45:2 45:11-12 45:14-15	110:1	110:2
3	5	1	1

zero

116:15	129:6-7	121:4	20:14 87:10
1	2	1	2

33:6	45:13	55:1	122:3
1	1	1	1

zero   zero

126:4	20:10	20:13	33:8
1	1	1	1

vb+*

33:9	55:2	72:11	75:9
1	1	1	1

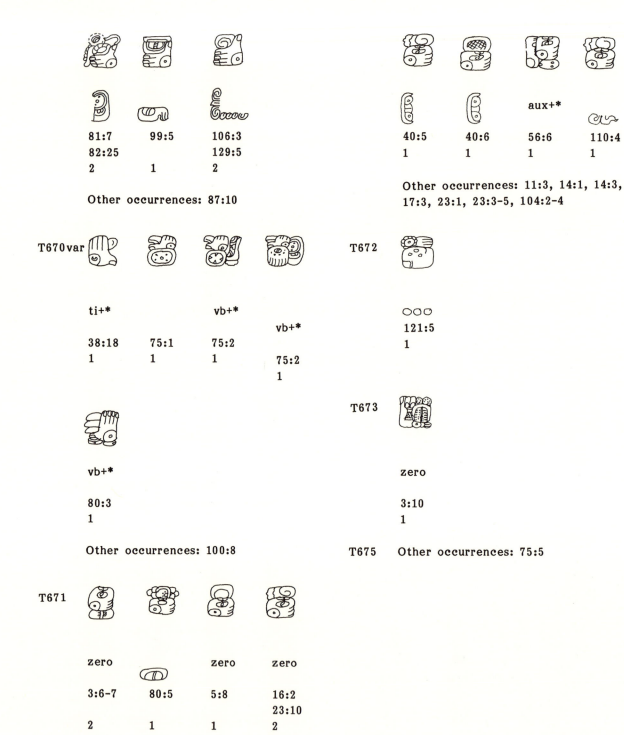

81:7	99:5	106:3
82:25		129:5
2	1	2

Other occurrences: 87:10

40:5	40:6	aux+*	110:4
1	1	1	1

Other occurrences: 11:3, 14:1, 14:3, 17:3, 23:1, 23:3-5, 104:2-4

T670var

	ti+*		vb+*	vb+*
	38:18	75:1	75:2	75:2
	1	1	1	1

T672

121:5
1

vb+*

80:3
1

Other occurrences: 100:8

T673

zero

3:10
1

T671

zero		zero	zero
3:6-7	80:5	5:8	16:2
			23:10
2	1	1	2

T675 Other occurrences: 75:5

T678

vb+*

45:3-7   109:7   110:1
5   1   1

T679

zero

3:6-7   56:4   81:2?   81:5
2   1   1   1

82:4-5   120:6   82:13   87:3
                   129:4
2   1   2   1

vb+*

62:19-20   82:27
2   1

Other occurrences: 3:6

T683

ti+*   ti+*

38:15   38:20?   113:7?   126:5
79:9
79:14
3   1   1   1

T684

           aux+*

zero   ti+*

7:1-13   37:4   45:1   48:6
40:3   53:1
14   1   1   1

63:2   71:1-23   99:3   102:1
1   23   1   1

106:11
1

T685

zero   zero

21:17-18   21:19
2   1

T694

vb+*

116:15
1

T700

zero   ti+*

9:7-12   38:28   117:1   128:1-2
          48:2   117:5-7
          79:4
5   3   4   2

130:3
117:2
2

T705

zero

20:2
1

T710

zero   aux+*   zero   zero

3:1-2   3:8   20:11   3:1
3:8-9
3:12-15
3:19
48:6
76:3
11   1   1   1

29:1-13   ti+*
           38:2   43:1-21   47:1-5
           38:29
13   2   21   5

59:2   56:1   61:1   61:3
           56:7
1   2   1   1

65:1-3   98:1   109:3-4   111:1-4
           98:13
3   2   2   4

T711

T712

zero

3:20
1

vb+*

3:21
20:21
35:4
35:6
37:12
37:22
37:25
37:27
132:1-4
132:8-9
132:11-14
132:18
19

aux+*

35:2
38:28
55:5-6
132:15
132:16
132:17
132:19
7

ti+*

35:5
39:7
98:5
98:6
132:10
5

vb+*

39:3
1

40:3
1

vb+*

75:9
1

76:7
1

vb+*

98:9
1

aux+*

101:2
1

128:5
1

T713a

zero

2:1-19
19

28:1-25
25

41:1-12
12

50:1
1

60:1
60:5
2

64:1
1

64:2
1

125:1-6
6

aux+*

zero

8:1-18
18

37:20
1

60:3-4
2

37:20
72:1-10
11

127:7
127:9
2

56:5
1

59:6
1

106:5-6
2

110:3
1

58:3
1

59:9
1

72:1
72:6-7
3

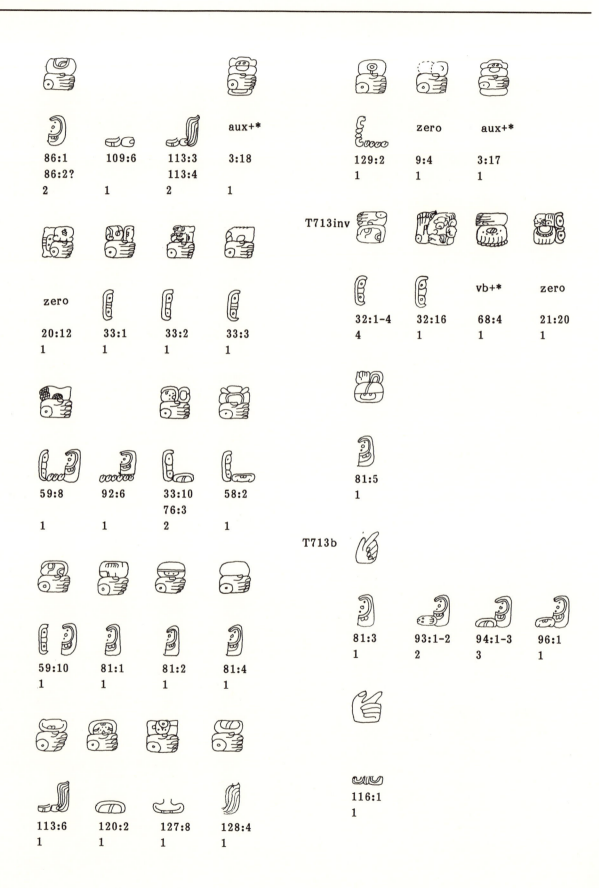

aux+*

86:1   109:6   113:3   3:18
86:2?   113:4
2   1   2   1

129:2   zero   aux+*
1   9:4   3:17
          1   1

zero

20:12   33:1   33:2   33:3
1   1   1   1

T713inv

32:1-4   32:16   vb+*   zero
4   1   68:4   21:20
                   1   1

59:8   92:6   33:10   58:2
1   1   76:3   1
                   2

81:5
1

59:10   81:1   81:2   81:4
1   1   1   1

T713b

81:3   93:1-2   94:1-3   96:1
1   2   3   1

113:6   120:2   127:8   128:4
1   1   1   1

116:1
1

T714

zero | aux+* | ti+*
15:1-6 | 37:26 | 38:12 | 39:1-7
6 | 1 | 1 | 7

46:1-4 | 55:3 | 76:1-2 | 94:4
4 | 1 | 2 | 1

96:5 | 116:14
1 | 1

T736

zero | | | zero
24:3-10 | 40:1 | 116:9-10 | 24:11
8 | 1 | 2 | 1

zero | | zero
24:12 | 116:8 | 21:27?
1 | 1 | 1

T738

80:3
1

T740

zero
20:5 | 33:1 | 73:1 | 88:1-17
20:15 | | 73:9
| | 73:12
2 | 1 | 3 | 17

89:1-25 | 91:1-13 | 94:7 | 95:1
25 | 13 | 1 | 1

97:2 | 98:14 | 101:1 | 105:1-8
| 99:1-2
1 | 3 | 1 | 8

116:3-5 | 118:1 | 119:1-6 | 127:1
3 | 1 | 6 | 1

ti+*

38:22
1

Other occurrences: 75:2, 127:12

T741a

zero   zero   vb+*

4:10   12:2   27:3   33:5
         12:5
1   2   1   1

113:8   116:7   21:23-24 26:25
                            zero
1   1   2   1

T741b

*+ti

3:5
5:12
2

T743

zero   aux+*

5:6   108:2-3 37:8   82:30
                  52:5   82:31
1   2   2   2

                 vb+*

108:6   126:3

1   1

Other occurrences: 10:14, 131:1-3

T744a

127:10   127:11   zero
(17:2)   (17:4)   26:11-12
1   1   2

Other occurrences: 3:2

T744b

ti+*

79:13
1

T746

zero

26:23
1

Other occurrences: 69:9, 76:1?

T747a

zero   vb+*

21:1   40:6   94:5
1   1   1

Other occurrences: 65:1, 67:2

T747b

zero

9:1
1

Other occurrences: 40:3

T751

vb+*

80:4-5   82:17
2   1

T756

aux+*   ti+*   vb+*   aux+*

124:4-5   38:11   23:1   37:23
            79:11-12
2   3   1   1

Other occurrences: 21:26, 60:2, 89:6, 127:13

T756c

aux+*   zero

17:4-6   22:1-55
17:8-9
22:56-59
37:24
10   55

Other occurrences: 84:4

T756inv   *upside down*

zero

5:5   64:3-4   124:1
5:13
2   2   1

T757   *rabbit*

T333+   T333+   T333+   zero

14:2   75:10   107:6   20:3
14:4   107:7
                        107:9
                        107:10
2   1   4   1

zero	zero		
20:6	26:19	36:1-16 132:14 133:1-6 133:8-11	51:1-9
1	1	27	9

55:4	56:3-4	78:3-4 133:7	92:4
1	2	3	1

	*+cm	*+cm	*+cm
	zero		
112:30	3:21	132:18	35:1-2 35:6-8 37:1-26 132:1-4 132:6 132:9 132:11-13
1	1	1	40

*+cm	*+cm	*+cm	*+cm
45:12	52:1-9 132:14	56:6	57:1-4
1	10	1	4

*+cm	*+cm	*+ti	*+ti
101:2	107:8	35:1 35:3 38:1-16 38:18-29	48:1-3 48:5-6
1	1	30	5

ti+*	ti+*		
		ti+*	vb+*
53:1-4	55:5-8	78:2	27:4 129:7
4	4	1	2

vb+*			vb+*
113:5	126:2 126:7	78:1	56:4
1	2	1	1

Other occurrences: 8:1-18, 9:4, 37:20, 60:3-4, 72:1-10, 188:2, 127:9

T758

zero	vb+*		zero
5:4	20:2	90:1 90:3	108:5
1	1	2	1

Other occurrences: 14:1, 21:17, 43:3, 43:11-14, 65:2

T759

vb+*	ti+*		
21:20	57:2-3	36:14	83:1-2
1	2	1	2

82:7
1

Other occurrences: 12:3, 21:18, 113:3

T764

aux+*	aux+*	vb+*	vb+*
17:8	21:20	38:14	76:2
	52:7-9		
	57:2-3		
1	6	1	1

T765d

74:39
1

T767

32:14-15
2

Other occurrences: 76:1?, 110:2

aux+*

52:2
1

Other occurrences: 21:8. 26:13, 67:1, 68:3, 69:3, 76:4, 84:5, 87:3, 87:6-8

T765

T807

zero		vb+*	ti+*
10:4	27:2	80:7	38:4
20:1	80:2		
20:4			
21:5			
21:22			
37:13-15?			
75:7			
9	2	1	1

ti+*		
3:5	31:1-2	44:8
1	2	1

T814

vb+*

109:6
1

T819

*+vb

zero   zero

20:6   53:3   64:5   82:29
26:18
53:3
3   1   1   1

82:30   84:1   59:1   5:6
82:31   98:5-6   98:7
                  98:8-9
2   1   5   2

84:2   98:11-12 103:3-4 116:20-21
1   1   2   2

3:19
1

Other occurrences: 16:3?

T834

zero

21:6
1

T843

zero   zero

13:1-5   13:6   82:20
13:7-9
8   1   1

T854

vb+*   zero

23:2   23:2-6   10:4
                  75:7
1   5   2

T1000a

vb+*   ti+*

9:4   38:7   45:8   80:1
1   1   1   1

95:9
95:14
95:18
3

Other occurrences: 17:8, 38:5, 94:3

T1001

ti+*

38:5
1

Other occurrences: 94:3

T1006

aux+*

52:3-4   82:24-26
2   3

T1010

aux+*

37:9
1

Other occurrences: 17:2, 21:5

T1011

32:16   130:12-18
1   7

Other occurrences: 46:3

T1014

*+cm		aux+*+cm
17:1-8		37:24
127:10		17:9
127:11		
10	2	2

124:4-5

T1016

zero

3:11
1

T1019

vb+*

21:27
1

T1030

ti+*	vb+*	zero	zero
18:6	39:5-6	54:1-2	108:4
	46:4		
1	3	2	1

zero			
20:14	33:6	45:13	55:1
1	1	1	1

122:3	126:4
1	1

Other occurrences: 20:8, 55:3, 57:1, 75:2, 76:1-2, 94:4

T1030o   Other occurrences: 112:9-10, 112:12, 129:2

T1032

vb+*	ti+*	aux+*
21:20	38:13-14	52:7-9
1	2	3

T1040

ti+*		vb+*	
18:3	32:12	45:8	5:14
18:5?	50:3		
2	1	1	1

Other occurrences: 20:10, 46:3, 48:6

T1041

zero		
24:1-2	120:3	120:4-5
40:6		
3	1	2

Other occurrences: 60:2, 95:6-7

T1045

95:16-17
2

T1073

ti+*	
18:4	132:5
1	1

T1082

vb+*

21:11
1

Other occurrences: 11:4

The following examples include main signs not listed in Thompson's (1962) *Catalog of Maya Hieroglyphs.*

zero

3:9
1

vb+*

56:2
1

vb+*

9:1
1

aux+*

37:5-6
2

zero

9:3
1

zero

11:1-7
7

99:7-8
2

27:6
1

40:13
1

zero

21:9
1

zero

21:12
1

32:5
1

vb+*

99:6
1

23:9
1

132:5
1

vb+*

26:4-5

2

vb+*

39:3
46:1
2

40:4

1

vb+*

45:2

1

vb+*

59:2

1

70:5
1

98:2-3
2

103:7
1

Appendix 3

Catalog Summary According to Site and Monument Designation

AGUAS CALIENTES
Stela 1
  B2   84:1

AGUATECA
Stela 1
  A2   43:6
  A5   40:11
  A7   56:2
  D1   47:4
Stela 2
  A2   10:12
  B12   71:6
  D1-C2   54:2
  E2   95:11
  G13   29:2
Stela 3
  C3   47:2
Stela 5
  A9   105:11
  C2-D2   103:2
  C5   47:1
  D4-E1   79:3
Stela 7
  G1-H1   22:36
  I1-I4   22:37

ALTAR DE SACRIFICIOS
Panel 4
  pC6-pD6   10:18
  B6-A7   25:15
  C6   133:1
Stela 4
  A8   106:1
  A10-B10   81:4
  D5-C6   132:1
Stela 5
  C3-C4   13:3

Stela 12
  A1-A2   37:19

ALTUN HA
Earplug   40:9
Jade   59:9
     75:3

ARROYO DE PIEDRA
Stela 1
  C1-C2   22:35
Stela 3
  C1-D1   67:4
  C2-D2   68:3
  C3   109:4
  E2   120:8

BONAMPAK
Collection A
  C2-D3   23:1
  C8   2:2
  E3-F3   2:3
  F5   20:13
  F6   99:5
  F7   40:7
Collection B
  A3   95:1
  D2-C3   81:1
  E1   36:4
  F1   36:5
Collection C
  B1   36:7
Collection D
  D1   66:6
Lintel 1
  A3   74:22
Lintel 2
  A3   74:23

Lintel 3
  A3   74:24
Lintel 4
  A2-A4   12:9
  F1   22:28
Sculptured Panel 1
  B1   9:6
  C2b-D2a   21:14
Sculptured Panel 2
  A1+   22:27
Stela 1
  G2   41:5
  G3   29:5
  P1   22:29
  Q1   22:30
Stela 2
  C1-C2   71:15
  D5-D6   76:3
  D6   3:14
  E6   33:10
Stela 3
  A3-B3   29:7
Temple 1
Room 1
  P2a-Q2c   16:11
  S2-T2   38:19
  Text 42   38:23
Room 2
  Text 32   38:20
  Text 31   38:21
  Text 21   38:22

CALAKMUL
Stela 43   6:1
  B9-B10   82:19
  A8   130:5
Stela 51
  G1   22:41
  G3   22:42

Stela 2		
C1	22:38	
D1	22:39	
LACANJA		
Lintel 1		
C1	41:2	
C6–D6	132:8	
L3–K4	100:7	
LA MAR		
Stela 1		
A2–A3	37:20	
E1	22:40	
Stela 2		
A1	36:13	
D1	51:9	
Stela 3		
A6	14:3	
B2–A3	72:9	
B2	41:8	
B11	116:13	
C1	74:25	
LA PASADITA		
Lintel 1		
A3	74:20	
Lintel 2		
A1–A2	48:5	
A3	43:8	
LOS HIGOS		
Stela 1		
D1–D4	121:9	
D5	44:11	
D6	37:25	
MACHAQUILA		
Stela 2		
B2	60:5	
Stela 3		
A2	127:9	
F3b	50:1	
Stela 4		
A2a	3:4	
Stela 5		
A3–A4	40:8	
Stela 6		
A2	60:1	
B1b	132:15	
Stela 7		
C1	45:10	

D1–D2	28:18	
E5b	20:6	
Stela 11		
A4b	44:1	
A6	132:7	
B5a	133:6	
MOTUL DE SAN JOSE		
Stela 2		
A8–A9	71:22	
C5	28:22	
D6–C7	123:21	
NAH TUNICH		
Group I		
a B2	26:16	
a G5	116:19	
a H4	82:28	
Group II		
a A4	121:7	
Group IV		
b A3–A5	26:18	
b B1	82:30	
b B1–D1	82:31	
d A3–A5	116:20	
e A3–A5	116:21	
f A3–A5	82:29	
h A3–A5	98:2	
i A3	26:17	
j A1	3:17	
l A1	26:19	
m A3	26:20	
Group VI		
a A2–B2	26:21	
a E1	26:22	
b A3–A5	26:23	
b B1	82:30	
e B1–D1	82:31	
e J1	40:13	
NARANJO		
Altar 1		
F1	26:1	
F11–G12	26:2	
H1–H2	21:3	
H5	28:2	
H7	28:3	
H9	28:4	
I10–H11	42:5	
K6–K7	1:2	
Hieroglyphic Stairs		
B1	10:3	
N1b	10:2	

Stela 1		
E12	117:3	
F6–E7	2:11	
Stela 2		
A1–A2	38:7	
Stela 6		
A3	71:16	
Stela 8		
E7–F8	132:14	
Stela 10		
A2	89:21	
A8	28:17	
Stela 12		
B2	89:20	
H1	22:34	
Stela 13		
A3–A4	2:15	
A5–A7	35:7	
E10	2:16	
G1	133:9	
Stela 14		
A3	28:16	
D9–C10	71:17	
G1	22:33	
Stela 19		
A2–B2	29:6	
A8–A10	35:8	
C4	36:16	
I1–J1	37:23	
Stela 20		
A3–A4	53:1	
Stela 21		
A3–A5	48:1	
E10	2:14	
E10	128:3	
Stela 22		
B13	89:6	
E10	130:2	
E16	11:1	
F14	12:6	
F18–E19	11:2	
H1–G2	12:7	
G12–H12	11:3	
H14	11:4	
G20–H20	2:12	
Stela 23		
E9–E10	11:5	
F18	82:14	
G9	128:4	
G18	123:10	
G19	2:4	
G21–G22	129:11	

E7	88:7	C5	118:1	P11-O12	62:19
E13	105:1	C9-D9	39:4	R2	31:3
E17	105:2	C13-D14	120:3	R4	62:7
F7-E8	8:5	F7-E4	8:4	R10-Q11	112:14
I1-K1	21:17	E5-E6	45:9	R12	28:15
K10	5:14	E6	50:4	S2-S3	4:17
M3-N1	72:3	G9	122:3	S9-S10	30:4
O4	8:15	L2-M3	23:4	S10	62:9
O5-O6	23:3	M6-L8	17:2	T5	70:1
O12	56:5	M13	59:6	T7	31:5
O9-O11	46:1	M10-M13	39:3	**Middle Panel**	
P1-Q1	8:6	M14-L14	21:8	A1-B1	30:5
P5	88:8	N7-N8	100:4	A9	70:2
P7	91:2	N8-O8	23:5	B4	86:3
Q7-P8	8:7	O2-P3	8:3	B5	86:4
P11	91:3	O12	82:6	C3	108:2
P13	91:4	O16	87:9	C5	62:10
Q15-P16	8:8	**Alfardas**		C6	45:3
S4	91:5	A2	32:3	C8	62:11
R6-S6	8:9	G1	81:6	D1	31:6
S9	91:6	K2-L2	87:6	D9	109:7
S11-R12	8:10	**Censor**		F1	62:12
R16-S16	8:11	A6-A7	113:8	F2	45:4
T3-U3	8:12	**Door Jamb Panels**		F4-E5	33:1
T13	105:5	A6a	104:2	F9-F10	30:6
T16	105:6	A7b	127:6	F12	117:4
T17-U17	8:13	B11	4:2	H2	108:3
U2	105:3	B12	87:7	H9	70:3
U7	91:7	**Temple of Inscriptions**		I2-I3	129:2
U9	105:4	**East Panel**		I4	62:13
U9	116:5 Alfarda	Various	129:1	I8	31:7
A2	32:2	A7	62:1	I9	45:6
G1	127:4	A11-B11	112:9	J10	62:14
K2-L2	87:5	D10	62:2	K3	62:15
Censor 1 (DO Cat 281)		E11	62:3	K7	31:8
E2	12:12	G8	28:11	K8	45:5
H2	4:15	G6-H6	112:10	L9	62:16
G4	73:11	I8-J8	112:11	M3	31:9
H7-G8	25:17	J6	62:4	M4	45:7
J2	89:24	K7	62:5	**West Panel**	
J7-I8	113:7	L3-K4	112:12	A7-B7	44:8
Censor 2 (DO Cat 282)		L5	28:12	A10-B10	3:6
C3	89:25	L10-K11	112:13	A11-B12	3:5
106:10	106:10	M1	28:13	B3-A4	33:2
Door Jamb Panel		M3-N4	70:4	B9	4:11
A3	127:5	M12-N12	115:1	C2	4:12
West Sanctuary Panel		N3	4:16	C3	31:1
B1	27:2	O2	28:14	C8-D8	31:2
D1	110:5	O4	62:6	D2	3:7
Tablet of the Foliated Cross		O7	31:4	E2	91:8
B14	90:3	Q4-Q5	62:18	E4-F5	8:1
B16	88:9	O7	62:8	E9	4:18

F12	113:1				Temple 18		
F12	117:4	Tablet of the Slaves			Jambs		
G6	55:8	A4a	105:6		B13	116:4	
G10	55:9	A5	72:4		B17	59:8	
H2	113:2	B1a	128:1		C7	99:2	
K9a	3:11	B2	32:6		C11	130:3	
K9b	119:1	C2	8:16		C11	117:2	
K12	119:2	C9a	32:7		D6	128:2	
O6	119:3	D3	110:6		D17	3:2	
O9	106:4	E1a	74:17		Stucco		
O11-P11	106:3	F3	122:4		pC2-pD2	25:3	
O11-P11	129:5	F5b	108:5		pJ1	113:5	
R4-Q5	17:7	G4b-H4a	127:8		e1	70:7	
R8-Q9	118:2	G5a	1:3		g1	70:8	
Q9-R10	25:1	H5b	127:1		Palenque Bodega Numbers		
Q11	106:2	J3a	4:5		404	113:5	
S6a	19:11	Tablet of the Sun			409	55:2	
S9-T9	8:2	A14	101:4		411	4:13	
S11a	62:17	B16	130:10		420	92:5	
S12a	32:12	C1	88:10		420	129:3	
S12b	50:3	C9-D9	98:2		425	20:10	
T7-S8	118:3	C9-D9	98:2		431	126:2	
Sarcophagus		C10	119:5		435	33:4	
3	97:2	C11-D11	132:4		435	120:2	
6	30:1	D17-N2	104:4		437	40:2	
7	19:1	E2-F2	21:18		439	86:5	
13	116:7	I1-J1	12:4		443	20:3	
17a	19:2	N5-O5	23:6		444	40:4	
19a	19:3	L2-M2	8:14		449	8:17	
21a	19:4	O8-N10	17:3		449	126:6	
24a	30:2	O8-N10	127:11		462	73:7	
26a	19:5	O13	46:2		464	5:13	
29a	19:6	N14-N15	87:8		471	73:6	
33	19:7	P3-Q3	113:3		472	3:13	
39	19:8	P4	21:6		478	129:4	
45a	30:3	P7	113:4		478	82:13	
47a	19:9	P8-Q8	21:5		483	21:10	
50a	19:10	P13	88:11		485	73:8	
Tablet of the 96 Glyphs		Q13	82:7		500	24:2	
A2	124:1	P16-Q16	12:3		501	88:16	
B5-B6	23:8	Alfardas			510	26:6	
D4-C5a	85:8	A2	32:4		446	95:8	
D5	32:8	G1	21:7		Fernandez 44		
E4	49:1	Temple 14				96:2	
F3	85:9	A2-B2	5:12		Throne 1		
G4	32:9	A6	82:4		G1	3:10	
H2	85:10	B2	121:4		D1	5:9	
H6	123:15	A10	21:9		E1	5:10	
J6	133:10	B10-A10	87:10		L1	5:11	
K6-L6	103:6	B8	45:11		N1b	4:14	
L4	22:32	C6-D6	23:7		Palenque region: fragment		
K2	123:16	D4	20:8			73:10	
		F2	82:5				

PIEDRAS NEGRAS						
Altar 1		Stela 1		Stela 13		
L2	31:17	B3	91:9	Front		
K2	1:5	F2	82:2	Panel a	22:7	
Altar 2		G5	95:2	Panel b	22:8	
A2	89:14	G10–G11	38:6	Stela 14		
E2	71:7	K15	45:15	B11	71:8	
G3	41:3	Stela 3		Panel a	22:19	
Altar 4		A8	89:8	Panel b	22:20	
J3	123:13	D3b	95:3	Panel c	22:21	
Burial 5, shell		D6	89:9	Panel d	22:22	
B1	89:23	E3	33:5	Panel e	22:23	
E1	99:1	F4a	123:7	Panel f	22:24	
E3	82:1	F9	123:8	Stela 15		
I2	95:4	Stela 6		C5	71:14	
L2a	95:15	A18	28:24	Front		
Lintel 2		Front		Panel c	22:9	
H1–G2	110:1	Panel a	22:2	Back		
M1–N1	39:2	Panel b	22:3	Panel a	22:10	
O2–P2	116:15	Panel c	22:4	Stela 16		
W4–X4	110:2	Panel d	22:5	C5	71:10	
K'1–L'1	7:4	Stela 7		Stela 23		
Lintel 3		B10a	105:8	I8–J8	23:11	
F2–H1	68:1	C3	25:18	Stela 25		
J1–I2	99:6	Stela 8		A15	7:2	
M1–N1	79:13	A9	89:3	I8a	7:13	
P1–O2	61:2	B19	82:3	I12	7:3	
U2–V2	25:10	E1	95:5	Stela 30		
V5	73:5	F2	59:7	pA5	123:22	
X1–X3	21:26	G3–H3	71:5	Stela 35		
X7–Y7	21:27	M5–N5	123:23	B12a	10:22	
A'1–Z2	7:10	Stela 9		Stela 36		
A'5–Z6	26:28	C11–C12	123:12	B8	7:5	
A'6	21:25	Stela 11		C5	88:4	
Lintel 4		E7	71:18	Stela 37		
M2	106:8	F5a	98:14	C7	10:23	
O3	82:35	Left	22:6	Stela 39		
Frame Panel a	22:1	Stela 12		D2	28:23	
Lintel 8		A17	107:5	Stela 40		
Y17–X18	13:9	B12	28:25	A14	98:13	
Lintel 12		B21	20:15	B17	29:11	
D1–F1	116:18	D1a	10:24	C15	56:7	
I1	110:7	Right	41:7	Throne 1		
I1	129:9	Panel a	22:13	H1–I1	82:32	
L1–N1	127:14	Panel b	22:14	Q1	89:19	
N1	20:7	Panel c	22:15	Z2	126.5	
Q1	36:10	Panel h	22:16	Z5–Z6	106:7	
S1	36:11	Panel j	22:17	Z5–Z6	129:10	
U1	36:12	Panel k	22:18	A'1b	21:26	
V1–V2	38:1	Panel l	22:54	B'1b–C'1	13:7	
		Panel m	22:55	D'1	21:15	

E'3–F'1	21:16		Monument K			E1	130:11
F'4–F'6	82:33		A7a	84:8		F4–F6	72:7
G'3	71:19		B11	84:5		G1	130:13
K'3–K'5	127:12		Monument O			H3	107:9
Panel a	22:11		Y2–Z2	9:13		H5	129:12
Panel b	22:12		Stela A			Structure 1	
			B16	29:9		Central	
POCO UINIC			Stela C			Door	43:15
Stela 3			A10	44:5		West Door	43:16
A18–B18	112:27		B6	68:4		Corner	123:17
B21	121:6		B7–A8a	44:4		Zoomorph O	
			C7–D7a	44:6		M1	110:3
POMONA			C13	43:10		Y2–Z2	9:13
Stela Fragment 4:6			Base			Zoomorph P	
Fragment 12?			G1	82:22		C4b–C5a	43:11
pA2–pA3	98:4		Stela D				
Hieroglyphic Panel 1			East			**RESBALON**	
pA3–B3	109:3		A22d	98:8		Hieroglyphic Stairs 1	
Panel X			B17	69:9		A16–A17	121:8
pB2	64:3		B18	43:13		Hieroglyphic Stairs 3	
pB3	4:7		B22a	73:12		B10	71:23
pB4–pC2	52:8		West				
pD3	41:6		A23b–A23c	43:14		**RIO AMARILLO**	
Panel Y			B17	123:14		Altar 1	
pA2	103:3		Stela E			M2–P2	17:9
pA3	122:1		East			M2–P2	37:24
pB3	4:8		A9	69:8			
pC1	4:9		A14a	108:6		**RIO AZUL**	
pD1	103:4		A16	60:2		Tomb	
pD2	103:1		B12b	107:10		A9	97:3
Wall Panel			B19	43:9			
pE1	66:9		West			**SACCHANA**	
pG1	4:10		A8	33:6		Stela 2	
pH1	43:7		A20	56:8		C1–D2	58:3
pI1	41:4		B12b	107:10			
pJ1–pL1	52:7		B17	69:9		**SACUL**	
pL5	68:2		B17b	98:1		Stela 1	
			Stela F			A5	29:3
PUSILHA			East			A8	20:11
Stela D			C9–C9a	65:2		B10	20:9
D11–D12	26:13		C11b	44:10		C3	86:7
D13	12:11		C14	101:7		Stela 6	
F12–E13	26:14		C17b–C18	14:2		A3	119:6
F14	82:27		West				
H10–H12	21:21		A12b	75:10		**SAN DIEGO CLIFT**	
Stela E			B6	126:4		A4–B4	3:21
C10	132:6		B15a	5:4			
D3	133:5		A16b	66:7		**SEIBAL**	
			Stela J			Stela 7	
QUIRIGUA			A14	44:2		A4–A5	53:3
Monument L			B13	50:5		B2	7:11
A2–A3	15:2		C4–C5	21:20			

Stela 8		H4–H5	6:2	Stela 21		
A2	41:10	H1	32:5	B10–A11	85:7	
Stela 9		MT 39a–b	12:8	B11	111:1	
B2b–C1	53:4	MT 40		Stela 22		
C2	33:8	A12–A15	34:9	B2	2:9	
Stela 10		MT 42a–b		B11–B12	100:6	
A3	43:18	A2–A4	34:5	B12	111:2	
		A5–A7	34:6	Stela 23		
SIMOJOVEL		A8–A10	34:7	B4	88:1	
Shell		A11–A12	34:8	Stela 24		
B1	90:2	MT 43	34:4	yA16	91:11	
B9	127:15	MT 44	34:4	Stela 27		
		MT 51a–b	21:12	D2	28:1	
TAMARINDITO			34:3	Stela 31		
Hieroglyphic Stairs		MT 180	34:11	A12	130:4	
A2	40:12	MT 181	34:10	A13–B13	66:1	
		Stela 1		C10–D10	42:1	
TIKAL		B5	123:3	C19	116:16	
Altar 5		Stela 3		C20	123:2	
3–4	20:2	A8–B8	42:4	D2	21:1	
12	116:9	Stela 4		D9	125:1	
15–18	80:3	C4–B5	37:4	D15	125:2	
26	82:15	C4–B5	71:1	D15–C16	42:2	
29	93:2	Stela 5		D23	75:2	
Altar 8		D5	36:8	D27	82:8	
A1	36:9	Stela 7		E6–E7	13:1	
Column Altar 1		A7	123:4	E10–F10	9:1	
A1–A2	35:6	B2	36:3	E17	125:3	
Leiden Plaque		Stela 8		E18–F18	42:3	
B9	97:1	A1–A2	37:10	F24	66:8	
MT 28a		A6	123:5	G28	75:1	
A3	24:3	Stela 9		H7–G8	66:2	
A3	116:10	A1	116:1	H8	72:10	
A16	24:4	B1–B2	37:8	H15	1:1	
A24	24:5	B1–B2	52:5	H26	123:1	
MT 28b		Stela 10		I1–J1	37:5	
A3	24:6	C11	76:7	M1–N1	37:6	
A8	24:7	Stela 12		Structure 5D-57		
A25	24:8	B4	2:18	C2	95:14	
MT 29	11:6	D2	82:11	Temple 1		
MT 30a	21:11	Stela 13		Lintel 3		
A3	24:9	B1–B2	37:7	A4–B4	12:5	
A10	24:10	Stela 15		B2	121:3	
MT 31	37:14	B2–B5	37:9	C2–D2	80:4	
MT 32	15:3	Stela 16		C3–C4	39:7	
MT 33	15:4	A3	123:9	F9–E10	100:5	
MT 34	37:15	B1	2:19	E12–F12	80:5	
MT 35	37:13	Stela 19		F4	132:16	
MT 36	15:5	A12	123:19	Temple 4		
MT 38a–b		B13	111:3	Lintel 2		
C1	10:11	Stela 20		B8	10:15	
		A4	2:10	B9–A11	107:1	

B10–B11	95:16	M113 E	122:2	E4–F5	112:3
C1–D1	80:8	M	61:1	E6–F6	21:4
Lintel 3		N–O	87:1	E6–F6	82:21
A2	3:3	M122A3	10:10	E11	130:18
B4	20:4	Pestac		F11	21:23
B5	95:17	Stela	91:10	F16–E17	132:2
D4	10:14			J2	21:24
D5–D6	80:7			P2	1:4
E3	38:17	**TORTUGUERO**		Sarcophagus	
E5–F5	52:4	Box		M	133:2
E8–F8a	80:6	B2	64:2	36	74:1
G2–H2	79:7	C2–D2	5:6	38	75:6
G5	78:3	C2–D2	98:7	43	10:7
G5	133:7	F2	102:2	44	74:2
G8	132:17	H2–I1	112:5	63–64	112:4
H3	87:11	L2–M1	112:6		
Temple of Inscriptions		N1	130:9	**UAXACTUN**	
D14	2:8	O1–P1	112:7	Murals	
I'3–J'3	16:7	R2–S1	112:8	A1+	36:1
		M'2–M'3	87:4	C1–C2	37:2
TONINA		Earplugs		Stela 7	
F33 pB–pC	25:13	a F–H	23:2	pC2	89:22
F34 pB3–pB4	71:2	b C–D	10:5	C7?	89:24
F35 B–D	96:1	I	10:6	Stela 13	
F37 pA2	86:2	Monument 1		A4	84:2
F43 pB	107:2	A2b	28:10	**UCANAL**	
F43b	92:2	A3b	130:7	Stela 4	
F71	73:9	A3c–A3d	59:12	A2	28:20
F92 C2–D2	16:9	A4a–A4b	112:28	B2	43:20
M7 L	58:2	A4c	130:8		
H	47:5	Monument 6		**XULTUN**	
M20 pC4	91:12	A6	130:14	Stela 3	
M30 A4–A6	84:6	A7–B8	112:1	A4a	20:5
M69 D1	25:16	A10	21:22	A4b	28:19
N1	27:6	A10–B10	75:7	Stela 5	
MNAH Disk		A10–A11	10:4	E1–E1	38:3
	25:11	A13	130:15	Stela 9	
B1	86:8	B5	88:14	E1–E2	37:12
M74 A3–A4	84:5	B14	75:4	Stela 15	
M84 pD	107:3	B16	130:16	C1–D1	37:16
M91	10:17	C1–D1	75:5	Stela 16	
pA–pB	124:2	C4–D4	116:11	A1–B1	37:17
M95		C6–C7	82:20	Stela 19	
M95 D1–E1	84:4	D2	130:17	A1–B1	37:11
M104G	47:3	D9	112:29		
M110K	43:5	D7–C8	60:6	**YAXCHILAN**	
P–Q	98:10	D10–C11	112:2	Collection 13	
P–Q	129:8	D11–D12	26:4	C5B–D5	86:10
M111S	43:4	C17–D17	26:5	Collection Lintel	
K	66:4	E2–F2	121:2	C1–D1	37:21
O	92:1				

Lintel 1			Lintel 21			Lintel 39	
B2–C1a	38:9		A7b–B7	127:13		A2–B2	39:5
C1b–D1	18:5		C6	86:6		A4	51:1
E1–F1	38:14		Lintel 23			Lintel 40	
Lintel 2			B2b–C3	103:7		A2–B2	39:6
C1–E1	64:4		M5b–M6a	16:4		Lintel 41	
F1–H1	38:11		E2–G1	113:6		A2–B2	10:16
K1–L1	79:11		Lintel 24			C1	74:19
Lintel 3			B1a–D1	55:5		C3	34:16
C2a–D2	18:4		G1	55:6		Lintel 42	
D1b–C1a	38:10		H1–H2	17:5		C1–B2	38:8
Lintel 5			H1–H4	22:56		C2–C3	18:3
B2–C2	79:12		Lintel 25			Lintel 43	
Lintel 6			B1–E1	46:3		B2	48:4
B1–B2	48:3		G1a	51:2		Lintel 44	
Lintel 7			O2–Q1	17:4		A3	74:14
B1–C1	79:8		O2–Q1	22:57		Lintel 45	
Lintel 8			O2–Q1	124:4		A2b	34:14
A3	74:18		Lintel 26			B1b	74:15
B1	32:14		D1–F1	17:6		C6	32:11
E1	34:17		H2–J2	16:3		D1	22:25
Lintel 10			O1–P1	124:5		Lintel 46	
A2b–B2	129:6		O3–R1	22:58		F3	74:16
A4a	10:20		S1–U2	48:6		F6	34:15
B7	74:27		T1b–U2	3:16		F8	32:10
C1–D1a	27:4		Lintel 27			Lintel 46	
D4	133:11		A2–B2	25:6		F3	74:16
D6	132:13		F2	25:7		F6	34:15
D8b–E1a	110:4		Lintel 28			F8	32:10
F5	129:7		S1b–T1	25:8		F9	61:4
Lintel 13			W1–X1	16:6		H1	22:26
A3	89:15		Lintel 30			Lintel 47	
C1–D1	38:12		E3	92:3		A4–B4	85:1
E1–E2	38:13		H4	71:9		Lintel 49	
Lintel 14			Lintel 31			B3	9:7
A1	51:4		H1	89:16		B7	9:8
D2–E2	76:1		J4	16:2		D4	9:9
E4	59:11		J5–K1	126:3		Lintel 52	
G1–G2	52:6		K5	5:5		A2–C1	80:9
Lintel 15			Lintel 32			Lintel 53	
A2–G1	76:2		C1–E1	38:28		B2–C1	79:4
C1	51:5		Lintel 33			E1–F1	48:2
F2–G3	15:6		C1–E1	38:15		Lintel 54	
Lintel 16			Lintel 35			A2–B2	79:10
A2a	26:7		B2	9:12		Lintel 56	
Lintel 17			Lintel 37			H1–J2	16:5
A1–A2	53:2		B1	9:10		Lintel 59	
A4–B4	77:4		B7	9:11		L1–M1	25:9
C3	88:17		Lintel 38			Stela 1	
D1	51:6		A2–B2	55:3		B3	29:4

Stela 3
  pA1-pA3   67:2
Stela 5
  A2   74:26
  B2   32:15
Stela 6
  C7b-C8   67:6
Stela 7
  Secondary   82:16
  pC6   132:11
  pD8   132:12
Stela 10
  pA1   133:8
  pD2   132:10
Stela 11
  C4-E1   63:2
  C4-E1   71:20
  G3-F4a   132:9
  T1b-T2a   79:9
  A'1   51:10
  C'6   84:7
  C'11   7:6
Stela 12
  A2-B2   25:5
  C2-D2   112:19
  E1-F1   55:7
Stela 15
  A2   74:32
  A3   34:12
Stela 18
  A4   74:7
  A8-C5   75:9
  A9-A11   35:5
  C2-C3   57:1
Stela 19
  A3   74:8
  A8   34:12
Stela 20
  A3   74:6

Structure 20
  Hieroglyphic Stairs
  52   76:6
  58   74:36
  72   74:37
  94   74:38
  105   74:39
  115   74:40
  126   32:17
  137   74:41
  148   74:42
  160   74:43
  169   26:25
Structure 33, Step 7
  A1-B3   107:6
  E1-F1   107:8
  S1   96:4
  S2   13:6
  S3-T4   52:9
  U1   3:15
  C'1   3:12
Structure 44
  Central Upper
  A3-B3a   34:2
  C3   74:13
  C9b   107:4
  D10-C11   3:18
  D11-C13   72:6
  Central Lower
  B1-A2a   16:10
  A2a-B2   52:3
  E1   86:9
  Northwest Upper
  A2a   74:9
  C8b   74:33
  D4   74:34
  D7a   96:5

Northwest Lower
  A2a   74:10
Southeast Upper
  A2   101:6
  A5a   59:4
  D6b   74:11
  D1b   74:35
  D4c   59:5
Southeast Lower
  A2   74:12

YAXHA
Stela 31
  A2   74:28

Appendix 4

Summary of the Chronology of the Verbs

This appendix should be used with care because it is constructed as a summary only of the dates, actions, and actors noted within the verb catalog and does not, therefore, include verbs recorded without dates, with undecipherable dates, or dates with no surviving verbs. And because events and dates from badly eroded monuments, such as those of Uaxactun, and dates from monuments in the northern lowlands were not included in the verb catalog, the sample by its nature is biased. Furthermore, because the dates of dedication are not included in this appendix, it is not possible to determine whether Early Classic events are recorded on contemporary monuments or in later inscriptions without consulting the verb catalog. Nevertheless, this summary gives a potentially important overview of Maya history so far available in no other form.

Caution should be taken also concerning the number of times a particular event is recorded or the number of different events recorded on one date. Very often the multiple occurrences of verbs are the result of couplet constructions or redundancy within particular inscriptions. However, the number of times an event is recorded and the number of different sites that celebrated certain dates, particularly period endings, may reflect the importance of particular dates and events to the Maya who originally designed the inscriptions.

This appendix gives the following information: (1) Long Count dates arranged in chronological order; (2) location of each example in the catalog; (3) the site of each example; (4) description of the event; and (5) the actor. The descriptions of the events, where possible, include information as to meaning and terms designed to create immediate visual connection to the glyph; however, where glyphs are not describable, T-numbers are used. Some phonetic values are used; these are written in italics in order to contrast to those Mayan terms, such as "cauac," used only as nicknames, not readings. Those examples registered with "deleted" agents in the catalog appear in this appendix with the actor recorded when reconstruction is possible.

DATE	CAT NO	SITE	ACTION	ACTOR
12.19.11.13. 0	91:1	Pal	T740 birth	GI the First
12.19.13. 4. 0	88:6	Pal	T740 birth	Ancestral Goddess
	88:7	Pal	T740 birth	Ancestral Goddess
	88:15	Pal	T740 birth	Ancestral Goddess
13. 0. 0. 0. 0	33:3	Pal	deer hoof-T713	
	44:4	Quir	T586 end of tun	GIII and Aged Stingray God
	44:5	Quir	T586 end of tun	Black-Skull God
	68:4	Quir	T153 era event	
	68:5	Coba	T153 era event	

DATE	CAT NO	SITE	ACTION	ACTOR
	98:2	Pal	T561 era event	
	104:3-4	Pal	T153 era event	
	1:5	PN	T218 completion of 13 baktuns	
	31:17	PN	T153 era event	Paddlers
13. 0. 1. 9. 2	17:1	Pal	God N/6-Sky	GI the First
	20:1	Pal	*oc ta chaan*	GI the First
	32:13	Pal	God C-in-elbow	GI the First
	98:3	Pal	T561 era event	GI the First
13. 4.12. 3. 6	106:3	Pal	scroll-in-hand	GI the First
	106:4	Pal	T501.117.506	Ahpo-Skull
1. 6.14.11. 2	101:4	Pal	T520H 819 Day Count	God K
1.18. 4. 7. 1	90:3	Pal	T520 819 Day Count	God K
1.18. 5. 3. 2	32:1-2	Pal	birth (Caban variant)	GI
	119:4	Pal	T740 birth	GI
1.18. 5. 3. 6	32:4	Pal	birth (Caban variant)	GIII
	88:10	Pal	T740 birth	GIII
	119:5	Pal	T740 birth	GIII
1.18. 5. 4. 0	32:3	Pal	birth (Caban variant)	GII
	88:9	Pal	T740 birth	GII
	118:1	Pal	T740 birth	GII
	120:3	Pal	birth metaphor	GII
2. 0. 0. 0. 0	39:4	Pal	fish-in-hand	Ancestral Goddess
	67:3	Pal	T218 completion of 2 baktuns	Ancestral Goddess
2. 0. 0.14. 2	117:2	Pal	T700var accession	Ancestral Goddess
2. 1. 0.14. 2	8:5	Pal	T713 accession	Ancestral Goddess
5. 7.11. 8. 4	105:1-2	Pal	T740 birth	U-Kix-Chan
5. 8.17.15.17	9:6	Pal	T713 accession	U-Kix-Chan
8. 4.16. 7. 4?	3:20	Hau	T712 blood-letting	Bone-Deer
8. 6. 0. 0. 0	116:2	Cop	T218 completion of 6th katun	
8.14. 0. 0. 0	42:1	Tik	T218 completion of 14 katuns	Jaguar-Paw I
8.14. 0. 0. 0	125:1	Tik	T713 end of tun	
8.14. 3. 1.12	97:1	Tik?	seating (accession)	Bone-Head
8.15.16. 0. 5	26:5	Tort	*ka*/smoke-shield	
	121:2	Tort	Chuen count/T606-waterlily-bone	
8.17. 0. 0. 0	2:1	Cop	T713 end of tun	Hooded-Ahau
	42:2	Tik	T218 completion of 17th katun	????
	82:8	Tik	T78-house	????
	116:16	Tik	T617	
	125:2	Tik	T713 end of tun	
8.17. 1. 4.12	75:2	Tik	axe+????	Jaguar-Paw I
	123:2	Tik	T218+????	Jaguar-Paw I
8.17. 2.16.17	9:1	Tik	accession?	Curl-Snout
	37:4	Tik	aux+T684 inauguration	Curl-Snout
8.18. 0. 0. 0	42:3	Tik	T218 completion of 18 katuns	Curl-Snout
	125:3	Tik	T713 end of tun	7-Ek-Kan/Eccentric Cauac
8.18.10. 0. 0	66:8	Tik	half-period of 1 cycle	Curl-Snout
8.19. 1. 9.13	97:3	RAz	T740 birth	Cauac-Waterlily
8.19. 6. 8. 8	91:3	Pal	T740 birth	Ruler 3
	91:4	Pal	T740 birth	Ruler 3
8.19.10. 0. 0	66:2	Tik	half-period of 1 cycle	Stormy-Sky

DATE	CAT NO	SITE	ACTION	ACTOR
	72:10	Tik	T713 accession	Stormy-Sky
8.19.19.11.17	8:8	Pal	T713 accession	Ruler 3
9. 0. 0. 0. 0	1:1	Tik	T218 completion of 9 cycles	Stormy-Sky
	20:14	Cop	God K-in-hand	Yax-Macaw
	123:1	Tik	T218 completion of 9 cycles	Stormy-Sky
9. 0. 3. 9.18	75:1	Tik	axe-T585	Spear-Thrower-Cauac
9. 0.10. 0. 0	66:1	Tik	half-period of 1 cycle	Stormy-Sky
9. 0.11. 0. 0	39:1	Tik??	fish-in-hand	Chaan
	64:1	Tik??	T713 end of tun	????
9. 0.19. 2. 4	127:14	Yax	T546/4-bat/house	Moon-Skull
9. 1. 0. 0. 0	44:6	Quir	T586 end of tun	Maize Lord
9. 1. 4. 5. 0	91:5	Pal	T740 birth	Manik
9. 1.10. 0. 0	91:6	Pal	T740 birth	Chaacal I
	123:3	Tik	T218 completion of 2 katuns	Stormy-Sky
9. 2.12. 6.18	8:9	Pal	T713 accession	Manik
9. 2.13. 0. 0	42:4	Tik	T218 completion of 13th tun	Jaguar-Paw-Skull
9. 2.19.12.19?	37:8	Tik	aux+turtle	Kan-Chitam
9. 3. 0. 0. 0	2:2	Bon	T713 end of tun	
	20:13	Bon	flint-in-hand	
	28:1	Tik	T713 end of tun	Jaguar-Paw-Skull
	36:3	Tik	T757	Jaguar-Paw-Skull
	37:9	Tik	aux+????	Jaguar-Paw-Skull
	116:1	Tik	T218 completion of 3? katuns	
	123:4	Tik	T218 completion	
9. 3. 0.14.13	40:7	Bon	*tu*-bone	6-Fishfin
	99:5	Bon	mirror-in-hand	
9. 3. 1.15. 0	21:6	Pal	T44:110/606?	Kan-Xul I
	113:3	Pal	T617:713 heir-designation	Kan-Xul I
9. 3. 2. 0. 0	37:10	Tik	aux+????	Bird-Claw
	123:5	Tik	T218 completion	
9. 3. 3.16. 4	23:1	Bon	T671/bat/house	Kan-Batz'
9. 3. 6. 7.17	8:10	Pal	T713 accession	Chaacal I
	112:9	Pal	seating as T1030o	Chaacal I
9. 3. 9.13. 3	88:1	Tik	T740 birth	Lady of Tikal
9. 3.10. 0. 0	2:3	Bon	T713 end of tun	
9. 3.19. 3. 8	81:2	???	????:T713	Skull
9. 3.19.12.12	110:7	PN	T518 office taking	Kin-Ma-Cu-??
9. 4. 0. 0. 0	2:8	Tik	T713 end of tun	????
	6:1	Cal	end ("tun") of his katun	
	21:2	Car	tun-head?	GIII
	62:1	Pal	T669b of his cycle	Palenque Triad
	82:19	Cal	????	????
	116:18	PN	T79-house/tun	
9. 4. 1. 0. 5	116:15	PN	ahau-in-hand/T110??	Ahpo-Kin
9. 4. 3.10. 1	20:7	PN	T221:60:515	????
	127:14	PN	T122:546	local ruler
9. 4. 8.14. 9	81:1	Bon	T669:713+????	Kan-Chuen and Fishfin
9. 4. 9. 0. 4	91:7	Pal	T740 birth	Chaacal II
	105:3	Pal	T740 birth	Chaacal II
9. 4.10. 1. 5	105:4-5	Pal	T740 birth	Chan-Bahlum I

DATE	CAT NO	SITE	ACTION	ACTOR
	116:5	Pal	T740 birth	Chan-Bahlum I
9. 4.10. 4.17	19:2	Pal	T585 death	Chaacal I
9. 4.11. 8.16	85:1	Yax	seating *ta ah le*	Ta-??-Skull
9. 4.13. 0. 0	2:18	Tik	T713 end of tun	Curl-Head
	82:11	Tik	T586 end of	????
9. 4.14.10. 4	8:11	Pal	T713 accession	Kan-Xul I
9. 5. 0. 0. 0	62:2	Pal	T669b of his cycle	Palenque Triad
	125:4	Car	T713 end of tun	Nen-Oc
	123:22	PN	T218 completion of 5 katuns	????
9. 5.19. 1. 2	85:2	Car	seating as ????	Ruler 2
	85:3	Car	seating as ????	Ruler 2
	99:4	Car	seating as ahau-T518	Ruler 2
	130:1	Car	T168:518	Ruler 2
9. 5.19.12.18	15:1	Cop	fish-in-hand/flint-shield	????
9. 6. 0. 0. 0	28:2	Nar	T713 end of tun	
	28:5	Nar	T713 end of tun	
	28:8	Car	T713 end of tun	
	81:3	Car	T218	Ruler 2
9. 6.10. 0. 0	7:1	Cop	T684 inauguration	Waterlily-Jaguar
	62:3	Pal	T669b of his cycle	????
	84:3	Cop	PE special with T520	????
9. 6.10.14.15	101:6	Yax	T515 capture of Etz'nab	Knot-Eye-Jaguar
9. 6.11. 0.16	19:3	Pal	T585 death	Kan-Xul I
9. 6.11. 0.17	26:1-2	Nar	T79-tun	Ruler 1
9. 6.11. 5. 1	8:12	Pal	T713 accession	Chaacal II
	112:10	Pal	seating as T1030o	Chaacal II
9. 6.12. 4. 6	88:12	Car	T740 birth	Ruler 3
9. 6.13. 0. 0	28:11	Pal	T713 end of tun	
9. 6.15. 6. 4	75:3	Altun	axe	Chac-Pax
9. 6.16.10. 7	19:4	Pal	T585 death	Chaacal II
9. 6.18. 5.12	8:13	Pal	T713 accession	Chan-Bahlum I
	112:11	Pal	seating *ta ahpo le*	Chan-Bahlum I
9. 7. 0. 0. 0	4:1	Chin	seating of tun	
	28:3	Nar	T713 end of tun	
	28:6	Nar	T713 end of tun	
	28:9	Car	T713 end of tun	
	30:2	Pal	seating of tun	
	62:4	Pal	T669b of his cycle	Chan-Bahlum I
9. 7. 0. 1. 0	101:5	Chin	T515 capture of ??-Ah Kan	????
9. 7. 1. 2. 6	37:26	Cop	aux + T714 blood-letting	local ruler
9. 7. 1. 7. 6	73:1	Cop	T740 birth	local ruler
	37:26	Cop	aux+fish-in-hand	????
9. 7. 9. 9. 5	19:5	Pal	T585 death	Chan-Bahlum I
9. 7.10. 3. 8	112:12	Pal	seating as T1030o	Lady Kanal-Ikal
9. 7.10.11. 3	21:3	Nar	T78?:628	Ruler 1
9. 7.10.16. 8	94:1	Car	T713b hand	Ruler 3
9. 7.11. 2.17	59:9	Altun	T713 accession	local ruler
9. 7.14.10. 8	88:13	Car	T740 birth	Ruler 4
9. 7.19.13.12	128:5	Car	*yax*.93:712	Ruler 4
9. 8. 0. 0. 0	3:1	Car	scattering	Ruler 3

DATE	CAT NO	SITE	ACTION	ACTOR
	4:8	Pom	seating of tun	
	26:3	???	????	Kankin
	26:13	Pus	fire/*te'-tun*	local ruler
	26:14	Pus	fire/*te'-tun*	local ruler
	28:4	Nar	T713 end of tun	
	28:7	Nar	T713 end of tun	
	28:12	Pal	T713 end of tun	
	42:5	Nar	T218 completion of 8th katun	Ruler I
	62:5	Pal	T669b of her cycle	Lady Kanal-Ikal
	66:3	Bon?	half-period variant	
	69:1	Bon?	T586 end of	5-Kix-Chan
	69:10	Car	T586	Ruler 2
	103:3	Pom	T819	GI-Jaguar
	122:1	Pom	T506	
9. 8. 0.15.11	74:10	Yax	T515 capture of ????	????
9. 8. 1.12. 8	2:11	Pus	266-shell	local ruler
9. 8. 1.12.17	82:27	Pus	T548:??	????
9. 8. 5.16.12	85:4	Car	seating *ti ahpo-*??	Ruler 3
	100:1	Car	seating *ti ahau*	Ruler 3
9. 8. 9. 1.17	71:22	MJos	T684 inauguration	????
9. 8. 9.12.14	85:5	Q	seating *ti ahau le*	Ahpo-Kuk
	100:3	Q	seating *ti ahau le*	Ahpo-Kuk
9. 8. 9.13. 0	88:3	Pal	T740 birth	Pacal II
	91:8	Pal	T740 birth	Pacal II
	97:2	Pal	T740 birth	Pacal II
9. 8. 9.15.11	12:9	Bon	T266-shell of Ah ??-Imix	Chaan-Muan I
9. 8.10. 0. 0	29:1	Car	scattering	Ek-Batz
	82:10	Car	????	????
9. 8.10. 6.16	7:2	PN	T684 inauguration	Ruler 1
	7:3	PN	T684 inauguration	Ruler 1
9. 8.10. 6.16	7:13	PN	T684 inauguration	Ruler 1
9. 8.11. 6.12	19:6	Pal	T585 death	Lady Kanal-Ikal
9. 8.11. 9.10	112:13	Pal	seating *ti ahpo* feline	Ac-Kan
9. 8.12. 7.18	37:27	Cop	aux+T712 blood-letting?	????
9. 8.12.12. 9	9:2	Q	seating *ti ahpo*	Ah Naab-Chaan
	85:6	Q	seating *ti ahau le*	Ah Naab-Chaan
9. 8.13. 0. 0	28:13	Pal	T713 end of tun	
	70:4	Pal	T669b/tun-seating	Ac-Kan
9. 8.17.15.15	23:10	Q	T207-671	Smoking-Jaguar
9. 8.18. 6.16	7:13	PN	T684 inauguration	Ruler I
9. 8.18.12.12	18:1	Q	aux+chuen-*be*	Ah Naab-Chaan
9. 8.18.14.11	19:8	Pal	T585 death	Pacal I
9. 8.19. 4. 6	19:7	Pal	T585 death	Ac-Kan
9. 8.19. 7.18	115:1	Pal	seating *ti ahpo le*	Lady Zac-Kuk
9. 8.19.10. 5	88:14	Tort	T740 birth	Ahpo-Balam
9. 9. 0. 0. 0	4:9	Pom	seating of tun	
	28:14	Pal	T713 end of tun	
	30:3-4	Pal	T586 end of tun	
	59:10	Cop	T526:713	Smoking-Head
	62:6-8	Pal	T669b of her cycle	Lady Zac-Kuk

DATE	CAT NO	SITE	ACTION	ACTOR
	88:5	Cop	T740 birth	Smoking-Head?
	103:1	Pom	T583 end of	
	103:4	Pom	T819	5-Jaguar
9. 9. 2. 0. 8	89:1	Q	T740 birth	Chac-Naab-Be
9. 9. 2. 4. 8	8:1	Pal	T713 accession	Pacal II
	32:16	Pal	T713-GI accession of Pacal II	Lady Zac-Kuk
	72:2	Pal	T713 accession	Pacal II
	106:6	Pal	T713 accession	Pacal II
	112:14	Pal	seating *ti ahpo* T518 *le*	Pacal II
	113:2	Pal	T168:518	Pacal II
	117:5	Pal	T700var accession	Pacal II
	128:1	Pal	T700var accession	Pacal II
9. 9. 2.17. 0	76:5	Cop	????	local person?
9. 9. 6.10.19	25:14	Pal	le-zac-ahau-ik	Pacal II
	127:3	Pal	T221:60:515	Pacal II
9. 9. 9.10. 5	93:1	Car	T713b hand	Ruler 3
	92:4	Car	T757	Ruler 3
9. 9.10. 0. 0	49:2	Cop	T79-house	GI?
	67:1	Cop	T218 completion of half-period	????
	98:5	Cop	T819/712/akbal	local ruler
	109:1	Car	half-period	Ruler 4
9. 9.12.10. 6	71:3	Q	T684 inauguration	Zac-Ma-??
	100:2	Q	seating *ti ahau le*	Zac-Ma-??
9. 9.13. 0. 7	17:7	Pal	God N-*nakaw*	Lady Ahpo-Hel
	118:2	Pal	seating as ????	Lady Ahpo-Hel
9. 9.13. 4. 1	88:4	PN	T740 birth	Ruler 2
9. 9.13. 4. 4	12:1	Car	T266-shell to He of Naranjo	Ruler 4
9. 9.14. 3. 5	12:10	Car	T266-shell	Ruler 4
9. 9.14.17. 5	112:31	Cop	T644 accession	Smoke-Head
9. 9.16. 0. 0?	79:1	Q	aux+????	????
9. 9.18.16. 3	10:1	Car	star-Naranjo	????
	10:2	Nar	star-Naranjo	Ruler 4 of Caracol
9.10. 0. 0. 0	28:15	Pal	T713 end of tun	
	4:17	Pal	seating of 10 katuns-half of a baktun	
	30:3-4	Pal	seating of tun	
	31:5	Pal	T586 end of tun	
	62:9	Pal	T669b of his cycle	Pacal II
	62:10	Pal	T669b	GI
	62:11	Pal	T669b	GII
	62:12	Pal	T669b	GIII
	67:17	Pal	T669b/565	Lady Zac-Kuk
	70:1	Pal	*tup*	????
9.10. 3.17. 0	106:1	ASac	T585 death	local ruler
9.10. 2. 6. 6	88:11	Pal	T740 birth	Chan-Bahlum II
9.10. 3. 2. 0	95:1	Bon?	T740 birth	Chul
9.10. 3. 2.12	10:3	Nar	star/flint-shield of 18 Rabbit	Ruler 4 of Caracol
9.10. 3.17. 0	25:15	ASac	wing-shell death	????
9.10. 5. 8. 4	89:25	Pal	T740 birth	Chac-Cauac

DATE	CAT NO	SITE	ACTION	ACTOR
9.10. 6. 2. 1	106:8	PN	T585 death	Ruler 1
9.10. 6. 5. 9	7:5	PN	T684 inauguration	Ruler 2
	99:3	PN	T684 inauguration	Ruler 2
9.10. 7.13. 5	19:9	Pal	T585 death	Lady Zac-Kuk
9.10. 8. 9. 3	12:3-4	Pal	T266-shell	Chan-Bahlum II
	21:5	Pal	*oc te'/kin-kin*	Chan-Bahlum II
	21:17	Pal	pyramid (heir-designation)	Chan-Bahlum II
	21:18	Pal	pyramid+*oc te'*	Chan-Bahlum II
	38:4	Pal	aux+*oc-te'*	Chan-Bahlum II
	82:7	Pal	*ocah*	Chan-Bahlum II
	113:4	Pal	T617:713 heir-designation	Chan-Bahlum II
	122:3	Pal	God K-in-hand	Chan-Bahlum II
9.10.10. 0. 0	5:14	Pal	PE	
	117:3	Nar	T168:518	????
9.10.10. 1. 6	19:10	Pal	T585-death	Kan-Bahlum-Mo'
9.10.10. 2.16	37:24	RAm	aux+God N	
	17:9	RAm	God N+ *lu* bat	Rodent-Bone-Turtle
9.10.10.11. 2	21:13	Pal	T548:575--819 day count	God K
9.10.10.15. 0	40:1	???	T736 death	T'ul
9.10.11. 3.10	112:1-4	Tort	seating *ti ahau le*	Ahpo-Balam
	112:28	Tort	seating *ti ahau le*	Ahpo-Balam
	112:29	Tort	seating	Ahpo-Balam
9.10.11. 9. 6	10:4	Tort	*oc*/inverted-sky/star-earth	
9.10.11.12.17	13:3	ASac	T843	a woman
9.10.11.17. 0	89:11	Pal	T740 birth	Kan-Xul II
	116:3	Pal	T740 birth	Kan-Xul II
9.10.12. 0. 9	96:3	Q	accession	Chac-Naab-Be
9.10.12. 3.10	75:4	Tort	axe	????
9.10.12. 4. 8	89:2	Q	T740 birth	Puma
9.10.13. 0. 0	26:10	Tort	T713 end of tun	
	59:12	Tort	T520 his tun	Ahpo-Balam
9.10.14.13. 0	74:9	Yax	T515 capture of Cauac-Bat	Bird-Jaguar II
9.10.15. 0. 0	21:21	Pul	????/fire	local ruler
	35:1	Cop	aux+akbal-kin	Bat-Uinal
	59:3	Cop	aux+T712+T819	????
9.10.15. 1.11	26:4	Tort	*ka*/smoke-shield	
9.10.16. 8.14	89:13	ECayo	T740 birth	Carapace-Skull
9.10.16.13. 6	75:5	Tort	axe	
9.10.16.16.19	89:4	Q	T740 birth	Jaguar-Paw
9.10.17. 1. 2	74:1	Tort	T515 capture of ????	????
9.10.17. 1. 9	75:6	Tort	axe of Chac-Ik-??	Ahpo-Balam
9.10.17. 2.14	10:5	Tort	star-over-earth	
	10:7	Tort	star-over-earth	Ahpo-Balam
	60:6	Tort	zac-ahau-ik/*tu-chaan*	Ahpo-Balam
	74:2	Tort	T515 capture of 4 Chuen	Ahpo-Balam
	82:20	Tort	T78:628/ballgame/????	Ahpo-Balam
9.10.17. 6. 0	89:12	Pal	T740 birth	Xoc
9.10.18.12. 8	3:19	Cop	scattering	????
	86:11	Cop	T819+????	????
9.10.18.17.19	20:12	Pal	T628:713	Kan-Xul II

DATE	CAT NO	SITE	ACTION	ACTOR
	92:6	Pal	deer hoof–T713	Kan-Xul II
9.10.19. 3.11	88:2	Cop	T714 birth	local person
9.10.19. 8. 4	10:6	Tort	star-over-earth	Ahpo-Balam
9.11. 0. 0. 0	3:10	Pal	PE (T673)	Pacal II
	3:11	Pal	God C-ing of tun	
	4:4	Pal	seating of tun	
	4:14	Pal	seating of tun	
	5:9	Pal	T151 of earth	supernatural
	5:10	Pal	T151 of sky	supernatural
	5:11	Pal	T1016 end of tun	
	30:5	Pal	seating of tun	
	31:6	Pal	T586 end of tun	
	33:1	Pal	T741–T713	Palenque Triad
	41:1	Pal	T713 end of tun	Pacal II
	43:3	Pal	scattering	Pacal II
	45:3–4	Pal	helmet his cycle	Triad God
	62:10	Pal	T669b	GI
	62:11	Pal	T669b	GII
	62:12	Pal	T669b	GIII
	70:2	Pal	*tup*	????
	70:5	Cop	????	Bat-Uinal
	86:3–4	Pal	split-earth	Evening Star
	108:2	Pal	T17.25:743	Pacal II
	109:7	Pal	helmet	GII
	123:6	Pal	T218 completion of 11 katuns	
	124:1	Pal	bat-expiration of 11th katun	Pacal II
9.11. 1.12. 6	70:6	Pal	*lah* completion of 13 haabs	Pacal II
9.11. 1.12. 8	87:3	Pal	T79/*te'naab-chaan*	
9.11. 1.16. 3	14:1	Pal	axe of Crossed-Bands-Sky of Site Q	????
	74:5	Pal	T515 capture? of ????	????
	81:5	Pal	????	Crossed-Bands-Jaguar
9.11. 2. 1.11	23:8	Pal	T207-fire	Pacal II
9.11. 4. 7. 0	58:1	Pal	T218:60:515 *tu balan-ahau*	GI
9.11. 4. 7. 0	80:2	Pal	*mucah/tu yoc/tu* flint	Kan-Xul II
9.11. 5.12. 2	78:1	Q	aux+*te'*-tree	Chaan-Muan
9.11. 6. 1. 8	82:35	PN	kin-helmet	Ruler 2?
9.11. 6. 2. 1	110:1	PN	ahau-in-hand/helmet	Ruler 2
	110:2	PN	ahau-in-hand/T110:764	Ruler 2
9.11. 6. 3. 4	65:1	Q	scattering	????
9.11. 6.16. 3	74:4	Pal	T515 capture of ????	????
9.11. 6.16.17	119:1–2	Pal	T740 birth	Skull-GI
9.11. 9. 8.12	10:22	PN	star-shell	????
9.11. 9.14. 9	59:13	Pal	????/T713	Batz'
9.11. 9.15.19	45:8	DPil	????	Flint-Sky-God K
9.11. 9.17.16	114:2	Q	T79-tun/house	????
9.11.10. 0. 0	38:2	Q	aux+scattering	Zac-Balam
	66:5	???	half-period	Rodent-Turtle
9.11.10.12.13	25:19	???	wing-shell death	Sky-Uinal
9.11.10.16.15	98:11	Q	T819	Lord of Site Q

DATE	CAT NO	SITE	ACTION	ACTOR
9.11.11. 9.17	74:3	DPil	T515 capture of Tah-Mo'	Flint-Sky-God K
	77:2	DPil	*malah*	Flint-Sky-God K
9.11.12. 7. 2	101:7	PN	T740 birth	Ruler 3
	89:3	PN	T740 birth	Ruler 3
9.11.13. 0. 0	45:2	Pal	ahau-in-hand	Kan-Xul II
9.11.15. 0. 0	67:6	Cop	T713 +tun variant	
9.11.15.14. 0	51:7	Cop	T757	Knot-Skull
9.11.16. 8.18	21:4	Tort	*kin-le/na*-cauac	????
	21:23	Tort	uinal-hand	????
9.11.16.10.13	67:6	Yax	anniversary of accession	Bird-Jaguar II
9.11.16.11. 6	10:23	PN	star-shell	Ruler 2
9.11.17. 3.10	23:2	Tort	T79-house	Ahpo-Balam
9.11.17. 8.19	74:31	DPil	T592-515	????
9.11.17.18.19	10:8	DPil	star-shell	????
9.11.18. 9.17	105:6	Pal	T740 birth	Chac-Zutz'
9.11.18.15. 1	16:10	Yax	T207-fire/bat	Shield-Jaguar I
	52:3	Yax	aux+maize	Shield-Jaguar I
9.11.19. 4. 3	10:11	Tik	star-over-earth	paddlers
9.12. 0. 0. 0	3:5	Pal	PE	????
	3:6	Pal	PE	????
	4:11	Pal	seating of tun	
	4:15	Pal	T713 end of tun	
	30:6	Pal	seating of tun	
	31:7-9	Pal	*tup*	Palenque Triad
	33:2	Pal	Jester God-T713	Palenque Triad
	44:8	Pal	T807	????
	45:5-7	Pal	helmet his cycle	Palenque Triad
	61:1	Ton	scattering	
	62:13	Pal	T669b katun of T672 title	Pacal II
	62:14-16	Pal	T669b his cycle	????
	70:3	Pal	*tup*	????
	87:1	Ton	T79-house	????
	108:3	Pal	T17.25:743	Pacal II
	129:2	Pal	T617:713/58.1030o	Palenque Triad
	123:24	Cop	T218 completion of 12th katun	Paddlers
9.12. 0. 6.18	25:1	Pal	wing-shell death	Lady Ahpo-Hel
	106:2	Pal	T585 death	Lady Ahpo-Hel
9.12. 0. 8. 3	10:19	DPil	star-shell	
9.12. 0.10.11	101:1	Pil	T740 birth	Shield-God K
9.12. 2. 0.16	89:8	PN	T740 birth	Lady Ahpo-Katun
	89:23	PN	T740 birth	Lady Ahpo-Katun
	91:9	PN	T714 birth	Lady Ahpo-Katun
	99:1	PN	T740 birth	Lady Ahpo-Katun
9.12. 3. 6. 6	119:3	Pal	T740 birth	Ti-??-Kin
9.12. 3.14. 0	35:2	Cop	aux+akbal+T712	Copan EG
	94:4	Cop	fish-in-hand	Knot-Skull
9.12. 4. 0. 1	122:2	Ton	seating *ahpo le*	Muluc-Jaguar
9.12. 5. 0. 0	28:23	PN	T713 end of tun	Ruler II
9.12. 5. 9.14	10:9	DPil	star-shell	Twist-Skull
9.12. 5.10. 1	11:7	DPil	T45-head	Flint-Sky-God K

DATE	CAT NO	SITE	ACTION	ACTOR
9.12. 6. 5. 8	99:2	Pal	T740 birth	Chaacal III
	116:4	Pal	T740 birth	Chaacal III
9.12. 6.16.17	12:2	DPil	T266-shell ????	????
	82:23	DPil	eccentric-flint of 13-Gourd	Flint-Sky-God K
9.12. 6.17.18	5:6	Tort	*mac*/T819	Ahpo-Balam
9.12. 7. 0. 0	64:2	Tort	T713 end of tun	
9.12. 7. 1.19	102:2	Tort	T585 death	Ahpo-Balam
	112:5	Tort	seating *ti ahpo le*	Black-Scroll
9.12. 7.14. 7	112:7-8	Tort	seating *ta* office	Ah Ka-??-Balam
9.12. 8. 3. 9	82:34	Cop	????	Smoke-Head
9.12. 8.14. 0	74:8	Yax	T515 capture of Ah Ahaual	Shield-Jaguar I
9.12. 8.14. 1	34:2	Yax	T515 capture of Ah Ahaual	Shield-Jaguar I
	74:13	Yax	T515 capture of Ah Ahaual	Shield-Jaguar I
	74:15	Yax	T515 capture of Ah Ahaual	Shield-Jaguar I
	74:32	Yax	T515 capture of Ah Ahaual	Sheild-Jaguar I
	107:4	Yax	T515 capture of Ah Ahaual	Shield-Jaguar I
9.12. 9. 7.12	87:4	Tort	T79/house	Ah Ka-??-Balam
9.12. 9. 8. 1	46:3	Yax	fish-in-hand/God K	Shield-Jaguar I
	72:6	Yax	T713/fish-in-hand accession	Shield-Jaguar I
	3:18	Yax	T617 mirror-in-hand	Shield-Jaguar I
9.12. 9.17.16	100:5	Tik	seating TI T74:528.515	Ruler A
9.12.10. 0. 0	37:15	DPil	T757	????
	37:18	DPil	aux+510d	Flint-Sky-God K
	50:2	Cop	scattering+half-period	
	59:1	Cop	aux+T501+T819	Imix-God K
	69:3	Cop	T586/*te'-tun*	????
	77:3	DPil	*malah*	Flint-Sky-God K
	79:1	Q	aux+????	Person of Site Q
	98:4	Pom	T559 PE	
	101:2	Cop	aux+T712/akbal	18-Rabbit
	103:5	Cop	kin-akbal PE special	local ruler
	113:7	Pal	T228:683/T174:501	Cauac
	116:14	Cop	fish-in-hand	18-Rabbit
9.12.10. 5.12	94:2	Nar	T713b hand+????	Lady 6-Sky
	94:3	Nar	T713b hand+????	Lady 6-Sky
9.12.10. 9.12	40:5	Nar	T207:671	Lady 6-Sky
9.12.11. 5.18	19:1	Pal	T585 death	Pacal II
	19:11	Pal	T585 death	Pacal II
	25:2	Pal	wing-shell death	Pacal II
	116:17	Pal	wing-shell death	Pacal II
	118:3	Pal	seating *ta ahau le* in T585 death	Pacal II
	120:4	Pal	T1041 death	Pacal II
9.12.11. 6. 9	9:6	Bon	seating on jaguar-throne *ta ahau le*	Ah-Hun-Chu-??
9.12.11.12.10	8:2-4	Pal	T713 accession	Chan-Bahlum II
	8:14-15	Pal	T713 accession	Chan-Bahlum II
	27:2	Pal	*tu-oc te'* accession	Chan-Bahlum II
	32:6	Pal	seating (accession)	Chan-Bahlum II
	60:4	Pal	T713 accession	Chan-Bahlum II

DATE	CAT NO	SITE	ACTION	ACTOR
	72:3	Pal	T713 accession	Chan-Bahlum II
	100:4	Pal	seating *ti ahpo le*	Chan-Bahlum II
	117:1	Pal	T700var accession	Chan-Bahlum II
	117:6	Pal	T700var	Chan-Bahlum II
	126:1	Pal	T528.1040:87	Chan-Bahlum II
9.12.11.11. 2	77:1	DPil	completion of 2 katuns?/*malah*	Flint-Sky-God K
9.12.12.13. 0	110:5	Pal	T671 of U-Kix-Chan	Chan-Bahlum II
9.12.13.17. 7	64:5	DPil	T819	Flint-Sky-God K
	71:4	DPil	T684 inauguration	Great-Jaguar-Paw of Site Q
9.12.14. 3.11	37:14	Tik	aux+T600	Chan
9.12.14.10.11	82:1	PN	*macah*	Lady Ahpo-Katun
	82:2	PN	*macah*	Lady Ahpo-Katun
	82:3	PN	*macah*	Lady Ahpo-Katun
9.12.14.10.14	25:18	PN	wing-shell death	Ruler 2
9.12.14.10.16	95:2	PN	*nawah*	Lady Ahpo-Katun
	95:3	PN	*nawah*	Lady Ahpo-Katun
9.12.14.10.17	95:4	PN	*nawah*	Lady Ahpo-Katun
	95:5	PN	*nawah*	Lady Ahpo-Katun
9.12.14.11. 1	59:7	PN	posthumous event	Ruler 2
9.12.14.13. 1	71:5	PN	T684 inauguration	Ruler 3
9.12.15. 0. 0	28:24	PN	T713 end of yax-tun	Ruler 3
9.12.15.13. 7	89:6-7	Nar	T740 birth	Smoking-Squirrel
9.12.16. 3.12	92:1	Ton	seating as ahpo	Kuk
9.12.17. 3. 7	37:15	Tik	aux+????	Chan
9.12.17. 8.16	112:15	Chin	seating *ti ahau le*	Flint-Rabbit
	112:16	Chin	seating *ti ahau le*	Flint-Rabbit
9.12.17.12. 0	74:14	Yax	T515 capture of Zac-Manik	Shield-Jaguar I
9.12.17.12.10	89:16	Yax	T740 birth	Bird-Jaguar III
9.12.17.13. 1	79:6	ECayo	aux+T515	Turtle-Shell
9.12.18. 5.16	21:8	Pal	*te'-naab/chaan*	GI
	23:3	Pal	inverted sky-*lu*	GI
	23:4	Pal	inverted sky-*lu*	GII
	23:5	Pal	inverted sky-*lu*	GI-GVII
	23:6	Pal	inverted sky-*lu*	GIII
	82:6	Pal	T606	Chan-Bahlum II
	87:8	Pal	T79/*te'-naab-chaan*	GIII
	87:9	Pal	T79	Palenque Triad
9.12.18. 5.17	17:2-3	Pal	God N/west/quetzal/house	Chan-Bahlum II
9.12.18. 5.19	39:3	Pal	fish-in-hand	Chan-Bahlum II
	46:1-2	Pal	fish-in-hand	Chan-Bahlum II
	56:5	Pal	T60:713	Chan-Bahlum II
	59:6	Pal	T60:713	Chan-Bahlum II
9.12.18. 7. 1	104:2	Pal	T520H 819 Day Count	God K
9.12.18. 9.16	37:13	Tik	aux+T600	Shield-Yax-Head
9.12.19.12.19	20:2	Tik	????	Lady Cauac
	16:1	Pal	T207-fire	GVI
	21:7	Pal	9-upended vase	GIII
	81:6	Pal	T221:60:515	GII
	87:5-7	Pal	T79/*te'-naab-chaan*	
	127:4-5	Pal	T221:60:515	GI

DATE	CAT NO	SITE	ACTION	ACTOR
9.13. 0. 0. 0	3:7	Pal	PE	????
	4:2-3	Pal	seating of tun	
	4:12	Pal	seating of tun	
	4:6	Pom	seating of tun	
	21:14	Bon	T548:575	local ruler?
	31:1	Pal	T807	????
	43:4	Ton	scattering	Kuk
	47:1	Agua	scattering	????
	66:4	Ton	half-period of 13 katuns	
	79:3	Agua	aux+T44:502	Flint-Sky-God K
	103:2	Agua	T218 completion of 13 katuns	Flint-Sky-God K
	109:3	Pom	scattering	????
	123:23	PN	T218 completion of 13 katuns	
9.13. 0. 4.12	113:8	Pal	????	Lady ????
9.13. 0. 7. 0	59:8	Pal	deer hoof:T713	Chaacal III
9.13. 1. 4.16	128:3	Nar	T168:518	Smoking-Squirrel
9.13. 1. 4.19	12:6	Nar	T266-shell of Chikin-Cab	Smoking-Squirrel
9.13. 1. 9. 5	11:1	Nar	smoke-head	
9.13. 1.13.14	11:2	Nar	smoke-head	
9.13. 2. 4.11	15:4-5	Tik	fish-in-hand	18-Rabbit of Tikal
9.13. 2. 4.13	106:10	Pal	T585 death	????
9.13. 2.16. 0	12:7	Nar	T266-shell of ????	Smoking-Squirrel
9.13. 3. 0. 0	2:5	Nar	T713 end of tun	Lady 6-Sky
	121:3	Tik	yax.124:528.528	
9.13. 3. 7.18	12:4	Tik	T266-shell of Jaguar-Paw of Site Q	Ruler A
9.13. 3. 8.11	95:14	Tik	nawah of Uuc-Bolon-Imix	????
9.13. 3. 9.18	39:7	Tik	fish-in-hand+T712+akbal	Ruler A
	80:4	Tik	T174:565/tu ????	Ruler A
	80:5	Tik	T174:671/tu ????	Ruler A
9.13. 3.13.15	12:8	Tik	T266-shell of Bone-Imix	Split-Earth of Site Q
9.13. 4.17.14	10:21	DPil	star-shell	Shield-God K
9.13. 5. 4.13	11:3	Nar	smoke-head	
9.13. 5.12.13	38:29	Yax	aux+T700	Shield-Jaguar I
	79:4	Yax	aux+T700	Shield-Jaguar I
	48:2	Yax	aux+T700	Lady Ik-Skull
9.13. 5.16. 4	73:2	Chin	T585 death	Feather-Shield
9.13. 6. 2. 0	45:14	DPil	ahau-in-hand	Shield-God K
	112:18	DPil	seating ti ahau le	Shield-God K
9.13. 6.10. 4	11:4	Nar	smoke-head to Kan-Flint	Smoking-Squirrel
9.13. 7. 3. 8	9:4	Nar	T713+????	Lady 6-Sky
	9:5	Nar	mul ti+????	Lady 6-Sky
	38:5	Nar	aux+T1001	Lady 6-Sky
	52:1	Nar	aux+T592	Lady 6-Sky
	80:1	Nar	nah ta nen-chaan	Lady 6-Sky
9.13. 9.14.14	74:6	Yax	T515 capture of Ah Kan	Shield-Jaguar I
9.13. 9.14.15	98:14	PN	T740 birth	Ruler 4
	89:14	PN	T740 birth	Ruler 4
9.13.10. 0. 0	2:11	Nar	T713 end of tun	????
	2:12	Nar	T713 end of tun	none

DATE	CAT NO	SITE	ACTION	ACTOR
	2:13	Nar	T713 end of tun	Lady 6-Sky
	3:9	Pal	scattering	????
	112:23	Cop	seating *ti ahau le*	18-Rabbit
	116:6	Cop	seating	18-Rabbit
9.13.10. 1. 5	24:1	Pal	T1041 death	Chan-Bahlum II
	73:3	Pal	T585 death	Chan-Bahlum II
	120:5	Pal	T1041 death	Chan-Bahlum II
9.13.10. 6. 8	32:7	Pal	seating (accession)	Kan-Xul II
	32:8	Pal	seating on throne	Kan-Xul II
	60:3	Pal	T713 accession	Kan-Xul II
	72:5	Pal	T713 accession	Kan-Xul II
	85:8	Pal	seating *ta ahpo le*	Kan-Xul II
	106:5	Pal	T713 accession	Kan-Xul II
	112:17	Pal	seating as T757	Kan-Xul II
	117:7	Pal	T700var	Kan-Xul II
	118:4	Pal	????/T51.617:561	Kan-Xul II
9.13.10. 9.16?	53:1	Nar	aux+T684 inauguration	Smoking-Squirrel
9.13.11. 5. 7	80:3	Tik	tri-lobe flint-in-hand	????
9.13.11. 6. 7	116:9	Tik	T736 death	Lady Ca-wa-c(a)
9.13.13. 7. 2	10:25	DPil	star-shell	Shield-God K
9.13.13.12. 5	25:6	Yax	wing-shell death	Lady Pacal
9.13.13.15. 0	23:7	Pal	T207-impinged bone	Chan-Bahlum II?
	87:10	Pal	T79/*yax* God K-in-hand	
9.13.13.16.11	15:2	Quir	fish-in-hand/T671	Smoking-Turtle
9.13.14. 4. 2	48:1	Nar	aux+???? house	Smoking-Squirrel
9.13.14. 8. 0	86:1	Pal	T617:713 heir-designation	Xoc
9.13.14.11. 1	45:15	PN	ahau-in-hand	Ruler 3
9.13.14.12.16?	53:1	Nar	aux+T684 inauguration	Smoking-Squirrel
9.13.14.13. 1	38:1	PN	aux+??-zero-*ma*	Lady Ahpo-Katun
9.13.15. 0. 0	2:14	Nar	T713 end of tun	Smoking-Squirrel
	43:1	DPil	scattering	????
	82:12	DPil	T586 blood-letting?	????
	94:5	DPil	T747b ahau	????
9.13.16. 4. 6	89:9	PN	T740 birth	Lady Ahpo-Kin
9.13.16.10. 3	92:3	Yax	T520H 819 Day Count	God K
9.13.17. 8.16	112:16	Chin	seating as lord	????
9.13.17.12.10	89:17	Yax	T740 birth	Bird-Jaguar
9.13.17.15.12	17:5	Yax	God N/*lu* bat	Turtle-GI
	55:5	Yax	aux+T712 blood-letting	Shield-Jaguar I
	55:6	Yax	aux+T712 blood-letting	Lady Xoc
9.13.18. 4.18	11:5	Nar	smoke-head	
9.13.18. 9.15	82:14	Nar	T586:563 of Person of Yaxha	Smoking-Squirrel
9.13.19. 6. 3	128:4	Nar	????:713	Smoking-Squirrel
9.13.19.13. 1	33:5	PN	ahau-in-hand/T580	Lady Ahau-Katun
	123:7	PN	T218 completion of 25 tun as ruler	Ruler 3
9.13.19.16. 6	82:15	Tik	T586:563	????
9.13.19.16. 9	93:2	Tik	T713b hand	????

DATE	CAT NO	SITE	ACTION	ACTOR
9.14. 0. 0. 0	2:4	Nar	T713 end of tun	Smoking-Squirrel
	2:17	DPil	T713 end of tun	Shield-God K
	2:19	Tik	T713 end of tun	Ruler A
	18:2	DPil	aux+TikEG	Shield-God K
	28:22	MJos	T713 end of tun	
	43:2	DPil	scattering	Shield-God K
	76:4	DPil	T586 blood-letting?	Smoking-GI
	123:8	PN	T218 completion of 14th katun	
	123:9	Tik	T218 completion of 14th katun	Ruler A
	123:10	Nar	T218 completion of 14th katun	Smoking-Squirrel
	123:20	DPil	T218 completion of 14 katuns	Shield-God K
	123:21	MJos	T218 completion of 14 katuns	local ruler
	125:5	DPil	T713 end of tun	Shield-God K
	129:11	Nar	????	Paddlers
9.14. 0. 3. 5	120:8	ArP	T573	Chac-Be-??
9.14. 1.17.14	74:16	Yax	T515 capture of Ah Kan	Shield-Jaguar I
	74:35	Yax	T515 capture of Ah Kan	Shield-Jaguar I
9.14. 2. 0.14	10:18	ASac	star-over-earth	
9.14. 2. 5.13	95:6	Pal	*nawah*	????
9.14. 2. 5.14	95:7	Pal	*nawah*	Lord of Palenque
9.14. 3. 0. 0	3:6	Nar	T713 end of tun	Lady 6-Sky
	35:3	Nar	aux+akbal	Smoking-Squirrel
9.14. 3. 8. 3	66:6	Bon	half-period variant of 13 tuns	Flint-Mandible
9.14. 8.14.15	127:7	Pal	T79.671/T713 accession	Xoc
9.14. 8.16.18	27:5	Pal	house	Xoc
9.14. 9. 0.12	24:3	Tik	T736 death	local person
9.14.10. 0. 0	69:11	NimP	T586 end of tun	local person
	37:22	NimP	T712 blood-letting	18-U-Ma
	43:5	Ton	scattering	Balam
	43:21	DPil	scattering	Shield-God K
	76:4	DPil	T586 PE/blood-letting?	Shield-God K
	95:18	DPil	????	Smoking-GI
	98:10	Ton	kin-akbal PE special	
	109:2	DPil	half-period	Shield-God K
9.14.10. 0. 1	115:2	NimP	T759	local person
9.14.10. 3. 3	24:4	Tik	T736 death	local person
9.14.10. 4. 0	79:5	DPil	aux+T218-house	Shield-God K
	125:6	DPil	T713 end of tun	Shield-God K
9.14.10. 4. 2	49:1	Pal	accession	Chaacal III
	72:4	Pal	T713 accession	Chaacal III
	85:9	Pal	seating *ti ahpo le*	Chaacal III
	128:2	Pal	T700var	Chaacal III
9.14.10.13.12	24:5	Tik	T736 death	local person
9.14.11. 2. 7	108:4	Pal	T207-God K of GI??	Kan-Xul II
9.14.11.12.14	8:16	Pal	T713 accession	Chac-Zutz'
9.14.11.15. 1	17:4	Yax	God N/*lu* bat	Lady Xoc
9.14.11.17. 6	74:17	Pal	T515 capture of Knot-Manik	Chac-Zutz'
9.14.13. 4.17	9:13	Quir	seating *ti ahau le*	Two-Legged-Sky
	33:6	Quir	God K-in-hand	Two-Legged-Sky
	72:7	Quir	T713/fish-in-hand accession	Two-Legged-Sky

DATE	CAT NO	SITE	ACTION	ACTOR
	126:4	Quir	God K-in-hand	Two-Legged-Sky
9.14.13.11. 2	110:6	Pal	axe-kin	Chac-Zutz'
9.14.14. 8. 1	103:7	Yax	25-tun anniversary of accession	Shield-Jaguar II
9.14.14.13.17	6:3-4	Yax	207-fire	Lady Xoc
9.14.15. 1.19	24:6	Tik	T736 death	Shield-God K of Dos Pilas
	25:4	DPil	wing-shell death	Shield-God K
9.14.15. 2. 3	27:3	DPil	*muc* burial of Shield-God K	Spangle-Head
9.14.15. 4. 3	24:7	Tik	T736 death	18-Rabbit
9.14.15. 4.14	26:24	NimP	water-scroll	6-Gourd
9.14.15. 5.15	71:21	DPil	T684 inauguration	Spangle-Head
9.14.15. 6.13	24:8	Tik	T736 death	local person
9.14.15. 6.16	21:11	Tik	chuen+????	????
9.14.15.17.11	35:5	Yax	T712 blood-letting	Shield-Jaguar I
	57:1	Yax	aux+T669b/snake/sky/God K	Shield-Jaguar I
	74:7	Yax	T515 capture of Ah Chuen	Shield-Jaguar I
	74:11	Yax	T515 capture of Ah Chuen	Shield-Jaguar I
9.14.15.17.11	75:9	Yax	snake/????/T712/sky-in-hand	Shield-Jaguar I
9.14.16. 9. 9?	119:6	Sac	T740 birth	????
9.14.16.13. 9	113:6	Yax	T23:713/house	Lady Xoc
9.14.17.12.18	122:4	Pal	axe-T110	Chac-Zutz'
9.14.17.14.17	95:15	PN	*nawah*	Lady ??-Bat
9.14.18. 1. 1	108:5	Pal	T87:758	Chac-Zutz'
9.14.18. 3.13	71:18	PN	T684 inauguration	Ruler 4
	71:7	PN	T684 inauguration	Ruler 4
9.14.18. 5. 7	71:11	ECayo	T684 inauguration	local ruler
9.14.18. 6.12	17:6	Yax	God N/*lu* bat	GI?
	48:6	PN	aux+T684 bundle/scattering	Shield-Jaguar I
9.14.18. 9. 8	127:8	Pal	????/T60 534 :713	Chac-Zutz'
9.14.18. 9.17	1:3	Pal	T218 completion of 3 katuns	Chac-Zutz'
	127:1	Pal	T740 birth (anniversary)	Chac-Zutz'
9.14.19. 5. 0	131:1	Cop	T586 expression	18-Rabbit
9.14.19. 8. 0	131:2	Cop	T586 expression	????
	70:9	Cop	T44:501	????
9.14.19.11. 0	131:3	Cop	T586 expression	????
	106:9	Cop	T585 death??	????
	116:8	Cop	T736 death??	????
	131:3	Cop	T586 expression	????
9.14.19.14.18	96:5	Yax	fish-in-hand	captor of Ix-Tun-Ahau
9.15. 0. 0. 0	4:5	Pal	seating of tun	
	41:3	PN	T713 end of tun	Ruler 4
	47:2	Agua	scattering	Spangle-Head of Dos Pilas
	51:8	Cop	T757	18-Rabbit
	56:1	Cop	scattering	18-Rabbit
	57:2	Cop	PE special	18-Rabbit
	59:3	Cop	T218 completion	
	67:4	ArP	T218 completion of 15 katuns	
	67:5	Cop	T218 completion of 15 katuns	
	68:3	ArP	????/*te'-tun*	
	69:4	Cop	T586 end of	18-Rabbit
	69:5	Cop	T586 end of	18-Rabbit

DATE	CAT NO	SITE	ACTION	ACTOR
	109:4	ArP	scattering	Chac-Be-??
9.15. 0.12. 0	74:32	Yax	capture of Na-Cauac-Manik	????
9.15. 0.15. 3	96:5	Yax	fish-in-hand	captor of Ix-Tun-Ahau
9.15. 1. 1. 7	82:24	Q	T200:506P	????
9.15. 1. 6. 3	24:11	ECayo	T736 death	Turtle-Shell
9.15. 1.12.13	24:10	Tik	T736 death	Ik
9.15. 2. 1. 5	26:17	NTun	T586.??	local person
9.15. 3. 6. 8	85:7	Tik	seating *ti batab le*	Ruler B
9.15. 4. 6. 4	10:12	Agua	star-over-Seibal	
	10:13	DPil	star-over-Seibal	
9.15. 4. 6. 5	54:1	DPil	axe	Spangle-Head
	54:2	Agua	axe	Spangle-Head
9.15. 4. 6.11	95:11	Agua	*nawah* of Jaguar-Paw-Jaguar of Seibal	Spangle-Head of Dos Pilas
	95:12	DPil	*nawah* of Jaguar-Paw-Jaguar of Seibal	Spangle-Head of Dos Pilas
9.15. 5. 0. 0	29:2	Agua	scattering	Spangle-Head
9.15. 5. 3.18	123:12	PN	7th tun as ahau	Ruler 4
9.15. 6. 5.12	116:20	NTun	T819-*mo-pan*	local person
9.15. 6.13. 1	16:5	Yax	T207-fire	Lady Xoc
9.15. 6.14. 6	75:10	Quir	axe of 18-Rabbit of Copan	Two-Legged-Sky
	107:9	Quir	axe of 18-Rabbit of Copan	Two-Legged-Sky
	107:10	Quir	axe of 18-Rabbit of Copan	Two-Legged-Sky
9.15. 6.16.11	15:3	Tik	fish-in-hand	Ahpo-Kin
9.15. 6.16.17	55:1	Cop	God K-in-hand	New-Sky-at-Horizon
9.15. 6.17. 0	9:3	Cop	????	New-Sky-at-Horizon
9.15. 6.17. 1	45:13	NimP	ahau-in-hand	Fishface
9.15. 7. 0. 0	31:15	NimP	T586 end of tun	local ruler
9.15. 7. 6.12	120:7	Cop	????	New-Sky-at-Horizon
9.15. 8. 8. 5	116:19	NTun	????	????
9.15. 8. 9. 4	82:28	NTun	*talah*	????
9.15. 9. 3.14	74:24	Bon	T515 capture of ????	Knot-Eye-Jaguar
9.15. 9.16. 1	40:11	Agua	????	Shield-God K of Dos Pilas
9.15. 9.16.15	56:2	Agua	????	God K-Mah Kina
9.15. 9.17.16	79:9	Yax	aux+T684/T563/sky	Shield-Jaguar I
9.15. 9.17.17	71:6	Agua	T684 inauguration	God K-Mah Kina
9.15.10. 0. 0	3:3	Tik	half-period of katun	
	5:4	Quir	T758 of the tun	
	29:10	NimP	scattering	Lahun-Chaan
	44:1	Mach	T586 end of tun	Etz'nab-GI
	47:4	Agua	scattering	God K-Mah Kina
9.15.10. 0. 0?	72:11	EPeru	*ahpo-le*-in-hand accession	local ruler
	121:7	NTun	T45	local person
9.15.10. 0. 1	39:5	Yax	fish-in-hand/God K	Bird-Jaguar III
	51:1	Yax	T757	Bird-Jaguar III
	52:6	Yax	aux+yax-mul+T712 blood-letting	Chac-Skull
	59:11	Yax	*balan-ahau*	Lady Zero-Skull
	76:1	Yax	fish-in-hand	Lady Zero-Skull
9.15.10.17.14	25:5	Yax	wing-shell death	Shield-Jaguar I
	25:7	Yax	wing-shell death	Shield-Jaguar I

DATE	CAT NO	SITE	ACTION	ACTOR
	55:7	Yax	aux+*balan-ahau*	Shield-Jaguar I
9.15.12. 2. 2	10:14	Tik	star-Yaxha	
	95:17	Tik	*bacwah*	GVI
9.15.12. 2. 3	80:7	Tik	????/T671 *tu yoc*	GVI
9.15.12. 3.18	123:12	PN	T218 completion of 7th tun *ti ahau le*	Ruler 4
9.15.12. 9.15	26:20	NTun	T45	Ek-??-Cab
9.15.12.11.12	20:4	Tik	*oc*+????	Ruler B
9.15.12.11.13	10:15	Tik	star-????	
	95:16	Tik	*bacwah*/????/T174:671	Kin-Balam?
9.15.12.17.13	100:7	Lac	seating *ti* T563.181	Knot-Eye-Jaguar of Bonampak
9.15.13. 0. 0	36:8	Tik	T757	Ruler B
9.15.13. 4.14	74:28	Yha	T515 capture of Zotz'	Chac-God K-GIII
9.15.13. 6. 9	3:12	Yax	scattering	Bird-Jaguar III
	13:6	Yax	ballgame	Bird-Jaguar III
9.15.13. 6. 9	52:9	Yax	na-chan blood-letting	Bird-Jaguar III
	96:4	Yax	????	3-Knot-Skull
9.15.13.11.10	26:16	NTun	T586:23	Muan
9.15.13.12. 1	17:8	???	God N/*lu* bat	Shell-Imix
9.15.15. 0. 0	41:2	Lac	T713 end of tun	Knot-Eye-Jaguar of Bonampak
	29:11	PN	scattering	Ruler IV
	56:7	PN	scattering	Ruler IV
	98:13	PN	scattering	????
9.15.15. 2. 3	52:4	Tik	aux+maize	GVI
	38:17	Tik	????+sky	????
	79:7	Tik	aux+????	GVI
	80:6	Tik	T174:565+????	Ruler B
	87:11	Tik	T79	Ruler B
9.15.15. 6. 0	39:6	Yax	fish-in-hand/God K	Lady Balam
9.15.15.12.16	109:6	Cop	T617:713	Ahau Chac-Ek
9.15.15.14. 0	80:8	Tik	????	Ruler B
9.15.16. 9. 3	26:18	NTun	T819	local person
9.15.17. 0. 4	35:6	Tik	aux+T712 blood-letting	7-Gourd
9.15.17. 5. 0	124:3	Cop	T79	New-Sky-at-Horizon
9.15.17.15.14	25:9	Yax	wing-shell death	Lady Fist-Fish
9.15.18. 3.13	68:1	PN	T559 completion of 1st katun as *ahau*	Ruler 4
	99:6	PN	T575 *ti* canoe	Jaguar of Yaxchilan
9.15.18. 3.15	79:13	PN	aux+body-macaw	Ruler 4
9.15.18. 3.16	61:2	PN	????	Ruler 4
9.15.18.16. 7	89:19	PN	T741 birth	Ruler 7
9.15.19.14. 3	25:8	Yax	wing-shell death	Lady Ik-Skull
9.15.19.14.14	84:7	Yax	T520 819 Day Count	God K
9.16. 0. 0. 0	2:10	Tik	T713 end of tun	Ruler B
	111:1	Tik	scattering	Ruler B
	123:13	PN	T218 completion of 16 katuns	Ruler 4
9.16. 0. 1.11	102:1	Cop	T684 inauguration??	????
9.16. 0.13.17	26:7	Yax	T515 capture of Ah Ca-be	Bird-Jaguar III
9.16. 0.14. 5?	38:12	Yax	aux+fish-in-hand	Lady Zero-Skull
	38:13	Yax	aux+hun uinic blood-letting	Bird-Jaguar III

DATE	CAT NO	SITE	ACTION	ACTOR
	53:2	Yax	aux+blood-letting?	Bird-Jaguar III
	88:17	Yax	T741 birth	Shield-Jaguar II
	89:15	Yax	T741 birth	Shield-Jaguar II
9.16. 1. 0. 0	7:6	Yax	T684 inauguration	Bird-Jaguar III
	18:5	Yax	aux+????	Bird-Jaguar III
	38:9	Yax	aux+ahau-in-hand	Bird-Jaguar III
	38:14	Yax	aux+na chan blood-letting	Lady Zero-Skull
	63:2	Yax	T684 inauguration	Bird-Jaguar III
	71:9	Yax	T684 inauguration	Bird-Jaguar III
	71:20	Yax	T684 inauguration	Bird-Jaguar III
	112:19	Yax	seating *ti ahpo le*	Bird-Jaguar III
9.16. 1. 0. 9	86:6	Yax	????/4-bat	Bird-Jaguar III
9.16. 1. 2. 0	18:3	Yax	aux+*kan*/skull	Bird-Jaguar III
	38:8	Yax	aux+ahau-in-hand	Bird-Jaguar III
	79:12	Yax	aux+cauac-bat	Bird-Jaguar III
9.16. 1. 8. 6	48:3	Yax	aux+*ti*+zip	Kan-Tah
9.16. 1. 8. 6	48:4	Yax	Zip (God K/basket staff)	Bird-Jaguar III
9.16. 1. 8. 8	79:8	Yax	aux+????	Bird-Jaguar III
9.16. 1.12. 0	84:4	Ton	T520/*lu*-bat/*kan-tun*	Dragon
9.16. 3.10. 4	40:13	NTun	????	Chaan-Ah Cauac
	82:31	NTun	T819+????	
9.16. 4. 1. 1	10:16	Yax	star-shell	
	32:14	Yax	T764 capture of Ahpo-Muluc	Kan-Tah
	74:18	Yax	T515 capture of Jeweled-Skull	Bird-Jaguar III
	74:19	Yax	T515 capture of Jeweled-Skull	Bird-Jaguar III
9.16. 4. 1. 5	98:12	NTun	T819/*mo/pan*	Chaan-Ah Cauac
9.16. 4. 3.15	89:17	ECayo	T741 birth	4-Panac
9.16. 4. 6.17	16:6	Yax	T207-fire	Lady Xoc
9.16. 5. 0. 0	18:4	Yax	aux+head	Bird-Jaguar III
	21:20	Quir	na-chan blood-letting	Two-Legged-Sky
	44:2	Quir	T586 end of	????
	38:10	Yax	aux+ahau-in-hand	Bird-Jaguar III
	50:5	Quir	scattering	Two-Legged-Sky
	69:6	Cop	T586 end of	New-Sky-at-Horizon
	79:10	Yax	aux+*kan*/????	Bird-Jaguar III
9.16. 6. 0. 0	38:11	Yax	aux+cauac-bat	Shield-Jaguar II
	64:4	Yax	bat-expiration of 5th tun as *ahau*	
	79:11	Yax	aux+cauac-bat	Bird-Jaguar III
9.16. 6. 1. 6	38:15	Yax	aux+cauac-bat	Bird-Jaguar III
9.16. 6. 9.16	7:10	PN	T684 accession	Bat-Jaguar of Yaxchilan
9.16. 6.10.19	21:27	PN	????	????
9.16. 6.11.17	25:10	PN	wing-shell death	Ruler 4
9.16. 6.12. 0	73:5	PN	*mucah* burial	Ruler 4
9.16. 6.17. 1	71:8	PN	T684 inauguration	Ruler 5
9.16. 8.16. 1	20:9	Sac	ahau-in-hand	Shell-Hand
9.16.10. 0. 0	20:11	Sac	wing-hand	????
	29:3	Sac	scattering	Ahau-Kin
	29:4	Yax	scattering	Bird-Jaguar III

DATE	CAT NO	SITE	ACTION	ACTOR
	44:10	Quir	T586 end of?	Two-Legged-Sky
	47:5	Ton	scattering	
	57:3	Cop	PE special	New-Sky-at-Horizon
	58:2	Ton	zero:T713	Ah Imix
	65:2	Quir	scattering	
	66:7	Quir	half-period	
	69:7	Cop	T586 end of	New-Sky-at-Horizon
	86:7	Sac	????	Ahau-Kin
9.16.10. 5. 2	116:21	NTun	T819/*mo*/pan	Chaan-Ah Cauac
9.16.11.12. 4	82:30	NTun	T819	Chaan-Ah Cauac
9.16.12. 5.14	55:3	Yax	fish-in-hand/God K	Lady 6-Tuns of the Ik site
9.16.12. 5.17	7:7-9	Cop	T684 inauguration	New-Sky-at-Horizon
	112:20	Cop	seating *ti ahau le*	New-Sky-at-Horizon
	112:21	Cop	seating *ti ahpo le*	New-Sky-at-Horizon
	112:22	Cop	seating *ti ahau le*	New-Sky-at-Horizon
	112:25	Cop	seating *ti ahau le*	New-Sky-at-Horizon
9.16.12.10. 8	71:10	PN	T684 inauguration	Ruler 6
9.16.12.14.10	71:12	ECayo	T684 inauguration	Ah Chac-Zotz'
9.16.13. 0. 0	16:2	Yax	T207-671	Mah Kina Itzam
9.16.13. 0. 0	126:3	Yax	seating/turtle/house	Bird-Jaguar III
9.16.13. 0. 7	32:9	Pal	seating on throne	Kuk II
	85:10	Pal	seating *ti ahau le*	Kuk II
9.16.13. 4.17	123:14	Quir	T218 completion of 2 katuns *ti ahpo le*	Two-Legged-Sky
9.16.14.17.17	16:8	Tik	T207-fire	????
9.16.15. 0. 0	43:8	LPas	scattering	Bird-Jaguar III
	43:13	Quir	scattering	Two-Legged-Sky
	43:14	Quir	scattering	Two-Legged-Sky
	48:5	LPas	aux+T280:501	Zac-Muluc
	73:12	Quir	T168	????
	80:9	Yax	????	Bird-Jaguar III
9.16.15.18. 9	37:21	Yax	aux+*nawah* of Ek-Chan	Bird-Jaguar III
9.16.16. 1. 6	38:15	Yax	aux+T683/563/Sky	Bird-Jaguar III
9.16.16. 2. 5	21:30	???	canoed	Ti-Kab-Cauac
	24:13	???	T736 death	Ti-Kab-Cauac
9.16.17. 2. 4	15:6	Yax	fish-in-hand	
	76:2	Yax	fish-in-hand/na-chan blood-letting	
9.16.17. 6.12	79:14	Yax	aux+T683/T630/sky	Bird-Jaguar III
9.16.17.14. 3	71:16	Nar	T684 inauguration	Ruler IIIa
9.16.17.16. 4	100:6	Tik	seating *ti batab le*	Ruler C
9.17. 0. 0. 0	2:9	Tik	T713 end of tun	Ruler C
	4:10	Pom	seating of tun	
	5:1-2	Cop	T586 end of tun	New-Sky-at-Horizon
	5:5	Yax	T756 expiration of tun	
	5:8	Cop	T671	New-Sky-at-Horizon
	7:10	Seib	T684 inauguration	Ah Tah
	13:4	Cop	T843	New-Sky-at-Horizon
	31:10-14	Cop	T44:502	
	41:4	Pom	T713 end of tun	

DATE	CAT NO	SITE	ACTION	ACTOR
	43:6	Agua	scattering	Shield-God K of Dos Pilas
	43:7	Pom	scattering	
	43:9	Quir	scattering	Two-Legged-Sky
	50:8	Quir	T819 PE	
	52:7	Pom	na-chan blood-letting	GI-Balam
	56:4	Cop	T679-757	New-Sky-at-Horizon
	66:9	Pom	half-period variant of 17 katuns	
	69:8	Quir	T586 end of 13 Ahau tun	Two-Legged-Sky
	82:16	Yax	????	Shield-Jaguar II
	98:1	Quir	scattering	Two-Legged-Sky
	111:2	Tik	scattering	Ruler C
9.17. 0. 0. 3	68:2	Pom	T559 kankin	????
9.17. 0. 2.12	89:20-21	Nar	T741 birth	Ruler IIIb
9.17. 1. 5. 9	71:13	ECayo	T684 inauguration	4-Panac-Ahau
9.17. 2.10. 4	109:5	Cop	T520H 819 Day Count	God K
9.17. 4. 1.11	24:12	Cop	T736 death	????
	108:1	Cop	T586.669b	????
9.17. 4.10.12	82:22	Quir	eccentric-flint?	????
9.17. 4.12. 5	25:16	Ton	wing-shell death	Chaan
9.17. 5. 0. 0	13:5	Cop	T843	New-Sky-at-Horizon
9.17. 5. 0. 0	29:9	Quir	scattering	Two-Legged-Sky
	43:10	Quir	scattering	Two-Legged-Sky
	43:11	Quir	scattering	Two-Legged-Sky
9.17. 5. 3. 4	33:7	Cop	ahau-in-hand+????	New-Sky-at-Horizon
9.17. 5. 7. 5	27:6	Ton	posthumous event	Chaan
9.17. 5. 8. 9	71:15	Bon	T684 inauguration	Chaan-Muan
9.17. 5. 8.12	37:28	Nar	T757	Ruler IIIb
9.17. 9. 0.13	99:7	Ixk	smoke-head	local ruler
9.17. 9. 0.14	75:8	Ixk	axe	local ruler
9.17. 9. 2.12	112:26	Cop	seating/T16.669b:140:178	Yax-Zotz'
9.17. 9. 3. 4	99:8	Ixk	smoke-head	local person
9.17. 9. 5.11	13:7	PN	T843	Ruler 7
	21:16	PN	T173.4:528+star-shell	Ruler 7
	106:7	PN	????	Ruler 7
	126:5	PN	T683.565	Ruler 7
	129:10	PN	T126.25:565	Ruler 7
9.17.10. 0. 0	2:15	Nar	T713 end of tun	Ruler IIIb
	2:16	Nar	T713 end of tun	Ruler IIIb
	29:5	Bon	scattering	Chaan-Muan
	29:6	Nar	scattering	Ruler IIIb
	35:7	Nar	aux+akbal-kin	Ruler IIIb
	35:8	Nar	aux+akbal-kin	Ruler IIIb
	37:25	LHig	T712 bloodletting	
	41:5	Bon	T713 end of tun	Chaan-Muan
	43:12	Ixt	scattering	Ah Yax-T'ul
	44:3	Ixt	T586 end of tun	Ah Yax-T'ul
	121:9	LHig	???? in his house	local person
9.17.10. 6. 1	21:15	PN	T548:575 (T550)	Ruler 7
	82:32	PN	T548:575 (T550)	Ruler 7
9.17.10. 9. 4	71:14	PN	T684 inauguration	Ruler 7

DATE	CAT NO	SITE	ACTION	ACTOR
	71:19	PN	T684 inauguration	Ruler 7
9.17.12. 6. 2	46:4	Cop	fish-in-hand/God K	New-Sky-at-Horizon
9.17.12.13.14	74:21	???	T515 capture of Balan-Ahau	Ah-Chac-Ma-??
9.17.12.13.17	95:13	???	*nawah* of the captive	Split-Earth
9.17.13. 0. 7	103:6	Pal	1st katun *ti ahau le*	Kuk II
	123:15	Pal	T218 completion of 1st katun *ti ahau le*	Kuk II
	123:16	Pal	T218 completion of 1st katun *ti ahau le*	Kuk II
9.17.13. 4. 3	71:17	Nar	T684 inauguration	Ruler IIIb
9.17.14.15.16	112:27	PUin	seating *ti ahpo lel*	Chac-Balam
9.17.14.16.18	110:3	Quir	T713 accession	Ruler 2
9.17.15. 0. 0	29:7	Bon	scattering	Chaan-Muan
	43:13	Quir	scattering	Two-Legged-Sky
	69:9	Quir	T586 end of tun	
	98:8	Quir	T819	Two-Legged-Sky
	127:12	PN	T546/????/house	Ruler 7
9.17.16. 3. 8	74:23	Bon	T515 capture of Zotz'	Shield-Jaguar II of Yaxchilan
9.17.16. 3.12	74:22	Bon	T515 capture of Ah 5-Skull	Chaan-Muan
9.17.16.14.19	107:5	PN	T515 capture of Ah Nabe	Ruler 7
9.17.18. 2. 1	123:19	Tik	T218 completion of 1st katun *ti batab le*	Ruler C
9.17.18. 6.19	37:19	LMar	aux+T713 accession	local ruler
9.17.18.15.18	3:14	Bon	scattering	Lady Cauac-Skull
	49:3	Bon	flint-T713 blood-letting	Lady Cauac-Skull
	76:3	Bon	T586 blood-letting	Lady Cauac-Skull
9.18. 0. 0. 0	4:7	Pom	seating of tun	
	28:16	Nar	T713 end of tun	
	28:21	Ixk	T713 end of tun	
	29:12-13	Ixk	scattering	Shell-Hand
	38:29	Ixk	aux+*ti*+scattering	local person
	41:6	Pom	T713 end of tun	
	52:8	Pom	na-chan blood-letting	????
	64:3	Pom	bat-expiration of 18 katuns	
	111:3	Tik	scattering	Ruler C
9.18. 0. 3. 4	38:19	Bon	aux+T518 heir-designation	????
9.18. 1. 2. 0	16:11	Bon	T207-fire	Chaan-Muan
9.18. 1. 8.18	14:3	LMar	axe	????
9.18. 1.13. 2	114:4	Cop	T79:565	????
9.18. 2.14. 6	121:6	PUin	eclipse	
9.18. 2. 8. 0	74:30	Cop	*tah*-T515	New-Sky-at-Horizon
9.18. 3. 0. 0	29:8	Ixl	scattering	????
9.18. 4. 2.19	116:13	LMar	T515 capture of Zac-Zotz'	Macaw-GI
9.18. 4.16. 7	20:15	PN	46th tun anniversary of birth	Ruler 7
9.18. 5. 0. 0	41:7	PN	T713 end of tun	Ruler 7
	41:8	LMar	T713 end of tun	Macaw-GI
	43:11	Quir	scattering	????
	84:9	Quir	T520	Ruler 2
	90:1	Cop	T758	
9.18. 6. 4.19	74:36	Yax	T515 capture of ????	Shield-Jaguar II

DATE	CAT NO	SITE	ACTION	ACTOR
9.18. 6. 5.11	32:15	Yax	T764 capture of ????	Shield-Jaguar II
	74:26	Yax	T515 capture of ????	Shield-Jaguar II
	74:37	Yax	T515 capture of Inverted Ahau	Shield-Jaguar II
9.18. 7. 6. 0	74:38	Yax	T515 capture of ????	Shield-Jaguar II
9.18. 7.10.13	101:3	Pal	T520H 819 Day Count	God K
9.18. 7.16. 9	74:39	Yax	T765d deer event	Shield-Jaguar II
9.18. 8. 3. 3	74:40	Yax	T515 capture of Ah-Zac-??-??	Shield-Jaguar II
9.18. 8.10.12	32:17	Yax	T573 changeover	Shield-Jaguar II
9.18. 9. 4. 4	72:8	Pal	T713 accession	6 Cimi-Pacal
9.18. 9. 6. 6	74:41	Yax	T515 capture of God K-Cleft-Sky	Shield-Jaguar II
9.18. 9. 7.10	86:10	Yax?	T563/*ku ti ma*	Lady ????
9.18. 9. 7.18	74:42	Yax	T515 capture of ????	Shield-Jaguar II
9.18. 9. 9.14	74:43	Yax	T515 capture of ????	Shield-Jaguar II
9.18. 9.10.10	26:25	Yax	capture? of Ahpo-Pah	Shield-Jaguar II
9.18.10. 0. 0	28:26	Ixk	T713 end of tun	Shell-Hand
9.18.10. 0. 0	41:12	???	T713 end of tun	Ah Cauac
	53:3	Seib	aux+????	Ah Ahpo-Tah
	60:5	Mach	T713 end of tun	
9.18.12. 0. 0	44:7	Itz	T586 end of tun	????
9.18.14. 7. 0	84:8	Quir	T520 819 Day Count	God K
9.18.17.12. 6	10:20	Yax	star-shell	
	74:27	Yax	T515 capture of Turtle-Bat	Great-Skull
	129:6	Yax	ahau-in-hand/T606/T757	Great-Skull
9.18.17.13.10	110:4	Yax	T207:671 *ti balan ahau*	Great-Skull
9.18.17.13.14	129:7	Yax	ahau-in-hand+????	Great-Skull
9.19. 0. 0. 0	28:17	Nar	T713 end of tun	
	43:15	Quir	scattering	Mul-Chaan
	43:16	Quir	scattering	Mul-Chaan
	123:17	Quir	T218 completion of 19th katun	????
9.19. 4. 1. 0	26:9	Nar	????	18-Rabbit
9.19. 4. 1. 1	7:11	Nar	T684 inauguration	18-Rabbit
9.19. 4.15. 1	26:11	Nar	*kuk:ma.??:ma:??*	
	62:20	Nar	T669b+????	
9.19. 5. 0. 0	50:1	Mach	T713 end of tun	Split-Kin-God K
9.19. 5. 9.12	26:12	Nar	T573-*kuk*+T669b	
	26:21	Nar	T669	
9.19. 9.15. 0	26:10	Nar	????	18-Rabbit
9.19.10. 0. 0	3:4	Mach	PE	
	41:9	Nar	T713 end of tun	18-Rabbit
	43:17	Car	scattering	Ox-Cauac
9.19.14.15. 1	127:9	Mach	T713 accession	Split-Kin-God K
10. 0. 0. 0. 0	1:2	Nar	T218 completion of 10 cycles	
	31:2	Pal	T807	????
	31:13	Cop	T44:502	
	84:2	Uax	T819	local ruler
	128:6	Cop	T79-house	
10. 0. 0.13. 0	28:18	Mach	T713 end of tun ??	
	45:10	Mach	????	local ruler
10. 0. 0.14.15	20:6	Mach	T819:757	local ruler
10. 0. 3. 3. 8	20:5	Xul	T741 birth	????

DATE	CAT NO	SITE	ACTION	ACTOR
10. 0. 5. 0. 0	60:1	Mach	T713 end of tun	
10. 0. 7. 9. 0	47:3	Ton	scattering	Ik-Skull-Dragon
10. 0.10.17. 5	40:8	Mach	????	????
10. 0.19. 4.15	44:9	Car	T596 end of	Ox-Cauac
10. 1. 0. 0. 0	28:20	Uca	T713 end of tun	
	33:8	Seib	God C-in-hand	Ah Bolon-Tun
	41:10	Seib	T713 end of tun	Ah Bolon-Tun
	43:18	Seib	scattering	Ah Hun-Kin
	43:19	Ixl	scattering	local ruler
	43:20	Uca	scattering	local ruler
	53:4	Seib	aux+??:kan	Ah Bolon-Tun
	65:3	Car	scattering	Ox-Cauac
10. 1.10. 0. 0	28:19	Xul	T713 end of tun	
10. 1.13.17.19	104:1	???	T520H 819 Day Count	God K
10. 1.14. 5.17	16:8	???	T207	Bat
10. 2. 0. 0. 0	5:3	Itz	T586 end of tun	local ruler
10. 2.10. 0. 0	41:11	Ixl	T713 end of tun	
	111:4	Ixl	scattering	Ah Kal
10. 3. 0. 0. 0	61:3	Jimb	scattering	local ruler
13. 0. 0. 0. 0	1:4	Tort	T218 completion of the 13th baktun	
1. 0. 0. 0. 0. 8	55:8	Pal	80th CR anniversary of Pacal's accession	
1. 0. 0. 0. 0. 8	55:9	Pal	80th CR anniversary of Pacal's accession	

The following events are those recorded as having occurred in the mythological past. "*" marks the amount of time before 13.0.0.0.0 4 Ahau 8 Cumku of the date of each event.

DATE	CAT NO	SITE	ACTION	ACTOR
9 Ik 10 Mol	5:12	Pal	*xoc ti* ahau-in-hand	Moon Goddess
	20:8	Pal	first ahau-in-hand	deleted
	21:9	Pal	T58.86:??	deleted
	121:4	Pal	chicchan-in-hand/God K	Moon Goddess

*5.18.14.13.17.16.18

13 Oc 18 Uo	45:11	Pal	ahau-in-hand	Bolon Yocte
	82:4	Pal	TI.679:528.528.181	supernaturals
	82:5	Pal	TI.679.177:23:180	supernaturals

*5.18.14.13.8.1.10?

13 Manik 5 Pax	107:6	Yax	axe	First Knot-Skull

*13.13.13.13.13.13.13.13.3.14.9.14.18

9 Kan 12 Xul	107:7	Yax	axe	2nd Knot-Skull

*13.13.13.13.13.13.13.13.3.8.10.14.11

DATE	CAT NO	SITE	ACTION	ACTOR
1 Ahau 13 Xul	107:8	Yax	axe	3-Knot-Skull

*13.13.13.13.13.13.13.13.0.0.0.0.0

DATE	CAT NO	SITE	ACTION	ACTOR
1 Manik 10 Zec	113:1	Pal	T168:518	supernatural

*7.17.13.0.0.7.13

Appendix 5

Split-Ergativity in the Cholan and Yucatecan Languages
by Barbara MacLeod

This discussion will focus on the phonemenon of split-ergativity, a feature which I have noted in all of the Cholan and Yucatecan languages. The pattern of splitting found in these languages, as well as in Pocoman and Pocomchi, occurs in simple sentences with intransitive verbs in incompletive (imperfective) aspect. Whereas the more common pattern in Mayan and other ergative languages is to mark the subjects of transitive verbs with one set of pronouns and the subjects of intransitive with another set, the Yucatecan and Cholan languages utilize the ergative (transitive) set with intransitive verbs in incompletive aspect, shifting to the set of suffixed absolutive pronouns in the completive. The ergative pronouns in the languages under consideration are prefixed to the verb; in many other Mayan languages these, too, are suffixed.

It has been proposed by Bruce (1968:41-42) that Lacandon, a Yucatecan language, has no verbs. The controversy focuses on incompletive intransitives such as *in hanan*, which can be understood as "I eat" or "my food." In Yucatec, the closest kindred to Lacandon, the distinction would be made by means of an obligatory preposed aspect marker, *k-*:

k-in hanal	"I eat"
in hanal	"my food"

The same morpheme *k-* occurs in Lacandon, but Bruce believes it to mark future time. My own data on Lacandon reflect the present-time ambiguity of which he has spoken, although I would argue that the language does, in fact, have verbs. For all practical purposes, however, incompletive intransitives might just as well be considered nouns. This nominalization is fundamental to the development of split-ergativity in all of these languages, although most have developed some sort of disambiguating or dodging strategy as well, as seen in the Yucatec example above.

Cholti and Chorti appear to have implemented yet another set of prefixed pronouns, a set with no function other than to mark incompletive intransitive constructions. More will be said of this set later, following several examples of its function. There is yet another strategy, one which serves to circumvent the ambiguity altogether. This is the "auxiliary verb + *ti* + verbal noun" construction, seen most often in Chol, but noted also in Cholti and to a lesser degree in Mopan. Thus in Chol one may say *woli-k wiyel* "I am sleeping," or *woli-y-on ti wiyel*, with the same meaning. The latter is the more commonly heard form, wherein the ergative pronoun *k-* has been replaced by the absolutive *-on*, now suffixed to the auxiliary, followed by the locative *ti* (to, at, toward). *Wiyel* "sleep" is ambiguous by itself; following *ti* it must be considered nominal.

A number of examples, selected from various Cholan and Yucatecan languages to demonstrate the contrast in inflection resulting from split-ergativity, appear in

Table 1. The function of ergative and absolutive pronouns in split-ergative languages
can be summarized as follows:

Ergative pronouns:
  (a) subjects of transitive verbs;
  (b) possessors of nouns and in most lan-
      guages with the split-ergative pattern
      (Cholti and Chorti excepted);
  (c) subjects of intransitive verbs in
      incompletive aspect.

Absolutive pronouns:
  (a) objects of transitive verbs;
  (b) subjects of intransitive verbs (except
      in incompletive aspect in split-
      ergative languages);
  (c) subjects of stative constructions.

From the examples in Table 1 we see evidence in all of the Cholan and Yucatecan
languages of a split pronominal pattern
based on aspect. A close look at the Cholti
examples reveals two third person pronominal
prefixes in addition to the suffixed pronoun, which is Ø in third person singular.
Fought (1972) gives the following sets of
pronominal prefixes for Chorti, designated
the "u-set" and the "a-set" respectively:

	u-set		a-set	
	sing	plur	sing	plur
1	vl/-ni	ka-	vn-	ka-
2	a-	i-	i-	is-
3	u-	u- -o'p	a	a- -o'p

Although Moran (1935) does not explicitly
recognize this second set of prefixes in

Cholti, he does provide numerous examples
using third person, and on page 30 of his
vocabulary he indicates that e- is a "second
person singular possessive"--the term that
is his usual classification for prefixed
pronouns. This e- looks suspiciously like
the second person singular of the Cholti a-
set above. Since there is now evidence of
the a-set in Cholti, I have assumed greater
antiquity of it than has previously been
proposed. Preliminary evidence from the
writing system indicates possible glyphic
analogues.

The u-set in both languages is reserved
for complex stems ending in -vl (a nominal-
izing suffix in all Cholan and Yucatecan
languages), apart from the expected transitive verb and noun morphology. A further
example from Fought's (1972) *Chorti Texts*
underscores the nominalized nature of intransitive "verbs" taking the u-set:

  u w-*ir-na-ar*   "their being seen"

Ergative splitting is clearly demonstra-
ble in all of the Cholan and Yucatecan languages, and it is apparent that a nominal-
izing process is at the heart of its evolution. Furthermore, the ancestors of all
these languages were likely participants in
the development and elaboration of the writing system. Syntactic and morphological
disambiguating strategies apparently developed side-by-side with ergative splitting
in most of these languages, and evidence for
all these patterns may be found through
careful attention to glyph morphology and
syntax.

Table 1. Split-ergativity in Cholan and Yucatecan languages.

LANGUAGE	ASPECT	ERGATIVE PRONOUN	STEM	ABSOLUTIVE PRONOUN		GLOSS
YUCATEC						
	incompletive	k-	u	han-al			"she eats"
	completive	(h)-		han-i	-ø		"she ate"
LACANDON						
	incompletive		a	ween-en			"you sleep"
	completive			ween-			
MOPAN						
	incompletive (progressive)	tan-	a	han-al	-eech		"you are eating"
	completive			han-	-ø		"you ate"
ITZA						
	incompletive	k-	a	taah			"he comes"
	completive			taal-i	-ø		"he came"
CHOL						
	incompletive (progressive)	woli-	k	wiyel			"I am sleeping"
	completive	tza-		wiy-i-y-	-on		"I slept"
		tza-		buch-l-e-y	-on		"I sat down"
CHONTAL (Acalan)						
	incompletive		u	tal-el			"he comes"
	completive	ø-		tal-i-y-	-ob		"they came"
		ø-		chum-wan-	-ø	ta ahau-l-el	"he became governor"
CHORTI						
	incompletive		a	cham-ay			"he dies"
	completive			cham-ay-	-ø		"he dies"
	incompletive		a	tur-wan			"he sits down"
	completive			tur-wan-	-ø		"he sat down"
CHOLTI						
	incompletive (progressive)	iwal-	u	koy-tal		padre	"the padre is lying down"
	completive			koy-wan-	-ø		"he lay down"
	incompletive (progressive)	iwal-	u	pas-k'a-el			"it is being revealed"
	incompletive		a	pas-k'a			"it is revealed"
	completive			pas-k'a-	-ø		

References

Aulie, H. Wilbur, and Evelyn W. de Aulie
1978 *Diccionario ch'ol-español, español-ch'ol*. Serie de Vocabularios y Diccionarios Indigenas, Num. 21. Mexico City: Instituto Lingüístico de Verano.

Balser, Carlos S.
1974 *El jade de Costa Rica*. San José, Costa Rica: Lehmann.

Berlin, Heinrich
1958 El glifo "emblema" en las inscripciones mayas. *Journal de la Société des Américanistes*, n.s., 47, pp. 119-121. Paris.
1959 Glifos nominales en el sarcófago de Palenque. *Humanidades* 2(10):1-8. Universidad de San Carlos de Guatemala.
1963 The Palenque Triad. *Journal de la Société des Américanistes*, n.s., 52, pp. 91-99. Paris.
1968 The Tablet of the 96 Glyphs at Palenque, Chiapas, Mexico. In *Middle American Research Institute, Tulane University, Publication 26*, pp. 135-149. New Orleans.

Blom, Frans, and Oliver La Farge
1926 *Tribes and Temples*, vol. 1. New Orleans: Tulane University.

Bricker, Victoria Reifler
1977 Pronominal Inflection in the Maya Languages. *Occasional Paper 1, Middle American Research Institute, Tulane University*. New Orleans.
n.d. A Morphosyntactic Interpretation of Some Accession Compounds and Other Glyphs in Mayan Hieroglyphs. In *The Fourth Palenque Round Table, 1980, Vol. 6*. Austin: University of Texas Press. In press.

Bruce S., Roberto D.
1968 *Gramática de Lacandón*. Mexico City: Departamento de Investigaciones Antropológicas, Instituto Nacional de Antropología e Historia.

Closs, Michael
1979 Venus in the Maya World: Glyphs, Gods and Associated Phenomena. In *Tercera Mesa Redonda de Palenque, Vol. IV*, edited by Merle Greene Robertson and Donnan Call Jeffers, pp. 147-172. Palenque, Mexico: Pre-Columbian Art Printers.

Coe, Michael D.
1973 *The Maya Scribe and His World*. New York: Grolier Club.
1974 A Carved Wooden Box from the Classic Maya Civilization. In *Primera Mesa Redonda de Palenque, Part II*, edited by Merle Greene Robertson, pp. 51-58. Pebble Beach: Robert Louis Stevenson School.
1976 Early Steps in the Evolution of Maya Writing. In *Origins of Religious Art and Iconography in Pre-Classic Mesoamerica*, edited by H. B. Nicholson, pp. 107-122. Los Angeles; UCLA Latin American Center Publications and the Ethnic Arts Council of Los Angeles.

Coe, William R.
1967 *Tikal: A Handbook of Ancient Maya Ruins*. Philadelphia: University Museum, University of Pennsylvania.

Durbin, Marshall

n.d.   A Discussion of Transitive Syntax in the Classic Maya Inscriptions. Paper given at the Taller Maya IV at Palenque, July 1979.

Dutting, Dieter

1979   Birth, Inauguration and Death in the Inscriptions of Palenque, Chiapas, Mexico. In *Tercera Mesa Redonda de Palenque, Vol. IV*, edited by Merle Greene Robertson and Donnan Call Jeffers, pp. 147-172. Palenque, Mexico: Pre-Columbian Art Printers.

Edmonson, Munro S.

1971   *The Book of Counsel: The "Popol Vuh" of the Quiche Maya of Guatemala. Middle American Research Institute, Publication 35.* New Orleans: Tulane University.

Fernandez, Miguel Angel

1954   Drawings of glyphs of Structure XVIII, Palenque, with notes by Heinrich Berlin. In *Notes on Middle American Archaeology and Ethnology* 119. Washington, D.C.: Carnegie Institution of Washington, Department of Archaeology.

Fought, John G.

1972   *Chorti (Mayan) Texts.* Edited by Sarah S. Fought. Philadelphia: University of Pennslyvania Press.

Gates, William

1931   Glyph Studies. *Maya Society Quarterly* 1, pp. 32-33. Baltimore.

Greene, Merle, Robert L. Rands, and John A. Graham

1972   *Maya Sculpture from the Southern Lowlands, the Highlands and Pacific Piedmont, Guatemala, Mexico, Honduras.* Berkeley: Lederer, Street, and Zeus.

Jones, Chrostopher

1977   Inauguration Dates of Three Late Classic Rulers of Tikal, Guatemala. *American Antiquity* 42(1), pp. 28-60.

Joralemon, David

1974   Ritual Blood-Sacrifice among the Ancient Maya: Part I. In *Primera Mesa Redonda de Palenque, Part II*, edited by Merle Greene Robertson, pp. 59-76. Pebble Beach: Robert Louis Stevenson School.

Josserand, Kathryn, Linda Schele, and Nicholas A. Hopkins

n.d.   Auxiliary Verb + *ti* Constructions in the Classic Maya Inscriptions. *Fourth Palenque Round Table, 1980, Vol. 6.* Austin: University of Texas Press.

Kaufman, Terrence, and William Norman

n.d.   An Outline of Proto-Cholan Phonology, Grammar, and Vocabulary. Paper presented at the SUNY Albany Conference on Maya Hieroglyphic Writing, April 1979.

Kelley, David H.

1962a   A History of the Decipherment of Maya Script. *Anthropological Linguistics* 4(8), pp. 1-48.

1962b   Glyphic Evidence for a Dynastic Sequence at Quirigua, Guatemala. *American Antiquity,* 27(3), pp. 324-335.

1975   Planetary Data on Caracol Stela 3. In *Archaeoastronomy in Pre-Columbian America*, edited by Anthony Aveni, pp. 257-262. Austin: University of Texas Press.

1976   *Deciphering the Maya Script.* Austin: University of Texas Press.

1977   Maya Astronomical Tables and Inscriptions. In *Native American Astronomy*, edited by Anthony Aveni. Austin: University of Texas Press.

Liman, Florence F., and Marshall Durbin

1975   Some New Glyphs on an Unusual Maya Stela. *American Antiquity* 40(3), pp. 314-319.

Lounsbury, Floyd G.

1974   The Inscription of the Sarcophagus Lid at Palenque. In *Primera Mesa Redonda de Palenque, Part II*, edited by Merle Greene Robertson, pp. 5-20. Pebble Beach: Robert Louis Stevenson School.

1976   A Rationale for the Initial Date of the Temple of the Cross at Palenque. In *The Art, Iconography, and Dynastic History of Palenque, Part III: Proceedings of the Segunda Mesa Redonda de Palenque*, edited by Merle Greene Robertson, pp. 211-224. Pebble Beach: Robert Louis Stevenson School.

1980   Some Problems in the Interpretation of the Mythological Portion of the Hieroglyphic Text of the Temple of the Cross at Palenque. In *Third Palenque Round Table, 1978, Vol. 2*, edited by Merle Greene Robertson, pp. 99-115. Palenque Round Table Series Vol. 5. Austin: University of Texas Press.

n.d. Letters on Venus Phenomena in the Classic inscriptions, especially at Bonampak. Written to Mary Miller, 1981.

Maler, Teobert
1901 Researches in the Central Portion of the Usumatsintla Valley. *Memoirs of the Peabody Museum of American Archaeology and Ethnology, Harvard University*, II, No. 1. Cambridge.

1903 Researches in the Central Portion of the Usumatsintla Valley. *Memoirs of the Peabody Museum of American Archaeology and Ethnology, Harvard University*, II, No. 2. Cambridge.

Marcus, Joyce
1973 Territorial Organization of the Lowland Maya. *Science* 180, pp. 911-916. Washington, D.C.: American Association for the Advancement of Science.

1976 *Emblem and State in the Classic Maya Lowlands: An Epigraphic Approach to Territorial Organization*. Washington, D.C.: Dumbarton Oaks.

Mathews, Peter
1979 The Glyphs on the Ear Ornaments from Tomb A-1/1. In *Excavations at Altun Ha, Belize, 1964-1970* 1, pp. 79-80. Toronto: Royal Ontario Museum.

1980 Notes on the Dynastic Sequence of Bonampak, Part I. In *Third Palenque Round Table, 1978, Vol. 2*, edited by Merle Greene Robertson, pp. 60-74. Palenque Round Table Series, Vol. 5. Austin: University of Texas Press.

n.d.a Notes on the Monuments of "Site Q." MS provided by author.

n.d.b The Inscription on the Back of Stela 8, Dos Pilas, Guatemala. Paper prepared at Yale University. Copy provided by author.

n.d.c Tonina Dates: 1. A Glyph for the Period of 260 Days? Maya Glyph Notes, No. 8. MS provided by author.

n.d.d On the Glyphs "West" and "Mah K'ina." Maya Glyph Notes, No. 6. MS provided by author.

Mathews, Peter, and David H. Pendergast
1979 The Altun Ha Jade Plaque: Deciphering the Inscription. In *Contributions of the University of California Research Facility*, 41, pp. 197-214. Berkeley: Archaeological Research Facility, Department of Anthropology, University of California.

Mayer, Karl Herbert
1978 *Maya Monuments: Sculptures of Unknown Provenance in Europe*. Trans. Sandra L. Brizee. Ramona, Calif.: Acoma Books.

1980 *Maya Monuments: Sculptures of Unknown Provenance in the United States*. Trans. Sandra L. Brizee. Ramona, Calif.: Acoma Books.

Miller, Jeffery H.
1974 Notes on a Stelae Pair Probably from Calakmul, Campeche, Mexico. In *Primera Mesa Redonda de Palenque, Part I*, edited by Merle Greene Robertson, pp. 149-161. Pebble Beach: Robert Louis Stevenson School.

Miller, Mary
n.d. The Murals of Bonampak, Chiapas, Mexico. Ph.D dissertation, Yale University, 1981.

Moran, Fr. Pedro
1935 *Arte y Diccionario en Lengua Choltí, a manuscript copied from the Libro Grande of fr. Pedro Moran*. Baltimore: The Maya Society, Pub. 9.

Morley, Sylvanus Griswold
1975 *An Introduction to the Study of Maya Hieroglyphics*. New York: Dover Publications.

Proskouriakoff, Tatiana
1960 Historic Implication of a Pattern of Dates at Piedras Negras, Guatemala. *American Antiquity*, 25(4), pp. 454-475.

1963-1964 Historical Data in the Inscriptions of Yaxchilan, Parts I and II. *Estudios de Cultura Maya*, 3:149-167, 4:177-201. Mexico City: Universidad Nacional Autónoma de México.

1968 The Jog and the Jaguar Signs in Maya

Writing. *American Antiquity* 33(2), pp. 247-251.

1973 The *Hand-grasping-fish* and Associated Glyphs on Classic Maya Monuments. In *Mesoamerican Writing Systems*, edited by Elizabeth Benson, pp. 165-178. Washington, D.C.: Dumbarton Oaks.

1974 Jades from the Cenote of Sacrifice, Chichen Itza, Yucatan. *Memoirs of the Peabody Museum of Archaeology and Ethnology, Harvard University* 10(1). Cambridge, Mass.

Robertson, Merle Greene

n.d. The Ritual Bundles of Yaxchilan. A paper presented at the Tulane Symposium on the Art of Latin America, 1972. New Orleans.

Ruz Lhuillier, Alberto

1958 Exploraciones arqueológicas en Palenque: 1953-56. In *Anales del Instituto Nacional de Antropología e Historia*, vol. 10. Mexico City: Instituto Nacional de Antropología e Historia.

Schele, Linda

1976 Accession Iconography of Chan-Bahlum in the Group of the Cross at Palenque. In *The Art, Iconography, and Dynastic History of Palenque, Part III. Proceedings of the Segunda Mesa Redonda de Palenque*, edited by Merle Greene Robertson, pp. 9-34. Pebble Beach: Robert Louis Stevenson School.

n.d.a Some Suggested Readings of the Event and Office of Heir-Designation at Palenque. Paper presented at the SUNY Albany Conference on Maya Hieroglyphic Writing, April 1979.

n.d.b Human Sacrifice among the Classic Maya. Paper presented at the Dumbarton Oaks Conference on Human Sacrifice. October, 1979.

n.d.c The Xibalba Shuffle: A Dance after Death. Paper presented at the Princeton University Conference on Maya Vase Painting, November 1980.

Schele, Linda, Peter Mathews, and Floyd Lounsbury

n.d. Parentage Statements in Classic Maya Inscriptions. Paper presented at the

International Conference on Maya Iconography and Hieroglyphic Writing, Guatemala City, July 1977.

Schellhas, Paul

1904 Representation of Deities of the Maya Manuscripts. *Papers of the Peabody Museum of American Archaeology and Ethnology, Harvard University* 4(1). Cambridge, Mass.

Schumann, Otto G.

1971 Descripción estructural del maya itzá del Peten, Guatemala, C.A. *Centro de Estudios Mayas, Cuaderno 6*. Mexico City: Universidad Nacional Autónoma de México.

1973 La lengua chol, de Tila (Chiapas). *Centro de Estudios Mayas, Cuaderno 8*. Mexico City: Universidad Nacional Autónoma de México.

Smailus, Ortwin

1975 El maya-chontal de Acalan; Análisis lingüístico de un documento de los años 1610-12. *Centro de Estudios Mayas, Cuaderno 9*. Mexico City: Universidad Nacional Autónoma de México.

Stuart, David

n.d. The Inscription on Four Shell Plaques from Piedras Negras, Guatemala. In *The Fourth Palenque Round Table, 1980, Vol. 6*. Austin: University of Texas Press. In press.

Swadesh, Mauricio, Ma. Cristina Alvarez, and Juan R. Bastarrachea

1970 Diccionario de elementos de maya yucateco colonial. *Centro de Estudios Mayas, Cuaderno 3*. Mexico City: Universidad Nacional Autónoma de México.

Thompson, J. Eric S.

1943 Maya Epigraphy: Directional Glyphs in Counting. *Carnegie Institute of Washington, Division of Historical Research, Notes on Middle American Archaeology and Ethnology*, 20. Cambridge, Mass.

1950 Maya Hieroglyphic Writing: An Introduction. *Carnegie Institute of Washington, Publication 589*. Washington, D.C.

1959 Systems of Hieroglyphic Writing in Middle America and Methods of Deci-

phering Them. *American Antiquity*
24(4), pp. 349-364.

1962 *A Catalog of Maya Hieroglyphs*. Norman:
University of Oklahoma Press.

Trik, Aubrey S.

1963 The Splendid Tomb of Temple I at
Tikal, Guatemala. *Expedition* 6(1), pp. 2-
18. Philadelphia: University Museum,
University of Pennsylvania.

Warkentin, Viola, and Ruby Scott

1980 *Gramatica ch'ol*. Serie de Gramáticas
Indígenas de Mexico, No 4. Mexico

City: Instituto Lingüístico de Verano.

Whorf, Benjamin Lee

1933 The Phonetic Value of Certain Characters in Maya Writing. *Papers of the
Peabody Museum of American Archaeology
and Ethnology, Harvard University*
13(2). Cambridge, Mass. Kraus Reprint,
New York, 1967.

Zimmermann, Gunter

n.d. *The Maya Codices (with Glyph Index)*.
Edited and trans. by Berthold Riese Norman:
University of Oklahoma Press (in
press).